...ootings

...book will no doubt save
lives."   ...hor, *Stop Laughing at Me*

"The book that finally puts it all together, connects the dots and
truly will help prevent the *next* school shooting."
—Nancy Willard, author, *Cyberbullying, Cyberthreats*

"Reading this, my heart hurt, but as a mother, I thought of my kids,
I thought every parent must read this book."
—Heather Buchman, former president, Costa Mesa MOMS Club

"Prescient and suddenly, tragically relevant."   —*Publishers Weekly*

"This is no mere gratuitous rehash. Lieberman reveals important information not made public during this community's most searing
event."   —Karen McCowan, *The Register-Guard*

"Heartbreaking and eye opening."
—Nancy Stapp, radio talk show host, KOPT/Air America

"Riveting! I read it in three days, learning more than I ever imagined about a subject I thought I knew."
—Madalyn Tower, Oregon School Counselors Association

"The students are totally into the book—many are reading ahead
because they can't put it down! An important book, which begs further thought into our societal tendencies towards violence."
—Vicki M. Pettus, professor, Kentucky State University

"Extensive, thoroughgoing, helpful, excellent . . . a tremendous service
to all of us who are trying to understand why rampage shootings are
increasing in frequency."
—Dr. Ralph Larkin, author, *Comprehending Columbine*

"EVERY school administrator should read this book! I did three times,
and it helped prevent a shooting at our school."
—Mike Johnson, assistant principal, Eugene, Oregon

"Powerfully written, thoroughly mesmerizing."
—Hans Kracauer, screenwriter, New York City

"An excellent examination of this continuing crisis. Lieberman's writing is thorough and shades the complexity of our world . . . a balanced, thoughtful examination of what cumulative factors collide into 'the day it all seems to fall apart.'"
>—Danny Ledonne, filmmaker, creator of the controversial interactive videogame Super Columbine Massacre RPG!

"An exceptional book—brilliant, insightful, informative."
>—Susan Magestro, criminologist and antibullying anger management consultant

"Lieberman has given the country information that by studying it (if people would just learn from this) might prevent these horrific things from happening again."
>—Bridget Kinsella, West Coast editor, *Publishers Weekly*

"The best analysis I've seen on what's been happening in the minds of these young killers. It's not only important and accurate, it's also fascinating."
>—Dennis Murphy, founder, Ribbon of Promise National Campaign to Prevent School Violence

"This work is deep. *School Shootings* targets isolation, rejection, antisocial behaviors, ready access to guns, and the accepted norm of violence in the media and in society."
>—Amy Pincus Merwin, independent radio and video producer, InForm Productions

"So valuable to seeing the big picture of why this happens."
>—Cindy Murdoch, parent of Thurston High shooting victim

"A compelling, informative read that delves into the missed signs of the world's most infamous school shootings."
>—Alan Lampe, webmaster, www.Columbine-Angels.com

"A book that is tragically timely."
>—*The Oregonian*

School Shootings

WHAT EVERY PARENT AND EDUCATOR NEEDS TO KNOW TO PROTECT OUR CHILDREN

. . .

Joseph A. Lieberman

Foreword by
Dr. Brad Sachs

CITADEL PRESS
Kensington Publishing Corp.
www.kensingtonbooks.com

CITADEL PRESS BOOKS are published by

Kensington Publishing Corp.
850 Third Avenue
New York, NY 10022

This is a revised, updated edition of *The Shooting Game*, published by Seven Locks Press.

All Kensington titles, imprints, and distributed lines are available at special quantity discounts for bulk purchases for sales promotions, premiums, fund-raising, educational, or institutional use. Special book excerpts or customized printings can also be created to fit specific needs. For details, write or phone the office of the Kensington special sales manager: Kensington Publishing Corp., 850 Third Avenue, New York, NY 10022, attn: Special Sales Department; phone 1-800-221-2647.

First printing: September 2008

10 9 8 7 6 5 4 3 2 1

Printed in the United States of America

Library of Congress Control Number: 2008922846

ISBN-13: 978-0-8065-3071-0
ISBN-10: 0-8065-3071-5

To my mother, Frances,
who passed during the making of this book,
and to every kid who took a bullet,
lost their childhood,
or lives in fear of their memories,
and to all the parents, siblings, teachers, admin, and counselors
who suffered along with them,
this work is dedicated.

Contents

Foreword by Dr. Brad Sachs   ix

Preface   xii

Acknowledgments   xvi

Chapter 1: It Begins with the Home   1

Chapter 2: "Stay Away from School"   11

Chapter 3: The Smell of Satan   18

Chapter 4: "Mr. Self-Destruction"   28

Chapter 5: A Minor Sentence   41

Chapter 6: "An Ideal American Family"   51

Chapter 7: A Chain of Events   64

Chapter 8: Copycats   74

Chapter 9: The Politics of Blame   85

Chapter 10: Love Hurts   93

Chapter 11: Stealth and Lies   99

Chapter 12: A Question of Pride   102

Chapter 13: "The End of the World"   114

Chapter 14: "Voices in My Head"   122

Chapter 15: An Explosive Mind-Field   138

Chapter 16: Hit List   158

Chapter 17: Who Knew?   169

Chapter 18: Acceptable Murder   176
Chapter 19: Face Value   194
Chapter 20: Fame and Immortality   202
Chapter 21: The Female of the Species   219
Chapter 22: Love in All the Wrong Places   230
Chapter 23: Damaging Relations   236
Chapter 24: Parents' Rights, Parents Wronged   244
Chapter 25: The Other End of the Gun   250
Chapter 26: The One Safe Place   262
Chapter 27: The Cutting Edge   284
Chapter 28: Why the School?   293
Chapter 29: Conclusions   304
Epilogue: Sins of Compassion   314

Appendix A: Warning Signs of Potential School Shooters   329
Appendix B: Further Research and Assistance   331
Appendix C: Chronolgy of Major School Shootings,
              1974–2008
Index   355

Foreword
by Dr. Brad Sachs

From my kaleidoscopic perspectives as a family psychologist, as a parent of three young adults, and as a citizen, it has become increasingly clear to me that the behavior of adolescents can never be completely divorced from the cultural narratives of which their behavior is always a part. In fact, adolescent behavior often elucidates, with great precision, the underlying themes and conflicts that a particular society is struggling valiantly to suppress, unmasking hidden truths that refuse to remain forever unseen.

So, for example, when teens are violent, they must be viewed not simply as creating violence, but as expressing and articulating the violence that roils beneath the surface of the society from which they emerge. Adolescent behavior provides us with an unerringly accurate mirror that reflects back to a community its most deeply held values and priorities, disturbing as this mirror may be.

It is through this lens that we must view the tragic horror of school shootings, because these murders, and the students who perpetrate them, reveal immensely important facets of our culture. It is tempting, of course, to write these massacres off as rare, isolated and deviant misdeeds, actions that emanate from disturbed, deranged minds, and that, because of this, have little to say to us about the world that we have created and reside in.

But, from my vantage point, the rage that these young adults carry, the rage that drives them to march into a school with automatic weapons and murder their peers and instructors, as well as, at times, themselves, is not entirely their own—it is that of our entire society, and these young murderers are the unfortunate bearers of this rage. They represent the cold tip of a dark iceberg, and we ignore what lies under the surface at our great peril.

For example, our supposedly child-centered culture, in reality, leaves too many children regularly exposed to a world of crime, homelessness, and poverty, where basic mental- and physical-health care for youth and families is at best poorly distributed, and at worst completely unavailable. When there are surging rates of marital discord and divorce, when discrimination based on race, gender, religion, and sexual preference abounds, and when our first response to troubled adolescents is to diagnose, medicate, and exile them to institutions rather than engage, embrace, and understand them, it should not come as a surprise that the response of the generation that we are passing the torch to thunders against the insensitivity and callousness that permeate the world that they are emerging into.

Indeed, the massive physical and emotional suffering that school shootings leave in their wake is horrible and traumatizing, but no more horrible and traumatizing than the everyday violence that we inflict on so many children and families in so many communities when we so sorely neglect their most elemental rights and needs, when divisiveness, remoteness, and isolation regularly triumph over belonging, empathy, and attachment.

By nature, adolescents are acutely attuned to matters of fairness and justice, and they will rail against unfairness and injustice using whatever tools are at their disposal. Sometimes, perhaps most often, they will use thoughts, words, and constructive action to do battle, and there are many wonderful, inspiring examples of students who do just this. But sometimes they will use aggression, weapons, and destructive action to do battle, because they are unable to find any more suitable way to articulate their outrage.

The despairing young adults whom Joseph Lieberman has limned so eloquently in this book must not be viewed as lunatics on the fringe of society, but as terrified and terrifying spokespeople for a generation that is yearning desperately to be heard, cared for, and thoughtfully encountered, rather than disregarded and dismissed, bought off and numbed by materialism and technology. Their acts do not occur in a vacuum, but must be seen as grotesque, misguided attempts to call attention to all that has gone awry. It is only when we grasp the ugliness of school shootings in the context of all that is alarmingly, unnervingly ugly for our youth that we can begin to understand these surreal executions, and, through that understanding, begin to successfully prevent their reoccurrence.

The new millennium began with the shared trauma of 9/11, and the specter of global terrorism continues to haunt the present and cloud the future. But there is a terror that is more immediate, one that emerges from *within* our community rather than from *without,* and it is this terror that we need to confront with just as much thought, strategy, vigilance, and immediacy. Homeland Security will remain oxymoronic unless we assiduously set ourselves to the task of making the homes in our land more emotionally secure for the children and families who inhabit them.

In this trenchant and revelatory work, Mr. Lieberman helps us to more carefully map and explore the complex psychological terrain of school shootings, and to analyze and comprehend the individual and cultural states of mind that are conducive to such grave and dreadful acts. While much remains to be learned about the issues involved with such shocking attacks, the author guides us in thoughtful, and ultimately hopeful, ways through their origins and aftermath, enabling us to envision the ways in which these frightening losses might ultimately be converted into social gains for our community as a whole.

As the world grows both more populated and more technologically interconnected, it is becoming increasingly evident that our choice as a race is an abundantly clear one—either we discover new ways to reconcile, heal, support, and bond with each other, or we all run the very real risk of ceasing to exist at all.

We are entitled to grieve in the face of school shootings—indeed, there can be no more legitimate response—but we must allow that grief to transform our sorrow, our loss, our anguish, and our horror into something that makes us more human, and more humane. Mr. Lieberman's book is an important catalyst for that transformation, and, because of this, deserves to be read and reflected upon by everyone who seeks to break the cycles of hatred and violence passed from one generation to the next, and who instead endeavors to fortify the strength of our most noble and compassionate spirit.

Preface

Just two years had passed since I'd written a book called *The Shooting Game—The Making of School Shooters*, trying to sound the alert to administrators, educators, and others that this problem was far from over. In spring and again in fall 2006, we saw record numbers of arrests for school-shooting plots and an escalating number of tragic incidents. Then in spring 2007 came Virginia Tech, followed in the fall and winter with a horrible attack in Finland and then mall and church shootings by young people in the United States. All were rooted in the same source. This situation demanded a rewriting of my book and a renewed effort to reach those in whose hands we place the safety of our children. This time, would they listen? Word came in that already my first book had been instrumental in preventing a school shooting in Oregon, but much more needed to be done.

For me, personally, it all began when I looked up and saw the piercing eyes of a slender, fragile-looking eighteen-year-old girl asking if she could share my table in the cafeteria of Lane Community College (LCC), just outside Eugene, Oregon. When I'd settled in for lunch on that cloudy October day in 2000, I had no idea my life would be changed forever by what was about to happen.

Although the student was smiling, I couldn't help noticing that her gaze had a kind of haunted look about it, as if she were staring at something distant but terribly disconcerting. Intrigued, I asked the girl I'll call "Crystal" to take a seat. After brief introductions, the sketch-pad she carried led us into a discussion of surrealistic art and psychology. It seems a teacher had once told her that her unconventional drawings were indicative of a disturbed personality and had sent her to a counselor, who in turn recommended that she see a school district psychologist. That seemed to me a rather excessive reaction, so I asked her which school, and she answered, "Thurston High," in neighboring Springfield.

The name was familiar. It was there that fifteen-year-old Kipland Kinkel had murdered two students in May 1998, and seriously injured twenty-five others—the highest number of wounded in any high school shooting in U.S. history—after killing his parents the previous afternoon. I asked the girl if she had been present during that infamous event. She had indeed. In fact, after a few seconds, she began giving me a detailed description of her terrifying ordeal that day; how she was splattered by the blood of nearby friends, and how she lay there gripping a bench while she witnessed her classmates screaming with panic and fear. During the shooting, Kinkel had come up to her and looked directly into her eyes. She accepted that she was going to die. Then, for some unknown reason, he turned away and once again continued firing at others. Since that cataclysmic moment, it had become an obsession for her to find out why the killer had spared her life.

Needless to say, I was held spellbound by her narrative. This very private outpouring had issued forth within ten minutes of meeting her. I had never before met anyone who had survived such a harrowing experience. It was also a curious coincidence. Less than a week earlier, I'd attended a meeting at the University of Oregon School of Law concerning adolescents and gun violence. At one point, the woman sitting next to me had inadvertently disclosed that she was a member of Kip Kinkel's defense team. I expressed an interest in the case, and we began exchanging e-mail about it.

In the following days, I tried to recall all I'd read or seen about the incident. I returned as a stranger to America in 1999, after spending over fifteen years working as a university lecturer and a traveling photojournalist in the "nonviolent" culture of Japan, writing hundreds of articles and authoring a few textbooks. Like most expatriates, I'd heard about school shootings and wondered what prompted kids to go to such extremes. Revenge for bullying had never been so lethal before. Although these acts in some ways resembled adult workplace shootings, most juvenile homicides up until now had been matters of personal vendettas, drug deals gone bad, a lover's jealousy, or gang-related brutality. I had an uneasy feeling that we were witnessing a transition into some new arena of violence, that this phenomenon was somehow different from all that had gone before.

Since the Thurston incident had taken place a year before I relocated to Oregon, I knew of Kip Kinkel only through media stories. I'd been searching for a topic for my next book, but never expected to encounter a subject of such profound proportions. Instead, it seemed to find me. After the meeting in the LCC cafeteria, I was astonished to learn that no books about Thurston had ever been written. I found this story even more compelling than Columbine because Kinkel was the only one among dozens of school shooters who'd also murdered both his parents. Did two crime scenes indicate two different motives, or was this more on the order of some kind of modern Shakespearean tragedy?

I began interviewing students and teachers who were present during the shooting, examining police reports, and reviewing transcripts of the sentencing hearing. Even as the reasons behind Kip's rampage became less of an enigma, contradictions remained. Kip had been arrested for having a stolen gun in school on the morning of May 20, one day before the shootings. Why on earth was he then *released* by Springfield police and not held for seventy-two hours as the law stipulates?

Then, on January 30, 2002, I got a phone call from a husky-voiced man who asked what I knew about the lead-up to the shooting. After giving him a brief synopsis, he laughed, but in a voice completely devoid of humor. Then he whispered sarcastically, "So, you don't know the half of it." I froze for a second, and then grabbed a pad and pen. I asked if he had anything to add to what I'd learned. He did, but he wasn't going to just hand this information over. I had to earn it. For thirty minutes, he gave me hints and asked me leading questions. When I got it right, he would say, "Now you're starting to see. Now you're getting it." After following his leads, I realized this could be the break I'd been searching for. In the end, I knew I had information that would change the picture of what really happened at Thurston High, and how the tragedy could and should have been averted. There appeared to have been a cover-up after all.

As my inquiry progressed, I was frequently amazed at the links between Kinkel and other school shooters, and among many of them to each other. Numerous similarities in regard to their influences, methods, and motivation appeared not only in the succession and grouping of events, but also geographically. This couldn't be mere coincidence. Yet, each time a nexus occurred, new questions immediately arose. How many of the shooters, for example, truly suffered from depression or exhibited psychotic symptoms? Why is it almost always boys, rarely girls, who do these killings? How alike were the American episodes to similar events taking place in other countries?

I started consulting experts in the fields of law, psychology, education, media, and family violence. As a journalist, I knew my limitations, but I was happily able to bring together a broad range of professional opinions and suggestions of tangible steps that could be taken to lessen the probability of future occurrences.

Although the original focus of this work was upon the life of one particular young killer and the singular tragedy at Thurston High, what took place there overlaps with dozens of other school shootings and incidents of mass murder. All of these malevolent activities eventually interface at some level. It was impossible to ignore, for example, adult attacks or terrorist sieges of elementary schools and other forms of related violence that are not typically defined as "school shootings."

My research took me from the Regents scholar who became a student sniper in 1974 to the college grad who perpetrated the Illinois campus shooting on Valentine's Day, 2008. It became evident along the way that the roots and extent of this violence cannot be discerned from merely observing one event or studying the phenomena from one scientific, philosophic, or academic angle. This book is not, therefore, just about individual shooters and others who have chosen a path of destructiveness. It is also about changing the way each of us looks at our society, our nation, our families, and ourselves. Understanding how and why these terrifying events took place is the first step toward prevention. It is the author's hope that this book will contribute to that end.

Acknowledgments

No work of this nature could be created without the contributions and support of dozens of individuals. The author especially wishes to single out and acknowledge the very substantial assistance of the following people, whose insights have proven to be invaluable: to retired Lieutenant Colonel Dave Grossman, author of *On Killing* and *Stop Teaching Our Kids to Kill*, for his creative thinking, early recognition of deeper issues, and constant encouragement to "stay staunch"; to former Thurston High assistant principal Dick Doyle for reaching out, keeping the faith, and staying the course; to Assistant Principal Mike Johnson for initiating monthly drills and a campus-wide Crisis Response Team, proven to prevent a school shooting; to University of Oregon professor Dan Close for filling in so many gaps, providing the expertise of his experience, and helping it all make sense; and to Springfield, Oregon, fire chief Dennis Murphy, founder of Ribbon of Promise National Campaign to Prevent School Violence, who willingly took on enormous burdens personally, financially, and politically in his devotion to stopping further acts of mayhem.

Research was the backbone of this work and for their help in that, I want to express my gratitude to Sue Klang, Louise and Nelson De Sousa, "Shianne" Shryer, Jennifer and Diana Alldredge, Cindy Murdoch and other families of school shooting victims for sharing their stories and trust; to Alan Lampe, for creating the most complete chronological listing of all acts of school violence globally at columbine-angels.com; and to Police Chief Bill DeForrest for taking the time to listen and respond without ever backing off the issues.

I also highly appreciate all the professors, lawyers, psychiatrists, and psychologists who offered advice; with special thanks to educator and lawyer Nancy Willard, executive director of the Center for Safe and Responsible Internet Use, who maintains a Web site devoted to stopping cyberthreats and cyberbullying; Dr. Kathy Seifert, CEO of Eastern Shore Psychological Services in Maryland, a specialist in Child and Adolescent Risk Evaluation (CARE); Ralph Larkin, Ph.D., author of *Comprehending Columbine* and *Suburban Youth in Cultural Crisis,* for insights on the problem of school bullying; Dr. Carole Lieberman (no relation), a renowned Beverly Hills psychiatrist who authored *Coping with Terrorism: Dreams Interrupted*; and Dr. William Sack for his professional expertise imparted over long-distance phone calls and audiotape.

Law enforcement certainly played their part. Special thanks to Park County Sheriff Fred Wegener in Colorado, Green Bay Police Department Commander Lisa Sterr, Joseph F. Lawrence, the Deputy Chief of Police at Plymouth Township, Richard Schmidt in the Juno, Alaska Department of Corrections, Deputy Warden Penny Hart and Yolanda Rodriguez at Red Rock Correctional Center in Arizona, Orange County Sheriff's Office Captain Charles Blackwood in Hillsborough, NC, Suzanne Singletary at the Mississippi Department of Corrections Office of Communications, Detective Dan Wolverton of the State Police of Oregon, Deputy Medical Examiner Frank Ratti, Eugene Sgt. Mike Gaylik, Sharon Ramsdale of the Springfield Police Department, and Sgt. Matt Keetle of the Lane County Sheriff's Office for their cooperation and forbearance; and to Sgt. Jim Fields, former Unit Supervisor of the Eugene Police Department's Metro Explosive Disposal Unit.

Dr. Maressa H. Orzack, of McClean Hospital's Computer Addiction Study Center, and attorney Elisa Swanson contributed considerable experiential counsel concerning addictive play on first-person video shooter games. Although attorney Jack Thompson, an activist campaigner against violence in media and entertainment, stands in complete opposition to the positions of game designer and documentary filmmaker Danny Ledonne, both men contributed valuable insights.

The author also wishes to rain praise upon the heads of those in the literary fields who gave of their time and endurance in guiding this work toward completion: to Michaela Hamilton, editor-in-chief of the Citadel imprint and executive editor at Kensington Books, for allowing me access to a first-class publishing house, believing in me against all odds, and getting these pages into print; Mike Gulledge, publisher of the *Billings Gazette,* Jystiin Summers of American Media, Inc., Cam Cardow and Leonard Stern of the *Ottawa Citizen,* Roy Ockert of the *Jonesboro Sun,* and former student Mandee Axtell who all stepped up with photo permissions; editor Ted Taylor, of the *Eugene Weekly,* for giving me ample opportunities to present controversial material; to spy novelist and former military intelligence agent John Reed for pointers on how to make it all work, covertly and otherwise; to author Jodee Blanco and criminologist Susan Magestro for their enthusiastic support; and most especially to Dr. Brad Sachs for creating a most excellent and insightful foreword to this book, capturing the underlying meaning of my research with clarity and deep perception.

• Chapter 1 •

It Begins with the Home

*Once they've drawn first blood, you usually can't talk them
down. They've reached the point of no return.*
                                    —John Nicoletti, Colorado
                                    police psychology expert

Shangri-La is a heavily forested bedroom community just east of Springfield, Oregon, surrounded by rustic foothills and edged by a cascad-
ing, snow-fed mountain stream. Hidden from the road, isolated by tall
scented pines, a solidly built double A-frame house sits snugly fur-
nished but devoid of life, an eerily silent shell lacking any animation
within. Below its broad wooden decks, a boy's bicycle rusts amid high
weeds. On a verge of driveway, an overturned canoe filled with cobwebs
is beginning to molder. Rustic wood shingles and a light-gingerbread
trim suggest the architecture of a cozy vacation ski chalet, yet there
is no frivolity about this dwelling, no joyful expectation of the sea-
sons ahead. All of that had vanished in the split second it took a
bullet to travel from the hand of a son to the target of his distress.

Once upon a time, Bill Kinkel and his wife, Faith, dreamed they
would set up a family haven for their daughter, Kristin, and her little brother, Kip, in this quiet subdivision beside the McKenzie River.
On the afternoon of Wednesday, May 20, 1998, when their auburn-
haired boy had reached his fifteenth year, any hope they still harbored of creating a paradise in this idyllic setting abruptly collapsed.

Sometime around 3:00 P.M. on that day, Kipland Philip Kinkel

1

took his dad's .22-caliber Ruger semiautomatic pistol downstairs to their kitchen and shot his father once in the head. Bill Kinkel died instantly, his back to his son, never knowing what hit him. It was an ironic death, for in a certain sense, Bill, a balding, bespectacled fifty-nine-year-old Spanish teacher, had never really had a clue as to what was going on in his son's deeply disturbed mind.

A little after six that evening, Kip's mother, Faith, returned to their two-story home from a retirement party for three colleagues. An energetic fifty-seven-year-old with midlength ginger-brown hair, Faith parked her Ford Explorer in the garage below the Kinkel dwelling and found her son nervously awaiting her. Kip dutifully helped her unload some groceries and her briefcase, followed her halfway up the garage stairs, spoke the words "I love you," and shot her twice in the back of the head with a 9mm Glock handgun. She tumbled backward, striking her forehead as she fell. Noticing that she was still breathing, Kip dragged her across the floor, turned her over, and shot her three more times in the face. His sixth and final shot pierced her heart.

Sometime soon after, Kip composed a confessional letter, trying to explain what he had done. His writing was rife with misspelled words (corrected here), due to a learning impairment he'd been struggling with since elementary school. Police would later find the following message on a coffee table:

> I have just killed my parents! I don't know what is happening. I love my mom and dad so much. I just got two felonies on my record. My parents can't take that! It would destroy them. The embarrassment would be too much for them. They couldn't live with themselves. I'm so sorry. I am a horrible son. I wish I had been aborted. I destroy everything I touch. I can't eat. I can't sleep. I didn't deserve them. They were wonderful people. It's not their fault or the fault of any person, organization, or television show. My head just doesn't work right. God damn these VOICES inside my head. I want to die. I want to be gone. But I have to kill people. I don't know why. I am so sorry! Why did God do this to me? I have never been happy. I wish I was happy. I wish I made my mother proud. I am nothing! I tried so hard to find happiness. But you know me, I hate

everything. I have no other choice. What have I become?
I am so sorry.

The fact that Kip had slaughtered both his parents put him in a unique position among teenage school shooters. Only four others— Clay Shrout, Luke Woodham, Jeff Weise, and Alvaro Rafael Castillo— out of hundreds we have on file, committed similar double crimes. In every school shooting, we tend to question the parenting, but in these five cases, close family members paid the ultimate price.

Clay Shrout was a seventeen-year-old senior honor student at Larry A. Ryle High School in Union, Kentucky. His forty-three-year-old father, Harvey, was an ordained church elder. His mom, Rebecca, and two younger sisters rounded out the family. Despite being called a "borderline genius," and growing up in a loving, religious, upper-middle-class home, Clay was jealous of his parents' attention toward his siblings. His lifelong friend Richard Brown attested, "I remember maybe two times that he got a hug and a kiss from his mom. I never saw any signs of physical love. But with his sisters, they were always hugging them and saying 'I love you.'" Clay later told police that he felt as if his parents had totally planned out his life for him "without asking me what I really wanted to be first."

The trigger to his rage came when Clay was suspended for bringing a stun gun to school. As punishment, his parents grounded him and confiscated his heavy-metal music CDs, his computer, and his knife collection. Clay decided it was time to leave home, but he knew his parents wouldn't permit that—and besides, he wanted his prized possessions back. So he made a plan. At five o'clock, on the morning of May 26, 1994, he stole into his dad's Jeep Cherokee to get a Colt .380-caliber pistol, which he knew was locked in the glove box. Then he crept upstairs to where his parents were sleeping. He shot his father first. As his dad rolled, wounded, out one side of bed, his mother awoke. Before she could scream, Clay shot her once in the face. He heard a noise coming from down the hall and knew that at least one of his sisters must have awoken. It was the fourteen-year-old, Kristen, getting out of bed. Clay reassured her that the gun had fired accidentally. His sister scolded his careless handling of the weapon and turned away. Clay shot her, and she, too, died.

He heard his father groaning as his dad struggled to find enough energy to reach the phone and call for help. His father kept repeating, "Oh, my God," until Clay came back in and sent another bullet into his brain. It was still too early for Lauren, the twelve-year-old, to get up for school, but now she was standing in the hallway, trying to rub the sleep out of her eyes. "What's going on?" she asked, and Clay gently answered, "Just a bad dream" as he guided her back to her bed and tucked her in. She was calm and relaxed as she told her brother she'd been having a really nice dream. Her eyelids fluttered closed again. Quietly Clay placed the muzzle of the gun near the top of Lauren's head and squeezed the trigger.

As if he had just finished a practical task, like cleaning out the garage, Clay decided to call Richard Brown to tell him what he'd done. "I killed 'em. I killed 'em all," Clay crowed. Brown would not believe it. "No, man, I did it," Clay insisted, encouraging his friend to come over and take away anything he liked, but also advising him, "Just don't go upstairs. It's a mess up there."

Clay wasted no more time as he hastened to reclaim his treasured belongings from his parents' bedroom. After cleaning himself up, he reloaded the gun and put it, along with over one hundred rounds of ammunition, into an old gym bag. On his way to school, he stopped at a convenience store to grab some breakfast, and then swung by the home of a girl he daydreamed about running away with. She had been his prom date two weeks earlier. He forced her at gunpoint to ride with him to Ryle High, where Clay started searching for the English teacher and assistant principal whom he held responsible for his suspension.

Unable to find them, Clay slipped into a calculus class that was taught by one of his favorite teachers, Mrs. Kanabroski. The boy sauntered up front, plunked down in the teacher's chair, and took out his gun. "I've had a bad day," he told the class. "I just killed my family." They believed him. He held the class hostage at gunpoint for thirty minutes until Mrs. Kanabroski convinced him to surrender. Although he had killed his entire family, he did not physically harm anyone at school. Unlike Kip, however, Clay never expressed any regrets—or even emotion—about what he had done. He did tell police that he never hated his parents and even got along well with his father, though he often argued with his mother. Shrout later pleaded guilty, but mentally ill, to four counts of murder. He was sentenced to life and remains today in the Kentucky State Penitentiary for dangerous offenders.

Luke Woodham was another shooter who seemed to have not the slightest trace of conscience—in fact, immediately after his arrest, he was positively glowing with excitement and was all smiles on his video police confession. The boy was aged sixteen at the time of his crimes in October 1997 (chapters 4 and 12). He believed his divorced mother hated and blamed him for her husband's abandonment, but he also blamed his mom for ending his brief relation with Christina Menefee, one of two girls he later killed at Pearl High School in Mississippi. When Kip Kinkel killed his mother, it was "to save her" from his own disgrace. By contrast, Luke Woodham said he brutally murdered his mom (by smothering her with a pillow, stabbing her with a knife, and beating her head with a baseball bat) because "She always never loved me." But he added, "I didn't want to kill my mother. I do love my mother. I just wanted her to understand."

Before Jeff Weise went on his March 2005 shooting binge in Minnesota, he used a .22-caliber gun to shoot to death his grandfather, veteran Red Lake tribal policeman Sergeant Daryl "Dash" Lussier, and Lussier's companion, Michelle Sigana, thirty-two, in their home on the Red Lake Chippewa Indian Reservation. The deceased couple left behind a son, who was just two years younger than Weise. Although Jeff supposedly felt close to his grandfather, there may have been some jealousy. Michelle had never mentioned Weise in conversations with her brother, despite living with Daryl for about fifteen years.

Internet postings attributed to Jeff Weise indicate that he had deep-seated resentment toward his mother, with whom he lived in the suburbs of Minneapolis until she suffered brain injuries in a car accident in 1999, when Jeff was ten years old. Since then, she had resided in a Minneapolis nursing home, while Jeff had to go live with his grandmother Shelda Lussier on the Red Lake reservation. Shelda, who was already separated from Dash, said that Weise's alcoholic mother was never a model parent. The mom often locked her son out of their house, and the mother's boyfriend would sometimes lock Jeff inside a closet or make him kneel in a corner for hours. Weise wrote on an Internet site that he felt alienated and lonely because his mother "would hit me with anything she could get her hands on" and "would tell me I was a mistake, and she would say so many things that it is hard to deal with them or think of them without crying."

Weise's stepfather, Daryl Lussier Jr., dramatically killed himself at home after a one-day standoff with police on the reservation in July 1997. Weise's grandfather "Dash" Lussier was one of the policemen surrounding the house, but he failed to negotiate a resolution with his son. Faced with the options of prison or self-annihilation, Lussier Jr. put a gun to his head and pulled the trigger, just as his stepson, Jeff, would do eight years later.

On the morning of August 30, 2006, in Hillsborough, North Carolina, nineteen-year-old Alvaro Rafael Castillo killed his father and then videotaped himself confessing what he had done and explaining what he was about to do. Soon after, he loaded his gray minivan with pipe bombs and weapons, and at 1:00 P.M. drove to Orange High School, which he'd graduated from in 2005. Speeding past the parking lot guardhouse, he jumped from the van, launched a smoke bomb, set off a line of firecrackers, and, using two rifles, fired eight times at cars. Students eating lunch outdoors began screaming and diving for cover. One senior girl was grazed on her right shoulder, and a male student was injured by shattered glass.

Within two minutes, the school resource officer (SRO), London Ivey, of the Orange County Sheriff's Office, and Russ LeBlanc, a former state trooper who taught driver's ed, confronted Castillo near the cafeteria. Ivey aimed his pistol at the youth, ordering him to put down his weapons. The young shooter complied, and LeBlanc, unarmed, rushed in to handcuff him.

Once in custody, Alvaro told deputies he had murdered his dad, Rafael Huezo Castillo, sixty-five, by shooting him several times in the head and neck as his father sat on a couch facing away from him. Castillo explained this act as "Sacrifice. The world is cruel. We all have to sacrifice. Somebody had to put him out of his misery. He abused all of us."

This claim was further enhanced in Castillo's videotapes when, clearly agitated, he tells how his father was verbally abusive, had mistreated his mother, and sometimes hit members of his family. Showing off a sheet that covered his father's corpse, he says, "Look at me. I'm not even crying. I just killed him and I feel fine." Later, Castillo laments, "Don't judge me for what I did. Based on what I did, you might think I'm a monster, a sick freak . . . but I tried to do good things. I tried. . . . I treated everybody with respect as best I could. All I wanted was respect in return."

Then, echoing two of Kip Kinkel's phrases, he says of his impending rampage, "I'm sorry for the pain I'm going to cause, but I'm not right in the head. I just want to die." This may not be mere coincidence. When arrested, Castillo told deputies he'd been obsessed for years with the Thurston shooting in Oregon, the Jonesboro, Arkansas, massacre, and, of course, the biggest event of all up till then: Columbine. "Columbine. Remember Columbine," he said while being led into his initial appearance at Orange County District Court. When asked why the fixation, Castillo replied, "I don't know, I was just attracted to it ever since I was ten." In fact, he had even traveled to Colorado the previous year to drive by the school and homes of the two teens that carried out that shooting.

In one more bizarre twist, Castillo e-mailed Frank DeAngelis, the current Columbine High School principal, the morning of his crimes, warning that he would attack his Orange County school. Unfortunately, DeAngelis didn't see that e-mail until after the incident. It read:

> In a few hours you will probably hear about a school shooting in North Carolina. I am responsible for it. I remember Columbine. It is time the world remembered it. I am sorry.

In addition to that message, Castillo mailed his videotapes and a letter to the *Chapel Hill News* (a twice-weekly newspaper), in which references were made to several school shootings. The letter ends with a fatalistic statement of his suicidal intentions: *I will die. I have wanted to die for years. I'm sorry.*

There had been a previous warning four months earlier, however. In April, Castillo had sent another videotape to a former high school friend whom he had a crush on, saying that he was going to kill himself. Anna Rose was away at college when the tape arrived, but her mother, Bonnie, watched it and called police. As it turned out, however, two days before the video arrived at the Rose residence, on April 20— the seventh anniversary of Columbine—Castillo's parents had him committed to a state psychiatric hospital because he'd told them he was going to kill himself with a shotgun. He was released eight days later.

How Alvaro was committed played a significant role in what followed. Mark Botts, a Chapel Hill School of Government law professor at the University of North Carolina, related how state law "encourages authorities to persuade a person to consent to treatment even when the person is considered dangerous and eligible for involuntary treatment. But when consent is given, the state no longer has control over the duration of the person's treatment because willing patients are allowed to voluntarily discharge themselves."

Castillo's parents initiated an involuntary commitment and a magistrate agreed that Alvaro was mentally ill and a danger to himself or others. A physician at UNC Hospitals concurred that Castillo was psychotic and needed inpatient treatment. However, Alvaro agreed at that point, with the state's approval, to voluntarily admit himself to the hospital.

Why does the state encourage this? You can thank the North Carolina gun lobby. Although federal law makes it illegal to knowingly sell guns to anyone who's been involuntarily committed to a mental institution or otherwise been found by a judge to be mentally ill, Castillo's consent to treatment allowed him to retain his right to buy a gun. An effort to amend that state law failed a few years ago.

Was Castillo aware of this gun loophole when he changed his stance to voluntary commitment? Judge for yourself: On June 2, less than five weeks after his release, Alvaro passed a federal background check and purchased a Hi-Point 9mm rifle. He repeated the process on July 7 to buy a Mossberg 12-gauge shotgun.

During his attack, Castillo was wearing the customary black trench coat, a black hat, and black sunglasses, but he also wore a white headband, just as Texas sniper Charles Whitman did in 1966 (chapter 26). Like Whitman, Castillo had some military skills. He'd completed North Carolina National Guard basic combat training in August 2005, but he never deployed because his officers concluded he was medically unfit for service.

Media obviously played an active role in Castillo's plans. There were his videotapes and e-mail, and numerous diaries in which he wrote about school attacks and how violence had shaped his life. Despite Castillo's use of media to both access information and publicize his torment, during his trial for first-degree murder and ten other crimes in spring 2007, the judge honored the defense lawyer's request to deny Orange County investigators access to information on two personal computers taken from Castillo's home after his arrest.

Many of these elements—videotapes sent to media, prior judgment of being mentally ill, the influence of violent films, an expressed death wish—will be taken up in later chapters when we reference the nation's worst-ever shooting rampage by Seung-hui Cho (pronounced Suhng-whee Choh) that ended the lives of thirty-two students and faculty members on April 16, 2007, at the Virginia Polytechnic Institute and State University in Blacksburg. Cho would use a similar legal loophole to buy guns, despite being referred for psychological counseling. That would result in a tightening of gun laws in Virginia and several other states, but those new laws would be insufficient to prevent the shooting ten months later at Northern Illinois University (NIU) in DeKalb, Illinois on Valentine's Day, 2008.

Twenty-seven-year-old former graduate student Stephen Kazmierczak (pronounced kaz-MUR-chek) had been placed by his parents in a Chicago psychiatric treatment center after high school because he had become "unruly" at home, was depressed, and he used to cut himself. Nevertheless, he had a valid Firearm Owner's Identification Card, as required for all Illinois residents who buy or possess firearms. Although such cards are seldom issued to those with mental health problems, Kazmierczak's stay in the Thresholds-Mary Hill House in the late 1990s left him off the radar. He was able to legally purchase a pump-action Remington shotgun, a Glock 9 mm handgun, a Hi-Point .380, and a Sig Sauer at a gun store in Champaign, where he was enrolled in the graduate school of social work at the University of Illinois, 130 miles away from NIU, which he had left after his graduation in 2007.

Ironically, other handgun accessories, including two empty 9 mm Glock magazines and a Glock holster, were sold to Kazmierczak ten days before his rampage by the same Green Bay, Wisconsin-based Internet gun dealer who had also sold a weapon to Seung-Hui Cho in 2007. The results were similar. By the end of his shooting spree, Kazmierczak had murdered one male and four female students, and had wounded sixteen others, before committing suicide.

Unlike Castillo, Weise, Woodham, or even Cho, Kip Kinkel had no obvious dysfunction or public drama in his family history. Unlike Shrout, he got on well with his own much admired and highly achieving sister, Kristin, and appreciated her unwavering support. At the same time, however, he realized he'd never be as outgoing and successful as she was, nor as greatly esteemed by their parents.

Psychologist Robert R. Butterworth, an expert on youth issues, has stated that "children who kill do not believe that they are emotionally important to their family and don't feel connected emotionally to others." When Luke Woodham was asked in prison why he killed, he said he thought his mother hated him. Luke declared, "I just felt like nobody cared. I just wanted to hurt them or kill them."

Dr. George B. Palermo, clinical professor of psychiatry and neurology at the Medical College of Wisconsin, wrote: *The juvenile mass murderers appear to hold their parents in low esteem and to disregard their authority, and they do not seem to be concerned with avoiding their disapproval. . . . Their moral judgment seems to be arrested at the early conventional stage, and their capacity to reason in moral terms impaired.*

Only these five school shooters referenced in this chapter took their personal sense of deprivation, and holding "their parents in low esteem," to the extreme level of killing close family members. But for all of them, that was just the first step, the private murders, the shedding of first blood. What they intended next would be far more public, spectacular, and coldly impersonal.

Chapter 2

"Stay Away from School"

I am so full of rage that I feel I could snap at any moment. I think about it everyday. Blowing the school up or just taking the easy way out, and walk into a pep assembly with guns. In either case, people that are breathing will stop breathing. That is how I will repay all you motherfuckers for all you put me through.

—Kip Kinkel, writing in his journal

During a sleepless night, Kip Kinkel primed himself for what he knew he had to do the next day. In the morning, he ate a bowl of cereal, taped two bullets to his chest in an X pattern, and hid two knives, the Glock handgun, the Ruger pistol, and a Ruger semiautomatic rifle with a shortened stock, beneath a long khaki trench coat. He filled a black backpack and gray military bag with extra ammunition clips and loose bullets. Altogether he carried enough firepower to kill 1,077 people.

Before leaving, Kip inserted the CD soundtrack from a violent 1996 movie version of Shakespeare's *Romeo and Juliet* into the stereo, turned up the volume to maximum, and set it to continuous play. Kip most likely expected the sound of the loud music would attract the attention of neighbors and eventually the police. His intention may have only been to insure that his parents' bodies would be discovered, but, more ominously, he also left behind a number of homemade bombs, some of them armed to detonate.

Kip put on a black baseball cap, packed his deadly arsenal into his mother's car, and, at seven-thirty that Thursday morning, began the fifteen-minute drive to Thurston High School. His goal was to reach the cafeteria by 8:00 A.M., when it would be at its most crowded. He parked some distance from the back entrance, near the tennis courts. Under overcast skies that threatened rain, he started on the last walk he would ever take to school. A school security camera recorded him as he entered the north parking lot, but the poor image showed nothing alarming.

The open breezeway was almost empty at 7:55 A.M. as Kip moved rapidly under its shelter. Near the entrance, he saw his friend Adam Pearse walking with two other boys. Kip called Adam's name as he caught up with them, and warned him, "You shouldn't go to school today. Stay away from the cafeteria." Confused, Adam asked Kip what he was talking about, and noticing Kip's grave appearance, added, "Are you gonna do something crazy?" Kip just hastened forward without replying, his face an expressionless mask. Adam quietly touched the shoulders of his two companions, signaling them to stop. A minute later, they would be running for their lives.

As Kip moved forward, Ben Walker was moving in the opposite direction, trying to catch up to his girlfriend, Shannan "Shianne" Shryer. They usually would have been hanging around outside under the trees at this hour, but today Shianne felt hungry and wanted a snack from the lunchroom. While there, they'd had a lovers' spat over the fact that he was going to a party that evening without her. On the verge of tears, Shianne stormed out of the cafeteria, Ben following close behind. She was just pulling away from her boyfriend when Kip passed them by, swung back around, and lifted the rifle from under his trench coat. Kip's friend Bryan Mabe, a witness, described that moment: "Kip just turned around, didn't even look at Ben . . . like he had no emotion about anything." Aiming at the back of Ben Walker's head, Kip pulled the trigger.

The gun clicked, but did not fire. Kip could have seen the misfire as a sign to end it all now, an omen, a second chance, but instead, annoyed and frustrated, he cocked the weapon and squeezed the trigger again. This time, the bullet left the gun and shattered in Walker's brain. Shianne turned to see her boyfriend falling forward as Kip rushed away in the opposite direction. She was too stunned to speak. As she bent down to touch Ben's wet hair, someone jerked her up and into a darkened music room, where she became hysterical. When she finally managed to break away from restraining hands and find her way back out through a darkened adjoining room, she dropped down sobbing near Ben, pleading forgiveness over their quarrel, and whispering words of love as she choked on her tears. But it was too late. Ben had been struck unconscious by the exploding bullet and could no longer hear anyone. He would be taken off life support and die early the next morning without ever regaining consciousness.

Meanwhile, Kip had hurried two dozen paces forward toward Ryan Atteberry, the next student in his line of sight. A large, cheerful lad with a carefree demeanor, Ryan was so preoccupied with his upcoming class, he hadn't noticed Ben getting shot. He was totally unaware of anything being amiss, for in the din of the hallway the rifle sound had been little more than a sharp crack.

Without hesitation, Kip fired at the side of Ryan's face. The bullet penetrated his upper jaw and lodged near the third vertebra of his neck. The gunshot blasted so close to his ears, it temporarily deafened him; his brain did not have time to register the noise and he never saw the spark of the gun being fired. Amazingly, Ryan would survive and later recall his puzzlement at what was happening to him. A few moments earlier, he said, he had been daydreaming, walking in the hall, and then . . . "the next thing I noticed, I was looking towards the cement—for no apparent reason, I never understood, I noticed a large puddle of redness coming down into the cement. I was paralyzed during the time. I could not move, and there was a large ringing sound in my ears. I can't tell if I screamed. . . ."

Kip had reached his goal and stood before the cafeteria's side doors. He took a breath, cocked the rifle once again, and pulled one door open. Inside, some students watching him enter assumed he was pulling some kind of prank related to that day's class elections. Then Kip swept his semiautomatic in an arc, firing off most of a fifty-round clip. Those seated behind the front students thought the popping sounds they heard were firecrackers. It was only when they saw blood flowing and heard terrified screams that shock and panic set in.

Considering that there were up to 270 students packed into the cafeteria and Kip was shooting at close range, it's perhaps not surprising that his aim was accurate enough to wound twenty-five in less than ninety seconds. Jennifer Alldredge, one of the first to be struck, had been planning with friends how to celebrate her boyfriend's seventeenth birthday that day. Her beau (and later husband), Jacob "Jake" Ryker, sat beside her. Jennifer recalled in a courtroom eighteen months later the sensation of being shot twice just after Kip entered the room: "I felt intense heat and pain hit and spasm through my hand. I watched blood spurt and pour out of two fingers as my entire hand throbbed. Nauseated and scared, I tried to scream, but [Kip] had shot me again, this time through my lung, and blood gurgled out of my mouth. I fell, and went in and out of consciousness."

By the time medical personnel arrived on the scene, they assumed from her stillness and the copious amount of blood staining her clothes that Jennifer was dead. Barely conscious, she managed to spit out a candy that she had placed in her mouth just seconds before Kip had entered the room. Paramedic Todd Ferguson, who had bent over Jennifer to feel her pulse, saw her expel the candy at that vital moment. By this slight action, he knew that she lived, and he began the rescue process. Ironically, the candy she spit out was a LifeSaver.

Jennifer would flatline three times in the next twelve hours, yet she managed to hang on to a spark of life. Despite her outward frailty, her inner determination ultimately allowed her to survive. Still, it would take her months to recover. Jennifer had been sitting at the same front table as Crystal, the student who was described in the preface of this book. Crystal had never specified whose blood had splashed upon her in the Thurston cafeteria, but now the connection was clear.

As it turned out, the two girls were best friends and had been for years. This could explain some of the superficial similarities in their appearance. Both shared the same slender, willowy figure, blond hair, and captivating large blue eyes. In personality, however, the two young women were miles apart. Whereas Crystal had seemed fragile and unsure, her tone confessional, her eyes darting nervously hither and yon or staring intently, Jen was steel and strength, a powerhouse of resolve packaged in a petite and graceful frame. What was most intriguing about the pair, however, was the fact that after the shooting, both also shared that haunted gaze that seemed to focus on some fearful yet distant threat. Perhaps this look is common to those who have been to the edge of death and back, an attribute of the ones who have returned from seeing what the rest of us will only face in those final moments before the flame of life is extinguished.

Each student in the cafeteria that day was traumatized, but all reacted differently at the time of the shooting. Gabe Thomas was able to remain calm and walk quietly over to the nurse's station with blood running down his arm, while, in his words, "everybody else [was] freaking out." He described how he was "sitting there, playing this game. Next thing I know, I feel like somebody punched me with a metal spike. . . . People are groaning and in pain. . . . You don't know what the hell is going on. . . . I see piles of writhing bodies."

Having recently transferred from another school, Melissa Taylor was sitting in the Thurston cafeteria for the very first time. Her response was to remain motionless in her seat, hoping she wouldn't be noticed. Only after being struck by a bullet in her shoulder did she catch on that she wasn't invisible and it was wiser to duck down between the tables.

For Amber Ramsey, who very nearly died from a bullet that lodged in her abdomen, time stood perfectly still. She said she first became aware of "a burning and stinging sensation" in her midsection, and then "turned around, and what I noticed was that everyone in the cafeteria seemed to be frozen. . . . It seemed like time was moving very, very slowly." When reality kicked in again, she hastily dropped to the floor, her ears now alerted to the sound of Kip shooting and "everyone in the cafeteria screaming like I've never heard anyone scream before."

Perhaps no student experienced a state of disbelief and suspended reality more sharply than Elizabeth McKenzie. While others ran or ducked for cover, she "stood and watched what was happening," as if this were all taking place on TV, and, according to her father, "never really understanding what peril she was truly in." As a bullet passed entirely through one of her legs and into the other, she still did not fathom that she had been shot. Instead, she turned to look down at her close friend Teresa Miltonberger, who had crumpled to the floor from hits to her thigh and forehead. "I remember Teresa lying on the ground, and I kept asking her to get up, and she couldn't, and I couldn't understand why," Elizabeth explained in a calmer moment. "It never occurred to me that this was all real." Incredibly, even when blood started flowing from Teresa's forehead, Elizabeth could not, in her bizarre state of shock, accept that it was real blood. Her fear irrationally channeled itself into anger against her friend for "stubbornly refusing" to get up. Teresa would also survive, but with permanent brain damage.

Even at the height of his rampage, Kip was rational enough to selectively target students. The night before, he had told a friend on the phone that he liked a girl named Cassidy. While he was shooting in the cafeteria that morning, Kip looked at Cassidy, but passed her by, just as he had with Crystal a few moments earlier. He also turned his gun away from a boy whom he knew as the brother of a girl he had dated a year previous.

Meanwhile, another student, Mikael Nickolauson, had fallen to the ground bleeding from a thigh wound. His friend Ryan Crowley looked on in horror from beneath a nearby table as Kip came up to Mikael, aimed a gun at the back of his head, and fired. Ryan Crowley watched Mikael's face as he died. Then Kip walked directly over to Crowley, held the semiautomatic up to Ryan's forehead, and squeezed the trigger. A sharp click sounded and . . . nothing! Kip pulled hard— twice more—but, miraculously, his rifle was out of ammo, and Crowley's life was spared. That was the turning point. Crowley's fear turned to rage and he lashed out at Kip with his fist, hitting him in the throat.

Jake Ryker had been shot in the chest at the same moment he had leapt up in reaction to his girlfriend, Jennifer, being cut down. A varsity wrestling team member with a sturdy six-five frame, he was not yet aware that he had been hit. Jake had grown up around guns in a military family that enjoyed hunting, so when he heard the rifle chamber click empty as Kip tried to kill Crowley, he knew it was time to act.

At first, his long legs got tangled under the cafeteria table, but then he stood up, propelled himself forward, and tackled Kip to the ground, with his brother, Josh, close upon his heels. Jake saw that Kip had a knife and he was trying to disarm him as Josh and five other boys piled on, but all were taken by surprise when Kip squirmed and, despite the pile of students pressing down upon him, managed to pull the Glock handgun out of his belt. Kip had the gun aimed directly at Jake's face when the wrestler got hold of the barrel just as Kinkel fired, sending a bullet through Jake's left index finger. The same bullet then hit student Joshua Pearson in the backside. It was the last shot Kip got off before he was finally overpowered. Some of the boys began beating him. Only then did Jake back off, realize the extent of his injury, and collapse to the floor.

All of the seven who neutralized Kip—including the two Ryker brothers, Douglas and David Ure, Adam Walberger, Joshua Pearson, and Travis Weaver—were featured in a *Life* magazine article, but Jake was reluctant to do interviews. His reticence was based on a belief that he and the others were not heroes, just students fighting for their lives. For his brother, Josh, the memory that endures was that as the Glock was kicked away and their attacker was finally subdued, belly down on the floor, Kip kept screaming, "Just kill me! Shoot me now! I want to die!"

Kip was still pleading to be killed when motorcycle officer Dan Bishop arrived. In the next few hours, the world would learn that Thurston High had just been added to a mushrooming list of school shootings that would eventually add up to hundreds of incidents and an equally morbid number of barely averted catastrophes.

While Kip's guilt is undeniable, the shooting and its aftermath raised many disturbing questions. How could a boy growing up in a stable, middle-class home with two well-educated, loving parents perform such deeds? Were Kip's acts really the result of insane delusions, or were they the cunning calculations of a murderous mind? If the warning signs were there, why didn't anybody notice them?

For now, however, the tragedy had just begun and another act was about to commence.

• Chapter 3 •

The Smell of Satan

People love to debate whether humans are essentially good or essentially evil. I find those alternatives unacceptable. [Recognizing that] good people can do evil and evil people can do good, I have to be on my toes with other people no matter what their essential nature is. Making assumptions about human nature can be dangerous.

—Rabbi Rami Shapiro

If religious law determined civil law, as it often did in the distant past and still does in certain Islamic countries, the question of good versus evil might be more clear-cut. To the majority of those who observe a school shooting, the act is, without question, evil. What about in the minds of the killers? Kip Kinkel wrote, *All humans are evil. I just want to end the world of evil. I don't want to see, hear, speak or feel evil, but I can't help it. I am evil.* The Columbine shooters had basically the same worldview, although they called themselves superior, not evil. But many of these young gunmen also fostered a purposely "wicked" image and were attracted to arcane subjects and diabolical interests.

Kip had not succeeded in his quest to end his life via "suicide by cop." Neither would Jeff Weise at Red Lake, nor Eric Harris and Dylan Klebold at Columbine, but at least those three individuals had the intestinal fortitude to do themselves in while police and SWAT teams were closing in on them.

Weise, armed with his slain grandfather's two handguns and a shotgun, and wearing Dash Lussier's bulletproof vest, had driven right up to the front door of Red Lake High School, about 2:50 P.M., in his grandpa's police cruiser. As he stepped out of the car, the wind caught his black trench coat, revealing three guns to security guards Derrick Brun and LeeAnn Grant. He then fired the shotgun twice into the air. Derrick, who was unarmed and manning his post at the school's main entrance metal detector, recognized the danger, but he stood his ground. Jeff shot him down and pressed forward. LeeAnn used the few moments Derrick bought with his life to swiftly hustle students away from the line of fire.

Teachers also herded their charges toward rooms more distant from the popping sounds of gunfire, locking doors. Student Ashley Morrison remembered hearing shots, then seeing the gunman peering though the entry window of her native culture classroom and holding her breath as he hammered on the door, trying to break it down. Teacher Diane Schwanz said, "I was still just half-believing it. I just got down on the floor and [said], 'Kids, down on the ground, under the benches!'" She then called police on her cell phone.

Weise abandoned that effort and walked farther down the hallway, where he found a room with a glass panel beside the locked door. He blew away the glass with a shotgun blast, reached in, and turned the handle. The teacher, sixty-two-year-old Neva Rogers, was an outsider who had volunteered to come to the reservation. This was not a high-end assignment, but Rogers loved her job. Her final words before Jeff shot and killed her, moments after breaking in, were "God help us."

When Weise burst into the room, some students who knew him still couldn't accept that this was real. Cody Thunder, fifteen, said he had "a mean face," and a girl described Jeff's visage as "a mixture of anger and fear." Thunder told reporters: "I asked myself, What's he doing? I thought he was messing around. I thought it was a paintball gun or something." The gunfire was such a shock, that Thunder felt no pain when a bullet struck his hip.

Student Reggie Graves, fourteen, was crouched in an adjoining classroom, listening as frightened voices penetrated the wall. Some pleaded with the gunman to stop, Graves said. "You could hear a girl saying, 'No, Jeff, quit, quit. Leave me alone. What are you doing?'" Inside the room where the rampage was happening, according to another student who survived, a friend of Jeff's was spared. "He pointed his gun at a boy and then changed his mind, smiled, waved at him, and shot somebody else."

Other students were not so lucky as they crouched under desks or on the floor. Five were killed. Seven others were injured. Roland Lussier Sr., the father of a fifteen-year-old student murdered in that classroom of death, could be justly proud of his son. Chase Lussier had sheltered a female classmate with his body. "They died heroes," Lussier Sr. said. He knew Weise "was trying to shoot the girls, and Chase jumped in front of the gun. They were real warriors."

After killing these students, Weise tried to leave, but he was driven back into the same classroom by police bullets in the hallway. Jeff shouted, "I have hostages!", but then he ended it all by replicating his stepfather's 1997 death. Surrounded by Red Lake police, he fatally shot himself in the head.

One further detail is sure to continue resonating from this disaster. In a reversal of the famous "life-or-death" query asked at Columbine (see below), Weise spared another student by questioning his faith in God. Immediately after shooting the teacher, Jeff had asked student Chon'gai'la Morris, "Do you believe in God?" Morris said no, and Weise turned to shoot others. This exchange is bound to add fuel to the claims of a scattering of religious leaders who label most school shootings as the work of the Devil made incarnate. And for their part, the shooters have made that connection all the more easy, for several of them were indeed mildly attracted to, or even obsessed by, Satanism, the occult, and witchcraft.

Just after Columbine, Pastor Bill Oudemolen, of Foothills Bible Church, in Littleton, Colorado, announced in his Sunday sermon, "I smelled the presence of Satan." A few weeks later, he broadened that with, "[Satan] wants us to see trench coats and people in Gothic attire and makeup and here's what he wants us to feel: look how powerful and scary Satan is." One of his parishioners stated that those who do not accept this "are playing right into Satan's hands." Their inspiration lay in the fact that the very same question—"Do you believe in God?"—had been supposedly asked by Eric Harris and Dylan Klebold to at least two female hostages during their killing spree. Jeff Weise, mimicking them six years later, must have surely been aware of that.

Though it was never conclusively proven whom they were speaking to, Harris and Klebold did make at least one student, and possibly two, reply to that challenge. When the reply was "yes," the gunmen shot them. The literary result of these incidents was a slew of books—six on Rachel Scott, and two on Cassie Bernall—that celebrated their martyrdom. One book title called Rachel "Columbine's Joan of Arc."

Although these sentiments brought comfort to their families, they also raised certain controversies. First, while several terrorized students overheard the gunmen ask "the God question" in the library, where most of the deaths occurred, no one knows with certainty in the confusion to whom these questions were actually addressed. Rachel was, in fact, not in the library—she was one of the first students shot at the school entrance. However, there is no question the seventeen-year-old girl was openly proud of her Christian faith and had expressed her beliefs to Harris and Klebold on more than one occasion. Whether she was targeted for that reason or was simply in the wrong place at the wrong time is still conjecture.

As for Cassie Bernall, two years earlier, "she was going down the road of Dylan and Eric," according to her pastor, the Reverend George Kirsten. Cassie was high on drugs, embroiled in witchcraft, and writing hate-filled letters to her parents saying she wanted to kill them. Then abruptly on a weekend youth ministry, she was "reborn," seemingly overnight. It was the born-again Cassie who came up against a bullet that day, but the only student inside the library who was definitely taunted for her belief in God was Valeen Schnurr. Valeen was wounded by Klebold but lived to tell about it. No books, however, were written about her.

The real issue underlying this disputation is whether the teenage killers in these incidents were specifically "out to get" Christians. Some of those who hold different beliefs feel the heavy focus on this question represents a distortion of the causes and motives of these shooters and was exploited to advance religious agendas by generating a sense of persecution.

The only bona fide "anti-Christian" among shooters, thus far, was Matthew J. Murray, twenty-four, who carried out attacks on December 9, 2007, killing five (including himself) at two evangelical organizations in Colorado because he blamed them for spurning his former missionary ambitions. Murray had been brought up just thirteen miles from Columbine High in a highly religious home with extremely strict rules regarding access to popular media. Matthew wrote, *I remember getting thrown around the room and hit while getting interrogated about whether or not I had video games and DVDs.* Matthew searched for alternate spiritual answers in the satanic lyrics of Swedish metal bands and in a Denver-based occult group called Ad Astra Oasis, which also rejected his membership.

You Christians brought this on yourselves, Murray wrote in a lengthy Internet posting before his rampage, claiming that all he'd found in Christianity was *hate, abuse (sexual, physical, psychological, and emotional), hypocrisy, and lies.* His diatribe ended:

> I'm going out to make a stand for the weak and the defenseless this is for all those young people still caught in the Nightmare of Christianity for all those people who've been abused and mistreated and taken advantage of by this evil sick religion Christian America this is YOUR Columbine.

At Virginia Tech, Seung-hui Cho also used persecution as his main theme. Although he compared himself to Jesus (chapter 15), he paradoxically blamed "Christian Criminals" for his pain (his parents were members of an evangelical church in Centreville, Virginia, and his boyhood pastor admitted that Cho had been bullied in his Christian youth group). Cho made sure we all knew who the real victim was here: "Jesus loves crucifying me. He loves inducing cancer in my head, terrorizing my heart, and wrecking my soul all this time."

Thus, it seems that most anti-Christian rants have emerged from students with evangelical backgrounds. Why might this be? Those who have studied comparative religion point out that in fundamentalist Christianity more than in other faiths, the dichotomy between good and evil is literally a black-and-white issue with few shades of gray. As President G. W. Bush famously said, "You are either with us, or against us." The predilection among shooters for wearing black and cultivating their "dark side" may be an attempt to rebel against a system that they feel gives them "no other options."

As for Harris and Klebold, it's undoubtedly a fact that in their videotapes and writings, they exhibited a hatred of Christians; but they also openly despised "jocks," "preps," and a wide range of other ethnicities, races, religions, and personal habits. In short, they "had it in for" the entire human race. Their chief desire was to shock and offend the people they despised. Patty Nielson, the only teacher in the library that fateful day, was certain the gunmen's real intention was to humiliate and torment their victims, no matter what their beliefs, before indiscriminately shooting them.

When Eric and Dylan prowled through the blood-soaked library casually deciding which of their classmates should live and which should die, they taunted one boy for being fat, another because he was African-American, a third for his style of glasses. They were doing it because, in their minds, they'd been ostracized, ignored, and ridiculed, though perhaps not by the students present there that day, and this was their moment of revenge. In the end, their lifeless bodies lay beside those of their victims, each shot once in the head in an apparent double suicide, although it's also possible they shot each other.

Kip Kinkel had no partner to do him in, but he got one more opportunity to coerce others into committing the one act he seemed incapable of—killing himself. He saw to it that the Thurston drama did not end when he was brought into the Springfield police station.

In point of fact, it was his second visit to that same building in as many days. Detective Alan Warthen, a tough but compassionate cop whose remaining fringe of hair was stippled with gray, had arrested Kip at school on the previous day for possession of a stolen gun. The boy had not been held in detention, as logic dictated and the law allowed, but instead he'd been released into his father's care. It was an act of lenience the detective was no doubt regretting at that moment.

It was Warthen who solemnly returned, once again, to the school to take over the case on May 21. The middle-aged career officer brought Kip back to the station to book him, and then left him alone in a locked interview room while he went out for a moment to set up photo equipment for the mug shots. Kip apparently had not been thoroughly frisked. Still handcuffed from behind and left alone in the room, he managed to loop his arms below his feet, enabling him to pull out the concealed hunting knife that had been taped to his leg. On the detective's return, the youth charged at Warthen, brandishing the blade and screaming, "Kill me! Just shoot me!" as he had in the cafeteria. Warthen hastily retreated and got the door closed between them, but Kip started jabbing at the cuffs with his knife. The officers thought he was trying to slash his wrists. Warthen rushed in with another detective and shot pepper spray at Kip's face while his partner knocked away the weapon.

When Kip calmed down, he was ordered to remove his shirt, somewhat belatedly, so he could be inspected for additional weapons. The detectives then found the bullets taped to Kip's chest. The boy explained their purpose, and admitted killing his parents. Acting swiftly, three Lane County sheriff's officers were dispatched to the Kinkel residence and arrived there just after 9:00 A.M. When they pulled up, one deputy thought he heard a woman screaming inside. It turned out to be an operatic portion of the *Romeo and Juliet* movie soundtrack that Kip had left blasting from the speakers. Through a glass door, the officers spotted several hundred .22-caliber bullets on the living room floor. Entering, they discovered the bodies.

At the same time detectives were searching his home, Kip was confessing to police, rationalizing why he'd shot Faith several times but his father only once. It was not, he said, out of any greater hostility toward his mother, but rather from an intense shame regarding himself, and a desperate affection for her. "She was still alive," Kip told Detective Warthen, "and I said that I loved her. . . . I shot her again so she wouldn't know that I killed her."

During this confession, Kip denied a rumor told to police by students who knew him well: he had left behind some homemade bombs. When the explosive devices were, in fact, discovered, the sheriff's officers stopped their search of the Kinkel residence and evacuated neighboring houses. There was also some concern that the corpses of Bill and Faith might have been booby-trapped, but this proved to be untrue. However, their bodies had to remain as found for another thirty hours until the site was declared safe.

Forensic experts were able to determine that Bill had been drinking coffee when the shot hit him from behind, just above the ear, and he'd slumped over the counter. Kip had dragged his father's body into the bathroom, closed his dad's eyes, and gently but illogically placed his father's glasses back on his face before covering him with a sheet. Kip meticulously cleaned up the blood in the kitchen next, mindful that his mother might return home unexpectedly. He later covered his mother's lifeless body in the same manner with a sheet. Forensic experts say that killers who murder a loved one almost always cover the corpse out of respect, but omit this if they slay a stranger.

Next to Kip's note on the coffee table, detectives found the May 21 *Register-Guard* newspaper. It was folded open to an article describing the trial of Conan Hale, a twenty-two-year-old killer who had murdered three teenagers at a local logging landing back in 1995, when he was nineteen years old. The headline ran: HALE THREATENED TO KILL "SOMEBODY SOMEDAY." Kip had warned of the same thing, and it's very likely he'd been reading that story the morning he made good on his own threats to kill. Ironically, Kip's attack on Thurston may also have influenced the outcome of Hale's trial (chapter 22).

As police were about to find out when they searched the Kinkel residence, Kip had been considering his own annihilation and that of others long before May 20, 1998. That discovery would send further shock waves through the community. As with most school shootings, no one in the town of Springfield had suspected that such a calculating, murderous, and unscrupulous mind could have dwelt so long among them undetected.

In Kip's room, there were two pieces of a demolished punching bag. On one was scrawled, *Mr. Self-Destruction,* and on the other, *Nothing can stop me now.* Kip misspelled the last word as "know" but he meant "now." Both expressions are taken from lyrics on *The Downward Spiral* album of the rock group Nine Inch Nails, recorded in the house where Charles Manson butchered Sharon Tate and her friends on August 9, 1969. "Mr. Self-Destruction" is a corruption of two similar song titles ("Mr. Self-Destruct" and "Self Destruction, Final"). The second phrase is a line from the song "Big Man with a Gun," which also includes the lyrics: *maybe I'll put a hole in your head / you know, just for the fuck of it.* Almost at the conclusion, the song says: *I'm every inch a man, and I'll show you somehow / me and my fucking gun / nothing can stop me now.*

Coincidental to several other school shooters, Kip was also a fan of Goth rock music. He had downloaded the words to songs by Marilyn Manson and other such groups from the Internet. On a single sheet of paper that Kip had printed, framed, and hung on his wall were the following:

- On the top third of the sheet, *no salvation, no forgiveness* was repeated fifteen times. (This song, "The Reflecting God," also contains the lyrics *shoot, shoot, shoot, motherfucker.*)
- From the same album, the lyrics, *every one will suffer now* were also repeated fifteen times on the bottom third of the sheet.
- In between was a jumbled mix of other phrases, including *Nothing here ever lasts Nothing but memories of what never was Living makes me sick, so sick i'd die,* taken from the group Smashing Pumpkins. Kip had underlined the final word.

Police also located Kip's journal. Although it was a full-sized diary, he had written his personal thoughts on only the first two pages. Page one stated just three words in block letters: HATE DRIVES ME. The next page was filled up to the margins with diminutive handwriting in minuscule script, which psychologists say is often indicative of a disturbed personality. Most of the following pages were completely blank, but some bomb-making recipes appeared toward the end of the journal. Kip's single-page memoir included the following lines, presented here with corrected misspellings:

> I sit here all alone. I am always alone. I don't know who I am. I want to be something I can never be. I tried so hard every day. But in the end, I hate myself for what I've become. Every single person I know means nothing to me. I hate every person on this earth. I wish they could all go away. You all make me sick. I wish I was dead. The only reason I stay alive is because of hope. Even though I am repulsive and few people know who I am, I still feel that things might, maybe, just a little bit, get better.
>
> I feel like everyone is against me, but no one ever makes fun of me, mainly because they think I am a psycho. There is one kid above all others that I want to kill. I want nothing more than to put a hole in his head. The one reason I don't: Hope. That tomorrow will be better. As soon as my hope is gone, people die. I ask myself why I hate more than anyone else. I don't know. But my head and heart want him dead. He only knows who I am through reputation, and I know he is scared of me. He should be. One

bad day, and there will be a sawed off shotgun in his face or five pounds of Semtex under his bed.

Oh fuck. I sound so pitiful. People would laugh at this if they read it. I hate being laughed at. But they won't laugh after they're scraping parts of their parents, sisters, brothers, and friends from the wall of my hate. Please. Someone, help me. All I want is something small. Nothing big. I just want to be happy.

Here Kip had divided the page and written, *new day*, then . . .

I feel like my heart has been ripped open and ripped apart. Right now, I'm drunk, so I don't know what the hell is happening to me. It is clear that no one will help me. Oh God, I am so close to killing people. So close.

Why did God just want me to be in complete misery? I need to find more weapons. My parents are trying to take away some of my guns! My guns are the only things that haven't stabbed me in the back. My eyes hurt. They hurt so bad. They feel like they are trying to crawl out of my head. Why aren't I normal? Help me. No one will. I will kill every last mother fucking one of you.

Kill me. Oh God, I don't want to live. Will I see it to the end? What kind of dad would I make? All humans are evil. I just want to end the world of evil. I don't want to see, hear, speak or feel evil, but I can't help it. I am evil. I want to kill and give pain without a cost. And there is no such thing. We kill him—we killed him a long time ago. Anyone that believes in God is a fucking sheep. If there was a God, he wouldn't let me feel the way I do. . . . Love isn't real, only hate remains. Only hate.

• Chapter 4 •

"Mr. Self-Destruction"

Every homicide is unconsciously a suicide and every sui-cide is, in a sense, a psychological homicide. Typically, the killer is afraid of killing himself, afraid of dying, and there-fore he murders someone else.
—David Abrahamsen, *The Murdering Mind*

Fortunate indeed is the adult who can recall his or her teenage years as a time of constant comfort, zero conflict, and unrivaled success. The more usual course of adolescence is to stumble through uneven periods of self-doubt, or even self-hate. In a best-case scenario, the pain associated with this downside of growth can lead to a strength-ening of character, but it can also sometimes cause suicidal depres-sion even within those households blessed by material well-being and/or strong religious convictions. Despite the fact that, in general, the affluence and technological conveniences of our society seem to be in a constant state of growth, teenagers are now killing them-selves at a faster rate than ever before in American history. Over the past several decades, the suicide rate for adolescents aged fifteen to nineteen has approximately doubled every twenty years. It is now the third leading cause of death among our young, after motor ve-hicle accidents and homicide.

If this trend merely concluded with teens who aborted their own youthful lives, the situation would be tragic enough. But it gets worse. Researchers have discovered compelling evidence that links suicidal ideation with homicide. Connections between self-loathing and aggression heighten the probability of a young person committing murder-suicide, for how can those who no longer value their own lives value the lives of others? The cement that bonds all these elements together is the dark catalyst of depression. Nearly every school shooter on record suffered from above average to severe depression. Many of them were either suicidal at the time of their rampage, contemplated killing themselves prior to it, or attempted to do so immediately after. And many succeeded.

When Kip Kinkel was brought into police custody and the .22-caliber and 9mm bullets were found taped to his chest, he explained that he thought he might need them to kill himself at the end of his shooting spree, so he'd prepared one of each type in case he ran out of ammunition. This is keeping in mind that he had brought over a thousand rounds into the cafeteria with him, evidently intending to use it all up. When it was recognized that Kip really had not planned to live through the day, a suicide watch was initiated and Dr. Suckow, a psychologist, was called in to monitor him.

In a taped interview, Suckow asked Kip what he was feeling when he killed, and the boy replied, "I just wanted to shoot myself, but I couldn't. I just wanted to die." Kip also told Suckow the only thing that made him happy was when he held a gun. As to why he went on his rampage, Kip proclaimed, "My head kept telling me I had no other choice," which at that time did not make any sense. Soon after, a court-appointed lawyer showed up and stopped the questioning.

Another teen shooter who resembled Kinkel in several respects was Michael Carneal, a fourteen-year-old high school freshman in West Paducah, Kentucky, who killed three students and wounded five at Heath High School in 1997, precisely two months to the day after Luke Woodham's assault in Mississippi. The first person he shot was Nicole Hadley, fourteen, a girl he'd wanted to date, but who had not returned his affections. Michael used a phrase almost identical to Kip's after his rampage ceased, pleading to student Benjamin Strong, who disarmed him, "Please, kill me now. I can't believe I did that. Kill me, please."

Benjamin was able to talk Michael into dropping the gun. He was the son of a pastor and leader of the student prayer group that Michael fired into just as they squeezed hands and said, "Amen." The day before, Michael had warned Ben, "Better not come to school tomorrow," because of kindnesses the older boy had shown him in the past.

When Michael was about twelve, friends pulled him off some railroad tracks where he had lain down in a game of chicken. A slightly built, B-average student who wore thick glasses, he told psychiatrists he felt worthless, had tried self-mutilation, and had thought of suicide, even to the point of playing with a gun. He was distressed by his inadequacy in making or keeping friends, and was diagnosed as suffering from depression. Like Kip Kinkel, Michael Carneal felt guns empowered him, and like Kip, he also got hold of a copy of *The Anarchist Cookbook* bomb-making guide, which he downloaded from the Internet.

In art class, Michael made a poster-sized collage featuring suicide themes: a decapitated man in a wheelchair and a stack of dead pigs. Anger and frustration were revealed in his school writing portfolio. An essay he wrote called "Halloween Surprise" concerns a bullied boy named Mike who surprises his mother by presenting her with the impaled bodies of "preps," i.e., schoolmates perceived to be snobbish and pretentious who had tormented him. In a close parallel, Columbine documents released in July 2006 revealed a graphic story by shooter Dylan Klebold about the slaughter of some "preps." Many of Virginia Tech killer Seung-hui Cho's written and video ravings were aimed at this same category of "privileged" students.

On December 1, after what was described as a normal Thanksgiving weekend spent with his parents, Michael Carneal wrapped five rifles in blankets, stuffed a pistol, earplugs, and almost one thousand rounds of ammunition into a backpack, and smuggled the lot into school, pretending he was carrying items for a science project. Michael stopped long enough to show his closest friends his stolen .22-caliber Ruger Mark II semiautomatic pistol, the same gun Kip used to kill his dad. Then he calmly put in ear protectors so the noise wouldn't bother him, and took a two-handed shooter's stance as he emptied a ten-round magazine into the circle of praying students. When asked later why he did it, Michael said he didn't know. On his eighteenth birthday, he was transferred to an adult prison, where he is serving a life sentence.

Luke Woodham told authorities that he thought about death as early as eight years old. In elementary school, he'd told his brother, "I just want to die," and said that often he "would sit around and think about death . . . mine." After being rejected by his girlfriend, Christina Menefee, Luke tried to kill himself at home with a gun on two occasions. Ironically, he was talked out of doing it during telephone calls with Christina, whom he would later kill, and in calls from another friend.

Kip, Luke, and Michael were hardly alone in planning to take "the easy way out" rather than face the consequences of their final act. In fact, because of the high percentage of school shooters who actually succeed in killing themselves, or who attempt to do so during their bloody siege, one could assume this to be an almost universal "given." Seung-hui Cho merely reinforced that point. In December 2005, he had told a roommate, "I might as well kill myself" after police warned him to stop stalking two women and secretly photographing students in class with his cell phone (he was never charged). The roommates reported his suicide threat, and police escorted Cho off campus this time. A county magistrate ordered Seung-hui to undergo a mental evaluation, declaring that there was probable cause the young man was "mentally ill" and an "imminent danger to self and others." He was involuntarily kept overnight at Carilion Saint Albans Behavioral Health Center (a move that should have prevented him from later buying guns), and he was prescribed medication for depression along with further counseling.

This suicidal bent also holds true for older adults who open fire on elementary schools or playgrounds, and even for those without access to guns who substitute various types of blades or explosives to wreak havoc. One of the few exceptions among this coterie of self-destructive killers were the two young boys at Jonesboro, Arkansas, in March 1998 (just two months before Thurston) who had a getaway vehicle and survival rations at the ready. However, even these culprits, Andrew Golden and Mitchell Johnson, did not seem blessed with anything that could be termed as long-term planning skills.

On rare occasions, a shooter has had a last-minute change of heart. On May 20, 1999, exactly one year after Kinkel killed his parents, and one month after Columbine to the day, sophomore Thomas "T.J." Solomon entered Heritage High School in Conyers, Georgia, at 7:55 A.M. as classmates ate breakfast. Solomon opened fire in the school commons area with a .22-caliber hunting rifle and a .357-caliber Magnum handgun taken from his stepfather's gun cabinet. Because he fired low, only at legs and feet, T.J. wounded six, but killed no one. The intended outcome was clearly suicide, as the fifteen-year-old next put the handgun into his mouth. However, Assistant Principal Cecil Brinkley talked the shooter into reconsidering. Solomon laid the gun down on the ground, then handed it to Brinkley, put his arms around the assistant principal, and tearfully surrendered.

Conyers is an affluent suburb of Atlanta and T.J. lived in a comfortable home with his mom and stepdad, an executive who loved hunting and kept a large collection of firearms. T.J. was being treated with a drug for hyperactivity and another for depression. After his girlfriend broke up with him, T.J. told friends he would bring a gun or bomb to school, or kill himself. He later plead guilty, but mentally ill. As a juvenile, the maximum sentence would have been five years in detention, but he was tried as an adult and sentenced to forty years in prison and sixty-five years of probation.

As the alert reader will have noted by this point, the use of antidepressant drugs (known collectively as Selective serotonin reuptake inhibitors, or SSRIs), such as Prozac, Zoloft, and Paxil, [stimulants such as Ritalin, antianxiety agents like Xanax, and antipsychotics like Thorazine] figure strongly in the histories of many school shooters, as well as in the backgrounds of numerous suicides, parricides, and workplace massacres. There has been a great deal written about the links between these drugs and violent or self-destructive acts, but for the nonprofessional, separating fact from rumor is no easy task. On the one hand, we realize that legitimate researchers are trying their best to produce safe drugs to treat depression and other ailments. Simultaneously we know that pharmaceutical companies are a multibillion-dollar industry, which, like any commercial interest, is trying to maximize profits.

Even a cursory glance at blogs and Web sites on this subject reveals that many people contend these drugs twist moral values, destroy ethical beliefs, and cause people to kill without feeling remorse. Dr. Julian Whitaker is a high-profile critic and practitioner of alternative medicine at his Whitaker Wellness Institute in Newport Beach,

California. He asserts there is credible evidence that the pharmaceutical industry, abetted by the FDA, has managed to keep crucial data from the public regarding the dangerous side effects of SSRIs discovered during clinical trials.

These drugs can cause Akathisia, mental and physical agitation that sparks self-destructive, violent behavior. They can also induce dissociative reactions, making those who take the drugs insensitive to the consequences of their behavior, Dr. Whitaker wrote in a November 1999 article titled "The Reason Behind the Madness," published in *Health and Healing: Tomorrow's Medicine Today.* Regarding mass murderers, such as school shooters, he writes: *Guns and movies don't cause these tragically frequent episodes of inexplicable violence. The real reason is written out on a prescription pad by psychiatrists and doctors all over the country—these monstrous acts were done not by criminals, but ordinary people high on prescription drugs.*

Whether the assertions of Dr. Whitaker and others are incontrovertible fact or educated opinion, the truth of the matter is that, as a suspect, SSRI drugs turn up in rampage shootings with more frequency than can be passed off as mere coincidence. In addition to Solomon, other users mentioned in this chapter include Michael Carneal and the Jonesboro duo, Andrew Golden and Mitchell Johnson (detailed in chapters 5 & 7), who were all believed to be on Ritalin. Published reports claimed Luke Woodham was on Prozac; Jeff Weise, taken up again at the end of this chapter, was on sixty milligrams of Prozac a day. Kip Kinkel had been prescribed both Prozac and Ritalin. The parents of Matthew Murray put him on two antidepressants after he shared his feelings about being suicidally depressed. Columbine autopsy reports confirmed that a significant amount of Luvox, an antidepressant, was found in Eric Harris's bloodstream. He had previously been on Zoloft, but was switched to the new drug when he reported suicidal and homicidal ideation.

Many other school shooters were supposedly using SSRI medications at the time of their crimes. Such data is often not disclosed to the public, but autopsy reports revealed that the body of thirty-year-old Laurie Wasserman Dann (chapter 21), who killed herself after a shooting spree at an elementary school in Winnetka, Illinois, on May 20, 1988 (ten years to the day before Kinkel's parricide), contained high amounts of Anafranil and lithium. Fourteen-year-old Elizabeth Bush, of Pennsylvania, another of the rare female shooters described in chapter 21, was on Prozac when she wounded a girl in March 2001. At age eighteen, Jason Hoffman (whose prison suicide is detailed later in this chapter) was on the antidepressants Effexor and Celexa when he wounded three students and two teachers at Granite Hills High School, in El Cajon, California, on March 22, 2001.

Prozac also played a role in the February 14, 2008 shooting at Northern Illinois University. Stephen Kazmierczak had stopped taking his medication for anxiety and obsessive-compulsive disorder about three weeks earlier, because "it made him feel like a zombie," according to his girlfriend Jessica Baty, who was twenty-eight. Kazmierczak's former psychiatric group home manager told reporters that as a teen, the young man had resisted using meds. "He never wanted to identify with being mentally ill," she said. "That was part of the problem."

Jessica Baty denied that her boyfriend's behavior after he ceased using Prozac had become erratic, delusional, or in any way unusual. Nevertheless, when Kazmierczak walked through a stage door on the right-hand side of Cole lecture hall at around 3 p.m. and calmly began firing at the teacher and students, "He had a blank look on his face," said witness Sam Brunell. "He was there to kill. Anyone that could walk into a room and just start shooting has no emotions."

Kazmierczak had paid cash to procure a DeKalb motel room three days before the shootings. The only "drugs" police found there were empty cartons of cigarettes, dozens of caffeinated energy drinks and cold medicine.

"Baby-faced" Cory Baadsgaard, of Mattawa, Washington, had been taken off Paxil and was receiving high doses (three hundred milligrams) of Effexor when he sneaked through a side door of Wahluke High School with a loaded big-game hunting rifle. The slender sixteen-year-old held twenty-three classmates and teacher Michelle Hanson hostage at gunpoint in his honors English class on April 10, 2001. To end the crisis, Principal Bob Webb and intervention specialist David Garcia came into the room and knelt in an unthreatening fashion in front of the boy, convincing him to put down the gun. They were aware of a deadly incident in nearby Moses Lake that had taken place five years earlier (later in this chapter, and chapters 20, 23 and 25) involving a deer-hunting rifle.

Canadian school shooter Todd Smith (chapter 20), who at fourteen required medications for a congenital heart condition, went into a coma for several months after he killed one student and injured another in Taber, Alberta, on April 28, 1999, eight days after Columbine. Later that year, on December 6, thirteen-year-old Seth Trickey fired off at least fifteen rounds with a 9mm semiautomatic Taurus pistol outside his Fort Gibson Middle School, in Oklahoma, wounding five classmates. At his first hearing, Trickey pleaded innocent to the charges, and SSRIs were part of his defense. He was convicted on seven assault charges, but after spending almost three years in Oklahoma's Office of Juvenile Affairs, he was released in 2003 to his maternal grandparents in Lawrence, Kansas. He graduated early from high school, took college classes, and did volunteer work at an American Indian resource center.

It's not only the students. A Chelsea, Michigan, high school chemistry and physics teacher named Stephen Leith, who was reportedly taking antidepressants, excused himself from a staff meeting on December 16, 1993, but returned a few minutes later with a semiautomatic pistol. He shot and killed Superintendent Joseph Piasecki and wounded another teacher and the principal.

Among other adult shooters who attacked schools, the 1966 University of Texas Tower sniper Charles Whitman (chapter 26) was a heavy user of amphetamines and prescription drugs. So was Patrick Purdy (chapter 8), aged twenty-six, who opened fire on a California schoolyard in January 1989. Former graduate student Peter Odighizuwa (chapter 28), who in 2002 killed three at the Appalachian School of Law, in Virginia, told a judge, *"I was supposed to see my doctor. He was supposed to help me out. . . . I don't have my medication."*

It's only common sense that those exhibiting depression would be treated with antidepressants, and the fact that some of them respond differently than others shouldn't surprise us. However, the possibility that side effects may include increased suicidal and homicidal behavior should certainly concern us.

Further, an Associated Press investigation released on March 10, 2008, revealed that trace amounts of a vast array of pharmaceuticals—

including antibiotics, anticonvulsants, mood stabilizers, and sex hor-
mones—have been detected in the reservoir systems of at least 41
million Americans, and that more than 100 variations of such drugs
have been found in drinking water supplies throughout the world.
We are all being touched by these medications whether we want to
be or not.

Of course, SSRIs are not the *only* factor in the suicide-homicide
equation. In fact, on one occasion, a shooter did not intend suicide,
but fate intervened. On January 23, 1995, eighth grader John Sirola
shot principal Richard Facciolo in the face and shoulder at Sacred
Heart School, in Redlands, California, with a sawed-off shotgun stolen
from a family friend. The reason for this act of cruelty was reportedly the school's insistence that John wear a uniform. As the thirteen-
year-old fled the principal's office, he tripped and dropped the gun.
It went off accidentally, resulting in John himself being shot and
killed.

Richard Facciolo recovered, but another principal was not so
lucky. On April 24, 2003, about fifteen minutes before classes started
at Red Lion Area Junior High School, in Pennsylvania, fourteen-year-
old James Robert Sheets pulled a .44-caliber Magnum handgun from
his backpack in the crowded cafeteria and fired one bullet into the
chest of principal Eugene Segro. As Segro collapsed and students began
to flee, the eighth grader took out another gun, this time a .22-caliber
pistol, and shot himself in the head. Both weapons, plus an unused
.357-caliber Magnum, were taken from the gun safe of Sheets' stepfather, just as Solomon had done at his home in 1999. This case was
unusual only in that Sheets, unlike most school shooters, had not issued a forewarning to anyone.

As indicated in the cases of Solomon, Woodham, Carneal, and possibly Kinkel, lost love is a prevalent theme in murder-suicides, whether
in or outside of school, with the romantic object of affection often
being a prime target of their bullets. On the same day as Kinkel's
Thurston shooting, Miles Fox, who was the same age as Kip, boarded
a school bus in Onalaska, Washington, and ordered his girlfriend to
get off at gunpoint. He took her to his home and fatally shot himself as the girl's father was breaking down the door.

The previous year, in late October 1997, an estranged boyfriend,

Khoa Truc "Robert" Dang, twenty-one, walked straight up to his sixteen-year-old former girlfriend, Catherine Tran, shot her to death with a 9mm Glock handgun, and then killed himself. The incident took place at John Glenn High School in Norwalk, California, from which Dang had graduated with honors in 1994.

On May 15, 2001, a young Texas man went to an English class at Ennis High School to do in a one-sided love interest, but he ended up merely blasting the classroom television before ending his own life with a second shot. Veteran teacher Andrea Webb became a true heroine when she bravely took a defensive position between sixteen-year-old Jay Douglas Goodwin and her students, including Jay's unrequited intended, Kim Crow. Though threatened at the point of Goodwin's .357 Magnum, Webb refused to obey the boy's commands to leave the room. Instead, she convinced him to release all the students except her and Kim, at which point Goodwin chose a different ending.

The only school hostage-cum-suicide situation in 2001 *after* 9/11 was also based upon a romantic breakup two days earlier. This Caro, Michigan, incident is described in chapter 26. However, one other school shooting–suicide based upon a frustrated infatuation is worthy of note for the strange twist it took. Douglas Bradley was having problems with his girlfriend, he had a history of depression, and he'd attempted suicide in the past. Friends in Palo Alto knew he'd been asking around for a gun, but didn't report it. Bradley decided to end it all with a plan uniquely Californian, involving cars, murder, and money. On February 8, 1996, the sixteen-year-old drove his navy blue Honda Accord onto the school playground and, stopping on an outdoor basketball court, started throwing dollar bills out the window. As classmates moved closer to scoop up the cash, Douglas fired three shots at them with a .38-caliber handgun, wounding a fourteen-year-old boy in the leg. With a fourth shot, Bradley terminated his own life.

Broken hearts are not always about romance. Fifteen-year-old Justin Allgood had recently lost two of his best friends in car accidents in Taylorsville, Utah. Despondent with shock and grief, on May 14, 1996, he got hold of a .357 Magnum and hijacked an empty Bingham Middle School bus after shooting the driver in the thigh. He may have wanted to die like his friends as he drove at high speed through a residential neighborhood, causing three accidents and finally crashing the bus into a two-story house. Dazed but still alive, Justin decided to finish it there with his gun.

While quashed emotions certainly contributed to the *"I'll show you!"* mind-set of suicidal school shooters, verbal harassment was an even more common factor. Being smart doesn't help if classmates constantly put you down as a nerd. Nathan D. Faris, twelve, was sick of being routinely teased about his weight and his reputation as a walking dictionary. On the final Friday of February 1987, he vowed he would put an end to the ridicule by bringing a gun to his school in DeKalb, Missouri, on the following Monday. His classmates didn't take him seriously, even when he pulled a .45-caliber pistol from his duffel bag on Monday, March 2, as threatened. The other students continued to taunt him for bringing a toy gun to school, so he proved it was real by killing Timothy Perrin, thirteen. In the uproar that followed, Nathan then turned the pistol on himself and pulled the trigger.

Another suicidal student took his resentment out on two math teachers at Blackville-Hilda High School in South Carolina even though it had been students who'd picked on him. True, Toby Sincino, sixteen, had also been suspended one week earlier for making an obscene gesture, and he was pretty upset about that. So on October 12, 1995, Toby returned to school carrying a .32-caliber revolver and wounded instructor Johnny Thompson with a bullet to his face. In the math teachers' workroom, Toby found and killed Phyllis Senn and then used the gun on himself.

By the time Jeff Weise put a bullet in his brain at Red Lake Indian Reservation in March 2005, the pattern had become consistently familiar. School officials later said they'd recognized behavioral problems in Jeff, but Weise himself had complained about harassment he received. In fact, it was one of the reasons cited for his transfer to the school's "Homebound" program in which students are tutored by a traveling teacher. His grandmother said that twice in the previous year, Jeff stopped attending Red Lake High and received tutoring because he was unable to handle teasing from classmates. At that time, he wrote about an inner anguish that *makes you so de-*

pressed you can't function, makes you so sad and overwhelmed with grief that eating a bullet or sticking your head in a noose [seems] welcoming.

Jeff was put on Prozac after a suicide scare during the summer of 2004 in which he sliced his wrists with a box cutter, *painting the floor of my bedroom with blood,* as he wrote on the Internet. Prozac was the only medication claimed to be safe and effective for children at that time, but in October of that year, the U.S. Food and Drug Administration (FDA) ordered that *all* antidepressants carry "black box" warnings of an increased risk of suicidal thinking, psychosis, or hostility (i.e., homicidal behavior) in young patients.

A "black box" is the highest-level warning in drug labeling. This one emphasizes the need for closely monitoring pediatric patients taking SSRI meds, especially when prescribers recommend any abrupt change in dose (up or down). The FDA also issued a warning of mounting evidence that during withdrawal from these drugs, there could be a temporary worsening of negative symptoms. The danger may begin from three weeks to four months after discontinuing the drug, and could last from a month to a year. Even though the medication may no longer show up in blood tests or autopsy reports, symptoms can persist as neurotransmitters in the brain continue "realigning" themselves.

In several 2005 online postings attributed to Jeff Weise, he spoke of depression and feelings of worthlessness. On January 4, he wrote: *I should've taken the razor blade express last time around. . . . Well, whatever, man. Maybe they've got another shuttle comin' around soon?* The last time Jeff saw a mental-health professional at Red Lake Hospital was on February 21, exactly a month before his killing spree.

Just a few days after Jeff Weise's hospital visit, eighteen-year-old Peter Keatainak shed blood at his high school in the far northern Quebec town of Salluit, on the Hudson Strait. Peter had been expelled, but returned with a gun on February 25. He shot his French teacher Hassina Kerfi-Guetteb in the neck, then shot himself. She survived; Peter didn't.

Even in imprisonment, some school shooters manage to complete their endgame. Anthony Barbaro, the first high school shooter in the

United States (chapter 8), hanged himself while awaiting trial in 1975, as did San Diego shooter Jason Hoffman a week before his sentencing in 2001, using bedsheets strung to a ventilation port.

Dr. George Palermo, writing in the *International Journal of Offender Therapy and Comparative Criminology*, observed: *These killers do not flee from the scene of their criminal offense, and they are not concerned about leaving evidence or being apprehended. Their homicidal fury clouds their self-preservation instinct.* Aware of the inherent wrongness of their crimes even as they commit them, *their hostility is directed both outwardly and inwardly. . . . It can be argued that they then punish themselves by becoming their own executioners.*

Dr. Palermo's words were published in March 1999. As valuable as this study is, it's interesting to note that it concluded, *Among juvenile mass murderers, there are no reported suicides (or attempts) by the offenders.* A month later, that observation would be very publicly disproven at Columbine. Even at the time, they had overlooked the suicidal aspects of Kinkel's earlier attack at Thurston, which was included in their report, and those of many other school shooters mentioned above.

Further, the cases listed in this chapter illustrate only the tip of a self-destruction iceberg. In fact, statistics that list all types of school violence show that for every combined school shooting–suicide, there are easily as many "classic" suicides at schools in which a young person makes a public display of taking him or herself out, but does no harm to others—at least physically. One of these incidents—the 1991 classroom suicide of Jeremy Delle in Texas (chapter 20)—became an award-winning rock video for musical group Pearl Jam. Sadly, that music video helped inspire Barry Loukaitis to kill a teacher and two students during his Moses Lake, Washington, shootings in 1996.

• Chapter 5 •

A Minor Sentence

The juvenile mass murderers believe that they have been wronged, assume a paranoid attitude, and are able to rationalize their emotions as follows: "I am alone. They don't appreciate me. I will show them who I am. I will dispose of them."

—Dr. George B. Palermo, clinical professor of psychiatry and neurology, Medical College of Wisconsin

The title of the Palermo report cited above and in the previous chapter is "Mass Murder, Suicide, and Moral Development: Can We Separate the Adults from the Juveniles?" Included within it were references to a number of earlier studies, some of which dated back to the 1980s. The following profile material from previous decades presciently describes shooter Seung-hui Cho at Virginia Tech:

According to one report, the killers were "motivated by revenge and despair, or by the desire to get even or to rectify perceived or received wrongs." Many showed signs of a superman complex and appeared to seek notoriety, even posthumous, due to their narcissistic personalities. They seemed unable to deal with common frustrations and tended to depersonalize their victims. While their anger may have focused on one individual, they targeted a larger number of others whom they viewed as equally responsible for their troubles.

Such comments could have been made with equal accuracy in the days following the Virginia Tech slayings, but another report quoted by Palermo comes even closer to Cho's profile, noting that many killers had a history of contacts with the psychiatric profession. All showed ambivalent feelings toward their families and seemed to carry grudges against society or their fellow students. "The idea of 'payback time' frequently is expressed just prior to the homicides, although there is always some event triggering revenge and retribution."

Two citations from previous studies suggest mass murderers also have experienced "impaired child attachments, formative traumatic experiences, and private internal worlds of thoughts and fantasies." As a result, the killers felt isolated and had none of the usual constraints on behavior.

These comments, which perfectly describe so many recent youthful school shooters, were actually made about adult mass murderers (average age twenty-five to forty). Cho was twenty-three and could be considered an adult, but the Columbine shooters, Jeff Weise, Kip, and many others were much younger. From the perspective of our present-day knowledge, we can now deduce that the inclusion of suicidal ideation in their attacks eliminates the last vestige of any "alternative distinguishing features" differentiating adult and juvenile mass murderers and crumbles the theory that younger shooters, at least in their mid-to-late teens, have a "less developed sociomoral conscience."

We can still concur with this study's observation regarding juvenile offenders that *from a legal point of view, the mass murders perpetrated by juveniles face the judicial system with a serious dilemma. . . . Their actions are incongruous with their status as children.* However, what are we now to make of the authors' conclusions regarding how this challenges the criminal justice system? The report states:

> Indeed, if the above assumptions are true—that the adult mass murderer is more mature than the juvenile and allegedly possesses a developed social and moral conscience—does the juvenile offender who may not yet have fully developed such a conscience possess substantial mental capacity to appreciate the quality and consequences of his actions?

Unfortunately, "the above assumptions," based upon a misperceived lack of any suicidal tendencies by juvenile mass murderers, have proven to be false. The report posits the question *Does the fact that they do not commit suicide after the killing support the assumption that they are unable to appreciate its wrongfulness?* Therefore, the revised query necessarily becomes *Does the fact that they do commit suicide after the killing support the assumption that they are indeed able to appreciate its wrongfulness?*

That question underpins the sentencing of Kip and other young, suicidal mass murderers who have survived their killing sprees. Internationally, an overwhelming majority of countries support the United Nations Convention on the Rights of the Child, which states that crimes committed by a juvenile should not result in life imprisonment without the possibility of parole, regardless of the circumstances. Execution of minors is, of course, also forbidden. According to the U.S. Department of Justice, America and Somalia are the only two UN members that have not ratified that accord.

However, on March 1, 2005, the U.S. Supreme Court ruled that the execution of killers who were under eighteen when they committed their crimes was unconstitutional, ending a practice used in twenty states. Justice Anthony Kennedy wrote, *The age of eighteen is the point where society draws the line for many purposes between childhood and adulthood. It is, we conclude, the age at which the line for death eligibility ought to rest.* The executions, the court said, violate the Eighth Amendment ban on cruel and unusual punishment. The 5–4 decision threw out the death sentences of about seventy juvenile murderers and bars states from seeking to execute minors for future crimes. Kennedy noted that *our society views juveniles . . . as categorically less culpable than the average criminal,* and that *the instability and emotional imbalance of young people may often be a factor in the crime.*

On May 22, 1998, Kip Kinkel was arraigned on four counts of aggravated murder, and in June indicted on fifty-eight felony charges. Over a year later, just as the trial was gearing up, Kip dropped his plea of insanity. Because many of his actions were deemed willful or volitional, his defense counsel no longer felt confident Kip could win a verdict of "guilty but insane," the state of Oregon's variation of what other parts of the United States might call "not guilty by reason of insanity." On September 24, 1999, after intense settlement negotiations, Kip's attorneys, Mark Sabitt and Richard Mullen, advised him to plead guilty to four counts of murder and twenty-six counts of attempted murder.

This meant there would be no criminal trial. Instead, a sentencing hearing was called for in the coming November that would last about a week. Prosecution and defense counsels provided evidence and called witnesses just as they would in a normal trial. The main focus of the hearing was Kip's mental state. Sabitt and Mullen held out some hope that issues of Kip's psychosis introduced as extenuating factors would result in a less harsh prison term. They argued that because of his psychotic disorder, his culpability was mitigated. Assistant District Attorney (ADA) Kent Mortimore disagreed and argued that Kip knew what he was doing, chose to do it, and should therefore "die in prison." He asked the court to lock Kip away for the maximum sentence of 222 years.

Defense psychiatrists testified that their medical exams confirmed Kip labored under a complex set of paranoid delusions, including a certitude that the Chinese Army was going to invade America, an outbreak of plague was imminent, and Disney dollars would soon take over our U.S. currency. They said he also experienced domineering auditory hallucinations, a further indication that he suffered from schizophrenia. Prosecution psychiatrists, including the celebrated Dr. Park Dietz, also examined Kip, but they were not called to testify or present reports.

Kip's counsel hoped for an agreement on a sentence of no more than twenty-five years. Besides the issue of Kip's mental condition, Sabitt reminded Judge Jack Mattison of Kip's minor status, arguing that "in a civilized society, we don't lock away our fifteen-year-old offenders without hope." Nevertheless, on November 2, Kip was sentenced to 111.67 years in prison *without* possibility of parole.

Public opinion ranged from those wishing to see Kip put into long-term treatment at a secure mental institution, to others favoring his execution. The latter course was impossible, since the lower age limit on capital punishment by lethal injection in Oregon was sixteen years old. Nevertheless, the police and detention center received many anonymous threats from people who wished to personally kill Kip with their own hands. A University of Oregon survey conducted in fall 1999 asked for the opinions of 420 Oregon adults. A majority of 56 percent "strongly agreed" with the nearly 112-year sentence, 32 percent thought it was too harsh or that it didn't include sufficient psychiatric counseling, and 21 percent thought his punishment should be death.

Many individuals were sympathetic to the mental deficiencies and youthfulness of the perpetrator, and they wished to see Kip being helped in a medical facility. Belief that juveniles in general should not be held liable for serious crimes in the same way as adults is based upon the principle that they are too immature to really understand what they are doing, and thus deserve greater compassion than the law presently provides, no matter how heinous their crimes.

A grad student at a New York forensic studies college shared an essay with the author that she'd written criticizing the fact that children who don't have adult privileges and responsibilities under the law while they are minors are suddenly considered to be adults if they commit a crime. Her point was that since the mind of an underage teen is not considered mature enough to handle such things as drinking alcohol, signing contracts, driving a car, or gambling, why, then, are they held legally responsible as adults when they break the law? She felt that society couldn't have it both ways.

This is a subject that stirs deep passions on both sides of the issue, with very little middle ground for compromise. During Kinkel's appeals, a letter written by a Canadian appeared in the January 12, 2003, Eugene *Register-Guard* condemning Oregon's juvenile justice system for allowing Kip to be imprisoned for life. The letter writer blamed the daily's editorials for contributing *to an atmosphere which drowned out any reasoned discussion of [Kip's] fate. Mob hysteria whipped up by the newspaper probably played a large part in his lawyers' decision to have Kinkel plead guilty. . . . [The* Register-Guard] *fanned the flames of hatred toward the child at the center of all this. . . . If Kip Kinkel had lived [in Canada], the maximum he would have received is six years. Is Oregon totally without mercy?*

This unambiguous sympathy for Kinkel's predicament reflected the continuing efforts of a coterie of like-minded people dedicated to lessening the severity of Kip's incarceration. One of them wrote a report on the subject of adult sentencing of minors in which she called these young offenders "sacrificial lambs." While she raised some legitimate concerns, her choice of metaphor seemed overly naive; *lambs*, after all, do not carry semiautomatic weapons and shoot people. Yet a surprising number of individuals expressed similar feelings about Kip to the author. As one University of Oregon professor who deals with children's legal issues put it: "While lots of folks in town wanted to hang [Kinkel], I wanted to take this child and hold him. I guess I kind of have a mother complex—especially when it comes to hurting kids."

Conversely, the parent of one of the shooting victims pointed out that Kip "was the one who decided to be motherless. He already had a deeply caring mom who loved, protected, and held him. . . . He shot her in the face and heart. These women who think they can do better than his real mother nauseate me." Another victim compared women who wanted to cradle Kip to those who send love letters to condemned murderers, seeking to resolve issues instilled in their own dysfunctional childhoods (chapter 22). Clearly, opinion was divided upon where the public's sympathies should lie.

All fifty U.S. states now have laws that allow juveniles as young as fourteen to be tried as adults. School shootings contributed mightily to the enactment of those laws, partly because the publicity surrounding them signaled a sea change in sentiment regarding the "innocence" and accountability of adolescents. Many prosecutors and law officials reject the notion that youthful perpetrators are guiltless and redeemable simply by virtue of their legal age. Their stance is that if a "child" kills another human being, that youngster has forfeited his or her rights of childhood.

Their argument goes something like this: When it comes to capital crimes, lenient sentiments of unconditional forgiveness underestimate the intelligence and cunning ingenuity of these young felons. Further, chronological age is not always a measure of maturity. Just as some youths exhibit impressive powers of reasoning and intuitive clarity, some older people display infantile reactions in response to challenging situations. If a yardstick of maturity is the ability to recognize the connection between cause and effect before a harmful and irreversible action is taken, can it truly be said that a middle-aged mass murderer is any more "mature" than an adolescent school shooter?

According to an October 2005 LA Times article, signs are posted in the Caucasus region of Chechnya, a spawning ground for terrorism, that display a legendary warrior's motto: HE WHO THINKS ABOUT

CONSEQUENCES IS NOT A HERO. By disparaging any consideration of cause and effect, terrorists encourage blind obedience to a mindless, antiempathic doctrine of hate. Even lacking a terrorism support network, many suicidal-homicidal youths decide on their own that examining consequences only interferes with their fatal objectives.

Blanket amnesties that remove the burden of responsibility from all young people make no allowances for the roots and causes of their criminal acts. A seriously abused child, born in dire poverty to alcoholic or drug-addicted parents, and brought up in brutal circumstances, may see little choice but to opt for violent solutions to problems. In this case, guilt might be mitigated by the hopelessness of the offender's past environment. On the other hand, a child of privilege, pampered by involved and loving parents, given a good education and offered counseling when problems arose, yet who still chooses murder as his only option, might be judged differently. A surprising number of school shooters appear to be firmly in that second camp.

An argument advanced by those opposing this view was summed up in the words of *Atlanta Journal-Constitution* editorial-page editor Cynthia Tucker. *Society*, she wrote, is not well served *by throwing violent juvenile offenders into facilities with hardened adult criminals, thereby ensuring that those youngsters will eventually leave prison even more deranged than they went in.* This reasoning, however, is faulty on several counts. First, young offenders are seldom if ever "thrown in" with adults; they are put into juvenile correctional facilities until they reach the age of twenty-one, or twenty-five in some states. At that point, they are transferred to adult prisons. Second, most are kept segregated from the more dangerous elements, are given at least weekly psychiatric care, and receive necessary medications. Their mental problems are not ignored. In cases where insanity is proven, there is no prison incarceration. Finally, in many cases, the crimes committed by these youths have been deemed serious enough to guarantee they will never be released back into society.

While the right of the state to hand down life sentences without the possibility of parole may seem excessive, and has been deemed so by the United Nations, this does not take into account the victims' points of view. Although they've done nothing to deserve it, their lives have been destroyed or permanently, negatively impacted by the perpetrators. It is only just that the person who caused this damage should lose his or her freedom for an equally significant amount of time. In fact, most campaigns of support for youthful killers contradict themselves by demonstrating greater concern for offenders than they do for the innocent victims, who have been injured or killed. If such concern exists, it's clearly secondary.

There are times, however, when even the supposedly harsh juvenile laws of the United States seem insufficient to provide just solutions to unjust circumstances. The sentencing of school shooters Mitchell Johnson and Andrew "Drew" Golden is a case in point. Two months before the Thurston attack, the age limit for mass murder was notched down to a preteen low when the first-ever set of paired school shooters opened fire upon fellow students and teachers at Westside Middle School in Jonesboro, Arkansas. Mitchell was thirteen and Andrew was only eleven at the time.

Just past noon on March 24, 1998, Andrew drew their prey into the schoolyard by setting off a false fire alarm. The two resourceful lads had set up a clever ambush, based upon young Andrew's extensive hunting experience. Dressed in camouflage, they had hauled guns and a large amount of ammunition into a copse of trees less than a hundred yards from the school's play area. After pulling the alarm, Andrew ran back to rejoin Mitchell on the wooded slope. Then they opened fire sniper-style from their hiding place in the thicket. Over two hundred students and teachers filed out of the building and directly into their line of fire.

Trapped in this open killing field, panicked classmates and teachers tried to reenter the school, but the doors had locked automatically. As bullets whizzed around her, an eleven-year-old girl later said the only thing going through her mind was the thought that "they're going to kill us, and I don't know why, or what to do." Amber Vanoven, also eleven, described in the *Jonesboro Sun* how her best friend, Natalie Brooks, got *"killed—shot twice in the head. . . . She started running over there on the concrete screaming, blood coming out of her head, yelling, 'This is real, this is REAL! Run, RUN!'"*

More than half of the twenty-seven bullets fired by the boys found their mark. When the shooting stopped, four students, all girls, lay dead: Natalie Brooks, Paige Ann Herring, and Stephanie Johnson were all twelve. Brittheny Varner was only eleven. Shannon Wright, an English teacher who was shot while shielding one of her pupils, died after surgery from abdomen and chest wounds. Lynette Thetford, another teacher, was luckier. She and the girl she was sheltering recovered.

Meanwhile, officers were pursuing the two young assassins as they bolted through the woods. They were captured and cuffed before they could reach a 1991 Dodge Caravan stolen earlier from Mitchell's stepfather, in which they had stashed more guns, over three thousand rounds of ammunition, and survival gear. Their three rifles and six handguns had all been stolen that morning from Drew Golden's dad, Dennis, the founder and head of the Jonesboro Practical Shooters Association, and his grandfather Doug, a wildlife conservation officer with the Arkansas Division of Fish and Game, a former gun dealer, and an avid collector who owned hundreds of firearms.

A day before the massacre, Mitchell warned friends that he had *"a lotta killing to do."* He told seventh-grader Melinda Henson, *"Tomorrow, y'all are gonna find out if you live or die."* No one related the threats to school officials or even to their own parents; most said they thought he was "just talking." Mitchell was also rumored to have pulled a knife on another student that day, but classmates were afraid to report him.

At a final adjudication hearing, Mitchell pleaded guilty to five counts of capital murder and ten of first-degree battery. He expressed remorse with tears in his eyes, holding his mother's hand as she cried uncontrollably. Somewhat dubiously, Mitch claimed, in a voice breaking with emotion, *"I really thought that no one would actually be hurt. I thought we would just shoot over everyone's head."* Many questioned his sincerity, seeing that their guns were fitted with telescopic sights and Andrew, taught to shoot in combat stance by his own dad, had been winning awards for marksmanship since he was nine.

After a juvenile court judge rejected his plea of temporary insanity, Andrew was declared guilty of murder. Under Arkansas law, however, the boys were too young to be charged as adults regardless of their crimes. Both could only be held in custody until their eighteenth birthdays. Federal gun charges kept them in prison until they turned twenty-one. Because they were charged as juveniles, their cases remained permanently sealed after their release and they had no criminal record. That entitled them to immediately regain the right to legally purchase weapons when freed.

Johnson lost no time in doing so. He was granted his freedom on August 11, 2005, and given a protective identity because of threats to his life. His cover was blown on New Year's Day, 2007, when he was arrested with a small bag of marijuana and a prohibited weapon (a loaded 9mm pistol) in a van that was weaving erratically down a city street in northwestern Arkansas. His companion was his roommate Justin Trammell, a boy who'd spent three years in prison for killing his father with a crossbow when he was fifteen. Far from being rehabilitated or thankful for getting a "second chance," Johnson appeared "arrogant" as he swiveled in his seat talking about the Jonesboro murders during a videotaped deposition taken from him on April 2 by an attorney.

Andrew Golden was released on May 25, 2007, for his twenty-first birthday, but because of his juvenile court status, not even the name of the institution where he'd been incarcerated was released to the public.

What sort of message did this restricted sentencing and erasing of criminal records send out to other young people bent on mischief? It was not necessary to look far. Two months after Jonesboro, on May 21, 1998—the same day Kip Kinkel attacked Thurston High—three sixth-grade boys with a "hit list" were arrested for plotting to kill their classmates on the last day of lessons at Becky-Davis Elementary School in St. Charles, Missouri. Their method was hardly original. It was modeled directly upon Jonesboro—pull a false fire alarm and shoot students, sniper-style, as they left the building.

• Chapter 6 •

"An Ideal American Family"

I don't know what to do at this point. Kip is completely out of control.

—Bill Kinkel to a friend, in what proved
to be their final conversation

Kip Kinkel's case went on to a series of sentencing appeals, but because a formal trial had been avoided, the most important question raised by the shootings—How did this happen?—was never addressed. To answer that here, we need to look more closely at his background.

There is, of course, no such thing as a perfect marriage, a perfect child, or a perfect family. There are only standards by which we gauge the success or failure of social units. By any measure, Kinkel's parents were well above average, as was the family of Clay Shrout and many other school shooters. What made their children's attacks especially disturbing was the very fact of the apparent normalcy of their homes. This is difficult to accept, and the parent within us yearns to discover some facet inside these households that was conspicuously *not* normal, giving reassurance that whatever happened in their homes could never happen in ours. And while it's true that any family, if examined minutely, might expose some less-than-flattering dysfunction, a closer look inside the Kinkel home does indeed suggest a host of questionable decisions and mistaken priorities. The Shrout home was similar. The consequence of their parents' unwillingness to honestly address Kip and Clay's underlying problems proved to be a fatal error in judgment.

51

In the aftermath of Thurston, only one person had three family members to grieve over. Kip's older sister, Kristin, was in her senior year at Hawaii Pacific University (HPU) when news reached her around 7:00 A.M. Oahu time that there'd been a shooting at her former school. A friend called to give her a running commentary. In Kristin's words: "She's watching the news, so she's giving me little bits of information. Finally I said, 'Is that why you're calling me? Is Kip hurt?' She said, 'Well, Kip was involved. I don't know any more. . . . I'll call you back.' Click."

Several hours later, she learned that her only sibling had murdered both her parents. In a single stroke, she simultaneously became an orphan and the sister of the killer who'd made her so. In addition, she discovered her kid brother had attempted mass murder at school. It couldn't have been a pleasant moment. Eight months later, Barbara Walters interviewed Kristin for the ABC News show *20/20*. When asked, "Did you ever suspect that Kip was a violent kid, that anything like this could have happened?" Kristin answered, "In my wildest dreams, never."

Sun-kyung Cho, sister of the Virginia Tech gunman, similarly told newsmen, "My brother was quiet and reserved, yet struggled to fit in. We never could have envisioned that he was capable of so much violence." It is fascinating to note how analogous Seung-hui Cho's family dynamic was to Kinkel's: two caring parents and a much admired, highly successful older sister who'd returned to Virginia and was living at home after graduating from Princeton University in 2004 with a major in economics. She had a job with a State Department contractor doing reconstruction projects in Iraq. A woman who'd done everything right, her brother's actions derailed all her achievements. Her family was shuttled between "safe houses" in protective custody because of retaliatory threats against their lives.

Kristin Kinkel was also well on her way to fulfilling the American dream. A pretty blonde, with an athletic figure, she deserved and received much praise for her grace and composure under extreme duress. Many were amazed at her ability to maintain calm, absolve her brother of blame in the name of sisterly love, and even display a measure of optimism. In fact, encouraging other people was not only her strong point; in a sense, it was her ticket to college. Kristin had been awarded a full cheerleading scholarship at HPU. Cheering others was what she did best.

Some felt that Kristin's stoic but sanguine disposition in the face of this devastating catastrophe was a self-imposed charade to protect her spirit and mental health from being submerged by profound and overwhelming grief. Despite an appearance of serenity, there were hints of something unsettling below the surface. One Eugene child psychologist pointed out that often, when there is dysfunction in a family, one sibling will work as hard at being "the good child" as the other will at gaining attention by being ill-behaved. Both have a stake in maintaining the status quo in order to meet their needs. This therapist gave as an example the fact that the Kinkels, like many in Lane County, were passionate fans of the University of Oregon (UO) Ducks football team. Obviously, Kristin could never be a football player, even to please her dad, but becoming a pro cheerleader was the female equivalent. Kip tried out for football at his father's request, but was never more than a mediocre benchwarmer at best.

With the addition of psychiatrists' reports, statements to police, and interviews with family friends, it became possible to trace Kip's descent from a frustrated child to an adolescent killer who, in the words of PBS *Frontline* correspondent Peter Boyer, "when visited by teenage despair, embraced it and set for himself a destructive course that followed the dark logic of a disturbed young mind."

Both Bill and Faith Kinkel were well-thought-of, popular, hard-working teachers. Bill had retired from Thurston High in 1991, but he was teaching part-time at Lane Community College. Faith was still teaching full-time. By all outward appearances, the family had few difficulties.

A yearlong sabbatical in Spain, just as Kip began schooling, left the five-year-old boy feeling discouraged. His bilingual family flourished there, while he withered in a school where the teacher spoke no English and a larger lad bullied him. When they returned to Oregon, Kip had to repeat first grade twice to sort things out.

Most of Kip's elementary-school teachers remembered him as a boy with anger management problems. To other kids, Kip was awkward and a class clown, yet his joking often had a rough edge. He'd tease others, but he flew into a rage when the same was done to him. In third grade, Kip's dyslexia was discovered. His handwriting and spelling were especially awkward. Even as late as eighth grade, he sometimes misspelled his own name "Kinkle." Nonetheless, IQ tests conducted later by prison psychologists showed Kip's mind to be well above average, as did intelligence tests conducted in grade school. In fact, his science and math abilities gained him entry into the Talented and Gifted (TAG) program.

The *Frontline* documentary stated that Kip came from "a nurturing home, a comforting community, and loving parents recognized for their special way with children—by all accounts an ideal American family." Although Kip's childhood relationship with his mother was close, Kip was aware of being a disappointment to his dad. Kristin, six years older, often served as a buffer, defending her brother's inadequacies. When she left for college, Kip lost a mediator in the escalating conflict with his parents. Perhaps feeling vulnerable, Kip insisted upon enrolling in karate classes, to which his parents reluctantly agreed.

At the age of twelve, Kip allegedly began experiencing auditory hallucinations. He told no one. Shortly after, Kip and a middle school friend were caught ordering a bomb-making text called *The Anarchist Cookbook* via the Internet. Delivered to the wrong address by mistake, their parents were notified and the book was confiscated. Kip got hold of another copy, insisting to his parents that the book was necessary because he hoped to someday join a police bomb squad. As both teachers and parents, the Kinkels felt simultaneously responsible and humiliated by Kip's shenanigans. Bill felt especially chagrined after his son entered the very school where he'd taught for thirty years.

Kristin knew Kip had got into trouble for secretly ordering the book. Like her parents, she accepted her brother's excuses and let it go at that. "One of his goals was to be on the bomb squad. He wanted to help people," she said in the *Frontline* interview a year later, still exhibiting a sense of denial. Then Kristin stated, "He and a group of friends had ordered a book about building bombs. And, in fact, I think he even did a report using that book for school. Just because you order a book doesn't mean that you're—oh, I don't know what to say about that . . . I mean, I . . . ." Her response trailed off, as if she suddenly realized her own naiveté. On the same program, questioned about Kip's gun obsession, Kristin replied, "My parents were both really, really concerned about it. He'd been interested in guns from as far as I can remember, from a little, little boy. And he was not allowed to have little soldiers. He was not allowed to have any kind of toy that had any kind of violent anything. I mean, violence in our house was a huge no-no."

Violence may have been a no-no, but Barbara Walters got it wrong on *20/20* when she stated, "Bill Kinkel . . . had never allowed guns in the house . . ." Bill outwardly disapproved of weapons, but three of the guns found in Kip's arsenal belonged to Kip's dad. They included a Marlin 336 rifle Bill had received as a young boy which he gave to Kip on his twelfth birthday; a Winchester lever-action rifle Bill had also kept from his youth; and a .22-caliber Ruger pistol Bill had owned for years, which he'd let Kip use for target practice.

Kip inevitably managed to obtain several more books about building explosive devices. His mother even helped him buy bomb-making materials after Kip told her the ingredients were for a science project. Kip went so far as to forge a note from his science teacher asking his parents to assist in purchasing the chemicals. Kip knew that the only store selling this merchandise required proof of being eighteen years old. This clever subterfuge typifies how Kip used his parents' gullibility to his advantage.

When Kip's mother finally learned the truth, she was livid. She told his dad and together they put Kip's bomb-making equipment into a large trash bag to await the next pickup. Their son quietly retrieved everything, hid much of it in the attic, and concealed completed bombs in a crawl space beneath their wide wooden verandah.

Kip's aptitude for designing explosives became formidable and he could rattle off chemical formulas like an expert. His proclivity was hardly kept secret; he gave an illustrated talk on the subject in speech class, blithely instructing his classmates on how to make deadly explosives.

Kip's obsession with pistols, rifles, and knives also intensified. His parents, against the use of all weapons, became increasingly alarmed yet submitted to Kip's demands with puzzling compliance. They bought him a BB gun, gave Kip at least three knives, and on his twelfth birthday, they gifted him with the rifle Bill had kept since boyhood. More firearms came later.

On his own, Kip accumulated nearly fifty knives, which he kept displayed in neat rows in his bedroom drawers—should anyone have cared to look. Only one person on record did. When Tami Griswold, the Kinkels' housekeeper of seven years, complained to them about their son's proclivities, the parents' response was "Thank you for telling us." The maid became so "uncomfortable" with Kip's interest in explosives and his knife collection, she quit.

Despite many attempts to pacify him, Kip continued to manifest signs of trouble. He had a hot temper and would kick holes in the walls at home. He was caught shoplifting CDs. He had a "habit of setting objects on fire," a major indicator of adolescent psychosis.

These were *not* normal activities. To verify that, we need only compare the habits of another boy who killed both his parents and his two little sisters. The parallels between Kip and Clay Shrout go so far beyond coincidence, they are truly bizarre, even to the point of Clay having a sister named Kristen.

Neighbors also described the Shrouts as an "ideal American family" living in a handsome two-story home complete with swimming pool, garden, several pet dogs, and a horse. Clay's well-educated parents were considered "very loving," and his two smaller sisters looked up to him, but by the time Clay became a freshman, he was exhibiting mood swings and outbursts of anger. He did have several close pals, including one who accompanied him on forays to steal CDs from a local record store, just as Kip and a buddy stole CDs from a Target store. Regarding his search for love, "he became obsessive," according to a friend, to the degree of writing "notebooks and notebooks of letters to one girl." Clay's romantic efforts were so frustrated by lack of response, he broke down in tears while confiding to a friend that he was considering suicide.

Clay Shrout began to prefer isolation, spending increasingly more time alone in his bedroom, where he hoarded a collection of around thirty knives kept in neat rows, ninja death stars, and brass knuckles. His bedroom walls were plastered with posters of heavy-metal bands that reflected his taste for Marilyn Manson, Danzig, and Cannibal Corpse. He taped up messages celebrating death and Satanism. Clay downloaded bomb-making information from the Internet and obtained a copy of *The Anarchist Cookbook,* just as Kip Kinkel and

Michael Carneal would do. At school, Clay boasted to classmates that he had the knowledge and means to build a pipe bomb that could "blow up the whole neighborhood." In English class, one of his poems morbidly detailed an amorous murder plot. (Kip also wrote strongly about his romantic frustrations.) Finally, when justifying to police why he did it, Clay Shrout explained, "They took away my weapons and something happened." Kinkel would also tell psychiatrists that the spark that ignited his rampage was fear that his parents would take away his guns. And when Clay Shrout explained to authorities, "I didn't want to be stopped, so I decided to kill them. . . . There really wasn't any way around it," how eerily similar to Kip's "I had no other choice!"

In Kip's downward spiral, the circumstances of his arrest on a felony charge in the central Oregon town of Bend on January 4, 1997, are crucial to much of what followed. The boy had gone there in order to attend a snowboarding clinic with his friend Gavin Keable. Faith suspected pals from Gavin's circle were encouraging her son's errant ways, but the athletic outdoor setting seemed like a healthy enough environment.

Supposedly on a whim, the two boys stood on an overhead railway trestle kicking and tossing rocks down at cars that sped along the narrow highway below. One struck a vehicle and the driver pulled over to call police. Both teens were caught and held on a charge of criminal mischief, but Kip denied his own role, claiming his friend had been the one who'd thrown the rock that hit the car. Gavin was arrested at the overpass, but when Kip was found hiding back in his motel room, he started crying and asked the arresting officer if anyone had been hurt. At 11:40 P.M., Bend police telephoned the Kinkels, who asked that their son be held until they could pick him up. Kip's parents drove hours to get there through the snowy Willamette Pass that night, and all three returned home early the next morning without pausing to rest.

Gavin and Kip were referred to the Department of Youth Services in Eugene for assessment at Skipworth Juvenile Facility (now the Serbu Youth Center). The conditions of their release were community service, paying $50 each in restitution, and writing a letter of apology to the driver, which Kip did, he told friends, very grudgingly.

Kip's show of tears during his arrest was later refuted by a personal profile on his Internet home page describing one of his hobbies as "throwing rocks off bridges at cars."

Psychologist Dr. John Crumbley did an evaluation of Kip and interviewed his parents at Skipworth on February 26, 1997, as part of a police appraisement. The Kinkels impressed him as being responsible parents. Kip played his role well, and was written up as being appropriately remorseful and forthright about his participation in this "boyish" crime. At this point, Kip's parents were hoping their son's felony charge marked the end of his venture into criminal mischief, not the beginning. They convinced themselves, and so they convinced Dr. Crumbley.

Privately, Faith had been apprehensive enough about Kip's behavior to set up appointments with Eugene child psychologist Dr. Jeffrey Hicks immediately after the Bend incident. Faith brought Kip to see the doctor nine times between January and June 1997, now more concerned about his fascination with weapons and explosives, and his antisocial behavior. Bill refused to go along, explaining he didn't think therapy would work and it would be too expensive. He regarded psychologists as unnecessary, the equivalent of chiropractors. In an early session, Kip told the doctor he thought his mom considered him "a good kid with some bad habits," while his dad viewed him as "a bad kid with bad habits." Hicks deduced that the source of Kip's difficulties was his strained relationship with his father.

Kip did not disclose suffering from any hallucinations or delusions. Instead, he conveyed to Dr. Hicks his difficulty in eating and sleeping, and his being bored and irritable. Kip denied feeling suicidal, but admitted being frequently angry and detonating homemade explosives at a quarry to release his hostility. While the psychologist found this disturbing and discouraged Kip from pursuing that practice, no more serious alarm bells were set off.

That April, Kip was suspended from school twice. Hicks diagnosed his patient with major depressive disorder, and in June, he recommended Prozac, an antidepressant that was dutifully prescribed by the family physician. Hicks testified he didn't know whether or not Prozac was approved for pediatric administration, nor did he know the protocol for continuing management of such medication.

He felt knowledge of these facts was the family doctor's responsibility. Unfortunately, many family doctors generally don't know the course of treatment, either. Much worse, the Kinkels mistakenly concluded that Kip's progress in therapy had cured him after just three months on Prozac. They decided both should be terminated, and Hicks reluctantly agreed. Most psychiatrists recognize that, regardless of whether the source of depression is situational or biological in nature, short courses of medication act as little more than a Band-Aid on a gaping wound. Once discontinued, there's often a relapse. Within weeks of being taken off Prozac, Kip's original symptoms reasserted themselves.

Before ending treatment, Dr. Hicks and Kip discussed weaponry. Considering the boy's obsessions, Hicks felt that *not* exploring the issue of guns would have been irresponsible. In fact, the doctor had guns of his own, and he enthusiastically told Kip how impressed he was with the reliability of his Glock pistol. Kip decided he had to have one. Just five months into therapy, and approximately a month before Kip's sessions wrapped up, Bill gave in to his son's persistence and bought him a semiautomatic 9mm Glock 19, the gun Kip would use to slay his mother. It was no cheap trinket. The invoice came to $497.65, including the gun, an Uncle Mike's brand hip holster, and a Butler Creek "Hot Lips No Fail" magazine of bullets. Kip promised to pay his dad back.

As a compromise, Bill insisted Kip take gun-safety classes and only use the pistol when he was present. Even so, the logic of this acquisition defies reason. Kip was still on Prozac at the time of the purchase. Not only did the Kinkels place themselves and others in jeopardy, they also seemed unaware their son might take his own life. The diagnostic "bible" of psychiatry known as the *DSM-IV* states: *Up to 15 percent of individuals with severe Major Depressive Disorder die by suicide.* For a boy who is both violent and depressed to be allowed firearms is reprehensible, but it got worse.

In September 1997, acceding again to Kip's demands, his father bought the boy yet another weapon, a .22-caliber semiautomatic rifle. Bill's denial of the true nature of his son's condition, his refusal to attend the counseling sessions, and his purchase of guns as a "cure" for Kip's depression and alienation went beyond bad judgment. On top of that, the Kinkels had no idea their son was also buying weapons illegally. A small arsenal was in the making, hidden in the bedroom of an angry, depressed teenage boy suffering from a psychotic disorder. Kip's final stockpile included his collection of hunting knives, a 20-gauge sawed-off shotgun he'd secretly bought in the summer after eighth grade, the .22-caliber Ruger pistol Bill had let Kip use for target practice, another .22-caliber handgun Kip secretly bought in ninth grade and hid in the attic, the Marlin 336 rifle Bill had given Kip, the Winchester lever-action rifle, the Glock handgun, the semiautomatic Ruger rifle with clips, which held fifty cartridges, and thousands of rounds of ammunition Kip had somehow acquired.

This lethal mix of firearms and an unstable personality reached combustion point with the final purchase of one more weapon Kip secretly arranged to buy on May 19, 1998. That evening, Kip's friend Korey Ewert managed to steal a loaded .32-caliber Beretta pistol from the father of a mutual acquaintance. Ewert telephoned Kip and made a deal to sell it to him the next day at school for $110, plus a music CD.

Kip was lightly built, but Korey was even smaller. Because of his stature, Korey had been at the receiving end of lots of bullying as he entered adolescence. This produced in him a nearly constant state of defensiveness and defiance, with the result that Korey was a frequent visitor to the disciplinary office. Football coach Don Stone doubled as the school's "enforcer" and was well aware that Korey was angry at the world, but he also took pity on the boy. One night, Stone drove him home because Korey had come to him frightened that two guys wanted to beat him up after school. Kip befriended Korey, and the smaller lad was eager to repay that friendship.

Kip traded cash for the weapon at 8:00 A.M. on May 20, and tucked the gun inside a brown paper bag in his locker. Scott Keeney, the pistol's rightful owner, called Thurston High that morning to say his handgun was missing and he was fairly sure one of his son Aaron's friends had taken it. He gave the school a list of roughly a dozen kids who might be involved, but the names of both Kip and Korey were not included. In fact, having taken Kip on camping and hunting trips in the past, the Keeneys stated to police on May 22 that "Kinkel was the last person we suspected of being involved."

Detective Alan Warthen happened to be at the school investigating another incident when the call came in from Scott Keeney. The account he typed up later that afternoon contradicts Keeney's and differs from other versions. Warthen wrote that after Scott's call, Aaron was summoned to the office and *provided us with a list of names of people who knew his dad had a pistol. . . . One of the names given was that of Kip Kinkel.* Two alternate accounts say that the first boys on Scott's list who were called in named other kids who might have done it, and the list grew. Whatever the exact sequence, since several students said that Kip and Korey might be involved, those two were finally sent for.

Warthen had Kip pulled out of a study session by hall monitor Jerame Wood, a college student and baseball coach getting his teaching credentials. On their way to the office, Kip attempted to toss his oversized pocketknife into a trash bin, knowing it was illegal to have one in school. Worried for a moment about the boy's intentions, Wood grabbed Kip's wrist. The knife fell to the floor unopened. Jerame retrieved it as Kip begged him not to tell anyone. Wood replied, "You know the rules, no weapons on campus."

Confronted by Detective Warthen in Assistant Principal Dick Doyle's office, the knife was handed over, and Kip assumed, or pretended to assume, that this was the reason he'd been called down. "I knew that knife would get me into trouble!" he blurted out, as if it were the knife's fault. "See, I washed my pants, and I forgot the knife was in the pocket, and . . ." Warthen told Kip he wasn't much interested in the knife; he was concerned about a stolen gun. Kip strongly denied any involvement at first, but when told that his locker, number 781, would be searched, he admitted buying the gun. "Okay, look guys, I'll be straight with you," Kip said as he confessed the gun was stored there.

At that point, Kip was advised of his Miranda rights and he confirmed he understood. Together, the detective, Kip, and Doyle went to retrieve the weapon. Kip nervously opened his locker and started to reach in for the bag. Warthen grabbed his arm and told him, *"No, Kip, I will retrieve the gun. Just back off and relax."* The boy quietly complied.

Wood was also asked to fetch Korey Ewert from class. Like Kip, Korey vehemently denied any association with the theft until he was asked to empty his pockets and had to explain the large amount of cash he'd tucked away. Then Ewert was also read his rights, and the whole story came out.

Don Stone had the job of impressing upon the two boys just how serious the situation had become; so, one by one, he took each of them into his office. Stone had dealt with plenty of "wise guys" in trouble before. Most made light of their predicament, toughed it out with *attitude*, or squirmed their way through a series of improbable excuses, as Kip had done earlier. This time, however, something different happened when the coach confronted Kip and made it clear that this was no game.

"In that moment of truth," Stone said, "Kip fell silent and just stared straight ahead with . . . well, with what I'd call 'shark eyes'— and by that, I mean his eyes just suddenly went cold and dead and empty. There was nothing human there. I've never seen anything like it before. And for the first time, I felt afraid something really bad was going to happen."

Stone's intuition was spot-on. His description was echoed years later by Derek O'Dell, a wounded survivor of the Virginia Tech massacre. Having looked at Cho's face as the killer tried to shoot him, O'Dell later said, "I saw into his eyes. . . . They seemed completely black and there appeared to be emptiness behind them. Sometimes you can look into a person's eyes and see their life story or the hardships they've encountered. With his, there was nothing."

If eyes are the windows of the soul, these cold, vacant stares indicate the shooter has retreated into the deepest recesses of his mind, no longer observable from the outside. Their pretense of humanity has been replaced by the true face of a murderer.

Kip and Korey were arrested, suspended from Thurston pending expulsion, and escorted off school grounds wearing handcuffs. At the police station, Kip was charged with a felony for receiving a stolen weapon and possession of a firearm in a public building. After holding him for a couple of hours in a cell, Warthen surprisingly released the boy into his father's custody around noon.

The school's head counselor was Bill Kinkel's personal friend Dick Bushnell, who called the Kinkel home around 1:30 P.M. Bill's main concerns at that moment were how to handle his son's academic situation and how to break the news to Faith. Bill was not yet entirely pessimistic. One option was to enroll Kip in the Youth Challenge Program, a "tough love" survival camp for wayward sons.

About an hour later, Scott Keeney telephoned Bill concerning his stolen Beretta. Bill, distraught, told Keeney he thought his boy "has some sort of disease" and needed help. He concluded, "I don't know what to do at this point. Kip is completely out of control." It proved to be their final conversation.

Bill did make one further call that afternoon, however. He rang up Keith Bonner, program director of the Oregon National Guard's boot camp in Bend, and told him, "I have a son who's probably going to be in serious trouble, and I'm looking for help." Bill was informed that unfortunately the minimum age for entry into the Youth Challenge Program was sixteen, and teens facing criminal charges weren't eligible.

That option was a father's last hope, but it no longer mattered. A few minutes later, Bill Kinkel would cease to exist. Whether over-hearing that call was the final event that catapulted Kip into deadly action, we may never know. Whether Kip or Clay Shrout—or many of the others for that matter—was too insane to fully comprehend what he was doing is another question.

• Chapter 7 •

A Chain of Events

*One of the key factors is that all children and most ado-
lescents do not understand the finality of death.*
—Scott Poland, chairman of the National Emergency Disaster
Team for the National Association of School Psychologists

While each school shooting is singular, all have certain elements in
common. The rampage at Virginia Tech in 2007 was not a unique
event, but rather one more link in a chain of such tragedies. Seung-
hui Cho and many others referenced Columbine as their inspiration,
but Cho also imitated North Carolina's Alvaro Castillo (chapter 1)
in sending videotapes out to the media between his two crime scenes.
In photographing himself brandishing weapons, Cho also copied
Kimveer Gill, who opened fire at Montreal's Dawson College on September 13, 2006.

Kimveer, in turn, was equally unoriginal. When Gill wrote, *Life
is like a video game, you gotta die sometime,* he was stealing almost
verbatim the words of eighteen-year-old Devin Moore, who murdered
two police officers and a dispatcher in Fayette, Alabama, in 2003
after obsessively playing Grand Theft Auto for hundreds of hours (a
lawsuit against the game maker ensued). After his arrest, Moore told
investigators, "Life is a video game. Everybody's got to die sometime."

Kimveer's attack was the third at an institute of higher education
in Montreal (chapter 8). A tall, well-built twenty-five-year-old of Indian heritage, Gill lived in the basement of his parents' home on a

quiet, tree-lined street in Laval, Quebec, with his younger twin brothers. He had no police record, was unemployed, and was not a student. After the shooting, his mother, Parwinder, told reporters, "He wouldn't hurt anybody. He was a different person, a very good person, and that's why we are in so much shock. . . . He became sad or depressed for some reason I don't know yet.

"Since Christmas," she added, "he started to spend more time on his computer playing video games." One of his favorites was the violent Postal series in which targets are ordinary people completing everyday errands. Another one Kimveer preferred was Danny Ledonne's controversial Super Columbine Massacre RPG! Ledonne's response: "My game contains absolutely no 'training' or 'murder simulation.' It's not a 'shooting game,' since the player never aims a gun. This is a role-playing game (RPG). The player takes on the identity of the shooters and the emphasis is on their choices rather than their actions. For me, the allegation that Kimveer trained on SCMRPG rings about as true as saying Mark David Chapman trained for the assassination of John Lennon using *Catcher in the Rye.*"

What Gill's mother didn't know was that her son had been visiting a local gun club, and that he frequented the Goth Web site VampireFreaks.com under the name "Fatality666." Online he vented his hatred, calling society *worthless, no good, kniving* [sic]*, betraying lieing* [sic]*, deceptive.* He singled out jocks, blaming them for school bullying, but added, *It's not only the bullies' fault, but the principal's fault for turning a blind eye. . . . It's the police's fault for not doing anything when people complain (ooops) my mistake, the cops are corrupt sons of whores, so it's not like they can do anything about it. Fuck the police.*

Kimveer Gill, like Kip Kinkel, was obsessed with firearms, writing, *I love guns. . . . I really do. The great equalizer.* In one log entry, he admitted, *Usually I have dreams about people being murdered, hung, getting shot, and stuff like that.* In another, he gave details of such musings, foreshadowing his killing spree: *The disgusting human creatures scream in panic and run in all directions, taking with them the lies and deceptions. . . . The Death Night gazes at the humans with an empty stare, as they knock each other down in a mad dash to safety. He wishes to slaughter them as they flee.*

Gill's image gallery held more than fifty photos. One shows him gripping his Beretta CX4 Storm semiautomatic rifle, sticking out his tongue, and making the sign of the Devil. It's captioned, *Rock and Roll baby!* Another, captioned *Anger and hatred simmers within me,* has him glaring at the camera with teeth clenched. In some pictures, Gill wears a red-and-black mask, a long black trench coat, and combat boots. He writes, *His name is Trench. You will come to know him as the Angel of Death.* This latter may have been a reference to Jeff Weise, who used the name "Angel of Death" in German on his Internet postings.

A photo of a tombstone with Gill's name on it is labeled: *Lived fast, died young. Left a mangled corpse,* a reworking of a phrase coined in 1947 by Willard Motley in his book about juvenile delinquents called *Knock on Any Door* (made into a movie with Humphrey Bogart two years later). The motto of street gang member Nick "Pretty Boy" Romano was "Live fast, die young, and leave a good-looking corpse." In the 2003 movie *Zero Day,* one of the fictional school shooters says, "Live fast, live hard, and die by any combination of those two."

Gill's final Internet entry praising whisky for breakfast was posted at 10:41 A.M. By 12:30, Gill had parked his car and removed from his trunk a 9mm semiautomatic rifle, a .45-caliber pistol, and a 12-caliber gun that can pump four bullets with each squeeze of the trigger. He walked purposefully toward Dawson College, firing as he went. (Gill had previously scouted a university—*Too big,* he had scribbled on a notepad—another college, and a high school before he settled on Dawson.) At 12:41 P.M., the first of more than four hundred 911 calls went out.

Two young policemen, who were in the area by chance, immediately followed Gill into the building with their guns drawn, yelling at him to drop his weapons. Dozens more officers arrived within minutes. Learning from the mistakes at Columbine, Canada's revamped policy is to go quickly inside to try and save lives even before the SWAT team arrives.

Meanwhile, Kimveer Gill had made his way up to the second-floor atrium cafeteria, firing haphazardly at anyone who moved. Once inside, he ordered everyone to get down. Most dropped to the floor in terror, but some, observing a man with body piercing, a Mohawk haircut, and combat boots, dressed in black with an assault rifle, thought it was a joke. One boy tried photographing him with a cell phone. Then Gill began shooting.

When police reached the cafeteria, they first tried to talk him into surrendering. Instead, he turned his guns on them, ducking behind vending machines as he screamed, *"Get back! Get the fuck away from here!"* Finally police let loose with a "hail of gunfire," as Gill had wished for on his blog. One bullet struck his arm. Realizing it was over, Kimveer Gill allegedly shot himself in the head.

Gill's body was dragged outside and covered with a tarp. Across the street, a girl fell into her mother's arms, sobbing, "He was going to shoot me! I was the closest to him, Mom. People were pushing me and he wouldn't stop shooting at us." She was lucky. Nineteen others were wounded, many critically, and eighteen-year-old Anastasia DeSousa lay dead.

Later, it became known that in 1999 Gill served briefly in the Canadian military, but like Alvaro Castillo, he was found unsuitable for service and didn't complete basic training. Those kinds of links among shooters are common. For example, in each of the two years prior to the Thurston High rampage, there had been seven similar attacks, including the incidents at Pearl, Mississippi, and West Paducah, Kentucky, late in 1997. When Kip Kinkel saw TV coverage of Johnson and Golden after the Jonesboro shootings in March '98, he told classmates Sean Marks and Gavin Keable that the massacre was "cool," and that "somebody should do that around here." For the next week or so, Kip tried to coerce another friend, Brandon Muniz, into joining him in a similar attack. Kip told Brandon, whom he considered to be a bit "slow and easily manipulated," that the kids in Arkansas did it all wrong, and that he had a better plan. Brandon didn't take Kip seriously.

At around the same time, in Edinboro, Pennsylvania, fourteen-year-old Andrew Wurst was also commenting to friends that he thought the Jonesboro slaughter was "really cool." But Andrew, a slim, bespectacled, and mild-looking eighth grader at James W. Parker Middle School, went a step further. He showed some friends a .25-caliber semiautomatic Raven pistol hidden in his father's unlocked dresser drawer and told them he planned to use nine shells to kill nine people he hated and then kill himself.

He acted on that promise precisely one month after Jonesboro, on April 24, 1998. That night, Andrew took his dad's pistol to his eighth-grade prom. The graduation dance was being held at a banquet hall called Nick's Place. Other teens were dressed up, but Wurst arrived around 10:00 P.M. wearing baggy pants and untied shoes. The *Titanic* movie theme, "My Heart Will Go On," was the song playing as popular science teacher John Gillette, forty-eight, was bringing the festivities to a close. Andrew simply walked up to John and shot him in the face. As Gillette collapsed to the floor, Andrew shot him again in the back, killing him. The crowd of teens panicked and ran screaming for cover.

One exception was fifteen-year-old Justin Fletcher, who confronted the shooter. Andrew fired the gun at Justin, but his aim was off and the bullet struck student Robert Zemcik's foot. Andrew shot again into the crowd and one bullet hit Jacob "Jake" Tury on his backside. As the song concluded, Andrew ran from the hall, but owner James Strand, carrying a shotgun, easily overtook him. With the assistance of two teachers, Andrew was tackled and held until police arrived. Wurst's alternating laughter and tears puzzled the officers arresting him. At his trial, the boy pleaded guilty to third-degree murder and was sentenced to thirty to sixty years in prison.

TV coverage of this attack, coming just one month before Kinkel's, may also have inspired Kip in his own deadly plans, but there's more. Only a week before his May 21 rampage, a fifteen-year-old named Buddy Morgan made the lead story on the local Eugene-Springfield TV evening news for being arrested with stolen guns in the trees behind Elmira High School, fifteen miles west of Thurston.

One would think that these newsworthy events, national and local, would have raised red flags in the minds of Kip's friends—or at least in the mind of the detective who arrested Kip for having a stolen, loaded gun in his school locker. *After* Kip stormed his school, the message that such threats must be taken seriously seemed to be getting through. One week later, Cody Hartle, eighteen, was arrested in Klamath Falls, southern Oregon, after threatening to kill fellow students at their graduation ceremony.

Across the country, problems continued. Three weeks after Thurston on June 15, 1998, a fourteen-year-old named Quinshawn Booker opened fire in a hallway of Armstrong High School in a depressed area of

Richmond, Virginia, while other students were taking final exams. Basketball coach Gary Carter, forty-five, and Eloise Wilson, seventy-four, a Head Start volunteer, were both wounded by Booker's .32-caliber Llama semiautomatic handgun.

Another shooting occurred at North Miami Senior High School on September 29, which appeared to be a gang-related incident. Two teens smuggled a semiautomatic gun past the school's security guard and five cameras, and opened fire in a hallway outside the cafeteria. At around 12:30 P.M., Felly Petit-Frere, a seventeen-year-old junior, and Occi Eliezer, eighteen, who was suspended from the school, began firing at another student who'd beat them in a fistfight a day earlier. Two students and a business ed teacher were wounded. Felly and Occi fled the scene, but were apprehended two days later and charged with three counts of attempted first-degree murder.

The slaughter at Columbine was still five months away when, on November 16, 1998, a more ominous event occurred in Burlington, Wisconsin. Police headed off a plot by five boys, aged fifteen and sixteen, to carry out a school-shooting spree. On a hit list, the kids specifically targeted fifteen students, two administrators, and a faculty member. However, their agreed goal was to kill ten times that number. This "Goth" clique formulated their plan with fanatical precision. It consisted of stealing firearms from their parents, cutting telephone lines at the school, taking the assistant principal hostage at gunpoint and forcing him to announce an emergency code over the public-address system. That would initiate a lockdown, meaning teachers would keep pupils inside classrooms. By accessing class schedules, they could fetch students marked for death, one by one, bring them to the office, and shoot them execution-style. At that point, they intended to station themselves outside five classrooms, sound a school evacuation alarm, and catch dozens of students in a deadly cross fire. Prosecutor Richard Barta also said the teenagers described their agenda as a suicide mission ending in a standoff with cops.

The five juveniles were arrested one day before their lethal act was scheduled to occur. It was only prevented because one of the teenagers' girlfriends overheard her guy trying to back out, and informed her parents who, in turn, tipped off the police. The authorities' first reaction was "These are just kids talking," but then one of them recalled, "Hey, didn't something like this really happen a few months ago in Oregon?" Because of Thurston, they decided to investigate.

The assistant police chief explained later that the students' vengeance was concocted because they were picked on and made fun of. "These are just kids they didn't like." In a pattern typical of derailed attacks, one of the youths claimed the entire project was not really serious—only a fantasy of revenge, fed by one member's anger over being sent to a foster home some distance away. The others maintained they went along with the game, mostly to make him feel good. However, from the boys' homes, police recovered six handguns, five high-powered repeating rifles, 6,500 rounds of ammunition, and detailed plans of attack. Much of this information wasn't released publicly.

A prosecution psychologist suggested the Burlington ringleader lacked self-identity and had no sense of moral responsibility. The judge agreed that this boy was disturbed and dangerous enough to require mental-health treatment. One method the boy had used for recruiting followers was to show them violent videos and gauge their reactions. Those who found the killing attractive passed muster, and those who didn't never knew what they were missing. Initially most parents felt police had overreacted, that the danger was blown out of proportion and the concern unreasonable. After Columbine, however, these same townsfolk belatedly understood they'd narrowly missed experiencing a similar catastrophe.

Then on April 16, 1999, just four days before Eric Harris and Dylan Klebold would kill fellow students in Littleton, Colorado, a sixteen-year-old high school sophomore with a death list boarded a school bus with a shotgun wrapped in a blanket. Shawn Cooper fired twice in a school hallway in Notus, Idaho, after pointing his gun at a secretary and some students; fortunately, no one was injured. He surrendered peacefully.

Finally, eleven months after Kip's rampage, on April 20, 1999, Harris and Klebold succeeded in their malefic plan to bring death and misery to Columbine High. Because a large number of books and articles have already been published on this watershed event, the author has confined mention of Columbine to only those aspects that interface with the central themes of this narrative. For the benefit of anyone unfamiliar with the exact sequence of events on that day, however, the following is a simple summary based upon the research of Alan Lampe, the guiding light at www.Columbine-Angels.com, and entered here with his kind permission.

Eric Harris and Dylan Klebold arrived at Columbine High School a little after 11:00 A.M. carrying two duffel bags filled with propane bombs into the cafeteria. They left the school and went outside to wait for the bombs to explode, but a faulty connection prevented them from detonating. The killers decided to storm the school with two sawed-off shotguns, a Hi-Point 9mm carbine, an illegal TEC-DC9 semiautomatic gun, and a plethora of homemade bombs. They crossed the soccer field and started walking toward the outside staircase. On this sidewalk, Eric met up with a former friend, Brooks Brown, and told him to go home.

At the top of the staircase, Eric began the massacre by killing Rachel Scott and injuring Richard Castaldo. Meanwhile, Dylan turned toward the staircase and fired into the backs of Daniel Rohrbough, Lance Kirklin, and Sean Graves. He continued shooting and injured Michael Johnson and Mark Taylor. Dylan then went down the stairs, blew off Lance's jaw as he cried for help, and killed Daniel. After finishing with Rachel, Eric turned to the open field and the baseball diamond, wounding Anne Marie Hochhalter. He then turned back around and blasted the set of double glass doors, just as teacher Patti Nielson and student Brian Anderson were about to come out. Patti ran into the library and dialed 911, while Eric and Dylan walked inside the shattered doorway, guns blazing.

Deputy Neil Gardner arrived and exchanged gunfire with Eric. Dylan, meanwhile, was shooting in the western hallway, wounding Stephanie Munson. Teacher Dave Sanders came up the stairs from the cafeteria after warning students there to stay down, and was shot in the back. He crawled out of the killer's line of sight down the eastern hallway toward science room three.

Eric and Dylan entered the library, with Eric's first shots striking Evan Todd as he stood at the copier. Evan was wounded and hid under the checkout counter. Dylan's first shots killed Kyle Velasquez, who was still sitting at a computer desk. Dylan also injured Daniel Steepleton, Makai Hall, and Patrick Ireland. Eric then killed Steven Curnow, wounded Kasey Ruegsegger, and then killed Cassie Bernall by sticking his gun under the table and saying "Peek-a-boo." Because of the way he was holding his gun, the kick from it gave him a bloody nose. Dylan shot Patrick again.

Eric taunted and killed Isaiah Shoels, the only African American student in the room, probably by first grazing the back of his head, then fatally shooting him in the chest. Dylan killed Matt Kechter, while Craig Scott lay in between his now-dead friends. Eric then tossed a bomb toward Makai, who grabbed it and threw it farther away from himself and anybody else. The bomb exploded causing little injury. Dylan walked to the other side of the library and injured Mark Kintgen, Valeen Schnurr, and Lisa Kreutz. He then killed Lauren Townsend. At this point, Valeen was ridiculed for her religious beliefs, but Dylan moved on without injuring her further.

Eric came over to where Dylan was and injured Nicole Nowlin and John Tomlin, but Dylan killed John shortly after. Eric killed Kelly Fleming. He hit Lauren's body in a spray of bullets, and injured Jeanna Park and Lisa Kreutz again. Dylan found one of his friends, and let him leave the library. Eric, meanwhile, killed Daniel Mauser. Corey DePooter was shot by both killers and died, while Jennifer Doyle and Austin Eubanks, who were hiding with him, were injured. Dylan slammed a chair atop the checkout counter that teacher Patti Nielson (who made the famous 911 panic calls) and Evan Todd were hiding under, and then the killers left the library.

They went back down to the cafeteria and tried to detonate the propane bombs with gunfire, but that failed as well. They ran back up to the library, but everyone who could move, except Patrick, Lisa, and Patti, had fled. Eric lit a Molotov cocktail, and then they committed suicide. Through all of this, Dave Sanders lay bleeding to death in the science room where two Eagle Scouts tried desperately to save him. Between three and four p.m., a SWAT team reached them, and against the pleas of the students, they escorted the youngsters out, leaving Dave behind. He died as the SWAT team carried him out.

The killers took thirteen innocent lives plus their own, left twenty-three others injured, created untold psychological trauma, caused over $1 million in damage to Columbine High, and made this the worst high school shooting in U.S. history. More will be said about this quintessential act of violence at varying points in this work, but for now, the author's purpose is merely to establish a timeline of events, and suggest how each shooting may have affected those that followed.

Although the percentage of shooters to the school population at large has remained minuscule, it became clear by the 1990s that a handful of youths without a shred of conscience or sympathy were prepared to annihilate themselves and their classmates. It seemed to some that America was producing homegrown adolescent mass murderers who, while their motivations differed, had at least a few factors in common with international terrorists. According to their early notes, the boys who attacked Columbine even had a fantasy of continuing their killing spree and eventually hijacking a jetliner to crash into New York City in order to massacre as many innocent people as possible. This was more than three years before such an event actually took place on September 11, 2001.

• Chapter 8 •

Copycats

Violence is so pervasive in our culture, I don't think any child escapes it. More children think about [committing acts of violence] than don't. For every one who acts on it, ninety-nine others think about it.
—Charles Patrick Ewing, clinical and forensic psychologist at the State University of New York, and author of the book *Kids Who Kill*

For those who wish a return to simpler times, it may be disconcerting to learn that both school violence and weapons in classrooms have been with us for centuries. Student mutinies and classroom vandalization were more common in Colonial America than they are today. Armed pupils in seventeenth-century France often dueled with one another and beat up teachers. Two centuries ago, schoolmasters in a corner of genteel England sought military intervention to calm their rioting scholars.

What has changed is not the possibilities of turmoil, but the means of accomplishing it. Scuffles and fistfights have been replaced by the blast of a sawed-off shotgun. Imitating workplace rage, mass murder is now deployed as a solution to adolescent angst. But "imitation" is the key word. Few school shooters are inventive, and most are merely trying to collect for themselves a piece of the infamy that was handed to their predecessors. Just as cheaters at school will copy homework or test answers from other students, so also will those with less imagination copy the methods and mayhem of others who have fallen to those depths before them—whether they do so consciously or not.

And it isn't just delinquents. A study of three hundred undergrad students at a college near Philadelphia in 2001 revealed that 60 percent of male students and 32 percent of females had harbored recent homicidal fantasies. Most said they got their inspiration for murder using a variety of weapons from TV, movies, news broadcasts, and popular songs.

The average person, young or old, is as fascinated by reports of school shootings as they are repelled by them. Only a tiny minority, however, is likely to be aroused or intoxicated by such killing. Still, there had to be a vehicle or method by which the adult crime of mass murder was conveyed to susceptible young minds in such an alluring manner that it stimulated emulation.

Studies by University of California Professor David Phillips and forensic psychologist Park Dietz concluded that "news reports—not movies or video games—are the prime media mover in begetting copycats." Phillips claimed that "you have to think of these stories as a kind of advertisement for mass murder." Dietz determined "the degree of imitation was inspired by sustained and sensationalized media coverage." Fred McKissack, writing in *The Progressive,* was one of many who suggested that endless media coverage of mass grieving over school shootings served to incite and instruct adolescent copycats.

This may explain why it was that after Anthony Barbaro's onslaught in 1974, the two very next such attacks occurred five and eight months later in a neighboring region. While Anthony most likely drew his inspiration from Charles Whitman's 1966 University of Texas Tower shooting spree (see chapter 26), the author considers Barbaro to be the first of the "new age" U.S. adolescent high school shooters. In the previous fifty years, the only other teenage school shootings reported in newspapers were in the nature of juvenile delinquents who got out of control, one in 1956, another ten years later.

The May 4, 1956, case involved a fifteen-year-old Maryland Park Junior High School student named Billy Ray Prevatte, who had previously been expelled from a school in North Carolina for pulling a knife on a teacher. Suspended again in Maryland, he got hold this time of a .22-caliber rifle, intending to murder his principal. Unable to find his quarry, he shot and killed his English teacher, Mr. Cameron, and wounded two other teachers. He was released from a juvenile facility at age twenty-one.

The October 5, 1966, case came a little closer to the pattern of later school shootings in that Grand Rapids High School student David Black was a victim of family abuse and teasing. He also had a reputation as someone not very grounded in reality; so when the Minnesota boy warned his classmates he was going to kill them the next day, they weren't much concerned. When David arrived, his friends were waiting calmly, but they broke out running when he pulled a .22-caliber pistol from his jacket. One member of the group, Kevin Roth, was rooted to the spot, unable to move until the shock of a bullet entering his body gave his feet wings. School administrator Forest Wiley came out to stop the attack, but was killed by six shots from David's gun. Kevin survived.

A decade between such shootings is not exactly high frequency. And although Anthony Barbaro attacked during a Christmas–New Year vacation and injured no students, he did kill three adults and wounded eleven others around his school. In addition, his modus operandi foreshadowed in some ways the plan of action that Mitchell Johnson and Andrew Golden implemented nearly twenty-four years later at Jonesboro, by using a fire alarm to draw out victims.

Writer Bonnie Culver created a play about this incident called *Sniper,* which opened off-Broadway in January 2005. Her fictional protagonist is renamed Anthony Vaccaro, but the story is based upon actual details of Barbaro's life. In the real world, Anthony was a Regents scholar who brought a 12-gauge shotgun and a .30-06 rifle with a telescopic site to Olean High School in upstate New York. He was also considered the best shot on his ten-man rifle team. On December 30, 1974, the eighteen-year-old entered the nearly empty building through an unlocked door and made his way upstairs. On the way, he came upon janitor Earl Metcalf and killed him with a shot to the chest. Next he started a small fire in the third-floor hallway, which he knew would draw a response. The alarm went off while Anthony set up a sniper position in a window and began firing at passersby, killing a man walking along the street, and a woman driving past the school in her car.

For ninety minutes, Barbaro shot at firemen who responded, wounding eight of them until state troopers and city police stormed the building using tear gas. The fighting ended at 4:30 P.M. when Anthony threw his weapons out one of the smashed windows. He hanged himself while awaiting trial, just as Granite Hills High School shooter Jason Hoffman would do twenty-six years later.

Because a story like this is bigger news locally than internationally, it's noteworthy that two subsequent school shootings occurred just across the Great Lakes in Ontario, Canada. Five months after Olean, on May 28, 1975, what might be called the first truly classic North American school shooting took place, inasmuch as it set a pattern that would be repeated dozens of times in the next thirty years. A student and teacher were killed and thirteen classmates wounded when sixteen-year-old Michael Slobodian opened fire at Centennial Secondary School in Brampton. True to form, Michael then took his own life.

It's ironic this happened in Canada, which is measurably less violent than the United States, but it's also significant that the very next incident occurred in the same province another five months later, almost to the day. On October 27, in Ottawa, eighteen-year-old Robert Poulin killed one student and injured five others with a sawed-off shotgun in a classroom at St. Pius X High School. Robert, too, committed suicide.

The overwhelming majority of teenage shooters from this time onward carried only rifles or handguns, and until Columbine, only one other utilized homemade explosives. That individual was Nicholas Elliot, sixteen, and his attack occurred fourteen years after Barbaro's rampage. Elliot carried a small arsenal—three firebombs, a semiautomatic pistol, and two hundred rounds of ammunition—into his school at Virginia Beach, Virginia, on December 16, 1988. In one of just a handful of U.S. high school shootings perpetrated by a nonwhite student, Nicholas, who was African-American, opened fire on a boy who had taunted him with a racial slur, killed one teacher and wounded another.

Had he been given enough time, Kip Kinkel would have plainly used bombs, but the rapid precipitation of events forced him to leave his collection behind at home. Like Kinkel, Harris and Klebold were very sophisticated in their knowledge of deadly pyrotechnics. In all, fifty explosive devices with timers were found in and around Columbine

High, as well as in their homes. These included highly lethal pipe bombs, propane-fueled shrapnel explosives, and plastic containers filled with gasoline. One of the bombs placed at the school exploded hours after their attack. Homemade bombs were found near the lifeless bodies of the two shooters, and Klebold's black BMW was wired with explosives in the school parking lot. After Columbine, school-bombing threats increased exponentially.

As mentioned above, Anthony Barbaro's fire alarm ploy was exploited with a different twist by Golden and Johnson at Jonesboro, the only "successful" school shooting other than Columbine that was carried out by a pair of male students as a team. Eric Harris noted this event in the journal he kept for a year before the Columbine attack. Perhaps a little miffed at the competition, he wrote, *When you [i.e., the media] write about [us] . . . we were planning this before the kids in Jonesboro, and we're going to die in there.*

In chapter 17, we make reference to an infatuation with Nazism by Harris and Klebold, Jeff Weise, and some Hoyt, Kansas, would-be shooters, but all were predated by Roger Needham, of Lansing, Michigan. Needham, fifteen, customarily wore a Nazi pin to Everett High School each day, but on February 22, 1978, his classmate Bill Draher razzed him about it. Roger responded by pulling out a .38-special and shooting Bill, first in the jaw and then directly into the fallen fifteen-year-old's head. The killer muttered, *"I'm tired of being pushed around. Now I'm even,"* according to a nearby social studies teacher. Then he handed the gun, a knife, and a box of ammunition to one of the school's bilingual specialists, saying, "Here, I give up."

Tom Wilson, a policeman who happened to be at the school, lecturing a history class, made the arrest. In a search of Roger's room, police found Nazi literature, swastikas, armbands, a huge Nazi flag, excerpts from *Mein Kampf* and other Hitler writings, and a detailed diagram of a Nazi extermination camp with gas chambers. Needham was charged with first-degree murder as a juvenile, pleaded no contest, and was ordered to undergo psychiatric treatment. Thirty-three juvenile homes across America refused to admit him, but one near Ann Arbor finally did, and assisted him in getting his high school equivalency diploma. He was then allowed, closely supervised, to take classes at the University of Michigan. He earned both a Bachelor of Science degree and a master's in mathematics in 1984 "with highest distinction." A year after receiving his Ph.D. in 1992, Dr. Roger E. Needham was hired by the City College of New York.

The theme of intelligent, privileged American youths committing atrocious crimes because they "want to know what it feels like to kill somebody" goes back at least as far as the Leopold and Loeb kidnap-murder of a fourteen-year-old boy in 1924. Millionaire's son Nathan Leopold, nineteen, was a University of Chicago law student and his lover, Richard Loeb, eighteen, was the son of a retired Sears, Roebuck & Co. vice president when they decided to kill little Bobby Franks, just to prove they were brilliant enough to get away with it. They weren't. This category of well-off, educated killer seems akin to several school shooters.

Dylan Klebold was an exceptional student whose father, a geologist, owned a sprawling contemporary home with a guest house and a half-dozen vintage BMWs. Anthony Barbaro was eighth in his class of 292.

John Christian was an honor student, and the son of President Lyndon B. Johnson's former press secretary George Christian, when he shot and killed a teacher at the elite Murchison Junior High School in Austin, Texas, on May 18, 1978. John, thirteen, casually walked into his eighth-grade English classroom with a .22-caliber rifle and shot twenty-nine-year-old teacher Wilbur Grayson Jr. to death as he sat on a stool conducting class. John fled the room, but he was caught by an athletic coach and held against a fence until police arrived.

A more bizarre school-related crime concocted by three sons of wealthy San Francisco Peninsula families took place on July 15, 1976, in Chowchilla, California. Frederick Newhall Woods IV, twenty-four, and two brothers, James and Richard Schoenfeld (twenty-four and twenty-two), hijacked a school bus out on a summer excursion and transferred twenty-six children and the driver into a moving van that had been buried in a quarry. The kidnappers' aim was to collect a $5 million ransom. After sixteen hours underground in the eight-foot by sixteen-foot space, the bus driver and two boys dug their way out and got help. The trio of failed criminals was sentenced to life. A 1993 TV movie called *They've Taken Our Children: The Chowchilla Kidnapping* was made about the incident.

Strangely, just three days earlier, the deadliest college massacre in Orange County history had taken place in Fullerton at California State University. Edward Allaway, a thirty-seven-year-old custodian, entered the campus library with a .22-caliber semiautomatic rifle and, in what was clearly an instance of workplace rage, shot and killed his boss and six coworkers. Two more were wounded. He left others unscathed, targeting only those on his hit list. The judge found him "not guilty by reason of insanity" and sentenced him to a state hospital, but every year since 1987, Allaway's been trying to prove he's not insane to get released back into society. These two California events were the only newsworthy incidents of school-related violence in 1976.

In fact, during the nearly two decades following Barbaro's assault, school shootings were sporadic, no more than a couple each year. For example, there were two in 1984, but only one each in 1979, 1980, 1982, 1983 and 1985. Two of those seven incidents were in Arkansas. The first took place on January 7, 1980, when Evan Hampton, sixteen, walked into his science class with a handgun his older brother had given him and shot Mike Sanders, a boy he disliked, three times, killing him. Hampton handed the gun to the teacher and calmly waited for the principal to arrive, but he never showed remorse.

Students who'd ignored Hampton bragging about his plan at a local hamburger joint the previous night had a difficult time coming to terms with the fact they did nothing to stop him. This event took place in the town of Stamps—the very place where seventeen years later, Joseph "Colt" Todd, an eighth grader, was charged in the 1997 sniper shooting of two students standing in his high school parking lot. Todd claimed he'd been humiliated by teasing and he wanted "somebody else to hurt." The fourteen-year-old took a hunter's shooting position hidden in nearby woods to fire at these kids, exactly as Johnson and Golden would do at Jonesboro, also in Arkansas, just three months later.

As to the 1984 Arkansas incident, this was one of the first college shootings instigated by a student. On the evening of January 27, James Howard Taylor, nineteen, a former freshman at the University of Arkansas, in Fayetteville, brought a 12-gauge shotgun into the Delta Delta Delta sorority house and held two University of Arkansas

Police Department (UAPD) officers and a number of students hostage. When he was distracted, Sergeant Reggie Houser shot Taylor three times, killing him before he could fire.

Lightning would strike twice at this same college when on August 28, 2000, a thirty-six-year-old grad student also named James brought a .38-caliber pistol and roughly a hundred bullets to a meeting with his faculty adviser, English professor Dr. John Locke. James Easton Kelly was seeking a Ph.D. in comparative literature from the Fulbright College of Arts and Sciences, but a six-member committee that oversaw the doctoral program dismissed him on August 21 because of poor attendance, and because he'd dropped required courses. Witnesses heard a heated argument between the student and the professor inside the office, then the sound of three pistol shots. Locke died from wounds to his face and chest. When the UAPD arrived, James shouted, "Don't come in! I'm hurt," then fired into his own chest, killing himself.

Through the 1980s, comparable school violence remained infrequent until 1988, when six incidents took place, all but one in southern states. Nicholas Elliot's December attack at Virginia Beach was the final act of the year, but prior to that, three assaults on elementary schools occurred one after the other. The first was in May by an adult female (chapter 22) in Illinois; the second took place in September in Greenwood, South Carolina; and the last happened in Moscotte, Florida, the following month. In the final incident, a nine-year-old girl was wounded by a camouflaged gunman firing from brush behind the playground who was never caught, but in the South Carolina shooting, two third-grade girls were killed, nine children and a teacher wounded by nineteen-year-old James William Wilson.

Wilson began his attack using a nine-round .22-caliber pistol in the Oakland Elementary School cafeteria. When he went into the girls' restroom to reload, physical education teacher Kat Finkbeiner bravely attempted to disarm him, but was shot in her hand and mouth. After wounding more students in another classroom, he simply dropped the gun and surrendered to Kat until police arrived. Wilson was sentenced to death after pleading guilty but mentally ill.

The year 1989 opened with another horrific elementary-school attack by an adult, and ended with the worst school shooting in Canadian history. On January 17, Patrick Purdy, twenty-six, opened fire with an AK-47 assault rifle at a playground in Stockton, California. Five Southeast Asian children died, twenty-nine children and one teacher were wounded. The gunman ended his rampage with a bullet to his head. Purdy, who also used the name Patrick West and a number of other aliases, had been a student at this very school sixteen years before. Ironically, this was the second shooting at a Cleveland Elementary School (the other was ten years earlier, again in January, by Brenda Ann Spencer, chapter 21).

In September, there was a high school hostage situation in Kentucky that ended peacefully when "quiet and bright" seventeen-year-old Dustin Pierce surrendered, and in October, another high school hostage situation, in Anaheim, California, didn't end as well. Anthony Lopez, one of the students being held at bay in his Loara High School drama class by fifteen-year-old Cordell "Cory" Robb, made the mistake of taunting his captor. "Oh, we've got a suicidal killer on our hands," Lopez teased, and, "If the gun is real, why don't you just start shooting?" Robb did just that, wounding him. Cory then let Lopez and most of the girls go before giving up to police.

Pierce's demand had been to meet his father, whom he hadn't seen since he was four years old. Robb's motive had been to get his stepfather to come to school so that he could kill him to prevent a planned family relocation to Northern California. The following month, the only objective stated by a thirteen-year-old Arlington, Texas, boy who shot his assistant principal in the back was "to get attention."

The year ended badly for Canada when twenty-five-year-old Marc Lépine, born Gamil Gharbi, walked into the University of Montreal, École Polytechnique, with a .223-caliber Sturm Ruger mini-14 semiautomatic rifle on December 6. In twenty minutes, Lépine brought death to fourteen female students, and serious injuries to twenty-seven others. He targeted only women, shouting at one point, "I'm here to fight against feminism!" He saved the last bullet for himself, wrapping his jacket around the barrel of the gun and firing at the side of his head.

Thankfully, 1990 was far quieter, with only one Las Vegas fatality in a crowded high school cafeteria. The number was just four in 1991, but in 1992, it jumped to nine. Two of those took place in New York, two in Texas, and in the same month, two in California. Regarding the latter, the first occurred when twenty-year-old Eric Houston killed a social studies teacher and three students, wounding thirteen others in an armed siege at his former school in Olivehurst on May 1. His attack upon Lindhurst High was in retribution for a failing grade in social studies, resulting in him not graduating and therefore losing a job. Houston was given a death sentence.

Two weeks later in Napa, fourteen-year-old John McMahan, claiming other boys had bullied him, shot and wounded two students in his first-period science class with a .357 handgun. The odds are good that the second event on May 14 was inspired by the first.

A potential shooter might not sit down, watch the news, and decide, "I will do that too" (although some have), but the concept as a potentiality may enter his mind consciously or subconsciously. Assuming that the paired incidents in New York, Texas, and California were not purely coincidental, 1992 marks the beginning of school shootings as a media-fed trend rather than isolated, freak occurrences. Within months of the California attacks, the addition of four prominent and one "minor" school shooting confirmed the impression that an expanding new phenomenon had commenced.

Despite Canada's reputation as a peaceful nation, it was once again in Montreal that another college shooting took place on August 24. This one could also be characterized as workplace rampage as the perpetrator was a former employee of Concordia University suffering from a severe personality disorder. Fifty-two-year-old Valery Fabrikant went to the ninth floor of a campus building and killed four faculty members, wounding a fifth. He was sentenced to life.

On September 11 of the same year, seventeen-year-old Randy Earl Matthews pulled a gun during a morning pep rally at Palo Duro High in Amarillo, Texas. Six students were shot and one was trampled, but all recovered. Matthews was charged with attempted murder and aggravated assault, and sentenced to eight years. Not long after, sensational shootings in Great Barrington, Massachusetts, and Grayson, Kentucky, occurred almost exactly a month apart.

The Massachusetts episode on December 14, 1992, is described in chapter 14 in relation to shooter Wayne Lo's claim of auditory hallucinations. Thirty-five days later, on January 18, 1993, seventeen-year-old senior Gary Scott Pennington took twenty-two students hostage in Deanna McDavid's seventh-period English class at East Carter

High in the Appalachian mountain town of Grayson. Using his father's .38-caliber pistol, Pennington shot the English teacher in the head, killing her. When custodian Marvin Hicks entered the room to help, Pennington shot the man in the abdomen, killing him as well. He later claimed what set him off was the teacher's questioning his increasingly morbid writings. Found guilty but mentally ill, Pennington was convicted as an adult on murder and kidnapping charges, and sentenced to life without parole for twenty-five years.

By the time of Kip Kinkel's attack in May '98, twenty-one school shootings had taken place in the previous thirty months, an average of one every six weeks. Eight were significant enough to be reported as international news. We indeed seemed to be in the midst of an escalating crisis in which out-of-control youths were savagely and inexplicably turning against their classmates in murderous killing sprees. Or, so said the media.

• Chapter 9 •

The Politics of Blame

There was absolutely no probable cause . . . to believe there
was any immediate danger to Kip or others.
—Springfield chief of police Bill DeForrest, May 22, 1998

Immediately after the Thurston tragedy, there was one legal issue still unsettled: the police claim that Kip was released after being arrested for possession of a stolen gun due to lack of "probable cause." On Friday, May 22, 1998, a press conference was called at Springfield's city hall. The first announcement of the day concerned sixteen-year-old Ben Walker. His life support had been disconnected when all hope had been lost; his donated organs would sustain the lives of nearly a dozen waiting patients.

Eventually Lane County district attorney F. Douglass Harcleroad was asked the crucial question. A reporter wanted to know: "Why this child who brought a gun to school a couple of days ago wasn't held at least for twenty-four hours? . . . He was expelled, but why wasn't he detained in custody at the juvenile center?"

"Sure, I can explain," Harcleroad replied. "Oregon law provides that when a youth is arrested for a crime such as the one you just described—possession of a firearm at school, which is a class C felony—that the police officer shall arrest the child, if appropriate, and then shall release the child to the parents or guardian unless, one, there is a warrant out for the child's arrest, which is not the case here . . . or, two, the officer has probable cause."

Harcleroad defined probable cause as "the standard in the law which means more likely than not, greater than fifty percent. If the officer has probable cause that there's an immediate threat to the child that he's arrested or to other individuals—and the officer had, from my reading of the police report and speaking to the officer, no reason to believe that. What he did was arrest the child for having a gun at school. The argument that, well, he had a gun at school, so that in and of itself is enough, is probably not probable cause."

Probably not probable cause? This is worth examining, for on that one thread hangs everything that followed. Harcleroad's definition is telling us that a single police officer was allowed to make the decision as to whether there was probable cause. If he had *no* reason to believe or suspect that Kip would harm himself or others, then the officer would be justified in his action. In fact, he would have been compelled by law to release the boy to his parents. The officer in charge of this case was the same one who arrested Kip: Detective Al Warthen. Unless he conferred with others, and there's no evidence of that, he alone made that weighty decision. Obviously, he knew the law and felt the risk wasn't sufficient to detain Kip.

Chief DeForrest later supported that decision strongly, stating, "There was absolutely no probable cause . . . to believe there was any immediate danger to Kip or others. The police department was in custody of the gun, he wasn't going to get it back, and he made no specific threats. Therefore the law says release the child to the parents' custody."

Reporters, however, had been talking to students who informed them Kip had indeed "been talking about killing people," that Kip "writes and speaks, openly making threats, saying one of his goals in life is to kill people," and, "he apparently had written in English-class journals about violence in front of teachers." So they questioned, why, "if this boy has this past of talking about killing, and all of a sudden you find a gun in his locker," was it not sufficient grounds to assume the "more likely than not" criterion of probable cause? One journalist asked, "Did the officer ask any questions . . . to the students who had a relationship with this boy?"

DeForrest responded, "That's not the kind of thing you'd normally do in this kind of an investigation, where you'd call in other students and inquire, 'What has Kip told you?' First of all, we wouldn't know who to talk to. This kind of information emerges after the fact."

Yet the school and arresting officer had indeed known which students to call in to ask on May 20. They'd used the list of names provided by the Keeneys.

Incredibly, it seems lack of probable cause was based only upon Kip's own protestations of his innocence. DeForrest told reporters, "Kip was asked, 'Why do you want the gun? What do you intend to do with the gun?' And his response was 'I just like guns.' You know, 'I wanted to buy this gun and so I have it.' 'Do you have any intention of using it?' 'No, I do not have any intention of using it against anybody.'" These statements were confirmed in the following excerpts from a taped confession made on May 21, 1998, soon after the Thurston rampage:

> DETECTIVE WARTHEN: Let's go back to the earlier case with the gun you bought from Korey. Why'd you buy that gun?
>
> KIP KINKEL: I don't know.
>
> WARTHEN: Did you buy it with the intention of hurting somebody?
>
> KINKEL: No.
>
> WARTHEN: When you brought the gun to school yesterday, or when you purchased it yesterday, did you know that was the right thing to do, or the wrong thing to do?
>
> KINKEL: I knew it was a wrong thing.
>
> WARTHEN: Okay . . . but you didn't have any intent yesterday, or at least that's what you told me yesterday, of hurting anybody. Is that correct?
>
> KINKEL: Right.

It appears again as if Kip's own denial of intent to hurt had been enough to permit his release. Or was it? Is it standard practice, when a person is arrested for possessing a stolen weapon, to let them go just because they swear they meant no harm? DeForrest claimed the Springfield police "went through normal investigative procedures." Later evidence suggested otherwise.

On January 30, 2002, the author received a startling phone call challenging what school and police officials had said at that press conference. The secretive phone informant had not only been at Thurston prior to, during, and after the shooting, he'd participated in Kip and Korey's arrest the day before. Once his identity was confirmed as former assistant principal Dick Doyle, there was no question about his legitimacy.

If what Doyle was saying could be proven true, it would completely alter the official portrayal of circumstances leading up to this tragic event. If there'd been a deliberate cover-up, the motivation wouldn't be hard to determine: saving face, reputations, and jobs, and avoiding the civil lawsuits that followed nearly every other school shooting.

Doyle offered a way to double-check the veracity of his statements: a report submitted on the evening of May 21, 1998, by Detective Rodric "Rick" Raynor, who'd been called over from neighboring Eugene to assist during the crisis. It confirmed that Detective Warthen and Dick Doyle were told by Korey Ewert on May 20 that Kip had purchased the gun with the intention of shooting someone. In two words: probable cause.

When I contacted Raynor (now retired) in 2003, he confirmed the report was accurate. After the arrests of Kip and Korey on May 20, Doyle informed Thurston Principal Larry Bentz of this threat. The principal let Doyle know after lunch that he'd put in a call to Springfield's assistant superintendent of Schools, Len Arney. Both Arney and Bentz had authority to lock down Thurston without needing a directive from Superintendent Jamon Kent, but this wasn't done. Bentz didn't think there was any danger even after being informed that Kip and Korey had been released. Many parents later felt these administrators failed to adhere to the Springfield School District's dictum: "We will hold the interests of children to be at the heart of all decisions."

Thurston was open and exposed on the morning of May 21, as if nothing unusual had occurred on May 20. Due to an appointment at his own kids' elementary school, Principal Bentz was absent when the shooting started. Other administrators were on hand early because of a "Senior Men's Excellence Breakfast" in the library, which was just ending when the attack came. The principal reached Thurston about half an hour later, coinciding with Arney and Kent.

In the Raynor report, it's explicitly stated that a clear, immediate threat was established on May 20. Raynor recounted how "Doyle told me Ewert said several times Kinkel wanted the gun to kill someone. I asked Doyle if Warthen was present when Ewert made the statement about Kinkel wanting to kill the person, and he was sure Warthen was present." Doyle later stated several students brought in prior to Ewert voiced similar concerns.

Doyle knew his good friend Warthen was hard of hearing. When Korey revealed Kip's lethal intent, Doyle looked at Warthen and asked, "Did you hear that, Al?" and the detective shook his head yes. When the information was repeated, Doyle again asked, "Al, did you get that?" and again Warthen nodded in the affirmative.

The Raynor report was never mentioned in any media coverage or court document. By chance or intent, this affidavit was ignored or buried. However, Doyle's testimony needed to be substantiated as the mental and emotional state of the assistant principal could be called into question. A large man in his mid-fifties, Doyle had suffered mightily in the months following the attack. He'd wanted to speak out publicly about Korey's warnings, but was warned off doing so by his legal counsel ("Keep your head down and your mouth shut"). Racked by guilt over what he knew but couldn't reveal, Doyle illogically took the blame for not preventing the shooting upon himself. A year later, he received a permanent leave of absence due to post-traumatic stress disorder (PTSD).

It would be easy for others to seize upon Doyle's symptoms as a sign that he was too disturbed to accurately recall Korey's threat thirty hours later when the Raynor interview took place. Fortunately, a second witness who did not suffer anywhere near that degree of trauma confirmed that everything Doyle said was true. Baseball coach Jerame Wood also heard Korey repeat the threat when the boy was sent alone into Don Stone's office. Wood also had the foresight to write an account of what he'd heard on May 20 when he came home from his job that afternoon. In his diary, Wood noted that as Korey entered the room he blurted, *"I'm fucked,"* then picked up a basketball and started bouncing it in a false display of indifference.

Wood took the ball away and calmly asked Korey, "Why did Kip need a gun?" Ewert replied, "A few kids were talking smack about Kip and we were going to get back at them, and it ain't over." The expression "talking smack" was slang for "putting someone down," but note the use of "we," not "he," and the final ". . . it ain't over."

Immediately after Korey was taken away, Jerame shared what he'd learned with Stone and Doyle. This, surely, should have been sufficient probable cause for holding both juveniles in detention, or for locking down the school after their release, especially in light of previous headline-making attacks.

Wood wasn't scheduled to work that fateful May 21. When he learned about the shooting, he wrote an addendum to his report: *I turned on the TV and it was all over the news. I immediately thought back to the day before and said the police must have released Kip and Korey. I immediately knew who was involved. I thought that it might have been Korey, for the fact that he was the one that was mouthy and threatening the day before. Kip, on the other hand, seemed to me like a normal, shy freshman that did not get into much trouble.*

Korey's parents, at least, had made a commendable attempt to push the law to accomplish what the authorities were failing to do. They asked that their son be detained at Skipworth Juvenile Facility to teach him a lesson. The officer in charge explained that Skipworth couldn't be used just to teach kids a lesson. It's presumed Bill Kinkel made a similar request because in his final phone conversation with Scott Keeney, Kip's dad stated he was concerned his son hadn't been taken to Skipworth.

None of this information was revealed at the May 22 press conference. Warthen made no mention in his report of interrogating Korey as to why Kip wanted the weapon. This seemed a strange omission, since it would be logical to ask of someone who's confessed to stealing a gun for a friend. Instead, Warthen details how, not *why*, Korey stole the gun and sold it to Kip. Also missing was the fact that when Kip was brought back into the interrogation room after Korey was sent out, Doyle reproached him in front of the detective, saying, "We know you wanted to kill someone here today with that gun." Kip protested, "That was just a joke." In other words, Kip was confirming he'd indeed made that threat.

Detective Warthen may have had the best of intentions when he made the choices that he did. He conducted all other aspects of the case in a capable and proper manner. Still, he's only human. During the court hearing months later, Warthen made his victim impact statement about how the shootings had deeply affected him. He told the judge, "On May 20, 1998, I was conned or led to believe it was safe to let Kip Kinkel go home with his father. On May 21, 1998,

Kip Kinkel again lied to me, which put many of my colleagues in harm's way because of his bomb making. We cannot be conned again to believe it will ever be safe for Kinkel to live among us."

The reference to May 21 was clear. After Kip's arrest for the school shooting, the sheriff's department heard from other students that the boy had made a large explosive device from a fire extinguisher. They suspected Kip might have booby-trapped the house. Al Warthen appealed to Kip, telling him, "Enough people have been hurt already, some people have lost their lives . . . and we must end this now." Then the detective asked him if the rumor of homemade bombs was true. For some unfathomable reason, Kip lied. He answered that he'd never done anything like that. Warthen pressed him. Kip said okay, he'd talked about it to other kids, but he was just bragging, wanting to impress people, and it wasn't true. Kip was employing once again the "I was only joking" tactic; it was the same maneuver he'd used so often in the past when "caught in the act." Indeed, he outdid himself, going so far as to express anger that "his friends would lie about him and say such a thing."

There was nothing Kip could possibly gain at that point by making false statements, yet his automatic response to being accused of wrongdoing was so ingrained, he could not stop himself even then from replying in the way he always did in such circumstances—with outraged denial. He seemed so sincere, Warthen believed him. When the truth became known, the removal of the parents' bodies had to be delayed while the bomb squad—the very group Kip had claimed he wished to join someday—risked their lives finding and removing a large number of explosive devices, including one made from a fire extinguisher.

The extinguisher bomb proved to be a prime example of Kip's technical prowess. A digital timer had been affixed to the top, deceptively rewired. If any button on the keypad were pushed, the timer would start counting down to detonation at one minute and twelve seconds. If a nearby cop keyed his radio mike, that also would set it off. The bomb squad transported it via armored trailer to their disposal range and remotely exploded it. It was so powerful, debris flew one hundred feet into the air despite being covered with sand in a hole two feet deep.

After cutting a hole in the side of Kip's house to remove bomb components, technicians uncovered dozens of smaller explosives. It must have taken Kip months to assemble them. Many were filled with fragmentation material in the form of tightly packed thumbtacks and straight pins to maximize injuries.

The myth perpetrated by a failure to establish probable cause allowed Oregon authorities up to the highest levels to maintain a posture of "plausible deniability." When Governor John Kitzhaber came to speak at the Thurston High library in the wake of the massacre, he promised the laws would be changed (they were). When he opened the session to questioning, Dick Doyle asked why Kip hadn't been detained. Kitzhaber replied that this case didn't fit the criteria. An indignant Doyle angrily shot back, "We knew on May twentieth that Kip wanted to kill someone. *How* does that not fit?"

Kitzhaber quickly took the next question. Sympathetic teachers later took the disheartened Doyle aside and quietly told him, "We understand where you're coming from"—their intention being to soothe his frustration. Their attitude was "It's over now, so let's move on." They had no idea how untrue that was.

• Chapter 10 •

Love Hurts

The greatest crimes do not arise from a want of feeling for others but from an oversensibility for ourselves and an overindulgence to our own desires.
—Edmund Burke (1729–1797), Irish statesman, member of the British Parliament

It may seem like a contradiction, but when Kip wrote in his farewell note, *"I love my mom and dad so much* just after slaying them, he was no doubt sincere. Kip didn't murder his parents because he hated them, but because he hated himself. He told Detective Warthen he loved his father, so that's why he had to kill him. The same holds true for him telling his mother he loved her even as he shot her. Love and hate are not mutually exclusive even in normal relationships, but Kip had so many emotional wires crossed, it's doubtful he knew how to separate one sensation from the other.

From the parents' side, there were obvious frustrations but also unconditional love. Faith kept a photo of Kip on her desk where she taught at Springfield High and still referred to the picture as "my little angel." Thurston High counselor Dick Bushnell, who knew the Kinkels personally, called their abode "a home with a lot of love." Yet, if this were so, why was Kip so full of hate? In his journal he wrote, *I hate every person on this earth,* and, *Love isn't real, only hate remains,* and then, *I know I should be happy with what I have, but I hate living.* In his suicide note, Kip wrote, *But you know me, I hate everything.*

The essays Kip composed in school were similar to his private jottings. In early May '98, Kip's literature class had been studying Shakespeare's *Romeo and Juliet*. Together, they'd watched a video of director Baz Luhrmann's excessively violent 1996 film version of the play, starring Leonardo DiCaprio and Claire Danes, to fire up their enthusiasm. The words were still Shakespeare's, but the youthful antagonists were members of street gangs. The kids at Thurston could relate, and even eight years later, Montreal shooter Kimveer Gill would write online that he wished to die "like Romeo and Juliet, or in a hail of gunfire." It was no accident Kip chose the musical soundtrack from this movie to leave blasting on his family's CD player as he drove off to his probable death at Thurston.

As his essay theme, Kip chose the point of view of Juliet's cousin Tybalt. The language he used looks disturbingly familiar, as Kip's Tybalt sounds off about the despised Montagues: *But you know me, I loathe all of them*, and, *I am no longer blind in my hatred, I can see with my hate*, and again, echoing another part of Kip's journal, *Blood will flow until they are all dead*. Perhaps Kip was projecting forward in his mind when he put the following words into Tybalt's mouth: *This was the first moment in my life where I had taken the life of another. I loved it, it dispelled all the anger and animosity I was feeling*. That last sentence is also nearly identical to expressions Kip used in describing to Dr. Hicks his release from stress each time he set off explosives.

When Kip did speak of love, it was in unfavorable terms. In a reply to a different essay question, he titled his paper "LOVE SUCKS," and wrote, *When you love something, it's always taken away from you. Everything I touch turns to shit*. And then, a flagrantly direct forewarning: *That's why you go to a pawn shop and buy an AK-15 because you are going to execute every last mother fucking one of you. If I had a heart it would be gray*.

Kip goes on to express his view concerning the emotions of love and hate:

> It is easier to hate than love. Because there is much more hate and misery in the world than there is love and peace. Some people say that you should love everyone. But that is impossible. Look at our history it is full of death, de-

pression, rape, wars, and diseases. I also do not believe in love at first sight. But I do believe in hate at first sight. Therefore love is a much harder feeling to experience.

He ends his paper:

I really wouldn't know how to answer this question because my cold, black heart has never and never will experience true love. . . . [Love] does more harm than good. I plan to live in a big, black hole. My firearms will be the only things to fight my isolation. . . . Love is a horrible thing. It makes things kill and hate.

These are some of the essays brought to the attention of Kip's mother by apprehensive teachers and counselors. A very similar thing happened at Columbine, and in the aftermath, Dylan Klebold's creative writing teacher, Judy Kelly, was added to a lawsuit charging that various school officials had ample warning of the coming firestorm. But Kelly had, in fact, met with a guidance counselor and Dylan's parents to discuss what she described as "the most vicious story I have ever read." In the English-class essay, Dylan graphically portrayed a violent protagonist in a black trench coat with a duffel bag brutally executing "preps." Once more, the ball was in the parents' court.

In the case of her son, could Faith Kinkel have concluded that all of Kip's tirades were simply a natural adolescent reaction to unrequited love? She was probably aware Kip was agonizing over the disappointments of an on-again, off-again flirtation with Stormy, a girl he once dated. Girls in this age group can be manipulative as they explore their maturing sexuality, and boys who become their admirers may be devastated by even minor downshifts in these relationships. Stormy and Kip were still passing notes to each other in class, but his insecure infatuation with her had left him feeling deeply resentful as she alternately encouraged or discouraged his affections. It was Stormy that Kip referred to in his journal when he wrote:

Every time I talk to her, I have a small amount of hope. But then she will tear it right down. It feels like my heart

is breaking. But is that possible? I am so consumed with
hate all of the time. Could I ever love anyone? I have feelings, but do I have a heart that's not black and full of animosity?

Kip was making an appeal for personal deliverance to a postpu-
bescent teenage girl who barely knew her own mind. Lacking any
certainty about their relationship, Kip nevertheless designated her to
be the sole source of his emotional salvation when he wrote, *I need
help. There is one person that could help, but she won't. I think I
love her, but she could never love me. I don't know why I try.*

Kip's melancholy was scattered between more caustic observations
in his journal. The next evening Kip wrote:

Today of all days, I asked her to help me. I was shot down.
I feel like my heart has been ripped open and ripped apart.
I gave her all I have, and she just threw it away. . . . The
thought of you is still racing in my head. Every time I see
your face, my heart is shot with an arrow. I think she will
say yes, but she doesn't, does she? She says, "I don't know."
The three most fucked up words in the English language.

In asking for her help, Kip seemed to recognize that he required
assistance in facing up to his fears of being emotionally unstable,
but Stormy was neither willing nor mature enough to handle that
kind of assignment. What Kip really needed was professional counseling. On another level, however, his feelings were not so different
from millions of other teenagers confronting the roller-coaster ups
and downs of first love and heartache.

During nearly the same period, three states away in Colorado, Dylan
Klebold was undergoing an almost identical bout of obsessive fixation. *I just hope she likes me as much as I LOVE her,* he wrote regarding his first attempt at romance. *The sound of her laugh, I picture
her face, I love her.* Then he drafted a message implying, like Kip,
that his crush could rescue him from the worst of fates. *The reason
that I am writing to you now is that I . . . want to go on to a new*

existence, he penned in a letter found later among his belongings. *However, if it was true that you loved me as I do you . . . I would find a way to survive.* In short, he was threatening to kill himself unless she loved him. Whether a copy of this missive was ever sent is unknown. Had it been, and had the girl responded positively, it's still a stretch to say this would have prevented the Columbine massacre.

Dylan's partner Eric Harris also had problems with the opposite sex. Harris perceptively wrote, *That's where a lot of my hate grows from, the fact that I have practically no self-esteem, especially concerning girls and looks.*

Similarly, eighteen-year-old German school shooter Sebastian Bosse (chapter 26) left a farewell message in 2006 lamenting the fact that he never had a girlfriend, and vowing revenge for a life of frustration.

Kids like this need to understand it's not the world's fault they don't have a girlfriend. They should know the situation will likely change in the future, but perhaps they're justifying to themselves their murderous intent.

As for Kip, because of his clear-cut conviction that he was an "unworthy son," the additional humiliation of being rejected in romance might have led him to adopt a general animosity toward any type of love. Depression, low self-regard, and a feeling that he was isolated ("nobody understands me") were the perfect fuels to feed his obsession with knives and guns. His weapons served as a protective coat of armor against the pain. For these tools of defense to be converted into an offensive arsenal, Kip only needed the catalyst of thinking that he'd been backed into a corner. That's exactly what he sensed when he was expelled for buying and having a gun at school on May 20. As he later cried out to Detective Warthen, "I had no other choice."

Contrary to the perception that no one could see the gathering storm, Kip didn't suffer in silence. He was constantly sending out signals of his intensifying rage. The English essays quoted earlier were just one aspect of those warnings, but they were *not* simply accepted, discounted, or dismissed. Concerned teachers passed them on to the appropriate staff. Kip was seen at least once by substitute counselor

Marcia Graham with respect to the violent "self-destructive" essays he wrote in the months before the shooting, and Kip's parents were notified about it.

The most blatant incident was the bomb-making lecture Kip gave in Marian Smith's speech class. The teacher reported this disturbing presentation to counselor Dick Bushnell. Smith wrote that Bushnell reassured her in a memo that Kinkel's father knew all about his son's obsessions. When Graham went on to recommend professional therapy to Kip's parents, Faith's response was to send an e-mail to Bushnell asking him to change her son's counselor.

At the press conference on May 22, Superintendent Kent was questioned about Kip's counseling history. "He apparently had written in English-class journals about violence in front of teachers," said one reporter, who then asked, if Kip had ever "been referred to counselors?"

Kent replied, "To my knowledge, he wasn't working with any counselors, and the staff reports to me this was an average, everyday kind of kid." Another journalist noted a discrepancy here, and tried to corner the superintendent, saying, "But, Mr. Kent, in other words, if you have a student in your school and he writes and speaks openly . . . about making threats saying one of his goals in life is to kill people, you do not then refer him to a counselor? That's an average, everyday kid?"

Kent defended his position, stating, "Oh, I didn't say we wouldn't refer individuals to counselors. What I'm saying is that if we detained every student that said they were going to kill someone on our campuses today, we would have a large number of kids detained."

After Columbine, such detentions were initiated and credited with stopping dozens of other school attacks.

• Chapter 11 •

Stealth and Lies

In my opinion, any other student, with teachers and coun-
selors calling attention to serious behavioral problems, would
not have been given the slack that this student and his
family received.

—Cindy Murdoch, Thurston parent

The close personal relationship of Springfield School District administrators with the Kinkels was no secret. After the gun arrest on
May 20, pressure came from both higher authorities and coworkers
to "give the boy another chance" or not go through with the expulsion at all. A female teacher called Doyle "a hard-ass" to his face
for refusing to reconsider Kip's punishment. She no doubt regretted
those words the next day. On May 20, however, none of these people seemed especially concerned that Kip having a gun in school
might foreshadow further problems, as if being the son of a teaching colleague eliminated such worries.

More damning to the Kinkels' stature, however, was the conversation that took place when Bill called Assistant Principal Doyle at
Thurston around lunchtime on May 20, after his son was arrested,
and demanded to know what could be done to save Kip's grades.
Doyle was staggered by Bill's sense of priorities. "Mr. Kinkel," he
told Kip's father, "we have a much bigger problem here than grades.
We have a problem with a gun."

In a response never released to the public, Bill then knowingly
lied in an effort to keep his son's options open, and by doing so, he

sealed his own fate, that of his wife, and of innocent children. Bill falsely assured Doyle of the school's safety, saying, "It's okay. We don't have any guns here at home. The police have the stolen weapon. My concern is Kip's grades."

Bill went on to say the school and police were making too much out of it. Doyle became more apprehensive. He had a gut feeling something was amiss, and that Kip's dad hadn't fully comprehended the gravity of the situation. He asked counselor Bushnell to call Bill back and discuss this "friend to old friend." Bushnell did so, between 1:15 and 1:30 P.M., and reported to Doyle that Bill again declared he was only "concerned about Kip's completion or credits for the academic year." Memories differ in details. According to Bushnell, the subject of guns in their home never came up. According to Doyle, Bill confirmed to Bushnell that Kip had no access to any weapons.

When Bushnell called Bill again "around 3:00 p.m." with the good news that Kip's teachers were in agreement to provide homework so the boy could finish the year with full credits, the phone wasn't picked up. The counselor left his message on the answering machine. Ironically, that's the estimated time Bill was shot while sitting near the kitchen phone.

Soon after the Thurston shooting, a badly shaken Doyle asked Bushnell, "Didn't you tell me yesterday Bill Kinkel said he had no guns?" To which, according to the assistant principal, the counselor sorrowfully replied, "I guess he lied." Bushnell has acknowledged he "may have said something of that nature" in the days following the attack, but it was a confusing time.

The Kinkels' antiviolence, antigun stance was an accepted fact in the community. Bill was outspokenly anti-NRA. Few had any inkling Bill had purchased guns for his son, nor that he owned several himself. His lie was accepted. That helps explain why the school didn't follow its own rules of initiating a lockdown on May 21, but it doesn't excuse it.

As for the police department allowing the boys to go free, this also had not made sense based solely upon Kip's protestations of innocence, but when further assurances of safety from Bill Kinkel are added into the mix, it sounds more plausible. After all, when Warthen said, "On May 20, 1998, I was conned or led to believe it was safe to let Kip Kinkel go home with his father," he didn't specify he'd been conned *only by Kip* that day. Therefore, it might be assumed Bill also made a declaration to police that no guns were kept in his house. If Bill could lie to Doyle, and possibly to Bushnell, an old friend and colleague, what would prevent him from using the same approach with police in an effort to "save" the son he loved? That would go far in explaining the riddle of how Detective Warthen might be inclined to release Kip to his father's care.

There's one further plausible factor in rationalizing that unbelievable release. Springfield is not an immense town. Personal networks form. Warthen's wife, Sherrie, had been Kip's fifth-grade teacher. Bill was aware of that fact, and he could have used that relationship to put additional emotional pressure on Warthen to release his son. That's speculation, but this personal association certainly added to the feeling of betrayal the detective expressed in his victim impact statement. "I can't tell this court enough," he said, "about the grief and emotional trauma Kip caused Sherrie. Not only did Sherrie know Faith and Bill Kinkel as parents, she also knew them as colleagues. Sherrie could not believe that one of her past Walterville Elementary School students could commit murder and mayhem to our community or attempt to kill her husband in his final act."

The fact was, Kip surprised a lot of people, but not everyone. Dick Doyle was accepting no excuses. "We'd crafted preventive measures," he said. "We'd created a safety wall, but the rules were ignored when the moment of truth arrived. They weren't followed because, quite simply, he was Kinkel. Instead of considering the fact of the gun, they considered the family of the boy who was caught with it."

Perhaps Kip would have found a way to act out his violent fantasies no matter how desperately his parents tried to appease or discipline him. But was it only up to the parents? Communities are supposed to have safeguards in place to protect the public against such disasters. The problem is, until recently, those safeguards were only aimed at obviously troubled kids with police records from high-risk homes and a history of abuse. Like a stealth bomber, Kip flew in under the normal radar screens, giving Oregon its first taste of how "commonplace" kids from decent homes could apparently turn into vicious killers overnight. The fact that both his parents were teachers in the school system that Kip attacked only served to make him more invisible.

• Chapter 12 •

A Question of Pride

*We're so into giving people their own space that the bound-
aries of normalcy for adolescence have become pretty broad.
And honestly, that's BS. A child talking about building
bombs, abusing animals and killing people is not normal.*
—Charles Patrick Ewing

Some acting out may be part of a child's natural stages of development, but when such conduct becomes constant and extreme, it can
be an early warning sign of serious problems ahead. When we see a
youngster throwing a tantrum in public, the first person we look at
is the attending parent, and the first question we are thinking is *Can't
you control your kid's behavior?* Similarly, when we hear of a rampaging adolescent committing mass murder, the first thing we silently
wonder is *What kind of family did he come from?* When a youthful killer has also murdered members of his own family, the question of parenting becomes more urgent.

The Kinkels were very careful to keep Kip's problems to themselves. By maintaining this proud facade, they cut themselves off from
the advice and counseling they so desperately needed. Only their closest friends got hints of the stress that was building up behind closed
doors. Once at a dinner party, Faith admitted being worried her son
had no conscience. When she'd reward Kip with positive attention,
he'd follow the rules—but only so long as it suited his purpose. When

his mind was set, the word "No!" had no meaning for him. The Kinkels confided in Denny Sperry, a friend of twenty years, that they were anxious about Kip's unhealthy attraction toward excessively bloody, violent films.

To counter Kip's antisocial attitudes, Bill and Faith tried interesting him in sports and outdoor activities. They tutored him after work and guided his homework. "The Kinkels did their best," Scott Keeney said, "but maybe they spoiled Kip. Anything he wanted, he got. They should've made him work harder for what he wanted." Ryan Crowley's dad, Michael, agreed that Kip took advantage of his parents. "Kip's attitude," he observed, "was I can do whatever I want." Berry Kessinger, another family friend, told how Bill and Faith "did everything right—tried everything. . . . He was an obnoxious kid. I knew right away they were going to have a hard time with him. He constantly challenged everything. I even wanted to take a swat at him."

When Kip was seven, Thurston teachers held a staff party at a public swimming pool. When it was time to get out of the water, Kip refused. Bill was renowned for running such a tight classroom, he never had to send students down for discipline. On this day, however, Bill's colleagues saw a side of him they didn't recognize as he waded back in, pleading with Kip to come out. Kip stubbornly refused, and Bill began to beg. It was a sight his shocked coworkers would never forget.

When Bill finally recognized how deeply rooted Kip's problems were, he was as lost as Faith in understanding how to deal with them. Though he shared this uneasiness with few friends, Bill impulsively opened up to a total stranger on December 14, 1997, at San Diego airport while waiting for a connecting flight. Professor Dan Close is coordinator of the University of Oregon's Family and Human Services and also does research for their Institute on Violence and Destructive Behavior. Bill struck up a conversation when he noticed Close carrying a book on adolescent disorders.

Bill happily described his home as a kind of paradise with only two things keeping his retirement from being perfect: his wife was still working, and their unpredictable, impossible-to-manage son had mood swings ranging from depression to wild paroxysms of fury. Bill's expression darkened and his voice lost all its former elation as he told Professor Close, "If Kip wants something, he throws a tantrum and persists with unyielding, constant pressure until he gets it." Kip was pestering his dad about driving lessons. Bill feared for his neighbors' lives, knowing how reckless Kip was, and how little impulse control he had. Bill was also distressed that his son had played with explosives and was obsessed with guns. He added that he was considering buying Kip a rapid-fire .22-caliber rifle.

Close thought Bill sounded like someone rationalizing an action, rather than asking advice. Still, the professor counseled Kip's dad to avoid buying the gun. In fact, Bill had already bought it over two months earlier, shortly after Kip stopped taking Prozac, the only thing that had restrained his violent urges. Denny Sperry, a gun collector, had advised Bill, "Hey, if you don't buy it, it's going to be like forbidden fruit." Sperry recommended a safer bolt-action rifle, and had no idea Bill was considering a semiautomatic. Sperry later said, "Bill thought he'd be a kid with a new toy. Obsessed at first, but then grow tired of it and move on to something else."

When neighbors informed Kip's parents that their son was secretly shooting at a human-shaped plywood target in their backyard when they weren't home, Bill knew he'd made a mistake. Furious, he threatened to take the guns away. He brought the Glock to his tennis club and secured it in his locker. However, other members asked him to remove it—they had a gun-free policy. Bill took it back home less than a week before it was used to murder his wife. The day before the shooting, he told a tennis buddy, "The guns are hidden and safe in a locked box in my bedroom."

From the year he started school, Kip kept pushing the boundaries, and his parents kept repairing the damage rather than addressing the cause. When Kip was just six, he went berserk after a twelve-year-old boy tried to take an eighteen-inch length of "rebar" they'd found. Kip chased David Scott, swinging the stick of metal above his head, and brought it down hard on the older boy's arm. Kip later expressed sorrow, but the scar still remained on Scott's arm a decade later.

When Kip hit adolescence, he badgered his parents into enrolling him in a karate class despite their dislike of martial arts. When he was caught shoplifting music CDs from a local Target store with pals Gavin Keable and Jesse Cannon, the manager worked it out privately with their parents. Friends later claimed Kip had stolen roughly a hundred CDs by cutting them out of their "steal-proof" packaging. Kip also avoided arrest after smashing the windows of a farmer's tractor with an ax. Until his arrest for the stolen gun, Kip had no police record.

Extreme cruelty to animals during childhood is a commonly observed trait among youthful psychotics. Kip took care of pets at home, but he boasted to classmates about shooting squirrels and torturing small animals. In middle school, Rachel Dawson claimed Kip told her he shot cats. When classmate Nissa Lund was fourteen, Kip boasted to her that he'd stuffed lit firecrackers in a cat's mouth. When a neighbor complained Kip had tortured her cat, Bill confronted his son. "He denied it and there wasn't any proof. But, yes, Bill believed he did it," Berry Kessinger reported.

Kip even claimed to have blown up a cow, a story he vehemently refuted later to prosecution psychiatrist Dr. Park Dietz. "It was just a joke," he claimed, but detailed accounts had circulated that Kip used duct tape to attach an explosive with a sixty-second timer to the heifer's side. Kip hid behind a tree, heard the explosion killing the beast, and then poked it with a stick "to see what sort of damage had been done," according to his pal Tony McCown.

For someone who delights in the torture and death of animals, it's not a great leap to consider doing something similar to human beings. Michael Carneal denied reports he'd tossed a cat into a bonfire at a neighbor's party weeks before his Kentucky rampage. Andrew Golden claimed he'd killed a neighbor's cat when he was five. Clay Shrout described how sometimes in a "frantic rage" he'd kick the family's two caged Dalmatians in the backyard. But Luke Woodham is the best example of this link between "zooicide" and homicide. The offenses he committed between spring and fall 1997 almost make other shooters seem benign by comparison.

Whereas Kip Kinkel felt at times "possessed" by inner voices, Luke Woodham claimed he was possessed by the Devil himself. Prior to his deadly rampage in Pearl, Mississippi, he maintained he'd seen several demons in association with his mentor, an older youth named Marshall Grant Boyette. Boyette had graduated from Pearl High School in 1996 and was attending Hinds Community College in nearby Jackson. Setting himself up as "the mastermind" of a band of bright but socially inept students, Grant formed a Devil-worshiping, anti-Christian cult called "Kroth," later renamed "Satan's Children." Referring to Boyette as "Father," the group met to plan how they'd kill their classmates at Pearl High, and afterward escape to Cuba.

Woodham and Boyette rehearsed for the slaughter in April 1997 by torturing and killing Luke's pet dog, a bantam-sized, long-haired Shih Tzu. They began by beating it on several occasions, but Luke became worried because his older brother, John, noticed the dog limping and suggested taking it to a vet, who might recognize the bruises for abuse. On April 12, the two boys decided to destroy the unfortunate pet in a way so inhumane and heartless, it defies belief.

In what may be one of the most repugnant diary entries ever written, Woodham recorded the event with loathsome enjoyment, beginning with the lines, *On Saturday of last week, I made my first kill. . . . The victim was a loved one. My dear dog Sparkle. Me and an accomplice had been beating the bitch for a while. . . .* Luke gleefully describes the manner in which they again beat the frightened pet, writing, *I will never forget the howl she made. It sounded almost human. We laughed and hit her hard.* It gets much worse, but the details are so revolting and depraved, the author in good conscience cannot include them here. Luke's narrative ends: *Then we put her in the burned bag and chunked her in a nearby pond. We watched the bag sink. It was true beauty.*

Although Woodham stood over six feet tall and weighed 267 pounds, Grant and another Kroth member, named Justin Sledge, teased him into submissive obedience, saying that if he ever wanted to amount to anything, he should commit murder. A year previous, Luke had become infatuated with classmate Christina Menefee. Woodham's possessive mother, Mary Ann, was so overprotective, she never allowed Luke to date Christina alone and always accompanied them. The defense psychologist later accused her, postmortem, of "emotional incest."

Mary Ann's constant chaperoning eventually caused Christina to break up with Luke. This devastated him. Rejected, Luke tried to kill himself with a gun on two occasions, but was persuaded not to do so by Christina on the phone. Nevertheless, she bore the brunt of his vengeance. "Grant knew I'd been hurt by Christina," Woodham told police, "and he said there was a way to get revenge on her. He said

Satan was the way. He said anytime Satan needs something, you put your thumbs on this pentagram and put it on your forehead and you ask Satan for whatever you want. . . . Satan would give me anything . . . money, power, sex, women, revenge."

According to Boyette, Luke first needed to rid himself of his mother. On the morning of October 1, 1997, the boy took a butcher knife from his kitchen, entered his mom's bedroom, tried smothering her with a pillow, shattered her jaw with a baseball bat, and then slashed and stabbed her while she fought for her life. At 7:55 A.M., Woodham arrived at school, driving his dead mother's car, just as Kip would do the following May.

Luke first handed a five-page will and "manifesto" to Justin Sledge, telling him to give it to Boyette. It included these melodramatic passages, which sound so similar to Kip's journal entries:

> I am the hatred in every man's heart! I am the epitomy [sic] of all Evil! I have no mercy for humanity, for they created me, they tortured me until I snapped and became what I am today! . . . Hate what you have become! Most of all, hate the accurssed [sic] god of Christianity. Hate him for making humanity.

Next consider the similarities between Luke's manifesto and the one sent to NBC TV news by Seung-hui Cho on April 16, 2007. Cho wrote, *You have vandalized my heart, raped my soul and tortured my conscience. . . . You had a hundred billion chances and ways to have avoided today. . . . The decision was yours. Now you have blood on your hands that will never wash off.* Cho also railed against the "*god of Christianity,*" but he compared himself to Jesus as well. Kimveer Gill (chapter 7) wrote in his blog the day before his 2006 Montreal rampage, *I hate God, I hate the deceivers, I hate betrayers, I hate religious zealots,* and *It's society's fault. . . . Society disgusts me.* All three blamed God and society for making them what they were, but Woodham blamed demonic forces as well.

After handing his manifesto to Sledge, Luke returned to his car to get a hunting rifle, stolen from his older brother, and concealed it under a long trench coat, the preferred attire for numerous school shooters from Kip to Columbine to Jeff Weise to Kimveer, and beyond. Woodham then walked through the front doors into the commons area, where everyone hung out.

This day had been chosen carefully. It was the one-year anniversary of Christina breaking up with him. Luke strolled over to his former girlfriend, and as she turned to run, he shot her twice in the upper body. He also slaughtered Christina's companion Lydia Dew, whose sister he had once brought to a prom. He then turned and fired low into a crowd of other students, wounding seven. He only stopped shooting when he ran out of bullets. He went back to his car and tried to escape, but he was stopped by Assistant Principal Joel Myrick, who held his own handgun to Woodham's neck until officers arrived.

From his innocent pet, to his mother, to the object of his infatuation, Luke had now murdered every being who'd ever cared for him. It meant nothing to him. In fact, in the heady moments following his arrest, he was as pleased with his slaughter of Christina as he'd been with the annihilation of his pet dog. In the police video made immediately after his capture, Luke's face shows positive delight as he brightly says, "I ran right up to Christina and, *bam,* right through the heart!"

In two separate trials, one for matricide, another for the school shooting, Woodham's demons were given their day in court, but they failed to assist him. Both juries refused to buy the delusional argument, partly because Luke himself had stated on the police video, "I'm not insane, sir. I knew what I was doing. I was just pissed at the time." Woodham was convicted as an adult on three counts of aggravated murder and seven counts of aggravated assault. The judge handed down three life sentences, plus 140 years, to be served in the Mississippi State Penitentiary at Parchman, including twenty-five years in solitary confinement. Police arrested six members of Kroth for conspiracy. Most were released for lack of evidence, but Grant Boyette got five years on probation in a plea bargain.

One other rampage killer spoke of demons. Red Lake shooter Jeff Weise was, like Woodham, over six feet tall, and at 250 pounds, he weighed just a tad less. He wrote that sometimes at night he would see small creatures sitting by his bed. He would reach out to touch them and then fall into unconsciousness. During the day, he would fashion his hair into two small points, like devil horns. In the words of a Chippewa classmate, "He looked like he was trying to be evil."

Around the time Clay Shrout (chapter 1) became enamored of heavy-metal bands that were famed for satanic associations, he also formed an interest in occult subjects, including witchcraft, sacrifices, and vampires. One of his friends described a series of roughly ten horizontal cuts down his forearm, which Clay claimed were part of a vampire ritual. Andrew Wurst (chapter 13) was nicknamed "Satan" because of his partiality to the music of Marilyn Manson. Patrick Purdy (chapter 8) wore a T-shirt with the word "Satan" on it when he gunned down five elementary-school children.

The real bedevilment for most school shooters is that, whether large or small of frame, they perceive themselves to be inconsequential and powerless in the eyes of their peers. In today's culture, having a tough outer image is standard equipment for school survival. Especially among boys, being perceived as overly sensitive is an open invitation to be needled by bullies.

The antidote for those who aren't by nature physically intimidating is to project an outer aura of evil, either by a simple costume of black, or more Gothic guises. Robert Steinhäuser used such dark trappings during his macabre 2002 rampage in Erfurt, Germany (chapter 26). Sebastian Bosse, another German student, "was always totally dressed in black, including a constant pair of sunglasses," said classmates prior to his 2006 rampage. In fact, he was called the "Man in Black." On the day of his shooting, he wore a long black coat and black gas mask (also chapter 26). Barry Loukaitis (chapter 20) cut the inner pockets out of his black trench coat so he could hold his gun and fire it while hiding his hands. Kimveer Gill wore a black mask, in addition to the trench coat. Jeff Weise outfitted himself in a hooded black trench coat, a black bandanna, black pants, and black military boots. By the time family annihilator Clay Shrout became a high school freshman, his search for an identity had become a steady diet of wearing solely black every day, accented by combat boots, a trench coat, and silver chains. Shrout's best friend, Richard Brown, commented, "I think Clay was trying to give himself a tougher, scarier image." Black was also the color of choice for Kinkel and several other shooters.

Another way these boys solicited attention was in uttering out-

rageous statements that intimated there was someone wicked lurk-
ing below the insipid exterior. The problem with such talk, however,
is that it will eventually be ignored if not backed up by some kind
of action. And so it was that Kip Kinkel's downward slide was propelled, in a sense, by his own boastfulness. No doubt he quietly rev-
eled in his gradual emergence as a character not to be tampered with,
but he desired further confirmation of this status with a larger audience.

Kip Kinkel's brushes with the law outside school were mirrored by
disciplinary problems within school. On April 23, 1997, Kip got a
two-day suspension for karate kicking a student in the head after
that boy insulted and shoved him getting off the school bus. Kip was
furious because the other boy was let off without equal punishment.
Days later, on April 29, Kip got another three-day suspension for
throwing a pencil at a different boy. In Thurston Middle School, Kip
was voted "The Boy Most Likely to Start World War III" in jest,
but behind the humor, there was a measure of truth.

Kip's delinquency file was expunged when he left eighth grade,
but high school counselors were still asked to "handpick teachers
that were capable of monitoring him a bit more than the average
student." Dick Bushnell was aware of the tight corner Kip's parents
were wedged into. "Bill and Faith had pride," he told *Frontline*.
"They were highly, highly respected people, highly intelligent people,
and it's one of those things where they had to wear whatever Kip
did, too, in the eyes of their friends."

A few weeks before his rampage, Kip and ten other students
sneaked out at midnight to wrap 454 rolls of toilet paper around
an elderly couple's house, beating the school "TP" record, but also
getting caught. Kip and the others cleaned off the house the next
day, but Kip's parents were not amused; they grounded him long-
term, while other kids got off with a stern lecture.

McCown said it was after this incident that Bill and Faith finally
searched Kip's room, broke open a padlock on his storage box, and
found his bomb-making books, chemicals, and some guns. They
threatened to get rid of all his firearms, which may have been the
spark that truly lit Kip's fuse. In his mind, losing his treasured arsenal would mean forfeiting the most important possessions in his

universe. It's surmised that this is when Kip wrote in his journal, *I need to find more weapons. My parents are trying to take away some of my guns! My guns are the only things that haven't stabbed me in the back.*

Kip started telling friends that his mom and dad had, in fact, already taken his cherished weapons away. If this were true, they couldn't have taken them far, for Kip possessed the entire trove of killing equipment on May 21. In the study hall from which he was pulled on May 20, just before he was arrested for buying the stolen Beretta from Korey, he told classmate Mickell Young, "My mom took my guns away." Young responded, "Oh, that sucks"; to which Kinkel replied, "It's not a problem. Something will happen."

Here again is another parallel with Clay Shrout. After Clay's suspension from school, the Shrouts hardened up. His closest friend reported, "They were pretty lenient as parents go, and then they finally got tough. Clay didn't seem too upset about it, but he was used to doing what he wanted." A week after his parents took away his weapon collection and other small treasures, Clay told friends he was in the market for a gun and wondered aloud whether it was possible for an air pistol to cause a fatal injury if it was positioned close against the head. When another friend asked how he was dealing with the loss, Clay replied that he "had things under control," a phrase akin to Kip's "It's not a problem. Something will happen."

Thurston parents were understandably perplexed regarding what Bill and Faith Kinkel did or didn't know. Diana Alldredge, Jennifer's mother, said, "We know the Kinkels weren't monsters or saints, they were human. They tried, but the father lost hope and patience, and the mother wore out, carrying the load herself. If you compound that with the extreme pride of their standing in the community and the purchase of weapons for their angry, aggressive son—it was a disaster waiting to happen."

Columbine lead investigator Kate Battan also echoed Diana's mention of monsters in September 1999 as she was trying to exonerate the Klebold family from a barrage of accusations that they had been incompetent parents. "It really does begin with the family, but . . . I've spent a lot of time with the Klebolds, and they're nice people," Kate stated. "It's not like they're these monsters that raised a monster. I mean, they truly are clueless about any warning signs that this was going to happen."

Battan was given further backup by Cornell University researcher James Garbarino, who wrote the book *Parents Under Siege* in coordination with the Columbine shooters' families. "The Klebolds are an extreme case of something quite common in terms of kids having secret lives," Garbarino told the press in Denver. He compared the Columbine parents' lack of enlightenment about their children's furtiveness to someone who's surprised to learn their spouse is having an illicit love affair. "It's not because they're blind or stupid. . . . People are good at keeping secrets, and it's hard to walk around thinking the worst of the ones you love. . . . Is every parent supposed to go around wondering about their kid: are you a mass murderer?"

Jay Beard, the parent of one of Dylan Klebold's classmates, disagreed. "How out of touch are you with your kid that you don't know he's making thirty bombs?" he asked. He had a point. The parents of the Columbine killers, as well as the Kinkels and many other moms and dads of school shooters, were intelligent, educated people. What they lacked was the acumen or intrepidity to recognize that their own offspring might somehow be sociopaths. Whether their blindness was willful, naive, or insensitive, the fact is they were outmaneuvered by sons who were equally intelligent, but totally lacking in conscience.

It is not only parents. The "monster" comparison was once again invoked by Northern Illinois University shooter Stephen Kazmierczak's girlfriend Jessica Baty. "He was anything but a monster," she told an interviewer. "He was probably the nicest, most caring person ever." Others agreed. Despite depression and psychiatric problems in his past, Kazmierczak was considered an outstanding student with a very good academic record, had received the Dean's award in 2006, and was formerly vice president of the university's Academic Criminal Justice Association. Professors called him rational and reasoned, engaging, motivated, and responsible, a gentle, quiet guy who had a passion for helping people. The man who did his macabre tattoos even called him "mousy." His interests also included political violence and peace and social justice. He sent his girlfriend a copy of Nietzsche's *AntiChrist* and two textbooks with a cell phone and a tender goodbye note on the day of the shooting. Having experienced cutting himself firsthand, he wrote papers about self-injury among the incarcerated and was working on a manuscript on the role of religion in the creation of early U.S. prisons. He worked briefly as a full-time corrections officer at the Rockville Correctional Facility, an adult medium-security prison. The monster—the Stephen Kazmierczak who burst through a stage door and started slaughtering people—was obviously a very different person than the one everybody thought they knew, including the woman closest to him.

• Chapter 13 •

"The End of the World"

"Why don't you just shoot me? I am such a bad mother."
—Faith Kinkel to her son approximately five weeks before he did just that

Although we might expect the figure to be higher, of all the school shooters in our study, only two were determined by psychiatrists to be paranoid delusional. One was Kip Kinkel, and the other was Andrew Wurst, whose rampage at his Edinboro, Pennsylvania, middle school preceded Kip's by just one month. Opinions on what constitutes insanity differ, but the legal definition is clear. While the average person would assume that the sudden mass murder of innocents and strangers is a crazy thing to do, seldom if ever has any school shooter been able to successfully plead "not guilty through reason of insanity," though almost every one of them has tried. Where true insanity exists, however, it is often linked to hereditary factors. If Kip were really insane, was there anything in his genealogical makeup that could have contributed to that? The answer to that question surprised many.

To most of us, it seems only logical that any kid who would shoot his classmates has to be a few cards short of a full deck. Carlene Higgs, sister of a boy Kip shot, spoke with frank simplicity when, facing the accused in court, she stated, "Kip, any person in their right mind thinks about consequences before they act." For that very reason, it would appear more likely that Kip was not in his right mind. Even so, a few victims, like Jacob Ryker, saw no reason to consider insanity as a mitigating factor. "If a dog was to go insane," he argued, "if a dog got rabid and bit someone, you destroy it." The law is somewhat more lenient concerning humans.

Part of the problem Kinkel's lawyers faced was that Kip kept any signs of mental instability hidden from those closest to him. After his psychiatric exams, it was claimed two main afflictions impacted Kip's mind: paranoid delusions and auditory hallucinations. At the time of this diagnosis, the defense team was still considering a plea of insanity. Doubters felt this was another of Kip's devious ploys to escape punishment, but there were indications of an unstable mind long before that.

Dr. William Sack is a child psychiatrist who interviewed Kip twice after his arrest and testified he was confident that Kip was "a very sick, psychotic individual." Sack described doing a "validity analysis" and concluded, "If he were lying to me, he would be the best actor I've ever seen."

Pediatric neurologist Dr. Richard J. Konkol presented illustrated evidence of abnormalities in Kip's brain via computerized image scans that he said showed empty gaps or "holes," as he unfortunately called them, within the boy's head. In truth, these "holes" were actually less active zones where blood flow was reduced to the frontal lobe, an area associated with emotional control and decision-making. Under experimental conditions, this situation indicates greater susceptibility to psychotic episodes.

Dr. Orin Bolstad, a clinical psychologist who works with violent youths in the Oregon penal system, conducted the most in-depth analysis and presented the largest body of evidence. All of these psychiatrists were hired on behalf of the defense, however; and it is customary in court cases to engage experts with a predetermined bias.

The district attorney called his own expert, Dr. Park Dietz, who had a national reputation for transforming even the most credible insanity plea into a victory for the prosecution, including such high-profile cases as Ronald Reagan's would-be assassin John Hinckley Jr. and serial killer Jeffrey Dahmer. Dr. Dietz examined Kip for over six hours in videotaped sessions, but his conclusions were never presented, because Kip and his lawyers dropped their insanity plea.

What *was* presented in court was a detailed psychiatric history of Kip's extended family that demonstrated a significant amount of psychosis in both his maternal and paternal lineage. Since genealogy is known to be an important factor in the inheritance of certain mental ailments, the defense hoped this disclosure would support their assertion that Kip suffered from congenital schizophrenia.

If one were to assume, then, that Kip's derangement was valid, what would that say about his culpability? The sentiments of those who oppose life sentences for juvenile killers increase greatly if there's any question of mental instability, but the criminal justice system seems to have little taste for it. The stance of the prosecution, and the feeling of many victims, was that if the boy was really so sick and delusional, why did no one—including his family—take serious note of his madness? Even Kip's psychologist concluded he'd been cured of his disruptive ways.

Except for Dr. John Crumbley, child psychologist Jeffrey Hicks was the only other therapist to examine Kip *prior* to the shootings. During treatment, Hicks saw no evidence that Kip was psychotic or delusional, nor did he diagnose a thought disorder. Hicks asked about auditory hallucinations during the intake screening, but Kip answered no, thereby decimating his later defense.

Dr. Bolstad reiterated a formidable array of Kip's beliefs that classified as paranoid delusions. Kinkel claimed he needed to arm himself and build explosives because the Chinese military was planning to drop nuclear bombs and invade the United States. He was concerned about a bioterrorist attack of plague. Kip was sure the Disney dollar would take over the American dollar. Moreover, Disney and the government, he insisted, were collaborating to censor lyrics in music.

Bolstad emphasized Kip's manner of saying things. "He said, 'I can see what Disney's doing. I can see the government as well'. . . . I told him I didn't see it that way. He became animated. He wanted to argue about it. . . . he said, 'No one of average intelligence sees it with Disney. You have to be smarter.' . . . It's not just the content of what's said, it's the way it's said . . . with a conviction that's characteristic of delusions. It's also said with a quality of grandiosity. When he said, '*I can,*' he's distinguishing himself from most everyone else in a grandiose way. . . . These are symptoms of psychotic thinking."

By the time Faith decided to end treatment, Dr. Hicks felt Kip had progressed in his ability to manage anger, and that with Prozac, his depression had lifted. How could even a professional miss the deeper problems?

Hicks was hardly alone in being deceived by his patient. When Seung-hui Cho was involuntarily kept overnight at Carilion Saint Albans Behavioral Health Center after saying he'd kill himself, in December 2005, he denied having suicidal thoughts. Psychiatrist Roy Crouse concluded that though Cho's "affect is flat and mood is depressed," his "insight and judgment are normal." Cho was ordered to continue outpatient care at Virginia Tech's on-campus Cook Counseling Services. Whether he ever showed up at that facility is unlikely, as follow-up on such patients was lax.

Long before Kinkel and Cho, mass murderer Charles Whitman (chapter 26) wrote, *"I definitely feel as though there is something unusual in my mental state.* This was two years before his 1966 college campus massacre. He then went voluntarily to see a campus psychiatrist, who was impressed by the clean-cut young man's "wholesome" image. A former altar boy, Whitman had once been the nation's youngest Eagle Scout. Now this ex-marine was a talented engineering student. Then a darker side emerged. Whitman described his father as a brutal man who'd abused Charles's mom, and he told how he hated his dad "with a mortal passion." He'd been court-martialed and given an early discharge by the marines due to "disciplinary problems." Most telling, he described thoughts of "going up on the tower with a deer rifle and . . . shooting people." Even so, the doctor judged Charles to be fit for classes, declaring, "I found no psychosis symptoms at all."

Like adult mass murderers, teen shooters may appear to be coherent, logical, and even charming—right up to their criminal act. Dr. Bolstad considered this point crucial to the defense, stating that the public, and often our legal system, doesn't realize "it's altogether possible for someone to be lucid one minute and very crazy the next. A distinguishing feature of the paranoid type of schizophrenia [is] you can have these symptoms of hallucinations and delusions, and at the same time have well-preserved cognitive thinking. . . . Even people with paranoid symptoms can shrewdly plan and complete a course of action. That doesn't mean they're logical."

The doctor explained that "the persecutory themes may predispose the individual to suicidal behavior, and the combination of persecutory and grandiose delusions with anger may predispose the individual to violence."

Kip told Bolstad he'd never revealed his hallucinations, but once came very close to doing so when his mother mentioned hearing ringing in her ears. He claimed he didn't follow through because she might get so distraught she'd "pull her hair out," an action he referred to on several occasions. Once, a teacher called his mom to warn her he'd been late for class twice. That day, he said, "She screamed at me, grabbed at her hair, went nuts. Said, 'You must hate me' and stuff like that. Like I was so embarrassing to her." But would she really have reacted so extremely? To her students and peers, Faith was universally described as gentle, positive, and compassionate.

Dr. Dorothy Lewis was one of the first defense psychiatrists to examine Kip and she concluded the reference was literal. In her report, she writes, *Kip's mother was described by several family members, friends, and herself to her doctors as given to extremes of emotion. At times she was suicidally depressed. Both Kip and Kristin recall times when, down on herself, she would say to Kip, "Why don't you just shoot me? I am such a bad mother."*

The vocalization of this prophetic utterance, even under stress, is macabre in its foreshadowing of later events. Kip's friend Tony McCown also reported that after finding their son's secretly obtained weapons and *The Anarchist Cookbook* about five weeks before the bloodshed, "Kip's mother was crying and told him to just go get the gun now and shoot her. Kip was upset that his mom said that to him." Upset, but the possibility remains that Kip was storing this suggestion subliminally for later action.

Another friend, Adam Pearse, told this same mother-son story with one important difference. Pearse said Kip told him he'd found it funny his parents got so twisted up about it. Still, when Kip was tackled in the cafeteria, and again at the police station, did he realize how closely his cry of "Just shoot me!" echoed his mother's words?

Faith's sister Claudia, describing her sibling, said, "She could get totally hysterical, unreasonably hysterical—it scared me." According to Claudia, when Faith went ballistic, Kip as a small child would try to calm her. If he couldn't, he and Kristin would seek a hiding place. The Lewis report adds, *Faith's other sisters . . . had similar mood disorders, further supporting the likelihood that Kip inherited a predisposition to bipolar mood disorder from his mother's side of the family.* Like Kip, Faith had been medicated for depression with Prozac.

Conceivably, Faith was unconsciously in denial, underestimating the depth of Kip's mental illness because of concerns about her own genealogical background. She would have had good reason to worry. A genetic predisposition to mental disease is now recognized as being as commonplace as the transmission of physical ailments, a stance supported by the 1999 U.S. Surgeon General's Report and the National Institute of Mental Health's 1999 publication, *Genetics and Mental Disorders.*

Kip's defense team hired a private detective, Joyce Naffziger, to investigate any history of mental illness in the Kinkels' immediate or extended family. Naffziger found both parents had an unusually large number of relatives with serious psychological problems. One example: Kip's great uncle, Robert McKissick, had delusions. Pulled over by a traffic cop in 1948, McKissick believed that the policeman was a Nazi soldier, attacked him with a knife, and was shot and killed.

On Faith's side, there were numerous cases of alcoholism and depression. One could argue that many people's family histories might include a few ancestors with these disorders, but at least eight of Faith's relatives had been or are currently institutionalized. Among the numerous diagnoses are bipolar schizoaffective disorder (a cousin), manic depression (another cousin and a nephew), and schizophrenia (a niece). Faith's mother and all three sisters suffered from depression, and all were medicated. Yet Dr. Hicks's treatment notes read as follows: *Mrs. Kinkel describes herself as quite emotional. The family history is negative for psychiatric illness.*

Bill Kinkel's lineage included similar problems. His father was a depressed "alcoholic gambler with a real temper" who lost his business and abandoned his family in debt. Bill's mother had two brothers confined to mental institutions for schizophrenia, which helps explain why Bill shunned psychiatrists. After her spouse left, Bill's mother filed for divorce, then rescinded it and took her husband back. Bill's dad responded by becoming a minister, who demanded his son learn from his errant ways, and pushed him to live a flawless existence. Bill seemed determined to pass on that tradition, expecting near perfection from his two kids. Kristin provided it. Kip did not.

Bill also had a darker side. He never got physically violent, but he was sometimes verbally abusive to Kip. While at school, he made each student feel special; at home, he was "utterly contemptuous of students in his classes who did not excel." When angry at his son, Bill categorized Kip among those he derided and considered "losers." Yet, even though many of Kip's inner demons could be traced back to his relationship with his father, the boy never blamed his parents for the way he'd turned out. In fact, quite the opposite. *I didn't deserve them. They were wonderful people. It's not their fault,* he wrote after killing them. In his confession to Al Warthen, he cried, "My parents were good people."

Joe Weigand, Faith's nephew, came to court to express his experience as a manic-depressive and borderline schizophrenic. He had been diagnosed as paranoid psychotic with delusions of grandeur, at one point believing he was the Second Coming of Christ. He'd once designed a bomb (shades of Kip's endeavors) and threatened the management at his workplace. Weigand has a sympathetic wife and friends who understood that when he acted strangely, "it wasn't me, it was the illness." He portrayed the sick individual as being separate from his true self, and described what it feels like to be actively delusional, when the conscience-controlling superego disappears, "and you don't realize it's gone. You're just the lower self. The lower nature of yourself is not [held] in check anymore. It's like being in a dream. . . . Rules and rationality don't hold."

Weigand's grandfather was permanently institutionalized, and his mother was psychotic. His cousin Teresa is a suicidal schizophrenic who "hears voices . . . telling her things to do." Weigand himself has sufficiently recovered and is now a music teacher, "thanks to medicine and modern science." But he pointed out he was a member of a generation that believed in love, peace, and saving the world. He says that mental illness "magnifies whatever your personality is. . . . There was no violence or hate in my episodes, but . . . if I'd been born thirty years later, into this generation where there is so much glorified violence and hate . . . kids being raised in child care centers . . . there's going to be a lot of tragedies like this."

*   *   *

A lot of tragedies . . . and one had taken place just a month before Thurston had. In only one case other than Kip's has a school shooter been clinically determined to be both paranoid and delusional. It's a condition Andrew Wurst remains in today, according to forensic psychiatrist Robert Sadoff. During Wurst's attack, when a student pleaded to know why he was shooting, Andrew shouted, "Because I'm crazy!" pointing the gun at his own head.

If Wurst was indeed paranoid, or perhaps even because of it, he delighted in scaring others. He often threatened people and then, like Kip, claimed he was only joking. He'd shown friends a gun hidden in his father's dresser drawer, telling them he planned to shoot nine people he hated. Andrew added he intended to kill himself at the end of his bloody offensive. No one told authorities.

Dr. Sadoff wrote, Wurst believes *that he's real but everyone else is unreal,* including John Gillette, the science teacher he killed, who in Wurst's mind *was already dead or unreal.* While waiting for police to arrive, Andrew told the men who subdued him, "I died four years ago. I've already been dead and I've come back. It doesn't matter anymore. None of this is real." Wurst informed Sadoff that the government has programmed everyone, except himself, by means of "time tablets" controlling thoughts.

As they withdrew into their fantasies, Wurst, Kinkel, Harris, and Klebold all found comfort in the lyrics of songs that echoed their private thoughts. By chance or a mutual attraction to violence, all of them especially enjoyed the raucous music of Marilyn Manson, known for such albums as *Antichrist Superstar.* The singer's real name is less exotic—Brian Warner wove his stage name from cult leader/serial killer Charles Manson and Hollywood icon Marilyn Monroe. In the Oscar-winning documentary *Bowling for Columbine,* singer Manson, despite his eccentric appearance, comes across as one of the saner voices in the movie. He's asked what he would have told the Columbine killers if he'd met them before their rampage. He replies, "I wouldn't say a single word to them. I'd listen to what they have to say. That's what no one did."

Chapter 14

"Voices in My Head"

When people hear voices, they are in reality externalizing internal cognitive processes. That's an absolute fact. It reveals a split in the self as a form of psychic protection, walling off the "bad me" from the "good me."
—Ralph W. Larkin, Ph.D., author, *Comprehending Columbine* and *Suburban Youth in Cultural Crisis*

It's possible that Kip Kinkel's buildup of an arsenal was motivated by extreme anxiety and delusion-based fears. However, he was never required to use his weapons based on those delusions, because none of those things ever happened. Instead, at some crucial point, his instruments of security became his tools for revenge. If it wasn't just his delusions, then what else could have pushed Kip into committing such savage acts?

When asked how his urge to kill originated, Kip himself directed the blame for what he'd done onto his inner voices, the auditory hallucinations that he claimed controlled, cajoled, and directed his life. This was his sole self-justification as to why he did what he did. Of course, this does not preclude that those aggressive, hate-filled voices represented or echoed the verbal abuse that his father occasionally threw at Kip in the privacy of their home.

Kip's belated disclosure that these voices had forced him to commit acts he knew were vile may have impressed his doctors, but they did not sit well with the lay community. Janet Taylor, mother of a wounded Thurston girl, reacted with bitter frustration to his claims. In court, she cried out, "Because you heard voices? Why didn't you just tell those voices you were in command . . . you take charge! You say no!" It was beyond her comprehension how anyone couldn't resist mere hallucinations.

Even among medical specialists, however, it's difficult to find universal consensus regarding the roots of auditory hallucinations. When the author asked defense psychiatrist Dr. William Sack, "Where do such voices actually originate in the brain?" His reply was "No one really knows. The answer to that would be worth a Nobel Prize." Dr. Sack pointed out how difficult it is for the unafflicted to comprehend this state of mind, which is utterly different from willfully fantasizing voices, pleasant or otherwise, in a daydream or reverie. If one has never experienced psychotic voices, he said, it's nearly impossible to imagine what it might be like to have a voice screaming in your head ordering you to do terrible things.

Whether Kip's claims are credible or not, analyzing this aspect of his case is critical to comprehending an otherwise senseless crime, for this is the only motive that Kip himself endorsed. Only a handful of other shooters made similar claims about hallucinations, and none described any as vicious as Kip's.

Eighteen-year-old Wayne Lo did not so much hear as experience commands that came "into his body directly, like an electrical charge, on several distinct occasions" ordering him to shoot people. Wayne was an atheist until that happened, but he believed the orders came from God. He murdered two and wounded four others at Simon's Rock, an exclusive college-prep boarding school in Great Barrington, Massachusetts, in December 1992. An outspoken gun lover who detested his father, Wayne was wearing a SICK OF IT ALL sweatshirt when arrested. The college administration was aware that Lo had received a heavy package of ammunition by mail, but they decided to let him keep it. A student there tried to warn counselors, but his account was ignored, reinforcing a tendency among colleges, up until Virginia Tech, to dismiss threats without thoroughly pursuing them.

Church shooter Matthew Murray (chapter 3) occupied a bunk near Richard Werner at one of their missionary training centers. Werner asked his roommate why he rolled around in bed, making noises, and Murray replied, "Don't worry, Richard. I'm just talking to the voices. You're a nice guy, the voices like you."

After Michael Carneal's rampage in West Paducah, Kentucky, his lawyer, Tom Osborne, argued for a "guilty but mentally ill" plea, claiming that the troubled youth suffered from a schizoid personality disorder brought on by relentless taunting by classmates. Other boys stole his lunch and sprayed him with water in the bathroom. When two boys threatened to beat him up, Carneal pulled out a .22-caliber handgun, only to be teased that he "couldn't hurt anybody with that." A week later, he carried a much larger assortment of firepower into the lobby of Heath High, and this time no one laughed.

According to one psychiatric exam, Carneal was obsessively shy. Nervous that people might see him naked, for instance, he habitually covered even the air vents in his bathroom. He often slept on the family room sofa to be near his parents, and claimed he heard voices calling his name and intruders tapping on windows. McCracken County Commonwealth's attorney Tim Kaltenbach responded that Carneal's claim of mental illness was a ploy to curry sympathy among jury members.

Another shooter, Jamie Rouse, of Lynville, Tennessee, told psychiatrists before his trial that he'd tried to drown out voices in his head by blasting his ears with heavy-metal music. Rouse was a self-proclaimed Satanist, who flaunted his image of being a dark-side character by dressing shirt to shoes in black, similar to so many others. In his junior year, Jamie held his brother Jeremy at gunpoint in their home, threatening to kill him. As punishment for that action, his parents took away his weapon. In an act reminiscent of Kinkel's dad buying him guns, Jamie's parents returned his rifle to him when hunting season began.

On November 15, 1995, upset over a failing grade, Rouse took his black .22-caliber Remington Viper to school. He calmly approached two female teachers in the hall, smiled roguishly, lifted the gun to their heads, and fired. One was killed, the other severely wounded. He also shot to death one student, fourteen-year-old Diane Collins, who stumbled into the path of a bullet Rouse intended for the football coach. Like most school shooters, Rouse, then seventeen, had forewarned a number of friends about his plan, yet again no one raised any alarm. At his trial, the voices Rouse claimed he heard were judged inconsequential. He was sentenced to life without parole.

In Kip Kinkel's case, test results strongly supported Dr. Bolstad's diagnosis of insanity. The psychiatrist explained to the court how the boy obsessed over his hallucinations constantly, and when he heard a song called "The Becoming" by Nine Inch Nails, it intrigued him to know others also heard voices. The day he attacked Thurston, Kip wore a black cap with the Nine Inch Nails logo, "NIN." The group meant a lot to him. Kip told the doctor the verse from "The Becoming" that attracted him goes like this: *Annie, hold on a bit tighter I might just slip away He won't give up He wants me dead. God damn this voice inside my head."*

Kip said that when he first heard the final line, it jolted him, because it fit him perfectly. He began repeating it to himself a lot. At least, that's the story according to Bolstad, but any Nine Inch Nails fan could spot the error immediately. Besides misquoting pronouns throughout, Kip rewrote the last line of that verse, which is actually "goddamn this *noise* inside my head."

God damn these voices inside my head! is also the phrase Kip wrote in his suicide note, but the only time others ever heard him say those words aloud, prior to his attack, was when he shouted them out during an English literature class on April 24, 1998, less than a month before the shooting. Kevin Rowan, a sensitive young teacher, reprimanded Kip for disrupting the class and asked him to fill out a disciplinary "respect sheet." Rowan was disturbed by the possibility that Kip was hallucinating, so he asked him bluntly if he really heard voices. Surprisingly, the defense lawyers never questioned Rowan in court as to how Kip replied, but prosecutor Caren Tracy did. Rowan acknowledged that Kip's answer was no, and that the boy claimed he didn't know why he'd shouted out that expression. If this was indeed an accidental disclosure that he was hearing voices, it was an episode quickly denied.

Rowan didn't simply accept Kinkel's explanation at face value, but alerted Kip's mother to it on the same day. Kip brought home the respect sheet for Faith to sign, which she did three days later.

To confirm she'd truly been made aware of her son's outburst, Rowan telephoned Faith as a follow-up. Counselor Marcia Graham also called her on the same issue. It's clear Faith knew her son had shouted out about hearing voices, but it's not known if Kip was able to dismiss any concern over real hallucinations by explaining to his mom it was "just a song." It's also possible Kip did *not* hallucinate that day, but was merely singing the tune in his mind, forgot himself, and spoke the lyrics out loud. This, however, is the only evidence we have prior to the suicide note that Kip's voices may have been authentic.

The cruel words that Kip reported hearing in his head were far more vicious than any song lyrics. His hallucinations began, he said, on an otherwise uneventful day in sixth grade. Only twelve years old, he'd just stepped off his school bus when, "I was on my driveway, looking at some bushes, and a voice said, 'You need to kill everyone in the world.' It scared the shit out of me. I was confused. . . . I ran into the house and cried in my room. It said, 'You're a stupid piece of shit. You aren't worth anything.'" Bolstad concluded that Kip's voices related to "fears about being evil, about other people being evil, about society falling apart. . . . It's not as if you can separate his hallucinations from his delusions. They're all interwoven."

Kip stated that he often heard two voices at the same time, and, periodically, a third. Dr. Pincus, one of many physicians who examined Kip, labeled the voices A, B, and C. Kip told Dr. Bolstad, "One voice always tells me what to do. It's authoritarian. Loud. The doctor gave that voice the title A. The B voice tells me I'm a piece of shit, a put-down kind of voice. . . . C just repeats what the others say over and over and over again. . . . I get angry, hearing these voices. I was very pissed at God, if I believed in him. What is this? Why do I have these voices?"

Kip said he heard voices a second time, while still in sixth grade. When his family got home from a weekend away, there was a school misbehavior referral in the mail. Kip recalled, "When my parents saw the referral, they went off, they really got angry, they were yelling at me. I went to my room, and the voices came after me, saying the same thing, 'Stupid shit, you can't do anything right.'" Bolstad described Kip crying in his room as voices screamed in his head and his parents yelled on the other side of the door. "Later on, he got on his bike. . . . He was bawling. He tried to ride away from the voices, but he couldn't get away from them. . . . He said they talked to each other about him, about how stupid he was."

Hearing multiple voices differs greatly from having multiple personalities. Auditory hallucinations are not the same as thoughts, but are actually experienced as voices of other persons, often hostile. Kip never believed he became any other character than himself, but like many psychotics trying to make sense of their illness, he developed a belief system involving exotic, preposterous scenarios. When Bolstad asked Kip, "Where do you think the voices came from?" Kip replied, "Well, I had some theories. Maybe it was from the Devil"— an explanation people believed for centuries, and one Kip's prison chaplain still subscribes to with all his heart today. In other cultures, voices were revered as oracles representing a direct line to the Divine. As an alternate source, Kip added, "At first, I thought the voices were outside of my head because they were so very loud, like surround sound. . . . The government might have put a chip in my head. Government satellites might have transmitted to the chip." Delusions of being wired or radio-controlled are relatively common among psychotics. Often it's the FBI or CIA that's the suspected perpetrator. Kip also claimed he believed one satellite gave voices to the microchip and another followed his every movement.

Many other bona fide paranoid schizophrenics have described hallucinatory voices that preoccupied, terrified and commandeered their thought processes. In tenth grade, De Kieu "Lisa" Duy, (pronounced DWEE), started hearing voices telling her that other students were spreading rumors about her sexual habits. Lisa's family had come to Salt Lake City in 1980 as Vietnamese refugees, and two of her older sisters had already been diagnosed with schizophrenia. While she was a student at the University of Utah, the increasingly intimidating voices caused her to attempt stabbing herself in the heart to silence them. She was hospitalized as a paranoid schizophrenic for two years. Later, believing a radio DJ had planted a mind-reading camera in her head and was broadcasting her sexual secrets, she attempted to attack him with a steak knife. When police came to arrest her, she shouted, "Just shoot me!" the same phrase Kip used after his rampage. A couple of years passed and Lisa was able to purchase a handgun, using a legal loophole. Finally, on January 14, 1999, she shot and killed a young mother and wounded a manager at a TV station for the same reasons as her earlier attack. A judge ruled her mentally incompetent to stand trial.

If indeed his voices existed, Kip denied himself personal relief and put others in harm's way by keeping his condition secret. Since he was unmedicated, the voices would augment or decrease according to levels of stress, depression, and anger. They might occur several times a day or once a week. Dr. Bolstad testified, "He tried . . . to get rid of the voices, but he said nothing worked. He used to tell them to shut up, but . . . it just made them get louder."

Then came the fatal day, May 20, 1998, when Kip was expelled from school and his dad picked him up at the police station to drive him home. Kip described that ride to Bolstad: "We stopped at the Burger King on the way home, and we ordered two Whoppers. We sat down. My dad said to me, 'You disgust me,' and he got up and went to the car to eat his hamburger. I couldn't eat because the voices had started. I just sat there. I threw the Whopper away and started to walk out, but then realized that there was too little time to have eaten it. So I went to the bathroom for a while before I went back to the car. I didn't want my dad yelling at me for not eating the Whopper, wasting money."

Kip said he felt his father's anger activated the voices ordering him to kill. "In the car, we drove home. The voices were all over me at that point, all three. B was saying, 'Look at what you've done, you stupid piece of shit, you're worthless.' The A voice said, 'You'll have to kill him, shoot him.' C was repeating this over and over. They got louder and louder." Kip also told Dr. Lewis that the voices were so overwhelming in the car, he couldn't even tell if his father was speaking to him. He compared the experience to having high-volume earphones on, impossible to remove.

When speaking to Dr. Bolstad, Kip began sobbing, his head on the table, as he related how the voices finally became impossible to resist any longer and he proceeded to transform what had only been thoughts into an irrevocable act: "I went into the house. I was crying. I went in my bedroom, up to the loft. There were two guns in the trunk, the twenty-two pistol and the sawed-off shotgun. I took them and hid them, because I thought Dad might look. Hid them in the attic." These words indicate Bill had given Kip a final ultimatum about taking away his remaining guns. Kip continued, "The voices kept saying, 'Get your gun, shoot him, shoot him.' I got the twenty-two rifle. My dad was sitting at the bar. His back was to me. The voice said, 'Kill him, shoot him,' so I did. The voices told me, 'You have no choice.' I had never heard that before."

Once again, despite the intensity of the situation and a possibility that Kip's memory may have been shaky, we have to keep in mind that it was proven by ballistics and an autopsy Kip did not use the .22 *rifle* to kill his dad, but the .22 *pistol*. There's such a considerable difference between the two weapons, this inaccuracy is puzzling, especially as Kip stuck to it, repeating it several times.

Dr. Lewis asked Kip if the voices wanted his father dead, out of anger or to spare him. Kip replied, "I guess with my father, both ways. . . ." Concerning his mother, it was "to protect her from what I did to my father. To protect her from what I am . . . from what I've always been . . . a disappointment. . . . It's the only way I could save her from me. . . ."

When Dr. Bolstad asked about Faith's murder, Kip replied, "When she came home, they said, 'Kill her. Look at what you've [already] done. You have no other choice.' So I killed her, too. I just wanted to kill myself." On this point, Bolstad was perplexed. "If that's the reason why he killed his parents, it doesn't explain why he shot people at school. . . . We'd have to have two separate theories about why he did these shootings."

Kip offered no other theories. Impassive after his arrest, during his confession to police, he became frenzied, often shouting, "Damn these voices!" Between periods of relative calm, Kip seemed to suddenly awaken to the horrible, unalterable reality of what he'd done. The following edited excerpts from Detective Warthen's audiotaped interrogation give some idea of Kip's distress, but no written description can adequately convey to the reader the emotional impact of listening to the actual recording of Kip's disturbing shrieks of anguish. The entire audiotape can be heard in full on the PBS *Frontline* Web site: www.pbs.org/wgbh/pages/frontline/shows/kinkel/etc/video.html.

The author recommends downloading this gripping testament so readers may judge for themselves how authentic Kip's emotions were. The following is a sample:

DETECTIVE WARTHEN *(asking about Bill, just before Kip shot him)*: Did he think that you were too young for a gun?

KIP: Yeah . . . I don't know what's wrong with me. . . . My head just doesn't work right.

WARTHEN: Why doesn't it work right?

KIP: I don't know, I can't—

WARTHEN: Okay . . . so was your dad . . . Did he hit you or anything like that?

KIP: No. *(He speaks as if that were the last thing his father would do.)*

WARTHEN: Okay . . . was he yelling or out of control?

KIP: *(cries)* I couldn't, I couldn't, I had no other choice—*(cries, then shouts)* God!

WARTHEN: Had I been a visitor in your home, would you have shot your dad?

KIP: I don't know, I just, I had no other choice. . . . He was saying all this, I—

WARTHEN: He was saying all that stuff, kind of . . . He was saying a lot of negative stuff about you. Like what was he saying about you?

KIP: *(crying)*

WARTHEN: Okay . . . He's mad at you because you got caught in school with the gun?

KIP: Right. And I [garbled] all his friends and everything knew [garbled cry].

WARTHEN: Okay, so he was feeling ashamed and embarrassed because you did something wrong, is that right?

KIP: Right. *(cries, then shouts)* I didn't *want* to! I love my dad! That's why I had to!

WARTHEN: You love him, so that's why you had to kill him?

KIP: Yes. *(cries)* Oh, my God! My parents were good people, I'm just so fucked up in the head, I don't know why [garbled].

WARTHEN: So what do you do from the time that you put the sheet over your dad and your mom comes home?

KIP: A few people called . . . some of my friends, and I just talked to them. I didn't say anything about that and I didn't know what to do because—*(cries)* oh, my God! My mom was coming home, and if she knew what I'd done, she'd—*(cries)* oh, my God!

WARTHEN: Okay. So your mom comes home about six, is that right? And she parks, where are you at?

KIP: I was waiting for her. *(cries, then shouts) I Just want to die!*

WARTHEN: So you told me that your mom gets out of the Explorer and starts up the stairs from the garage or basement, is that right?

KIP: Yes.

WARTHEN: Do you say anything to her?

KIP: Yes. I told her I loved her.

WARTHEN: And then you shot . . .

KIP: Yes. *(suddenly screams)* God *damn* these *voices* inside my *head*!

WARTHEN: All right, hey, [garbled] Kip . . . *(Kip is sobbing uncontrollably.)* Kip, settle down, settle down, it's all right, it's all right. . . . Just settle down, okay, just settle down.

KIP: *(long cry)* I had no other choice!

WARTHEN: Okay . . . you shot her several times?

KIP: 'Cause I dragged her up into the basement after I shot her and she was still alive and I said that I loved her and I shot her. . . . I shot her again so she wouldn't know that I killed her. . . . I loved my mom.

WARTHEN: So what did you do the rest of the night? Did you talk to more friends?

KIP: No, I just . . . I didn't . . . I didn't know what to do. . . . I held . . . I just held my Glock to my head and I wanted to kill myself so *bad*, but I *couldn't*. . . . I don't know why.

WARTHEN: Why did you go to school and start shooting people?

KIP: *I had to! I had no other choice! (cries)* I couldn't do anything else!

WARTHEN: Why did you feel that you didn't have a choice with the kids at school?

KIP: I don't know, I can't . . . My head is [garbled]. I had to, I just had to.

WARTHEN: Kip, let me ask you this, if you had it to do over again, what would you do?

KIP: I'd try so hard to kill myself! I can't do it! I want it more than anything!

Kip's confession is riveting and pathetic. There's nothing phony about the agony he expresses, yet we come back again to the question of whether the supposed voices were powerful enough to overcome his natural, human, moral resistance and drive him to do this. When Bolstad, like Janet Taylor, asked Kip why he didn't refuse the voices, he answered, "It didn't seem real. I hate everybody, myself especially. I hated the voices most of all. The B voice said later, 'Get guns and bullets. Go to school and kill everybody.' I argued with them. I told them to shut up. They ignored me. All night long, I didn't sleep."

The prosecution pointed out there were twelve hours between Kip's parricide and the attack on the school, time enough to reconsider what he'd done and, if he were truly remorseful, to avoid more bloodshed. Instead, he was busy preparing for his grim onslaught the next day. He switched the stock on his rifle from a long one to a short (the shortened stock in itself further evidence of preplanning), so that he could better hide it under his trench coat. Even between the murders of his father and mother, Kip chatted nervously on the phone in a three-way call with his good friends Tony McCown and Nick Hiaasen, and later with a girl he liked named Jayne. He also fielded a couple of checkup calls from English teacher Kevin Rowan.

Rowan had first called the Kinkel home around 10:30 A.M. on May 20, leaving a message for Bill on their answering machine. The teacher got a note at 2:30 P.M. saying Bill had called him back at school. Rowan tried calling the Kinkel residence again at 3:25 P.M., (soon after Bill was murdered), and this time Kip picked up the phone.

Rowan had seen Kip as a fair pupil academically, and felt he'd improved his sometimes inappropriate behavior. Nevertheless, the teacher's intuitive concerns on this day may have been prescient. Rowan was trying to gauge how dangerous the situation might be. Earlier that day, he'd found it necessary to send a few students out to counselors because "they weren't composed"—or to put it more bluntly, being well aware of other recent school shootings, they were "freaking out" over Kip's gun arrest. (Why wasn't the administration?)

During this call, Rowan told Kip that other students wondered what Kip intended by having a gun in his locker. Kip acted "shocked and a little surprised that people thought he might actually use the gun there at school." Kip asked incredulously, "People wouldn't really think that I'd do something with it there?" Remember, Kip had just killed his dad when he said this, he'd written earlier about killing kids at school, and he was already assembling his arsenal.

Kip then mentioned the possibility of attending private school and (perhaps significantly) the National Guard, as if he were truly considering these options for the future. He caught Rowan's nervousness about the gravity of the situation, and his ingratiating remarks were intentionally designed to be misleading. The disarmingly repentant pupil assured his teacher that he'd made a mistake and the worst was over. The gross insincerity of this ruse not only reflects Kip's lifelong habit of being contrite when it served his purpose, but it is stunning in its cold-blooded manipulation of Rowan so as to keep him and the school off-guard and exposed to his murderous plans for the following day. He had come this far, and nothing was going to get in his way.

Rowan was still concerned, however, because he called back around 4:45 P.M., again asking to talk with Kip's dad. Kip had just started speaking with Jayne when they were interrupted by a call-waiting signal. Kip told her the incoming call was from Rowan, so they temporarily disconnected. Kip explained Bill's absence to his teacher by saying his dad "was probably out drinking, he did that sometimes." Kip had also lied to his friends Tony and Nick that Bill was out at a bar, and he relayed this same message to Jayne, adding that his dad was going directly to work at Lane Community College after that. The girl found this very odd, as she was sure Bill Kinkel never drank before work.

In Kip's only references to anxiety, he complained to Jayne that his head ached, he hadn't eaten, and though he felt exhausted, he couldn't sleep. Then he apologized for complaining. Kip told Tony and Nick that his stomach hurt and he felt like throwing up. He needed to laugh, he said, so he planned to watch *South Park,* an adult cartoon show.

When Jayne telephoned Kip again, around 6:30 P.M. (shortly after he killed his mother), it was her third call to him that day. This time, they talked nearly two hours. Kip said he thought it unfair he was in so much trouble, as it was Korey who'd brought the gun to school. He wanted the school to listen to his side of the story and he hoped to convince them to change his expulsion into a suspension. Without any notion of how close she was to the mark, Jayne replied, "With all the shootings they've had at schools recently, our school probably wouldn't be willing to do that." Kip mumbled back, "Yeah, you're probably right."

Just before the call with Tony and Nick, Kip had deflected one from a member of his father's advanced Spanish class at LCC. Bill had never before been absent nor even five minutes late, and his students were concerned. Kip coolly told them his dad wouldn't make it there this time, due to "family problems."

Kip's interludes of apparent "normalcy" on the telephone contrast starkly with the raging inner turmoil he reported later. His explanation to Dr. Lewis was that the phone calls temporarily suppressed the hallucinatory voices, which started up again the minute he hung up. "I know it was about twelve hours," he said. "It didn't seem like that. When the voices are there . . . It feels like they take thoughts. They change thoughts . . . like I'm not in control of my thoughts."

Kip told Dr. Lewis he couldn't remember driving to school and he battled the voices even as he entered the hallway at Thurston. "I talked to the voices. I said, 'I don't want to do this.' I see a kid staring at me. I think, 'Run! Run! You need to run.'" Yet Kip did manage to verbalize a warning to a friend before shooting his first two victims. In Dr. Bolstad's version of Kip's walk down the corridor, the voices disputed each other. "He saw three kids in front of him. He heard a voice that said, 'Shoot them now,' another voice said 'Wait, wait.' He heard, 'Look at what you've already done,' and 'It's *their* fault.' . . . They said, 'Go into the cafeteria and kill everybody.'"

Kip fired randomly as he entered the cafeteria. "I just started shooting. It was all rolled together, the voices saying, 'You've ruined their lives. Shoot them. You've got no other choice.'" Yet Bolstad insisted the boy understood that killing was evil because "he begged the voices not to make him do it. He knew it was wrong. He has a moral code."

A *moral code*? Personally, the author finds this last statement disingenuous and even absurd, considering Kinkel's observable actions. Further, in describing the torment he claimed his voices and delusions were putting him through, Kip told of an agony so intense that "I wanted to bash my head against the wall or stick my finger in my eye to make [them] stop." Yet, despite this distress, he never confided these symptoms to anyone who could help him.

When Dr. Bolstad asked him why not, Kip admitted he was frightened of what the voices might indicate. "He didn't want anyone to think of him as mentally ill. . . . He particularly didn't want girls to think that." Kip's apprehension about his social status and what his parents or friends would think outweighed his "agonizing" concerns about insane, demanding voices, bioterrorism, and the end of the world.

Educator and lawyer Nancy Willard, an expert on cyberbullying, feels those priorities are perfectly normal among disturbed adolescents. *I know of no teen that isn't totally concerned about his [or her] social status,* she wrote. *In fact, I think the vast majority of sick kids strive mightily to not allow others to know how sick they are or what they're feeling. And certainly being sick would not be living up to Kip's parents' expectations. He'd failed them in every other way, so the pressure to keep "voices" a secret would be high.*

Kip himself had said, "I didn't want to go to a mental hospital. I didn't want my friends to know because that would end my friendships. . . . I'd be ostracized. . . . My parents might think I was nuts. They would be disappointed with me. I had caused enough problems for them already."

In the final analysis, we may never be able to prove conclusively if the voices really existed; yet even if they did, they simply mirrored Kip's emotional state. By echoing painful accusations he'd previously heard from real sources around him, those abrasive voices aroused destructive impulses, providing Kip with the excuse his conscience needed to bridge the moral chasm. They offered a dark channel of escape for the inner conflict of a boy consistently failing to live up to his parents' expectations.

At the same time, the alleged voices also told him to perform sinister deeds that, on some level, he really wanted to do anyway. In the case of his schoolmates, the actions his voices demanded were consistent with Kip's earlier written and spoken threats. While there was no previous indication he ever wanted or planned to kill his parents, hallucinations might have propelled Kip over the edge. If his guns were a defense against anxieties brought about by delusions, the possibility that his parents might deprive him of them played directly into his fears of vulnerability.

As if it were logical, Kip explained that he slew his parents to save them from disgrace. Dr. Bolstad saw that as further proof of mental illness. "Would you kill your parents because you're saving them the embarrassment? I think his behavior was dominated at the time by psychotic thinking." On the other hand, when Kip said that he killed his parents so as not to embarrass them, it may not have been, as he claimed, because of what he'd already done (getting expelled for having a gun in school), but rather for what he knew he was about to do (attacking his school). To honestly admit that his school rampage was premeditated would have damaged his defense.

Perhaps Kip thought he could handle his mental problems for a while, but by the third year of his psychotic symptoms, he was no longer in control. His minor misdemeanors, spurred on by his paranoid delusions, had also gotten out of hand. His immaturity was no match for his disease. The plan that first presented itself to his mind was to commit suicide at home, which Kip claimed he considered on several occasions. Once, he told Dr. Lewis, he wanted to cut his carotid artery. He informed Dr. Dietz that another time he sat with a loaded rifle pointed at his forehead.

We've seen how Kip prepared for his suicide together with his plans for shooting up Thurston. If his intent to die was real, but his hallucinations weren't real, then why would he bother to confess, *God damn these VOICES inside my head* in his suicide note?

One could theorize that whatever remained of Kip's more humane nature set up a power struggle within, challenging the corrupted part of his persona. One voice would tell him to kill himself, another would order him not to. Ultimately, fulfilling the voices' demands to kill others must have appeared to Kip as the only option—"no other choice." The voices then cut a deal with Kip's suicidal aspirations. He could be free of them at last if he committed certain homicidal acts. Kip reported that after hearing the voices say hundreds of times "You have to go to school! Kill everybody!" he begged them to "Promise me you'll let me kill myself after. . . ." The voices assured him that he could do so, or, alternately, that someone (most likely the police) would surely kill him in response to his actions and end his self-described life of misery. Seeking out "suicide by cop" is not unusual. Given Kip's mind-set, it was an event waiting to happen. Being unexpectedly expelled for having a gun at school was the catalyst that put it all into irreversible motion, probably sooner than Kip had anticipated.

This is the story that emerges when certain pieces of the puzzle are put together, the "irrational reason" that makes the most sense. If the depth of Kip's psychosis had been revealed sooner, if he'd remained on Prozac, or if he'd trusted anyone enough to admit hearing voices, there might not have been a tragedy at Thurston.

Accepting that Kip's voices and delusions were authentic at least grants us a means of comprehending how he could murder his parents and twelve hours later shoot kids at school. If, on the other hand, we deny the reality of the overpowering voices and dismiss the delusions, we are left with only volcanic, explosive rage. Indeed, that is exactly what some experts are saying happened.

• Chapter 15 •

An Explosive Mind-Field

Violence can only be concealed by a lie, and the lie can only be maintained by violence.
—Alexandr Solzhenitsyn, Nobel Prize–winning Russian novelist

Although the insane logic of Kip Kinkel's voices in combination with delusional paranoia might cover most of the bases in his reasoning process, it leaves unanswered a couple of questions. First, if the finality of "suicide by cop" was Kip's underlying motivation for his raid on Thurston, why didn't he attack a police station or a military base instead of unarmed students? His extinction would have been practically guaranteed. Second, and especially pertinent from a legal point of view, why did he narrow his indiscriminate killing by sparing some students he liked, and going up to others and shooting them at point-blank range in the head, execution-style?

The distinction between the two styles of killing makes all the difference in Oregon sentencing laws, at least for adults. Indiscriminate shooting may justify a first-degree manslaughter charge with a minimum sentence of just ten years. Specific targeting merits an aggravated murder charge, and is the *only* offense punishable by death in Oregon.

A further insight into Kip's mind-set came from his best friend, Tony McCown, three years after the ordeal. He recollected how other school shootings had been a hot topic in the months preceding May '98, both in classroom discussions and in school gossip. McCown also recalled that Kip reacted to these attacks by talking about how the other shooters, such as the two boys at Jonesboro, were losers who had "failed" by waiting to be arrested. "Kip kept saying they were stupid, they were dumb little kids," Tony reported. "He said they should have just killed themselves, which would be better than spending their lives in prison." (Note: The Jonesboro shooters were released at age twenty-one.) Kip also proclaimed that if he were to attempt such an act, he'd be certain to kill himself to complete the drama. He also said that if he were going to die in that fashion, he'd try to take out as many people with him as he could.

Tony's disclosure was corroborated by at least eight other students who were interviewed by police. Bryan Mabe told PBS *Frontline*, "He wanted to take out himself, and he wanted to take out his schoolmates—some of them—just not go out alone. Being alone was his weakness. He was always worried about being alone all the time, isolated."

Tony McCown isn't certain if Kip's voices were real, but even if Kip made up some of his symptoms, that doesn't mean he wasn't insane. The judicial laws of Oregon reject the idea of "not guilty by reason of insanity" (NGRI), which is accepted in several other states. Instead, Oregon's alternate defense is called "guilty but insane," a small but important difference. Traditionally, NGRI means that while the defendant may have done the crime, he lacked a guilty mind. Because the defendant was incapable of forming an evil intent, he isn't held culpable for his acts. "Guilty but insane" is dissimilar in that the defendant is held culpable for his crime, but instead of being punished, he is sent for treatment in a secure, prisonlike hospital.

Kip and his lawyers finally decided not to follow that line of defense. The issue wasn't so much "Was Kip crazy?" as it was "Could he have stopped himself from doing that?" That's the point of law around which all else revolves.

The question, then, becomes what sort of mental disease would cause a person who acts normally and appears rational in most respects, and who is even likable and popular, to suddenly go ballistic in a rampage of mayhem and murder? Throughout recorded history, there have been murderers who suddenly erupted in unpredictable violence aimed at apparently indiscriminate targets. Only in the past few decades, however, have psychologists coined a term to classify this type of homicidal behavior. It's called "intermittent explosive disorder" (IED), and contemporary school shooters, workplace shooters, and other modern mass murderers typify this syndrome. Individuals designated with IED exhibit not just a single occurrence but several escalating episodes of rage. On a repeated basis, they suddenly lose all semblance of self-discipline and allow their hostility to explode in uncontrollable fury. Kip's history of tantrums at home certainly suggests he met this requirement. The only debate is whether or not he had any "alternative diagnoses" that could explain his frequent outbursts of anger and his final frenzy at Thurston.

A professor at the University of Oregon, who had more than a passing familiarity with the Kinkel case, offered another point of view regarding the nature of Kip's illness. In his line of work researching juvenile violence, Professor Dan Close has seen a fair share of disturbed young offenders, but it was his chance meeting with the father of one of them—a fellow he met at the San Diego airport named Bill Kinkel—that will stay in his mind forever. It was Professor Close to whom Bill had confided his deep-seated fears about Kip, five months before his son murdered the concerned father.

Professor Close shared with the author details about that coincidental meeting, explained his theories on "the binary mind," and interpreted data on affective conditions such as "extinction behavior" and IED, as defined in the *DSM-IV-TR*. Close included a disclaimer that "based on Bill Kinkel's description and the high degree of damage done, I speculate that IED could be what happened. Since I'm not a licensed clinical psychologist or psychiatrist, I leave those diagnoses to the appropriate professionals.

"On the other hand," the professor added, "I've been on the receiving end of several of these explosive events in my work as the director of Oregon Supported Living and Oregon Community Support. During those times, I experienced such incredibly powerful aggressive and destructive acts that I believed I was dealing with IED. The primary difference is that I served individuals with low IQs, while Kip appears to have at least normal IQ levels. Still, I cannot rule out IED in Kip's case."

From the 1970s onward, America and several other nations witnessed a dramatic rise in incidents of workplace rage that resulted in a considerable number of deaths. Terminated and/or depressed employees would return to their place of employment and begin shooting down former colleagues or bosses. After an incident at the Edmond, Oklahoma, Post Office on August 20, 1986, in which fourteen employees were shot dead and six wounded by postman Patrick Sherrill (who then committed suicide), the cynical expression "going postal" joined the common lexicon. Contiguous with these workplace events were a number of adult attacks on primary schools, as well as sensational massacres at other locations where families and young people gathered, such as playgrounds and fast-food restaurants.

Like other mass murderers, rampaging students often allow their hidden frustrations to fester until they explode in sudden, deadly acts of violence. According to researcher Jack Levin, of Northeastern University, school shooters "were just like their older counterparts—this was the teenage equivalent of a workplace massacre."

Not every school shooter can be explained away with an evaluation of IED, but some certainly match that description. Not long before he shot and killed Principal John Klang in the tiny farm town of Cazenovia, Wisconsin, on September 29, 2006, Eric Hainstock had erupted in anger in a classroom after being caught using a spitball shooter fashioned from a pen as a phallic object protruding from his pants. Weston K-12 School vocal teacher Alyssa Brewer told how she ordered the fifteen-year-old to another room to cool off when he refused to hand it over. Instead, he stood up, threw a chair across the room, and came at her, challenging a fight, shouting as he grabbed her arm so hard he left a numbing bruise, "Do you want to fucking go? We can fucking go right now!"

This outburst only helped to solidify his reputation as a kid with few friends who was "just weird in the head." In fact, he'd been in what he termed "useless" anger management classes for years. He thought the counselor was too patronizing. "He's like, 'Your choices are based on your beliefs,'" Hainstock later said. "Like, 'duh.' It gets annoying." The special-ed student's main complaint was that school officials wouldn't do anything to stop a group of kids picking on him, calling him names, and rubbing up against him. That latter bit doesn't make much sense until we factor in that he'd been the target of sexual and physical abuse by family members and classmates. According to defense psychologist Michael Caldwell, anyone touching the boy reminded him of that molestation and raised his aggression several notches higher.

The red flags were flying in profusion. Sophomore Shelly Rupp said, "He always used to kid around about bringing things to school and hurting kids." Hainstock told three friends that Klang would "not make it through homecoming." This was 2006, and still no one reported it. Then the principal gave the freshman boy a disciplinary warning for having chewing tobacco on school grounds, which would likely mean an in-school suspension.

Hainstock fumed all night and decided the next morning that going to school with guns was the only way to get officials to listen. He pried open the family's gun cabinet and removed a shotgun. Then he unlocked his parents' bedroom and took a .22-caliber revolver. Entering the rural school, "he was calm, but he was on a mission," custodian Dave Thompson told police. The boy pointed the shotgun in the face of a social studies teacher, but Thompson grabbed it away. The custodian wrestled with Hainstock, but he broke free and took out his handgun.

Just then Principal Klang, forty-nine, entered the hallway and clutched the gunman from behind using a bear hug. Hainstock maintains that he didn't mean to kill Klang, despite an earlier announcement to the custodian that "I'm here to fucking kill someone." He "just freaked out," he claims, when the principal grabbed him, triggering his memories of abuse and escalating his rage. He put the revolver under his left armpit and shot the principal three times, in the head, chest, and leg. Badly wounded, Klang still managed to courageously wrestle Hainstock to the ground and brush the gun away. The principal died a few hours later in a Madison hospital.

Since they were very young, Brooks Brown was best friends with Dylan Klebold, one of the Columbine shooters. Brooks told about getting into a playground brawl with his childhood buddy in elementary school. *The fight was the first time I ever saw Dylan's temper,* he wrote in his book, *No Easy Answers: The Truth Behind Death at Columbine,* cowritten with Rob Merritt. *Because Dylan internalized things so much, he would let his anger build up within him until one little thing finally set it off. When that happened, it was like an explosion.*

It's interesting to note that Klebold, like Kip Kinkel, was also not allowed to have any toy guns or "war toys" at home when he was a child. Perhaps that fact requires further consideration. The idea

The empty Kinkel home in the Shangri-La subdivision of Springfield, Oregon, after the murders, and *(below)* the family in happier times, a decade earlier.

Kip Kinkel's "suicide note" left on the coffee table (with the phrase "God damn these VOICES inside my head"), and his single-page diary describing his suffering, ill will toward others, frustration in love, and his plan to attack Thurston High.

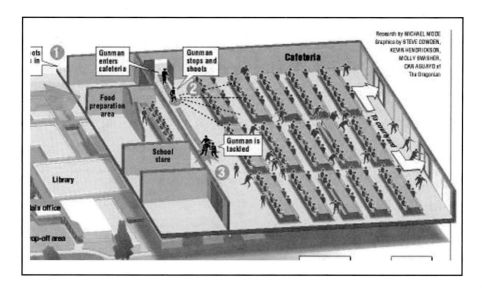

A graphic showing Kip's attack in the Thurston High cafeteria (© 1998 *The Oregonian*. All rights reserved. Reprinted with permission). *Below:* Student Ryan Atteberry, who had been shot on the side of his head, being led to an ambulance. Ryan survived (*Springfield News* photo reprinted with permission of Lee Enterprises).

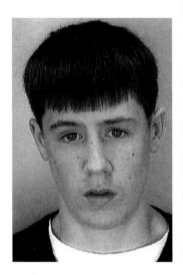
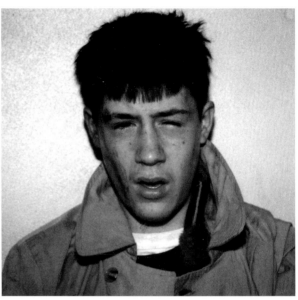

Kip Kinkel's Mug Shots. *Above left:* after his May 20, 1998 arrest for having a gun in school; *above right*: after being tackled by students who stopped his rampage on May 21; *below left*: upon entry to Skipworth after the school shooting; and *below right*: in 2007, age 25, at the time of his transfer to the Oregon State Correctional Institute in Salem.

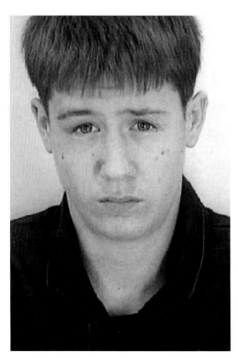

Stunned and tearful Thurston High student Mandee Axtell watches the tragedy at Thurston High (*Springfield News* photo, reprinted with permission of Lee Enterprises and Mandee Axtell). *Below:* Detective Al Warthen of Springfield Police gently walks Kip through the crime scene later that day.

Clay Shrout annihilated his entire family *(above left)* in May 1994, and then took his gun to school in Union, Kentucky. *Above right:* Clay in 2007, age 30, with his current prison ID number. He is serving 999 years.

Luke Woodham *(left)*, in high school yearbook photo. He killed his mother and several students at Pearl High School in Pearl, Mississippi, in October 1997. *Right:* Luke's prison portrait in 2005 as a Mississippi Department of Corrections inmate.

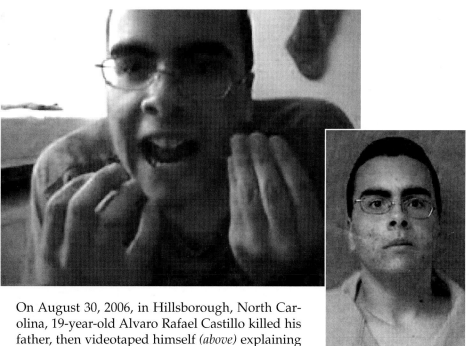

On August 30, 2006, in Hillsborough, North Carolina, 19-year-old Alvaro Rafael Castillo killed his father, then videotaped himself *(above)* explaining why he had done it and what he was about to do. Soon after, he loaded his minivan with pipe bombs and weapons, and drove to Orange High School.

Bullied student Charles "Andy" Williams, 15, killed two students and wounded thirteen in an eight-minute shooting spree on March 5, 2001, at Santana High School in Santee, California, near San Diego. His photo at age 12 *(below left)* and again in 2004.

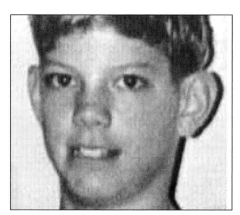

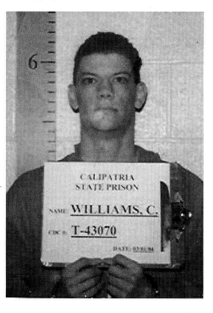

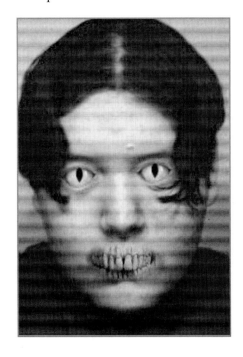

Before Jeff Weise's deadly March 2005 rampage in Red Lake, Minnesota, he murdered his grandfather, a tribal policeman. He had been creating graphically violent cartoons, and *(below right)* this self-portrait on his Internet profile.

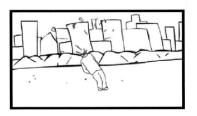

Prior to Columbine, the only paired school shooters were Andrew Golden, 11 *(above left)*, and Mitchell Johnson, 13 *(right)*, in March 1998. Four young girls and a teacher died in Jonesboro, Arkansas, that day, but since they were tried as juveniles, both boys were released at age 21. Mitchell *(below right)* was rearrested on New Year's Day 2007 for illegal gun and drug possession. *Bottom left:* A memorial sculpture at the Westside Middle School (courtesy *The Jonesboro Sun*, David Stout, photographer).

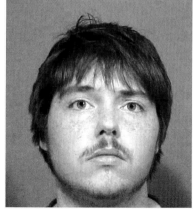

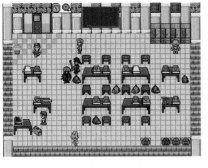

Eric:

Yes, Shakespeare said it best:

Good wombs hath borne bad sons, Vodka.

Danny Ledonne's 2005 video-game Super Columbine Massacre RPG! *(top left and above)* earned both harsh condemnation and professional praise. *The National Enquirer* on June 4, 2002 *(left)*, published the only two photos ever released of Eric Harris and Dylan Klebold lying dead in their own blood on the library floor. Both endeavors were criticized. However, the *Enquirer* photos succeeded in de-glorifying the killers by showing the ugliness of their deaths, and Ledonne's creation sparked useful dialogue. *Bottom left and below:* Scenes from the Columbine cafeteria surveillance camera as Harris and Klebold nonchalantly attempt to set off more homemade bombs.

L 11:45:39-55 AM 04/20/99

L 11:57:20-53 AM 04/20/99

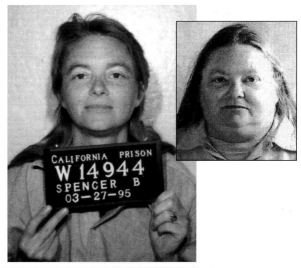

Top left: The one who started it all—1966 University of Texas tower sniper Charles Whitman, who murdered fifteen and wounded thirty-one; *top right:* aging murderess Brenda Spencer, who at age 16 in 1979 was the first female school shooter, shown here in 1995 and 2007; *below left:* teacher Gwen Mayor and over half her class of kindergarten students (sixteen in all) were killed by a 43-year-old psychopathic gun collector, Thomas Hamilton, on March 13, 1996, in Dunblane, Scotland; *right:* South Korean policeman Woo Bum-Kom, drunk and upset with his girlfriend, committed the worst solo mass murder in history, killing fifty-seven in 1982.

Above: Cartoonist Cam Cardow in the *Ottawa Citizen* comments on parents who blind themselves to all the warning signs.

Commander Lisa Sterr *(left)* confiscated a large arms cache *(below)* from the homes of two youths who were "one bad day away" from a Columbine-style attack in Green Bay, Wisconsin. William Cornell *(top right)* and Shawn Sturtz *(bottom left)*, both 17, were arrested on September 14, 2006; Bradley Netwal, 18 *(bottom right)*, shortly thereafter.

Anastasia DeSousa, 19 *(left)*, was killed and nineteen other students were wounded when Kimveer Gill, 25 *(below)*, opened fire at Montreal's Dawson College on September 13, 2006. Media-hungry Gill also put up Internet images of himself, taken by his longtime friend Rajiv Rajan (who was arrested for alleged chat room "threats" after the attack, but released), that show Gill posing in the black trench coat he planned to wear to the slaughter, with the Beretta semiautomatic Cx4 Storm rifle he would use that day.

Above right: Panic in the hallways as a surveillance camera records Asa Coon *(left)*, wearing a Marilyn Manson T-shirt, just before he opened fire with two revolvers, wounding two students and two teachers before killing himself at SuccessTech Academy on October 10, 2007, in Cleveland, Ohio. Two days later, a student in Norristown, Pennsylvania, tipped off police that Dillon Cossey, 14 *(below left)*, was planning a similar attack. Police found over thirty weapons in his bedroom, and Dillon admitted to the plan. His mother, Michele *(below right)*, was arrested soon after for purchasing his high-powered rifles.

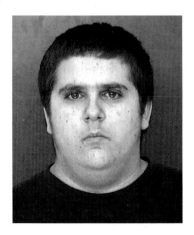

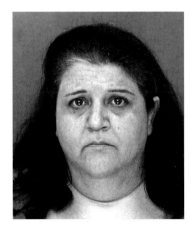

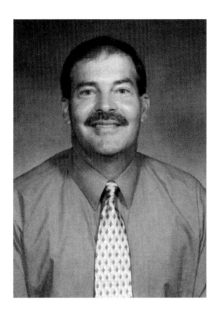

Above: Beloved Principal John Klang *(left)* was shot and killed by fifteen-year-old Eric Hainstock on September 29, 2006, in Cazenovia, Wisconsin. Only two days earlier, on September 27, 2006, Duane Morrison, 53 *(right)*, took six female students hostage at Platte Canyon High School in the small mountain town of Bailey, Colorado, and sexually molested them before killing one. Morrison then turned the gun on himself.

Below: Charles Carl Roberts IV, 32 *(right)*, lived quietly with his wife and three children in the rural Amish community of Paradise, Pennsylvania. On October 2, 2006, he took students hostage at the one-room West Nickel Mines schoolhouse. Police stormed in to find three girls and the gunman dead and seven badly injured. Two more girls died overnight.

Over a year prior to his bloody April 16, 2007, rampage at Virginia Tech, Seung-hui Cho *(above)* was declared "mentally ill" and an "imminent danger to self and others" in a December 2005 evaluation. He was still able to legally purchase guns. That loophole has since been tightened.

Below: Graduate student Stephen Kazmierczak, who also had mental issues, legally purchased guns to shoot and kill Northern Illinois University students *(top row)* Julianna Gehant, Catalina Garcia, *(bottom row)* Gayle Dubowski, Daniel Parmenter, and Ryanne Mace on Valentine's Day, 2008.

that boys may need outlets in which to channel their natural aggressive tendencies does not always match up to the dictates of those who consider themselves "politically correct." Toy soldiers or fighter planes are no different in a boy's mind than dolls are for girls—they're simply a way of exercising some degree of control over a miniature world that isn't as unpredictable or unsettling as the real world. Eavesdropping on that play may tell a parent a lot about their child's dreams and fears. Giving a child a realistic replica of a handgun or rifle may not be in their best interests, but even kids who pretend that sticks are guns or spears are mainly acting out fantasies inspired by what they see in the media they're exposed to. Even if parents are willing to eliminate those media influences, they cannot totally banish all assertive or unruly behavior in their offspring. It's part of growing up, but parents should be aware of the point at which such conduct crosses the line. If toy weapons represent a buffer against feelings of insecurity in a child, it's worthwhile to analyze where those insecurities originate.

Real weapons are another story. Outside of a hunting culture in which guns represent a widely accepted form of male bonding, a desire for firearms by young people is always cause for concern. Just as the age of mass murderers has dropped over the years, the location of killing sprees has also shifted. Compared to youth disturbances in the past, which were usually confined to violence-prone teens living in crime-ridden urban zones, most school attacks have taken place in predominantly white, rural, or suburban middle- and upper-middle-class districts. The "new breed" of perpetrators have insignificant or nonexistent histories of disorderly behavior; they get good to average grades in school, are characteristically quiet, even timid types, and are often raised in conventional two-parent homes free from any kind of material deprivation. They are not "the usual suspects."

Murders committed by urban ghetto kids in gangs make a perverse kind of sense in terms of the dynamics of commonly acknowledged personal and social conflicts. They hunt down specific targets, or pursue a particular enemy marked for death out of vengeance, territorial competition, or jealousy. Their hated rival is often considered an equal, and thus deserving of their hostile attention. With rampage killers, however, retribution is more generalized.

School shooters seldom have any idea of precisely whom they're aiming at. They've entered a state of total alienation from their peers, viewing them as expendable extras in an egocentric melodrama of self-inflicted pain. They shoot at "targets of convenience." In this way, they duplicate the patterns of adult mass murderers, such as Charles Whitman (chapter 26), who in 1966 shot forty-six people from the bell tower of the University of Texas, in Austin, without knowing a single one of their identities.

Another contrast between school shooters and gang members is that the latter have a shared social group, which allows them the luxury of diminished responsibility. They aren't trying to die by their dangerous conduct or murderous acts, but are hoping to elevate themselves in the eyes of their peers. School shooters, thus far, have largely been individuals seeking personal infamy in the expected blaze of negative glory and media coverage that will accompany their spectacular homicide-suicide.

Because of these differences, according to Professor Close, juvenile delinquents and school shooters are thought to represent two separate genres of antisocial adolescents. As prototypes, researchers further categorize them in relation to the age at which their disturbing characteristics begin to manifest themselves: "early onset" for the ones we recognize even before they reach preschool, and "late onset" for those who begin to express hostility toward the end of elementary school or at the start of puberty.

Most early onset antisocial kids can be identified by age three, and some as young as eighteen months old. Almost from the start, they give clear signs of future developmental problems. Unlike tots who pass through the usual "stages" of childhood evolution, these children are consistently aggressive, defiant, and oppositional, seldom listening, never obeying. Some tantrums are normative, but healthy youngsters grow out of them. Early starters challenge virtually every exchange they have with parents or other authority figures, wearing their caregivers down. Their worsening behavior is given an expanded audience as they enter elementary school, act disruptively in class, disregard teachers, congregate with other disobedient pupils, and bully weaker children. If their attitudes are not curtailed by third grade, their problems become chronic and thenceforth can never be cured, only managed. They will often be labeled "severely emotionally disturbed," and most will end up in juvenile detention before they reach high school.

By comparison, late onset antisocial children show few signs of such problems prior to age nine. They're more likely to be "led" into disruptive behavior by early onset antisocial friends around the time of puberty, but unless they're ripe and eager for this type of misconduct, it's unlikely they'll follow that route for very long. While early starters make themselves known to authorities in their first years of grade school, late starters generally manage to steer clear of confrontations with the law, counselors, school officials, or social service agencies until they finally surface years later.

Professor Close also sees a social class issue at work here. "Unlike typical juvenile delinquents from so-called 'bad' neighborhoods," he says, "the early antisocial behavior of most school shooters is limited, not overt, so when hints of trouble arise, their middle- to upperclass parents can bring in resources such as professional counseling. The families of urban ghetto kids couldn't generally afford that, so the violence poorer kids exhibit is exposed early. While the upscale antisocial child's anger remains better hidden, it swells up slowly and eventually explodes further on down the line."

Parents in the Kinkels' income bracket can indulge in the luxury of rationalizing their children's behavior away. They may deny incidents that psychologists would identify as telltale signs of psychosis, purchase the "toys" (a computer, a gun) they believe will stave off their child's further slide into disrepute, and convince any cops who intercede that a kid who comes from such a nurturing, well-educated, and law-abiding family won't ever get into trouble again.

When Kip's middle school delinquency file was expunged, as is standard practice for graduating eighth-grade students, his high school counselors were left in the dark regarding his past misdeeds. This well-intentioned practice is designed to give kids a fresh start, but in reality it blindsides secondary-school administrators who really need to be informed about potentially high-risk students. The assumption being made is that labeling youngsters as "bad seeds" at an early age will make them so, yet the idealized belief that "all children are by nature innocent" has proven itself to be overly naive.

With his thoughts guarded and his activities concealed, a late onset antisocial child creates a greater risk, because his pain and anxiety are deeply internalized. These kids are often prone to depression and suicide, but given the opportunity, those traits can abruptly externalize and swing strongly toward aggression. Kip Kinkel obviously fit that profile.

Kip showed some early onset symptoms as well: temper tantrums when required to follow the rules, lies and stealing, threatening others, disruptive behavior on playgrounds and in classrooms, kicking and screaming, ridiculing others, and venting a short, nasty temper when he himself was ridiculed. The reason he was not diagnosed sooner may have been, as Professor Close suggested, that his parents were better able to downplay his problems at the time.

For outsiders who observe the kinds of inappropriate behavior described above, it's easy to conclude that the child is simply spoiled. Another way of putting it is that he or she is excessively narcissistic. By definition, narcissists see themselves as being at the center of the universe. They acknowledge other individuals only as objects for their own use, and become enraged when they encounter obstacles to their demands. Some analysts believe this condition is rooted in depression and develops as a coping mechanism for maladapted self-esteem and lack of self-love. High self-esteem entails respecting oneself, whereas narcissism involves creating a grandiose self-image.

In July 1998, the American Psychological Association released a summary of two related studies conducted by Dr. Brad J. Bushman, of Iowa State University, and Dr. Roy F. Baumeister, of Case Western Reserve University. Both psychologists explored the connection between narcissism, negative personal feedback, and aggression. Narcissists, they found, are emotionally invested in establishing their superiority over others, yet are not convinced that they've achieved this, making them exceptionally aggressive toward anyone who offends or threatens their highly favorable views of themselves.

Unfortunately, this theory came home to roost five years after this report was published. On May 9, 2003, Case Western itself was the site of a shooting by an adult graduate who was frustrated because he'd lost a lawsuit filed against a staff member there. Biswanath Halder, sixty-two, entered the campus wearing a bulletproof vest, a wig, a World War II–style army helmet, and carrying two guns. As he walked the halls of the business school, he fired hundreds of rounds. One student died and two were injured.

Dr. Hervey Cleckley is author of *The Mask of Sanity,* arguably the most widely read book on the sociopathic personality yet written. Cleckley wrote that egocentricity is always a factor in psychopathic individuals; they know of no other way to think and can only visualize in terms of themselves. For a narcissistic boy, an ordinary case of rejection or frustration can generate extraordinary responses. When things don't go the way he had it planned, he may blame those closest to him for his discontent, just as Luke Woodham did by annihilating his mother and his girlfriend.

When Kip became infatuated with Stormy and projected all his needs upon her, her sensible refusal to be his savior threw him into a tailspin. Kip clearly was at the high end of the sensitivity scale, and he very likely believed that a solid boy-girlfriend relationship would go far in making up for the inadequacies he felt as a son. When the romance didn't work out quite as he'd imagined, he felt wounded and thus justified in his thoughts of wounding others. It was only a matter of time before his smoldering sentiments erupted into violent plans of retribution.

Along the route to his final frenzy, Kip got some technical assistance. The World Wide Web holds the greatest store of knowledge ever devised by mankind, both for good and for less altruistic purposes. Unrestricted by parental controls, a computer-savvy teen can electronically explore worlds that previous generations had not even imagined existed. To a pubescent boy, Internet pages that offer hardcore pornography or recipes on how to build bombs are, in a sense, condoning these things. It's as if the authors of these Web sites are saying, "It's really okay—there are lots of people who think like you do."

When Bill Kinkel spoke with Professor Close in San Diego, the one thing that he was proud of about his son was how Kip seemed to be a whiz at using his computer. The fact that his child was busy on the Internet instead of out gallivanting with rough companions was a satisfaction in itself. He might have been less pleased if he'd realized where Kip's cyberjourneys were leading him. Like many of their generation, Bill and Faith were not especially computer literate, and naive in their belief that no harm could come of Kip's adventures on the Web. Instead of wondering, "Do I know where my child is?" and feeling satisfied, they should have been inquiring,

"What Web sites is our kid visiting?" Even with the best intentions, they still exercised a failure to supervise.

If the "innocence" of Kip's parents concerning his Internet activities and bomb-making skills makes them appear somewhat gullible, Bill's attitude about buying weapons for Kip was the worst form of denial. He presented his son with guns to emotionally connect with him and divert Kip's fetish into a supervised hobby. If his dad saw this as a kind of warm and fuzzy "bonding," Kip's view, as spoken to his friend Mike Joseph, was "When I snap, I want the firepower to kill people." When Kip wasn't satisfied with a single gun or even a pair, a huge red flag should have shot up. Each time Bill gave in, both the price tag and killing power of Kip's weaponry escalated.

Kip was familiar with how to work this game of manipulation to his advantage. He played skillfully upon the sympathies of others while cataloging his own misfortunes in detail, taking a certain pleasure in his pain. Although in his diary he seemed unable to move into new relationships after Stormy took the wind out of his sails, on the very night he killed his parents, Kip several times told Jayne, the girl he spoke with for two hours, that he loved her.

Professor Close left his phone number with Bill Kinkel, but never got a call. His feeling was that Bill was worn down from the constant struggle ("I don't know if I can take this much longer," he had sighed) and asking for help, but at the same time, Bill believed he could handle it without professional assistance. One of Bill's concluding remarks came back to haunt Close as a foreshadowing of what followed. The professor had said, "Raising kids can be a pretty stressful job," and Bill shot back, "If we survive."

Close believes the Kinkels were victims of their own support and advocacy for the son who kept betraying their trust. They were skilled in protecting him from exposure and protecting themselves from the shame. At some point, Kip realized how the system functioned and took over its operation. He had a pair of older parents, with sound financial means, who gave in to his demands on a regular basis. When they told him no, he flew into a rage, whined, persisted, and wore them down, using every means at his disposal until he gained what he wanted. He got used to having his way, and he reacted with fury if he was not appeased quickly. He recognized that his parents were squeezed between his ultimatums and their standing in the community, and he milked that vulnerability for all it was worth. When it convenienced him to act contrite, he would express regret for embarrassing them. At the same time, he knew exactly what he was doing.

Bill and Faith had to intervene again and again to keep Kip from exposing their dysfunctional dilemma. In a series of desperate bids to keep his antisocial mannerisms hidden from public knowledge, they would make deals, do homeschooling, buy gifts, or get him private counseling and medication. In return, he would briefly calm down, and then, with renewed energy, he'd again begin punching holes in their Bubble Wrap of denial. Inevitably the destructive force that Kip's exhausted parents tried to suppress could no longer be contained. The final explosive event brought them all down, and blew away the serenity of Thurston High.

"At what point," Close asked, "do you stop mending the breaches and start connecting the dots? When do you stop denying and start recognizing the damage?"

For Bill Kinkel, that moment may have come on the day his son was arrested for having a gun at school. This could well have been the first time Kip's father really put his foot down. One can almost imagine Bill that afternoon shouting, "That's *it*!" as his fist slammed onto the counter. "I'm not gonna take this one day longer! You can kiss those guns good-bye!" Professor Close theorizes that it was Bill's tough, no-nonsense words—not voices in Kip's head—that backed the boy into his corner of extreme desperation.

Concerning Kip's repeated phrase, "I had no other choice," Close talks about a mind-set he terms "the binary nature of extremism," an expression he feels fits both terrorists and school shooters. The reference is to the binary language of computers that reduces all knowledge down to "bits" with a numerical value of "0" or "1." An equivalent pattern of reducing human thought into simplistic "yes/no, A or B" responses can be applied to the "binary minds" of those who attempt to eliminate the complexities of life by condensing their options into nothing more complex than "good" or "bad" resolutions to any given situation.

Ultimately, Close states, "impressionable young males lose the ability to examine several options in a reasonable manner, or to consider the relative consequences of their extreme acts." Confined by their binary minds, restricted in their choices, these kids face problems, but they don't see the various alternatives they have available, nor any way to reason their way out. In this context, the expression "I had no other choice" makes perfect sense.

Seung-hui Cho, in his video messages, said, "You forced me into a corner *and gave me only one option. . . .* When the time came, I did it. *I had to.*" Sebastian Bosse (chapter 26) wrote in a suicide message he posted on the Internet, "If you realize you'll never find happiness in your life and the reasons for this pile up day by day, *the only option you have* is to disappear from this life." Nikhil Dhar (chapter 28), who tried to kill a teacher at UMass in 2005, had a note in his pocket that contained the words: "I'm sorry I'm having to do this. But *I have no options left. . . .* I have nothing to lose." And Robert A. Hawkins, the December 2007 Omaha shopping mall shooter (chapter 20), wrote, "I've just snapped. I can't take this meaningless existence anymore. . . . It seems *this is my only option.*"

While there have always been people who limit themselves to fixed, inflexible responses, Close theorizes that binary thinking is a relatively recent trend. He attributes it in part to the enthusiastic adoption of modern technologies by younger folk, who may have limited experience in the real world. There is a downside for individuals who isolate themselves by spending excessive amounts of time fixated on video games or TV, or immersed in solitary explorations of the Internet. Many become preoccupied with violence or porn, while in the real world they might be experiencing rejection by their peers or passing through the typical discomforts of adolescence.

As these youngsters pull back from normal social exchanges, they sink deeper into their own private fantasies of how they imagine the world really operates. As a result, their zone of solitude expands, their social skills plummet, and their ability to interact in any meaningful way with others is trivialized. Their minds imitate the machines they bond with, reinforcing binary notions that reduce the complexities of human relations down to superficial simplifications. They lose the ability to think through all of the possibilities in any given situation.

Psychiatrists use the term "splitting" to describe something very similar to this condition. Dr. Neil Kaye calls it a defense mechanism common to borderline personalities. *A person looks at things as good or bad,* he wrote, *but can never see them as good* and *bad.* Dr. Park Dietz adds, "In splitting, the individual highly values some object or person, then shortly after devalues it. He or she idealizes an object or person, then does the opposite." This partly describes what happened to Kip with Stormy when she did not return the love he expected, or even his relationship with his parents.

For those whose minds are circumscribed in this manner, the choices of how to overcome a dilemma are never colored in shades of gray. No problem is ever delineated beyond a "black or white" solution. Like players in a video game, they are capable of planning only one level or "map" at a time before going on to the next stage, unable to see what the future consequences will be "in real time." Eventually they reach a degree of difficulty that's beyond their ability to resolve with the limited mental skills they've been able to cultivate. When cornered, the binary mind truly "has no other choice" because it's literally incapable of imagining any other alternative. Eliminating the problem by destroying it becomes the only option.

Psychologists describe people whose actions involve engaging in extreme self-destruction as exhibiting "extinction behavior." An example of this is when an abused wife manages to escape from an abusive husband, and then the abandoned spouse considers killing his former mate and committing suicide. It's not so much the loss of the woman he's continually threatened and beaten that he mourns, but rather it's the loss of the selfish pleasure and comfort he took in controlling her. His future becomes too difficult to face as he contemplates losing the one person he depended upon to depend upon him. Instead, he chooses the total extinction of them both.

Something similar may have happened between Kip Kinkel and his parents. He defined himself by the firepower he possessed. Explosives were his obsession, and guns were his drugs. Kip had succeeded for a while in manipulating his parents into the position of supplying him with the fixes he required in order to maintain his sense of self at their expense. The ax he held over their heads was social and professional shame. Finally he went too far. His father threatened to take away the very things that shaped his existence. Facing the loss of what he felt he needed so desperately, his thinking became *I'll eliminate the problem by eliminating the people cre-*

ating the problem that's upsetting me. After that, I'll eliminate my-self in a spectacular way.

For a mind in this condition, the normal human aversion to death no longer applies. Suicidal ideation, i.e., the glorification of one's own annihilation, is the means by which an individual faces down his fear of mortality by embracing it. By choosing the time, location, and manner of his suicide, Kip could feel he had an element of control over his demise. Even so, that was not enough—he wanted more drama and he absolutely demanded more attention. He dreaded dying as just another obscure teen who'd achieved nothing of significance in his life. By including others in his lethal plans, he could avoid the sad, lonely anonymity of a silent, uneventful suicidal death.

Here we might suggest another correlation between Western school shooters and young suicidal bombers who commit mass murder on behalf of Middle Eastern terrorist organizations, such as Islamic Jihad, Hamas, Hezbollah, or al-Qaida. An American boy seeking vengeance against those who do not accept him straps on a cluster of bullets and guns, and sets out to kill people in a crowded school cafeteria. A young terrorist seeking vengeance against those who do not accept his beliefs straps on explosives, and sets out to kill people in a crowded market. Is there any connection? Perhaps not in motive, but certainly in method. Both wish to inflict as much harm as possible upon others, and both care nothing for their own lives. Neither feels the least compassion or empathy for those they are about to slaughter, because they both believe their victims "deserve" to die.

In each case, it's necessary to dehumanize and even demonize the innocent victims who will be murdered as a result of the attack. Terrorists believe that all citizens of the nation, religious persuasion, or ethnic group they target are guilty, that even babies and children share complicity in the system they detest. School shooters, likewise, accuse the entire student body of complicity in their torment, often including faculty. They all must die "for laughing at me," as Kip put it, much like the victims trapped in the burning gym in *Carrie,* Stephen King's first successful horror novel (twice made into movies).

Unlike serial killers who look forward to the repetition of their crimes, mass murderers plan for just one single action, as striking as they can make it. Most have no intention of keeping their identities secret during or after their rampage, although a rare exception to this rule was Virginia Tech's Seung-hui Cho, who filed the serial numbers off his guns and carried no IDs, but then conversely mailed materials and left a note that guaranteed his infamy to the widest possible audience. In calling himself a martyr, comparing his death to Jesus and raving about how he was cleansing our world of the unpure, Cho also represents the most blatant interface yet between school shooters and terrorists. Like al-Qaida suicide bombers, Cho, the Columbine shooters, Sebastian Bosse, and Alvaro Rafael Castillo all recorded their final messages on video, expressly for use by the media after their deaths.

Terrorists and school shooters share other similarities. They both exhibit covert strategies, intelligent minds, the element of surprise, and easy access to weapons. They show deep, long-term planning skills and cleverly insinuate themselves into the surrounding society. Many volunteers for Islamic terrorist groups are well-educated young adults who came from middle- to upper-class homes, just like many of the shooters. The main difference between the two kinds of killers is in the purpose for which they're willing to die. Islamic extremists claim they're sacrificing themselves for the betterment of their people or religion. School shooters seem to be seeking only personal satisfaction. Even so, whenever a school rampage takes place, fan clubs spring up almost overnight on the Internet, lionizing the shooter for striking back at the system on behalf of all those downtrodden students who feel they have been unjustly ignored, teased, or bullied. In his final statement, Luke Woodham wrote, *I am not insane. I am angry. I killed because people like me are mistreated every day. I did this to show society, "Push us and we will push back."*

However, it was not until the massacre perpetrated by Seung-hui Cho in 2007 that all of these diverse elements came together—and this marks the real significance of the Virginia Tech shootings. In the "suicide note" left in his room and in the tapes he sent to NBC News, Cho took the hitherto unspoken connection with terrorists to a new level, openly and brazenly injecting an aura of religious fanaticism into school shooting for the first time. In his lengthy manifesto, he many times mimicked Islamic extremist philosophy, railing against materialism, wealth, and privilege, and claiming the right to purify the earth of the undeserving and the unclean by destroying them: "Your Mercedes wasn't enough, you brats. Your golden necklaces weren't enough, you snobs. Your trust funds weren't enough. Your vodka and cognac weren't enough. All your debaucheries weren't enough. Those weren't enough to fulfill your hedonistic needs."

At the same time, despite making anti-Christian statements, Cho utilized familiar Christian symbology to convey his message: "Do you know what it feels like to be humiliated and be impaled upon a cross, and left to bleed to death for your amusement? You thought it was one pathetic boy's life you were extinguishing. Thanks to you I die, like Jesus Christ, to inspire generations of the weak and the defenseless people. . . . I didn't have to do this. I could have left. I could have fled. But no, I will no longer run. It's not for me. It's for my children, for my brothers and sisters that you fucked. I did it for them."

Cho went on at length about his own agony, dismissing everyone else's distress ("You have never felt a single ounce of pain your whole life") and listing the myriad ways he had been made to suffer, as if that would justify the agony he would soon inflict on others: "Do you know what it feels like to be spit on your face and have trash stuffed down your throat? Do you know what it feels like to dig your own grave? Do you know what it feels like to have your throat slashed from ear to ear? Do you know what it feels like to be torched alive?"

Further, in speaking of the "martyrdom of Eric and Dylan" (at Columbine), Cho was including himself in a distinct subclass of mass murderers whose stipulated purpose is divine retribution. This sets up a disturbing picture for the future as more would-be shooters consider joining this "exclusive club." Thus far, the trend has been for each succeeding generation to be more "Look at me!" From their MySpace page to their video on YouTube, it's paradoxically the ones least able to communicate in the real world who most desire to leave their mark in a virtual world.

Two months prior to his November 2006 school shooting in Emsdetten, Germany, Sebastian Bosse wrote a diary entry that proclaimed in German: *ERIC HARRIS IS GOD*. In his farewell video, he said, "I learned there's just consuming life and then death. In 2003, 2004, my life changed and I wasn't human anymore. I was godlike. And I began planning this massacre. I wanted to kill them all because they'd ruined my life." The "kill them all" phrase was also a favorite of the Columbine duo.

One consistency among school shooters is that they show little originality and even less modesty. Dylan Klebold had said in a video, "I know we're gonna have followers, because we're so godlike. . . . We're not exactly human. We have human bodies, but we've evolved one step above you human shit." In *Natural Born Killers* (chapter 20), Harris and Klebold's favorite film, Mickey the psychotic killer says, "We're not even the same species. I used to be you, then I evolved." The Mickey character was based upon the real-life spree killer Charles Starkweather, who claimed he'd transcended his former self to reach a new plane of existence following his first murder. In the 2003 movie *Zero Day*, one of the two fictional school shooters says, "We're gonna be more powerful than God!" His partner replies, "We *are* God." And finally, from the videotaped manifesto of eighteen-year-old Finnish gunman Pekka-Eric Auvinen (chapter 26), an "antihuman humanist . . . and godlike atheist" (his words) who killed eight people before committing suicide at Jokela High, on October 10, 2007: "I cannot say that I am of the same race as this miserable, arrogant, and selfish human race. No! I have evolved a step higher." In this narcissistic manner, these egoistical killers seek to excuse their actions by placing themselves on a higher plane than their victims, whereas in evolutionary terms they more closely resemble a cancer on the underside of society.

Bosse, like Cho, was setting up a club of "godlike" outcast heroes (i.e., martyrs) that included himself, Harris, Klebold, Kip Kinkel, and Kimveer Gill, all of whose names were mentioned in a single diary entry. He hoped his violent actions would lead to other school outcasts being treated better, but history has shown such events are more likely to engender the opposite reaction from bullies who feel more justified, not less, in marginalizing kids they think are both freaky and dangerous.

Similar to Cho's rambling condemnation of wealth and materialism, Bosse wrote that he understood he was living in a *world in which money rules everything, even in school it was only about that.*

You had to have the latest cell phone, the latest clothes and the right "friends." If you didn't, you weren't worth any attention. I loathe these people, no, I loathe people. He concluded, *The only thing I learned intensively at school was that I'm a loser.* Maybe so, but shooting people doesn't make someone a winner. The real issue underlying this angst about not being accepted by "cool kids" may have more to do with envy than Utopian ideology, and that can be cured by growing up, getting a job and a life, and leaving such sophomoric, superficial relationships behind.

Binary notions are not unique to those who suffer from psychological disorders. For many deeply religious people, the only acceptable relationship to the world is one of unquestioning "right" and "wrong," as defined by their sacred canons. When Professor Close mentioned in 2005 that he "hadn't yet figured out how the religious aspect of terrorist thinking could be paralleled or tied into Kinkel's school shooting," my suggestion was that religion might be defined as "whatever a person thinks about most." Kip claimed he didn't believe in God, yet even those who declare themselves atheists may find their thoughts continually turning to one particular obsession—be it money, sex, food, health, a political cause, or dreams of revenge. That becomes the basis for their fanaticism. For Kip, weapons were his ideology.

Still, we wonder what it is in their makeup or upbringing that leads a few young people to embrace and dwell in a dark culture of death, while countless others follow a far more optimistic path toward personal fulfillment, social interaction, and a dedication to the betterment of mankind. Is it intelligence, instinct, spirituality, external guidance, or common sense that enables some people to patiently consider all the options, and others to see "no other choice"? One thing is certain: how we each learn to deal with the vicissitudes of life is a process that starts at the earliest stages of childhood.

From puberty, Kip couldn't stand being without some kind of weapon on his person or near at hand at every moment. Since second grade, he'd risked bringing knives to school and kept a collection of them under his bed. Adam Pearse and Tony McCown recalled the day a bunch of the guys did a sleepover and decided to play a trick on Kip by hiding his precious hunting knife under a sofa. Furious, Kip ran to the kitchen, grabbed a butcher knife, and came at them. The boys retreated to a bedroom, but Kip went ballistic and was screaming, "Give me my knife back!" as he stabbed desperately through the locked door. Genuinely frightened, his friends told him where to locate his missing treasure. As soon as Kip retrieved it, he immediately calmed down, as if he'd regained possession of his "security blanket."

Kip's knives, bombs, and guns were the possessions that gave meaning to his life and formed the core of his religion. The intolerable thought of these totems of power being forcibly taken away was enough to provoke his decision to commit both homicide and suicide.

When we analyze the components of intermittent explosive disorder, a binary mind, and extinction behavior, there seems to be substance enough to explain Kip's rampage even without the addition of any deeper psychosis. If these reasons are sufficient to cause a boy to snap into a killer rage, how, then, can we recognize others among our student population who are suffering from similar afflictions? If late onset antisocial kids can hide their symptoms so well, what subtle signs might alert us to potential dangers?

According to the FBI, often signs are not so subtle. Their research shows 95 percent of school shooters tell friends about their toxic plans, often quite explicitly. Parents may not be picking up on these signals, but many of the kids certainly are. What they're prepared to do with that information becomes the crucial factor.

Chapter 16

Hit List

I have it all and I have no choice *but to*
I'll make everyone pay and you will see
You can kill yourself now because you're dead in my mind
The boy that you loved is the monster you fear.
　　　　　　—Marilyn Manson, "Man That You Fear"

When Kip Kinkel attacked Thurston, it was the first high school shooting in Oregon history. There had, however, been a college campus shooting at the University of Oregon's Autzen Stadium, in Eugene, on Veterans Day, 1984. Michael E. Feher, a university dropout who was dressed in camouflage clothing and black face paint, began firing at random. First he shot and killed Christopher Brathwaite, thirty-six, a former Olympic sprinter who was jogging near the stadium. Eleven other athletes were working out and one of them, a twenty-two-year-old college wrestler ranked fourth in the nation, was slightly wounded before Feher committed suicide. As odd as it sounds, Rick O'Shea was hit by a ricochet bullet that grazed his leg and neck.

Feher had tried to kill himself at the same site in July of that year, so there was a prelude to his action. Were there similar forewarnings before other attacks? Jeff Weise, Kip Kinkel, and scores of others broadcast their alarming intentions to dozens of friends, yet few took them seriously.

In 1997, sixteen-year-old Evan Ramsey's pals did believe his threats, but they still did nothing about it. In fact, a few helped him carry it off and others luridly came along just to watch. One even planned to photograph the shooting as it took place.

Evan was a relentlessly bullied sophomore at the Bethel Regional High School in remote Bethel, Alaska. He'd been wanting revenge for the grief he'd suffered, so when Principal Ron Edwards confiscated his Discman, Ramsey decided to get it back at gunpoint. Evan shared his strategy with a number of friends, saying that "he was going to go in and get it, and then he was going to start shooting and wasn't going to stop until it was all over," according to Sergeant Marrs, who investigated the incident.

Two of Evan's closest friends became intimately involved in planning the carnage. One of them showed Ramsey how to load and fire his foster brother's 12-gauge shotgun the day before Evan brought it to school. A second friend suggested that they take pictures of the event. At the given time, the designated photographer carried his camera up to a balcony that overlooked the agreed-upon location, but in his excitement, he forgot to use it until "nearly the end."

Ramsey strode into the common area of his school on February 19, pulled out his gun, and shouted, "Why didn't everyone just leave me alone?" as he circled the cafeteria like a caged tiger. Popular basketball player Josh Palacios, aware of the danger, but hoping to defuse it, got up from his table and approached Ramsey, saying, "What are you doing with that gun?" Evan held no grudge against Palacios; in fact, there were other boys, his real tormentors, whom he would have shot unhesitatingly—had they been there. They weren't, but Josh was, and so Evan opened fire, shooting the sports hero in the stomach.

More than twenty eyewitnesses whom Evan had told to be there in order to observe his "evil day" had congregated up on the mezzanine above. Why there? Evan had specified, "Don't be in the main lobby. It will be a bad day." As if they were spectators in a miniature Roman Coliseum, all who'd gathered watched as Ramsey cut down Palacios, and then saw him shoot Principal Ron Edwards, who'd tried to approach Evan from behind. Edwards's wife happened to be there, and she cradled her husband as he died in her arms. Palacios also lay dead, and two other students were wounded. Unlike Kip and some other shooters, Evan didn't beg to be killed, although his original intention had been suicide. Instead, he fled to a nearby stairwell and shouted several times, "I don't want to die!"

Ramsey later claimed he intended only to scare three of his tormentors, but his friends convinced him to expand his list to fourteen targets, including Principal Edwards. They also suggested he take stronger measures than just spooking people by showing off a gun. They said he should use it. Ramsey had been talking about killing only himself, but his pals suggested that as long as he was considering taking himself out, why not take along a few others he disliked?

He wasn't hard to convince, seeing as how it was the same half-dozen kids who'd been beating him up, spitting at him, ridiculing him, and bullying him on a daily basis. Most teachers looked the other way, and when he attempted to explain his pain to the principal, he was told, "Try to ignore it." He tried to abide taunts of "you've got shit for brains," "stupid motherfucker," "homo," and "faggot," but being called "half-breed" hurt the most. The Division of Family and Youth Services had taken Evan and his brothers away from their Native American mother when he was in third grade, due to her inveterate alcoholism. For the next three years, the boys were placed in eleven different foster homes. In half of them, Evan claims, he was physically, sexually, or verbally abused.

This may explain where his anger came from, but it cannot justify killing. Ramsey was convicted as an adult on double counts of murder and sentenced to two consecutive ninety-nine-year terms. The pair of fourteen-year-olds who helped in the planning were charged as juveniles with complicity and first-degree murder.

Clay Shrout (chapter One) also shared with friends a detailed plot to execute an English teacher about three months before he slaughtered his family. He said the teacher had been picking on him and gave him poor grades. His best pal, Richard Brown, later told police that Clay "described how he was going to walk into her fifth-period class, calmly sit down, wait awhile, then pull out the gun and kill her, right in class." Shrout fantasized that afterward, he'd run away with a girl he liked and just disappear.

It took many more deaths before enough kids finally got the message that they were saving their own lives and those of their friends by taking these threats seriously and telling someone in authority. Unfortunately, the shooting at Thurston High took place long before this awareness really kicked in.

In considering the warnings Kip dispensed to classmates, we may decry the naiveté of those who heard him, yet never reported the danger. In juxtaposition with current teen standards, however, Kip's remarks become almost commonplace. For example, on the day of Kip's infamous bomb-making speech, a girl in that same class gave a talk on how to join the Church of Satan. By comparison, Kip's subject didn't seem overly bizarre. As appropriate topics for speech class, bomb-making tips and Satanism may seem a far cry from the traditions of an earlier era, but they're routine for a generation brought up on slasher films, adult Web sites, violent TV, and first-person-shooter video games. For those readers who don't live in close proximity to adolescents with a chip of rebellion on their shoulders, we may forget that love, sex, death, and violence are just channels young people surf through on the television of their inner minds. These items are fun for them to watch or play, but the realities, commitments, and responsibilities involved in those subjects have not really taken hold.

The proudly offensive language that contemporary youth revels in, brought to an "art" of sorts by "gangsta rap," illustrates how far we've traveled toward a moral wasteland in a half century of increasingly unethical mass-media saturation. Today, a general acceptance of obscene jargon has gained laissez-faire legitimacy if not outright approval in popular media, where it's often coupled with scenes of astounding violence. Even within this context, however, it's still surprising to learn the degree to which Kip's forewarnings progressed without provoking alarm. His extraordinarily graphic messages escalated as the date of his actual attack approached. After the event, interviews from the bloody scene carried hints of what would later become a flood of confessional data about threats heard and ignored.

For example, Aaron Keeney admitted in police interviews that he knew Kip had "lots" of thirty-round clips for his rifle, had viewed several of his guns, and had heard about, not seen, Kip's bombs. Korey Ewert contradicted those statements in an interview with Eugene police, claiming that Aaron "was also involved in the manufacture of bombs and explosive devices," and had assisted Kip in breaking into a storage shed where "black powder, fuses, and other explosive materials" were kept. Ewert added, "Keeney had in the past hidden bomb-making supplies, such as fuses and black powder, underneath his dresser in his bedroom." Police searched Aaron Keeney's premises and found nothing.

Aaron was the son of the man whose gun Korey had stolen. Minutes after the shooting in the cafeteria, head counselor Richard Bushnell had run into Aaron just outside school as he and a friend arrived on bicycles. "Kinkel had told him he was going to do something like this," Bushnell reported later. The same expression was echoed by dozens of others, including student Robbie Johnson, who told reporters, "He always said that it would be fun to kill someone and do stuff like that. Yesterday, he told a couple of people he was probably going to do something stupid today, and get back at the people who had expelled him."

Kari Stoddard was one of several students to whom Kip had boasted that he wanted to become "the next Unabomber." Kip claimed he could already make the same kind of bombs Ted Kaczynski had fabricated, but his abilities now had surpassed those of the infamous American terrorist.

Generalized threats are one thing, detailed plans are another. During Kip's 1999 sentencing hearing, District Attorney Kent Mortimore presented a specific list of assault strategies that Kinkel had articulated to his classmates. "Two weeks before these shootings, he told his friend Brandon Muniz that he wanted to lock the doors except for one, put a bomb in the cafeteria, and then pick people off, one by one, after the bomb exploded and they tried to escape," Mortimore told the packed courtroom. "Jesse Thorn overheard him on May twentieth (the day he was arrested for the stolen gun) saying he would lock the two front doors in the cafeteria, shoot everyone who tried to get out the back door, run down the hallway to the girls' locker room, climb up on some vending machines, and gain access to the roof where he would snipe at people."

These very graphic and precise descriptions of plans, so similar to the reality of what later took place, give us a clue as to what Kip's full intentions may have been—had he not been tackled by those seven intrepid students who brought him down. At the same time, it's disturbing to discover that such clear-cut statements of intent could be so totally dismissed by Kip's acquaintances, even given Kip's history of mockery. Indeed, more than a few of Kip's comrades suffered taunts during the following weeks for what was perceived as their silent acquiescence to Kip's deadly designs. Brandon Muniz and Destry Saul caught additional flak because Kinkel had tried to buy a gun from each of them earlier (both refused). Destry's family considered getting a lawyer to represent him because he'd "said too much" to police about what he'd known of Kip's schemes—as if telling the truth is now a bad thing.

For every student who described Kip as "scary," there were others who portrayed him as such an invariable joker that they never took anything he said seriously. In their defense, it should be pointed out that, not only among school shooters, but also in the case of many serial killers, snipers, mass murderers, and terrorists, that friends and family members often describe the perpetrator as "such a nice person" prior to the crime. Only later are acquaintances shocked to learn that someone they thought they knew so well was in reality a totally perverse individual.

During his research, Professor Dan Close had many opportunities to confront career criminals. He concluded there were several factors common to almost every offender he encountered. "You'll often find that some of the most horrendous people guilty of the most ghastly crimes were wonderful to their moms, pleasant to their neighbors, nonobtrusive to their coworkers, and kind to their friends," he said, "but none of that is accidental. Every single act in their lives is committed with the sole purpose of gaining some advantage. In the case of their 'being nice' to those around them, the advantage is that they're establishing 'plausible deniability.' Their socialization is task-oriented. They are compartmentalizing their relationships, one by one, for the sake of manipulation, true to the nature of their binary minds.

"The basic flaw of this thinking," Close continued, "is that, while others are easily deceived, it's also self-deluding. They take a position, believe it, and act upon it without regard for the fundamental laws or rules of society, defying the most universally shared values of mankind. At the same time, they blame those they attack for not understanding them. This 'extrapunitive' position allows them to minimize their victims as well. By the time everyone realizes this, it's too late." Considering these aspects of the criminal mind and its power to exploit those around them, it's easy to understand why at Thurston, and in countless other cases, there were so many people—Kip's parents included—who underestimated the destruction that was about to befall them.

After it was revealed that Kip's threats were already known to a number of students prior to the catastrophe, journalists on May 22 asked Chief DeForrest, "Do you know if anyone at all inside the cafeteria was targeted yesterday in this random shooting?" The police chief replied, "I have no information that would lead us to believe that any specific students were targeted."

That statement was true only for those *inside* the cafeteria. Every student shot there was simply a target of convenience in the wrong place at the wrong time. The two particular boys Kip had recently held a grudge against and supposedly intended to shoot were not there that day. One of them was Jacob Sisler, the school football star. He would later be voted the team's Most Valuable Player and go on to college football fame; but Sisler was absent on May 21, later claiming he overslept. When Kip's room was searched, police found a photo of the football team. Sisler's name was underlined, his face circled in black ink, and a piece of paper with the word "kill" had been taped to it. Next to it was a student locator card, with Jacob's home address, courses, teachers, and classrooms. Handwritten on the card was *I hate myself and want to die,* and beside that a black note which read, *You're gonna blow up and die.*

Why the animosity against this particular boy? Jacob was interviewed by a private investigator just over a year later. Although his mother had recalled in an earlier interview a verbal altercation between her son and Kip, Jacob now denied that ever happened. He allowed that he frequently drove past the Kinkel residence on visits to his girlfriend Allana's home. Allana was a neighbor of the Kinkels, had known Kip for years, and distrusted him. Kip told friends he himself was "interested in" Allana and he resented Jacob, whom he called "a stuck-up jock" for "hustling in" on her. Kip's antagonism was expressed clearly to his buddies—according to whom, Kip "talked quite a bit about wanting to hurt Mr. Sisler a lot, including killing him."

After his arrest for murder, Kip told Dr. Bolstad that one time Sisler had slowed his car long enough to say, "You're Kip Kinkel, I'm going to kick your ass." (Sisler claimed he couldn't recall ever having spoken to Kip, although they were both on the football team.) Kip said he didn't know why Jacob disliked him, but surmised it might stem from his reputation for being dangerous. He wondered if Sisler wasn't a bit scared of him. Then he said, "I really hated that guy." Bolstad wondered if these events were real or part of Kip's paranoid delusions, but his patient added another piece of information that made more sense. Kip told the doctor that his dad, a football fan, held Sisler up as an ideal. Bill Kinkel would say, "Why can't you play [or run] as fast as him?"

These particulars seem to offer corroboration that Korey was telling the truth on May 20 when he said Kip was targeting someone. But there was more. In the three hours between the murder of Kip's dad and mom, he spent part of that time in a three-way conference call with buddies Tony McCown and Nick Hiaasen. During the call, Kip alternated between indignation and being upset over his expulsion. In an angry outburst, he asked his pals if they knew who he "really hates," then declared it was Brian Havelock.

Nick and Tony knew why. Brian, a baseball team member, had recently come over to Kip in the cafeteria and "called him a faggot. Kip didn't react in any way, shape, or form, and, in fact," said Tony, "he didn't say a word." The two boys on the phone now told Kip not to worry and joked they would help beat Havelock up the next day, since Kip wouldn't be in school. "No, I'm going to kill him. Tell him I want him dead. And scream it in his face!" Kip shouted, agitated now. The other two boys urged Kip to settle down. "If we tell him that," Tony said, "you know how much trouble you'll be in, since you had the gun with you at school?" Kip became calm then, and responded, "Yeah, I know, forget it." The prosecution later pointed out the obvious chill factor here—Kip uttered a death threat "just after he's committed a murder."

Kip also said several times in the call that he had a "hit list," which included others besides Brian. This kind of talk, however, was nothing new to Kip's two associates, who'd heard it all before. Whereas a majority of school shooters were frequently bullied, Kip's experience of being the victim of such taunts was minimal, probably less than what passes for "normal" in many schools. Instead, he was more often the one who intimidated others. Kip had issued a similar death threat against student Josh Metzger during the previous spring break after verbally harassing the boy and putting him in a headlock. He'd also told classmate Cheyenne Houghton that he was going to kill him because he found him "annoying." He wrote in the boy's Spanish book, *I will hunt you down and put a hole in your head with explosives. You must die. Have a nice day.*

McCown later said, "Kip teased and laughed at other kids, but the one thing he hated most was being laughed at himself." One time at school, Tony put gum in Kip's hair as a prank. Kip was cutting it off with a pair of scissors, but he got frustrated and began crying. Some classmates started laughing at him, mocking, "He's crying! Crybaby! Crybaby!" Kip went berserk. Someone had to pay for this humiliation, and Kip saw Tony as the instigator. Kip claimed later his voices suddenly kicked in again at this point, telling him, "Stab 'em! Get 'em!" Filled with rage, he came at Tony with the scissors, point first.

Tony, larger physically, said, "I wasn't really scared, more like surprised. I just took the scissors from his hand, not too roughly. But it made me think." Kip had exposed his vulnerable, sensitive side when he cried, and hearing kids laugh at that played into his worst fears.

During the three-way call, Kip reiterated many times to Tony and Nick that he was nervous about how his parents would look in front of their colleagues when everyone found out about his expulsion, how Bill and Faith would lose face and be terribly shamed. Tony could imagine Kip pacing back and forth and constantly looking out the window as he kept repeating, "Where's my mom . . . when's she gonna be home?" Kip explained to them he was worried she'd hear something from other teachers at the retirement party she was at, and he wanted to be the one to tell her himself.

In fact, she had heard—Bill had telephoned Faith at the end of her lunch break. A graduate assistant was asked to take over her next class for a few minutes while she took the call. Faith returned to her classroom, looking anxious and puzzled, not at all like her usual exuberant self. "Thanks for taking my class," she told the assistant. "You're a lifesaver!" The younger woman never forgot those final words.

Faith said nothing to friends at the party she attended after school, but her reaction later was revealing. On the drive home, she stopped at an Albertsons supermarket, and at the checkout, she recognized a cashier, who happened to be the daughter of a Thurston High employee. To the surprised girl, Faith released a few caustic remarks against "that damned Dick Doyle" for so unfairly "throwing her son out of school."

If her first reflex was anger, however, her secondary response was more pragmatic. Somewhere between the supermarket and her home, Faith may have used a cell phone to seek outside help. Just as her husband's final phone call that day had been to solicit support from the Oregon National Guard's Youth Challenge camp, it's possible Faith's final call was to a hotline known as Parents Anonymous. A crisis call-taker there named Tina Murry reported to police that an unidentified woman telephoned sometime between 6:00 and 6:30 P.M., asking for advice on how to deal with her fifteen-year-old son who was "heavy into guns, had been in trouble with police in the past for minor infractions, and was now in trouble at school." Since she got very few calls about kids with guns, Murry remembered the woman as sounding "mature and well-educated, able to express her thoughts in a clear and concise manner." The anonymous caller said she was afraid her son, whom she dearly loved, might grow up to become a criminal, and she wanted to intervene. Murry's advice was to contact a program such as Tough Love, Scared Straight, or another boot-camp-style environment. Ironically, that is exactly what Bill Kinkel had tried and failed to do three hours earlier.

While this call may have been taking place, McCown was trying to encourage his friend on the phone to remain optimistic. Every time he did so, Kip repeated, "Tony, you don't understand. It's over. . . . Everything's over. . . . It's done. There's nothing we can do about it. . . . Nothing matters now." Only later did McCown connect "it's done" with Bill's death. Once Kip had shot the first bullet, everything that followed was preordained in his mind.

After multiple confessions by students to police and the press immediately following the shootings, denials came close on their heels. It came as no surprise that in an interview with Eugene police officer Sergeant Mark Montes a few hours after the shooting on May 21, Korey Ewert now admitted only that Kip had said "on several occasions that it would be cool to shoot people," and added that he "never took those statements seriously due to Kip's sense of humor."

Ewert also told Sergeant Montes "that he didn't know of any plan by Kip to go to school and injure anybody," and that, in fact, "the sale of the gun was because Kip wanted a handgun for protection, due to the fact that his parents had taken all his guns away from him."

Korey finally specified to Sergeant Montes that he "wasn't aware of any list of friends or associates targeted by Kip." In short, Korey told a different story the day of the massacre than he had one day earlier, and it doesn't take a rocket scientist to figure out why. As the boy who stole the weapon, Korey was in a very tight situation. At the time of his May 21 interview, he was facing prosecution for selling a stolen handgun to Kip on the day before his friend would shoot fellow students. Korey would have had tremendous motivation to "edit" his May 20 commentaries. His family couldn't afford the advice of a lawyer, but with both his stepfather and an uncle working for the Lane County Sheriff's Office (LCSO), resources were available to at least raise the possibility that his police interview could have been coached beforehand. However, his statements were not sworn testimony, and even if he withheld the complete truth, it's doubtful he'd broken any law.

CNN correspondent Greg Lefevre commented toward the close of the May 22 press conference, "They go back over and over again, and they ask the same questions: What could we have done? Were there signs we should have seen?" The greater damage produced by those who denied the truth of what they knew before the event, or who changed their stories out of fear of repercussions, was that they helped perpetuate the myth that there was "no way of knowing and no warning signs." This fallacy helped lay the groundwork for Columbine and all that followed.

Among those students who knew Kip well, some may still feel a measure of guilt or regret for lacking the sensitivity to discern his genuine anguish, lacking the vigilance to recognize the very real danger, or lacking the courage to do something about it. In the final analysis, however, it was Kip, and only Kip, who pulled the trigger.

Chapter 17

Who Knew?

I didn't tell anybody because, who would have believed me?
—Friend of Clay Shrout, who had told him
a month earlier he was planning to shoot
his English teacher on May 26, 1994

Whether or not Korey Ewert was the only boy to disclose Kip's secret to any adults before the massacre, there were plenty of others who heard Kip talk openly about his deadly intentions. "Complicity by inaction" was the informal charge leveled against many of those who at their own peril chose to discount Kip's "boasts" about the gruesome crimes he was about to commit. A few admitted they believed Kip, but they were too afraid of him to confide in responsible adults. Some simply didn't want to get involved. Others figured he was just kidding. Most, however, were simply observing the unspoken student "code of silence" by which to "inform, squeal, rat, snitch or narc" on any classmate is a peer violation of the highest magnitude.

This same pattern also occurred in almost every other school shooting to date. In the years following Thurston and Columbine, students in many other locales still believed the illusion that "it can't happen here." That was certainly the case at Santana High in Santee, California, on March 5, 2001. After fifteen-year-old Charles "Andy" Williams killed two students and wounded thirteen in an eight-minute shooting spree, classmates admitted, "He told us he was going to bring a gun to school . . . but we thought he was joking." Kids need to realize that joking about a school shooting is like joking about a bomb in your hand luggage at the airport security screening. It's no joke, and *every* threat is serious.

Andy's best friend, Josh Stevens, reported that the shooter bragged all weekend he was going to do this on Monday, and even invited his friends to join in. "I didn't want to get him in trouble if he was just kidding," Josh said, adding that Andy was "not the kind of kid to do something like this." Student Vanessa Willis, warned by Williams to stay home that day, confessed, "I said, 'Whatever.' I didn't take him serious."

On the morning of Andy's attack, a few friends were concerned enough to search him for weapons before class. "You're not gonna do a Columbine?" they asked as they frisked him, but they neglected to check his backpack, where the gun was hidden.

The undersized ninth grader, who'd only moved to California from Maryland the previous summer, was often mocked as a "dork, freak, and nerd." Bullies stole his skateboard, and even the shoes off his feet. Survivors said Andy was smiling as he fired his father's Arminius long-rifle revolver, and the thrill of revenge may have been the reason. On the other hand, several school shooters have been described as having "a maniacal grin." Those who escaped from the carnage at Red Lake Chippewa Reservation in 2005 said gunman Jeff Weise was "grinning and waving at a student his gun was pointed at." Then he swiveled to shoot someone else. Witnesses at Columbine said Harris and Klebold were giggling and laughing triumphantly as they meted out death. One student described them as "like, orgasmic." A girl sobbed as she told a reporter: "He put the gun right in my face and started laughing and said it was because people were mean to him last year."

After police arrived at Santana High, they charged into the boys' bathroom and found Williams kneeling on the floor holding the loaded revolver. "It's only me," Andy said as he surrendered. It would've been nice if that statement were true, but in the first forty-eight hours following Andy's rampage, twenty-three American children were arrested or detained for threatening various acts of copycat violence at their schools. (In the month after Columbine, the number was close to four hundred!) Among the suspects were three students from the California School for the Deaf, a fifteen-year-old Catholic schoolboy from Davenport, Iowa, and a fifteen-year-old honor student from Camden, New Jersey, who threatened to kill off a high school clique during woodshop class.

In Twentynine Palms, California, seventeen-year-old Victoria Sudd watched the Santee horror unfold and then told her mom that she'd heard two boys talking on the bus about killing people. Sudd's father contacted the authorities, who quickly obtained search warrants. The cops found a rifle and a list of sixteen students whom the boys had targeted. Far from being ridiculed as a tattler, Sudd was hailed as a heroine. Fellow students hugged her and the city honored her.

Then on March 22, 2001, less than three weeks after Williams's rampage, another student opened fire just six miles away from Santana High at a school in El Cajon. Jason Hoffman, an eighteen-year-old with a shaved head, got out of his car, assumed a sniper position, and began shooting at fellow students outside Granite Hills High, wounding two boys, a girl, and two female teachers before police shot and wounded him. Student Esme Agiler, fifteen, told reporters soon after, "I didn't think that anything like that could happen here, because I thought it was over with Santana High. I thought people had learned, but obviously they haven't."

Media maker Danny Ledonne wrote, "Kids need to trust parents and school officials enough to warn them when an acquaintance is veering toward the edge, and shake off the mind-set that 'it can't happen here.' It can and it does." But this has been a learning curve with a long trajectory. Prior to these two San Diego shootings, a vigilant eighteen-year-old girl in California made headlines by preventing an attack that should have increased statewide awareness of the ongoing danger. Kelly Bennett, whose father is a police officer, worked in the photo lab of a San Jose drugstore. Pictures she developed of a young customer posing with his arsenal of explosives and guns alarmed her. She showed the photos to authorities, who searched the home of Al DeGuzman, nineteen, a student at De Anza Community College. They found thirty pipe bombs, twenty Molotov cocktails, and a small armory of other weapons and ammunition. They also turned up a Web site DeGuzman had created on which he praised the Columbine shooters and lashed out at his own school, his classmates, and all ethnic groups, including his own, Filipino-Americans. It turned out that for nearly two years DeGuzman had been planning to plant bombs in the school's main cafeteria at 4:30 A.M., on January 30, 2001, and set them off around lunchtime. He was arrested on January 29, a very close call indeed.

Between that date and Santee, there were a number of other averted attacks across the nation. During eight days in February, there were four. On February 6, three students were charged with planning a Columbine-style massacre at Royal Valley High, in Hoyt, Kansas. Richard Bradley Jr., eighteen, was charged with conspiracy to commit murder. Two juveniles, aged sixteen and seventeen, faced charges of conspiring to use explosives and witness intimidation. Police found firearms, including a modified assault rifle, four hundred rounds of ammunition, bomb-making materials, bomb recipe books and computer discs, and a hand-drawn floor plan of their high school. They also found white supremacist and Nazi drawings and three black trench coats, similar to those worn by Klebold and Harris. A student's tip triggered the arrests.

Two days later, Colorado residents were appalled to learn that lightning could strike twice, just sixty miles from Columbine. Three ninth-grade teenagers were charged with a plot to commit mayhem at Preston Junior High, in Fort Collins. The conspiracy involved two fourteen-year-olds, one of whom said he'd been picked on and made an outcast, and a fifteen-year-old. Once again, police found weapons and plans to reenact the Columbine carnage on its second anniversary in April.

On February 11, sheriff's deputies arrested a Palm Harbor Middle School eighth grader in Florida after finding a partially assembled bomb in his bedroom. Fourteen-year-old Scott McClain had written detailed e-mails to two friends in which he described plans to detonate the bomb at school the next day. His bomb-making info came off the Internet.

Finally, on Valentine's Day, student Jeremy Getman, eighteen, was arrested in Elmira, New York, after he carried bombs and guns into the Southside High cafeteria. Getman had a gym bag containing fourteen pipe bombs, three smaller bombs, a propane bomb, and a sawed-off shotgun. He was armed with a loaded .22-caliber Ruger pistol. He was stopped because a female classmate turned in a threatening note Getman had given her.

In total, between April 1998 and April 2001, it's estimated that over four dozen school attacks were averted, some at the last moment, because of information passed on by alert students. After 9/11, the numbers of both school shootings and arrested students declined, but they did not disappear.

The "reawakening" (as it might be called) of school shootings, at Red Lake, Minnesota, in March 2005, contained many familiar elements, but some of them seemed out of place. For example, Jeff Weise was not a Caucasian from a comfortable two-parent home, like so many other shooters, but neither was he an inner-city delinquent. This was an area of down-and-out rural deprivation, where boredom and substance abuse ran high. Of the 355 students—all of them Native American—at Red Lake High, 81 percent lived in poverty, 23 percent were in special education, and the graduation rate was just 57 percent.

While many previous young killers, like Luke Woodham and Harris and Klebold, admired Hitler and the tenets of Fascism, the fact that Weise was also attracted to Nazism was curious, to say the least. After all, as a member of a minority group, Jeff was more likely to be targeted than embraced by white supremacists. As it turned out, however, the aspect of Hitler's National Socialist movement that most appealed to Weise was racial purity.

In the chat room of a pro-Nazi Web site he wrote: [*The teachers*] *don't openly say that racial purity is wrong, yet when you speak your mind on the subject you get "silenced" real quick by the teachers and like-minded school officials.* He claimed that when he talked in school about maintaining the tribe's ethnic purity by not marrying outside the bloodline, *I get the same old argument which seems to be so common around here. "We need to mix all the races, to combine all the strengths."*

Weise used two aliases online: "NativeNazi" and "Todesengel," which meant "angel of death" in German. Under these pen names, Jeff wrote, *I guess I've always carried a natural admiration for Hitler and his ideals, and his courage to take on larger nations.* Another posting said, *When I was growing up, I was taught that Nazis were evil and that Hitler was a very evil man. Of course, not for a second did I believe this. Upon reading up on his actions, the ideals and issues the German Third Reich addressed, I began to see how much of a lie had been painted about them. They truly were doing it for the better.*

On April 19, 2004, Weise referred online to being questioned by police as a suspect: *I'm being blamed for a threat on the school I attend, because someone said they were going to shoot up the school on 4/20, Hitler's birthday, and just because I claim being a National Socialist, guess whom they've pinned in.* Five weeks later, he said he was cleared, but he described with obvious delight the fuss at school when dozens of FBI and police turned up. Regrettably, they were premature.

Harris and Klebold had not randomly chosen the date of April 20 for their grisly butchery. The Columbine massacre was their way of honoring Hitler's birthday (although earlier they'd also considered the joint Waco, Texas /Oklahoma City bombing anniversary of April 19). Both boys enjoyed speaking in German and wearing swastikas, and a shout of "Heil Hitler!" would issue from their mouths when the two would get a strike while bowling. As mentioned earlier, this infatuation with Nazism was reprised in materials found at the homes of those Hoyt, Kansas, students arrested in 2001. If the object, after all, is to offend as many of your peers as possible, and to make a statement against contemporary society, what better way than to embrace the twentieth century's most abhorrent political leader and one of its worst mass murderers? Or, perhaps, one of his deputies—it was discovered that German shooter Robert Steinhäuser (chapter 26), a neo-Nazi, may have chosen April 26 for his 2002 shooting, which killed more people than Columbine, as a tribute to Rudolf Hess, whose birth anniversary fell on that date.

Chippewa tribal leaders at Red Lake knew little of Jeff Weise's background and lead-up to his rampage. Treasurer Darrell Seki described the tribe's feelings after the shooting as "terrible. We see things like this happen outside the reservation, but now it's happened here, in our home. It's an awful situation." Floyd Jourdain Jr., chairman of the Indian Council, told the press, "Our community is devastated by this event," and called it, "the darkest day in the history of our tribe."

It was an ironic turn of phrase, for Floyd's son Louis Jourdain, sixteen, was a member of a clique of about five students known as "the Darkers," who wore Goth-style black clothes and chains, spiked or dyed their hair, and loved heavy-metal music. Jeff Weise was also a member. Just over a week later, Louis was arrested and charged as an adult with conspiracy to commit murder. E-mails that police had found suggested Weise and Jourdain planned the school attack together. Their computer conversations included vivid discussions about logistics and targets. Louis couldn't deny the electronic evidence, but he told investigators he'd never had any real intention of going through with it. Up until it happened, he said, he didn't believe Weise would, either. So says every boy who is caught.

On January 13, 2006, Louis Jourdain, now seventeen, was sentenced in Minneapolis. The original charge was dropped in a plea agreement that also allowed Louis to be sentenced on a lesser charge as a juvenile. The sentence terms were not revealed because, as a juvenile case, it became a closed-court hearing. However, Floyd Jourdain Jr. later told reporters that the judge's ruling proves that his son is a "good kid" who was not directly involved in the shooting and "never intended any harm to anyone."

Still, federal prosecutors revealed that a total of thirty-nine people knew of Jeff Weise's planned school shooting beforehand, but told no one, and that at least four classmates had very specific knowledge of his intentions. Have we learned anything since then? Well, yes. On April 25, 2006, *another* student on the same reservation was arrested for planning a new attack. This time, someone spoke up and stopped him.

• Chapter 18 •

Acceptable Murder

*We, as a society, have become systematically desensitized
to the pain and suffering of others. . . . We are reaching
the stage at which the inflicting of pain and suffering has
become a source of entertainment: vicarious pleasure rather
than revulsion. We are learning to kill, and we are learning to like it.*

—Lieutenant Colonel Dave Grossman (ret.), *On Killing*

One of the most shocking aspects concerning the aftermath of nearly
every school shooting is that fan clubs of like-minded young people
spring up, mostly on the Internet, dedicated to honoring the murderers. After the 2006 murder of Principal John Klang by student Eric
Hainstock (chapter 15) in Wisconsin, Klang's wife, Sue, told how the
young killer's many supporters posted messages saying her husband
deserved what he got for not stopping bullies from harassing Eric.
Bullying is a terrible thing, but to suggest that it justifies shooting
an administrator is insane. Sue herself was harassed with anonymous
notes telling her to quit feeling sorry for herself, and that she was
a poor excuse for a Christian because she favored adult court for
Hainstock.

Thurston was not immune to this trend. Wounded student Jacob
Ryker was outraged by such messages and could not fathom why it
was happening. In court, turning toward Kip, he asked, "Why was
it when I got out of the hospital, when I was trying to recover, I received hate mail? Why was it that Internet fan sites were set up—

for you? Why is it people are writing me, telling me how much they loved what you did? And why is it that I had to be the enemy? I don't understand. I don't pretend to understand."

To answer Jacob's questions, one must examine factors that influence contemporary thinking. The most ubiquitous is electronic mass media. News coverage designed to inform us of terrible events, such as school shootings, and awaken our sympathies for the victims has the opposite effect on a few aberrant juvenile minds that identify with the shooter's alienation, applaud his actions, and find in him a worthy role model. Rather than being repulsed by the horror of these crimes, some teens view these young killers as heroes fighting the same anxieties they themselves face—bullying, isolation, uncaring adults, and rejection by the opposite sex. Dylan Klebold's parents said their son was set off by the "toxic culture" of Columbine High, where athletes were worshiped and bullying was tolerated.

As Jake Ryker sensed, a few students view school shootings with a kind of pleasure. Why? One theory: Consider the legions of adolescents who adore superhero comic books and films. What's the appeal? The teenager identifies with the hero, imagining what he (the reader) could do if magically granted those same superpowers. If the student has been picked on or bullied, those abilities could be directed against one's tormentors. In reality, the comic or film fan knows he'll never be able to fly, be invisible, or have superstrength, but owning a gun can give him power over life and death. Guns make real the daydream of "What if I possessed a superpower mighty enough to frighten those who frighten me?" But power is a potent drug that few adolescents can handle well. It takes wisdom and experience to know how to use it, and not be seduced by it.

At their best, cinema, music, the Internet, and video games can educate, inform, and inspire us, filling our hearts as well as our minds. Movies, which for five generations have been a great escape from the harsher realities of existence, are now heightened by brilliant sound, brighter images, and stunning special effects that stretch the boundaries of imagination. The big screen adds a shared communal experience to the adventure, allowing us to be part of an audience that laughs, screams, and sighs together in the anonymity of a darkened theater, and reassures us that all of our orchestrated emotions are in synch with one other. We belong. While some filmmakers respect this opportunity to offer us thoughtful and profound cinema, others exploit the medium, emphasizing a shallow or nonexistent sense of values in how they present images of sex, violence, and gore.

Does violent media truly encourage violent behavior? Definitely. This has been demonstrated in numerous case studies. Should media be blamed for violent behavior? Only partially and very selectively. As matters stand, the vows of media producers to maintain codes of decency are repeatedly compromised by bottom-line profits. Bloodshed, brutality, vulgarly presented sexuality, and rough language sell. Short of total censorship, these media products will remain permanently on the shelf. Although they may be temporarily withdrawn or toned down, a nearly constant and never-ending supply is a certainty. Since by the law of supply and demand, the supply is unlimited, all that's left to dispute is demand—our own and the demands of those within our sphere of influence. That is the only point over which we have any possibility of control. After all, if audiences did not willingly pay to see violent acts, such images would evaporate from contemporary pop media. Ultimately it is our own decisions and actions, not commands from media producers, that determine the course of our lives.

It goes without saying, however, that our decisions and actions are not always in our own best interests. Maybe it's because of our communal nostalgia for a self-reliant, frontier mentality, but many Americans seem to take pride in cultivating a rebellious streak. We have a long and (some would say) puzzling tradition in this country of making heroes out of villains. Think of Jesse James, Billy the Kid, Butch Cassidy, Bonnie and Clyde, the "Birdman" of Alcatraz, and even Al Capone, to name but a few—all of them murderers, notorious and celebrated in their time. What people admire in these reckless individuals is that they've dared to do things that others may briefly consider, but reject because they're not willing to pay the price of punishment by imprisonment or death. While we may condemn their actions, we simultaneously approve of them as rebels against the conventions of a repressive society. Obviously, the more a person feels marginalized or frustrated by their surrounding culture, the more he or she is likely to identify with these antiheroes.

Perhaps we should be more careful about whom we esteem. Although their message was malevolent, Eric Harris and Dylan Klebold achieved this same cultural resonance with many youths who iden-tified with their manifesto. At the time Columbine occurred, for in-stance, Danny Ledonne was a bullied kid in a Colorado high school. He wrote:

> I didn't fit in, and I was surrounded by a culture of elit-ism as espoused by our school's athletes. So were Eric and Dylan. Until their rampage, bullied teens had no context in which to visualize some potential retaliation. The Columbine mascot is the Rebels and, in a way, Eric and Dylan *became* that mascot. CHS created the rebels that rebelled against them, their system and the way of life they tried to inculcate. What Harris and Klebold "stood for" and what that ultimately led to were troubling, terrifying things, but nonetheless the shooters were seen by their ad-mirers in a macabre way as genuine but reckless ideo-logues.

In 2005, Ledonne created Super Columbine Massacre RPG! (SCM-RPG)—an Internet role-playing game, which has sparked strong con-demnation and even death threats. The game was Danny's way to critique the mass media's wholesale vilification of video games, rock music, and "Goth culture," to fulfill a potential for interactive elec-tronic media to confront cultural problems, to reshape the discourse on video games and school shootings, and to make a statement that would cause others to consider a different point of view.

Although Ledonne created a firestorm with his invention, his in-tentions were not to spark imitators of Columbine, but rather to probe beneath specious perceptions of where the blame lay and reach an underlying truth. He wrote:

> What really frightened people about Columbine is that it confronted America's concealed inner soul. In SCMRPG, Eric looks over downtown Denver and says, "I live in Den-ver, and God damn it, I would love to kill almost all of its residents." These words were actually written in Har-ris' journal just months before the shooting. These were upper-middle-class white males who had the potential to

do anything at all, and what they ended up wanting was
to blow it all up. How could this happen? Let's look a little deeper. Eric and Dylan were the canaries in the mine,
representing something larger than themselves that has gone
amiss. I was sorry for the killing, but at the same time it
was empowering to see two oppressed, marginalized kids
like me rise up. Maybe now the jocks and bullies would
remember what happened in Colorado and think twice—
like, what if the kid I pick on today shows up tomorrow
with a gun?

The game struck a raw nerve. Its detractors reckoned it, "a sad
and sick thing to make a video game out of a tragedy where thirteen innocent people were murdered," and "It disgusts me. You triv-
ialize the actions of two murderers and the lives of the innocent."
Its supporters included video game analysts such as Georgia Institute of Technology assistant professor Ian Bogost, who wrote, *While
it is a challenging subject, I think the effort is brave, sophisticated
and worthy of praise. . . . SCMRPG is disturbing because it is meant
to be. . . . This game is not fun, it is challenging and difficult to
play—not technically difficult, but conceptually difficult.*
Attorney Jack Thompson is a vociferous critic of the entire video
industry and has aggressively brought several lawsuits against game
makers on behalf of parents of students killed in school shootings.
Despite the seeming disparity in their views, both Thompson and
Ledonne share a surprisingly similar outlook in advocating for stronger
parental supervision of electronic media and in being outspoken critics of the society that spawned school shooters. Thompson takes a
traditionalist, conservative view. Ledonne wrote:

> Parents need to get more involved in their children's
> choices, to be there assisting them in making informed de-
> cisions about their own financial, emotional, academic, re-
> productive and spiritual lives. But parents also need to
> listen, to give young people opportunities to self-actualize
> on their own terms instead of imposing a set of cultural
> expectations they must adopt.

Each generation needs to create their own icons and their own forms of expression. Although their elders may not always understand or appreciate these manifestations, kids want to identify with someone their own age who expresses what they feel inside. When that expression is anger and rebellion, the outlet may be as "harmless" as rap music or Goth clothing, or it may be as deadly as a school shooting. By being more attuned to their feelings, we may be in a better position to influence and contribute to the choices they embrace. We can but hope that adolescents will also be prepared to hear the counsel of more experienced voices without automatically rejecting such advice.

Where Thompson and Ledonne differ is in the degree of blame that can be ascribed to media. Thompson's view is supported by psychologist Phil McGraw (TV's "Dr. Phil"), who said on *Larry King,* "Common sense tells you that if these kids are playing video games where they're on a mass killing spree, [and] it's glamorized on the big screen (i.e., movies), it's become part of the fiber of our society." But Dr. Phil qualified that with, "You take that and mix it with a psychopath, a sociopath, or someone suffering from mental illness and add in a dose of rage, the suggestibility is too high."

Ledonne concedes that if video games can teach kids geometry, they can also teach them how to aim a firearm. But he feels cable news networks and opportunistic politicians have exaggerated the risks they represent:

> While games like "Doom" may have taught the shooters how to strafe around corners while holding their shotguns, they certainly didn't create in them the desire to destroy their entire world. Rather, we ourselves have done this by saturating them in a society in which they're marginalized and rejected. Focusing the debate on violent entertainment or some shocking musician comfortably deflects the examination away from ourselves. The real answer to "Why did they do it?" implicates the core pillars of our collective identity. That's why shootings like Columbine are a painful look in the mirror—an uncomfortable perspective. Inasmuch as videogames are a tenuous part of that larger

dehumanizing force, they are culpable—though they bear no more responsibility than any of the other numbing palliatives of the consumer lifestyle obsession. To acknowledge that, is to tacitly indict the totality of society.

Well before Ledonne's game, there seemed to be a widening gulf developing between those who view violence as a last resort, and those who accept it as a legitimate way to resolve disputes, whether at a personal, local, or international level. Nowhere is this clearer than in the fan clubs that sprang up praising school shooters.

Mark Walker, father of one of the slain students at Thurston, spoke about how each attack spins off into others through approbation. "Just a short time ago," Walker stated, "four young men in Cleveland were arrested for planning a school shooting. Their friends said they thought it was cool." This last sentence echoed both Andrew Wurst's and Kip Kinkel's responses to the Jonesboro shootings. It also reflects the phrase uttered by Michael Carneal in West Paducah, Kentucky, who had told schoolmates before his attack that "it would be cool" to shoot into a student prayer group.

In his book *Without Conscience*, Dr. Robert D. Hare, professor of psychology at the University of British Columbia, argues that we live in a "camouflage society" in which certain psychopathic traits—such as egocentricity, lack of concern for others, superficiality, being cool, in the sense of showing no emotion, becoming skilled at manipulation for personal gain, and so forth—are increasingly tolerated and even valued. As a society, maybe it's time we asked, when did being "cool" become equated with being cold-blooded?

Let's take a moment to focus on the significance of this, because it's essential to understanding why school shootings and other forms of terrorism committed by youths have been occurring with such regularity during the past few decades. During that time, electronic media of all sorts became so all-pervasive that its influence now easily outweighs that of parents, schools, and religion for most young people. That's a major change in how society works, and we need to recognize the deeper, long-term effect of this change. In a sense, the very things that parents worked so hard to prevent their kids getting into are the very things being made available to them in every possible way. Parents feel helpless to stem this tide, especially when they consider how it seems to be increasing exponentially each year.

No one wants to halt progress, but something very basic and of enormous consequence has been altered in both our own culture and in many nations around the world during the last quarter century. We know that every society is based upon smaller units—communities, institutions, families, and individuals—that hold in common, to some degree, a collective accumulation of shared values. Whether or not everyone adheres to these values, they are apparent in each culture's general laws, customs, and codes of conduct. Societies may recognize or even condone variations or deviations, depending upon how strictly their principles apply, but the absence of all ethical and cultural restriction is universally condemned as a formula for chaos and moral disintegration.

Until the advent of advanced and cheaply available personal electronic media, functional families were able to keep less desirable cultural elements of their surrounding environment at a tolerable distance, so long as their children were living at home. When television first appeared, most families could only afford one, which took center place in the living room, where viewing was largely a shared experience, just as radios had been until the arrival of inexpensive transistors. As America's affluence rose through the '80s and '90s, televisions in nearly every room of a house became more commonplace. Today, small TVs are even embedded in refrigerator doors or in bathroom units, and the average American watches television four and a half hours a day. At the same time, personalized portable entertainment devices evolved from Walkmans to iPods, which give individuals constant access to immediately available musical pleasure. Mobile cell phones did something similar for telecommunications and candid photography, but all these mechanisms pale beside the potential vistas opened up by personal computers and access to the Internet.

For all the benefits these electronic marvels bestowed upon humanity, their combined influence decimated the ability of parents to fully supervise the moral and ethical content of their children's lives. Many adolescents viewed this as a positive thing—a chance to achieve freedom at an earlier age, exercise their own choices, and explore the secret byways of adventure and rebellion. More mature minds took a different view, especially when it became apparent that all of these freedoms carried a price—not just the cost of the electronic device or service itself, but the fact that all of these items hold the potential for manipulation of attitudes, opinions, and beliefs.

Why else would the corporations that market these things spend millions upon millions of dollars each year influencing youngsters to demand and receive these "must-have" devices? In the battle for the hearts and minds of the young, parents are being outspent and out-maneuvered. The ability of families to maintain a moral or ethical center is challenged every waking moment of every day. The influence of parents or communities doesn't even come close to what the kids are being fed by those who don't necessarily have their best interests in mind. In the past, the negative influences of the surrounding culture were what we were trying to protect our kids from. Today, those same influences dominate adolescent development.

Throughout history, parents have been confused or flabbergasted by their teenagers' behavior—nothing new in that. One unprecedented contrast with previous generations, however, is in the disturbing lack of empathy among some of today's youth—an apparent absence of concern for the welfare of other human beings. In her book, *The War Against Boys,* author Christina Hoff Sommers ascribes this to an education system that promotes a "do your own thing" idealized "Rousseauian philosophy of ethical romanticism" rather than practical and meaningful moral education with responsible discipline. Radio talk show host Michael Medved suggests this new attitude is tied to and bolstered by violent action films and TV. Dr. Laura Schlessinger pointed out on her radio show that if an eye-catching thirty-second TV commercial can influence teenagers in their lifestyle choices, how can they claim they are *not* influenced by three hours or more of daily video game play?

The results of an Indiana University School of Medicine study released on December 2, 2002, seem to confirm this. Research conducted by the Departments of Radiology and Psychiatry found the first hard evidence that the brains of aggressive adolescents diagnosed with disruptive behavior disorders (DBD) show less activity in the frontal lobe compared to nonaggressive youths when both groups viewed violent video games. The frontal lobe is the area of the brain responsible for decision-making and behavior control. This is simply saying that kids who already have problems will develop bigger problems with violent gaming. So the dilemma becomes, how do you keep violent games out of the hands of only those kids? However, the study also concluded that even normal adolescents registered differences in brain function dependent upon the amount of violent media exposure they experienced on television and in video games. In short, they suggest that overexposure affects everyone to varying degrees.

Lieutenant Colonel Dave Grossman, a psychologist and retired U.S. Airborne Ranger Infantry officer who both studied and taught at West Point Military Academy, agrees with those assessments and adds his concerns regarding a rapid spread in the popularity of first-person shooter (FPS) video games during the last three decades. Author of *Stop Teaching Our Kids to Kill* and *On Killing*, Grossman presents insightful research on "enabling violence," *i.e.*, overcoming natural, instinctive barriers to killing, an essential task for armed forces and law enforcement agencies. He contends that the computer simulations originally used for this training have been far outstripped by new video games that condition children to kill without any of the stimulus safeguards used by the military and police.

After their acts of extreme violence, school shooters often describe a detached state of mind as if there had been another person in control of their body, as if their "true self" only passively observed the events unfolding—in other words, as if they were watching a movie or playing a video game.

Many of these games originated in technologically advanced Japan. In reality, the nonviolent culture for which that nation is justly famed still requires a safety valve by which frustrated members of society can blow off a little steam. Ultraviolent comic books and samurai dramas generally served that purpose before video games almost universally seduced Japan's youth. As a result, *we have raised a generation that thinks nothing of killing*, wrote journalist Yoichi Masuzoe a few years ago. *In the games, you do not bleed or feel pain when hit. When you kill your opponent, nothing real comes out of the wound and there's no anguish. You don't get any sensation of how dangerous real fighting is, or what suffering you cause. You do cruel things with a light heart.*

We try to comprehend how a young man with a gun can be so blinded by his own egocentricity that he misses the obvious fact that the people he's about to hurt are real. These two elements—lack of empathy and obsessive immersion in virtual reality—may help cultivate a mind-set by which young people view those they dislike as inanimate objects. Dehumanization of one's victims is a factor common to all mass murderers, be they isolated psychopaths, school shooters, terrorist groups, or governments that advocate "ethnic cleansing."

In reference to mass murderers in general, Dr. Palermo wrote:

> They frequently depersonalize their victims. Although their feelings of revenge usually are directed primarily against one person, their acts become "over-killings." Unable to contain their destructive emotions, they target a larger number of people who may assume a symbolic meaning for them and are blamed for the killers' problems. . . . Violent individuals look for surrogate victims to replace the persons who aroused their anger, chosen only because of the victims' vulnerability and proximity.

According to Dr. Hare, a lack of empathy for victims is typical of those with antisocial disorders, which at their most extreme result in individuals who have no qualms about hurting others, and can kill brutally with very little guilt. A wide diversity of similar ailments may emanate from the damaged reservoirs of early youth. Criteria characteristic of "conduct disorder" include bullying or intimidating others, shoplifting, initiating physical fights, conning others to get one's way, starting fires, using a weapon that can cause serious harm, or being physically cruel to people or animals. Kip Kinkel had displayed every single one of these traits by the time he'd reached his fourteenth birthday.

Dr. Hare describes the characteristics of an antisocial personality as a distorted sense of entitlement, intolerance of frustration, being unremorseful, quick-tempered, apathetic to the needs of others, blameful, manipulative, affectively cold, disregardful of social obligations, nonconforming to social norms, and irresponsible; in short, people prepared to use any amount of violence to attain their massively selfish ends. Most school shooters seem to have some variation of these disorders, especially those that display a "pervasive pattern of disregard for and violations of the rights of others." Almost all of them casually joked to friends about violence and murder as if these were desirable goals. Many wrote menacing essays that dwelt heavily in blood and gore.

All of these attributes have been around for centuries, but we must now add to this mix the ingredient of current technologies, many of them so new that what occurred six months ago is already outdated. The ability to escape tedious homework, nagging parents, or peer pressure via powerful personal computers, realistic video games, and high-speed Internet access is accomplished by a simple flick of a switch. Most kids know more than their parents about the ins and outs of recent innovations. In reliable hands, this science can lead to positive, creative developments, and a worthwhile enhancement of knowledge. To a generation raised in an environment saturated with acceptable violence, this sudden access to unlimited information, coupled with a premature familiarity with adult themes, may bear different fruit.

Compared with public theaters in which we share our feelings with like-minded strangers in a communal way, the Internet opens doors to the most private and personal realms of our imaginations. Accessing taboo Web sites is as easy as declaring you're over eighteen. Obscure and distant chat room partners with made-up names are trusted with intimate details that might shock our daily acquaintances. We can partake of anonymous involvement in forbidden adventures with almost no risk or loss to our self-esteem.

Dr. Nancy Willard, who operates a Web site for "Safe and Responsible Internet Use," studies the effects of information and communication technologies on the ethical behavior of young people. She sees a generation overly involved in interactive pursuits that reward simulated violence and diminish compassionate responses. Willard suggests that the Internet has, in a sense, become a kind of magic Ring of Gyges for some young people. Her reference hails back to a story by Plato in which a shepherd finds a magical ring that makes him invisible, allowing him to slay the king and claim his realm. This ancient tale raises an ethical question—namely, if we're invisible, will we do whatever we want because nobody can catch and punish us, or will we do the right thing? This sense of invisibility on the World Wide Web complicates the already difficult task teens face in developing a clear moral code.

"When a young person recognizes that his or her inappropriate action has caused harm [to] others, it should lead to an empathic response and feelings of remorse," Willard contends. "Understanding that others disapprove of this action should lead to a sense of shame. Finally the threat of being detected by a person who has the authority to punish should lead to feelings of regret." All of this influential feedback is missing on the Internet. "With violent video games," Willard declares, "an additional element is added. Not only are game players not able to feel the pain of those they 'virtually' hurt, they are rewarded for this activity. And behavior that is rewarded, will be repeated."

Echoing Willard and Grossman, Toronto-based media activist Valerie Smith asserts that "first-person shooter games function as killing simulators or conditioning devices. . . . [They] teach the user to hit a target and help rehearse the act of killing." Smith offers as an example the fact that the U.S. Marine Corps once licensed Doom and used it to train their combat-fire teams in killing tactics.

Primitive by today's standards, Doom was the one game Kip Kinkel was known to have played—although thousands of others did as well with no conspicuous effect. Both Harris and Klebold became obsessed with Doom, playing it almost every afternoon. Harris even designed higher levels of play for the game. Mortal Kombat and Duke Nukem were other favorites. Players win by racking up the most kills and are rewarded for harming others in their virtual world.

What's the appeal? The answer may not be as obvious as we think. Try "predictability and stability." Surprised? Brooks Brown, one of Dylan Klebold's best friends, explained their point of view regarding video games in his book, *No Easy Answers,* as follows:

> In real life, things don't make sense. . . . In a video game you only get what you know; nothing changes. So video games are a sort of haven, an escape to a logical, exciting world. . . . Everything happens through your own doing, your own mistakes, and your own achievements. Eric and Dylan got sucked into this appealing fantasy because it was an escape from the troubles of everyday life. When you have a place to go—whether it be home, school, a bar, a drug den, or a video game—where things seem

perfect, then you go to that place as much as you can. It's
a type of drug—a fantasy—where happiness exists because
things make sense.

Just as with drugs, dependency can occur. Medical professionals
around the world are increasingly viewing this with concern. Dr. Maressa Orzack, a clinical psychologist, sees many similarities between
video gaming or Internet addiction and people with traditional behavioral disorders, such as compulsive gambling. As founder of the
Computer Addiction Service at McLean Hospital in Belmont, Massachusetts, she hears from a half-dozen new patients a day seeking
treatment for electronic media dependencies. "The same reward center in the brain—the dopamine system—is being tapped for all types
of compulsive behavior," she says. Dr. Orzack points out that massively multiplayer online games (MMOs) such as World of Warcraft
have as many as 8 million players. Some argue that such games have
genuine social and educational value as a way to teach adolescents
the virtues of planning, teamwork, and self-reliance, but they can
also involve players in excessive amounts of time spent on that and
nothing else. "Even if there's five percent who can't quit," Dr. Orzack
says, "that's huge. I hear from lots of them, and my sense is that
we're just seeing the tip of the iceberg. Addictive gameplay can result in lost jobs, downward grades, forgotten friends, broken marriages, and damaged lives."

Hard-core gamers may admit their hobby can be addictive, but
many are in denial that what's a pleasurable pastime for them can
be lethal for others. The evidence may be circumstantial, but it's still
compelling. When they set up their propane and pipe bombs in
Columbine just before lunch that day, Eric and Dylan arranged them
in a formation designed to set off a chain reaction, a strategy borrowed from Duke Nukem. Eric's final journal entry on April 3 talked
about getting *a few extra frags on the scoreboard*. "Frags" are FPS
slang for "kills." Some parents of victims responded with a $5 bil-
lion lawsuit against game manufacturers Nintendo, Sega, Sony, Time
Warner, and the creators of Doom. A judge dismissed the action. A
nearly identical lawsuit, filed after Michael Carneal's attack in Kentucky, was also thrown out of court.

Carneal had spent hundreds of hours honing his skills on FPS video games, yet prior to stealing the pistol he used in that crime, he had never discharged a real handgun. Of eight shots fired that day, each one hit a different student. To appreciate what this signifies in terms of accuracy, the FBI suggests an average experienced law officer at the same distance would hit a moving target with less than one bullet in five. Michael made five head shots and three to the upper torso. Many FPS games give bonus points for head shots and most encourage users to shoot at one target after another, trying to hit as many as possible within a short time. According to law enforcement analysts, the natural human instinct is to keep shooting at one target until he goes down in the interest of self-preservation. Michael, Kip, and several other school shooters simply kept firing until they ran out of ammunition or were otherwise interrupted, trying to hit as many students as possible, exactly as instructed by gaming.

Controversy surrounds the question of whether Seung-hui Cho had similar training. In his college dorm, his roommates never saw Cho playing video games and he owned neither a TV nor a gaming console. The official report says that Cho's favorite video game was Sonic the Hedgehog, designed for kids. That doesn't preclude having other games, and his roommates did say, "He was on the computer all the time." According to an article that ran in the *Washington Post*, which has been challenged elsewhere: *Several Korean youths who knew Cho from his high school days said he was a fan of violent video games, particularly* Counterstrike, *a hugely popular online game published by Microsoft, in which players join terrorism or counterterrorism groups and try to shoot each other using all types of guns.*

Counterstrike is one of many games in which players stalk through rooms and move down corridors, seeking out as many victims as possible and firing multiple shots into targets to assure their demise. During his nine-minute rampage, Cho unleashed 170 rounds as he stalked through the classrooms and corridors of Norris Hall, killing all twenty-seven students and five teachers with multiple shots. Dr. Joseph Cacioppo, of Montgomery Regional Hospital, reported, "There wasn't a shooting victim that didn't have less than three bullet wounds in them."

While there may or may not be a clear connection in Cho's case, this is not the first time that Counterstrike has been named as a mo-

tivator. The worst high school shooting in history was Robert Steinhäuser's massacre in Germany on April 26, 2002 (chapter 26), which
resulted in eighteen deaths. Steinhäuser trained himself on Counterstrike and wore an outfit similar to one of the game's characters for
his rampage. In Berlin, the shooting ignited a debate calling for a
ban on violent computer games. Certain types of knives were out-
lawed, gun controls were tightened, and the minimum age for buying guns was raised from eighteen to twenty-one.

Four years later, no legislation had been enacted in Germany pro-
hibiting games, but once again Counterstrike was cited in the Emsdetten school shooting by Sebastian Bosse (chapter 26). Sebastian
spent many of his waking hours intensively playing various violent
computer games and named one of his guns Jill, after Jill Valentine,
his favorite character in Resident Evil. This naturally provoked renewed calls for the German Parliament to take action, and a bill was
introduced soon after that forbidding the depiction in video games
of violent acts committed against human characters.

In the United States, attorney Jack Thompson wrote to Microsoft
CEO Bill Gates on April 18, 2007, warning him that his company
is potentially legally liable for the harm done at Virginia Tech. "Cho
and Steinhäuser were able to do what they did the first time because
it was not the first time," he said. "This is why the military uses
this same virtual reality simulation to train soldiers to want to kill
and *how* to kill calmly."

According to his dorm mate Ben Woloszyn, Stephen Kazmierczak
played a lot of video games at high volume, and most especially
Counterstrike, during the 2003/2004 period when he was studying
sociology at Northern Illinois University. The Glock handgun and
pump-action Remington shotgun Stephen purchased for his 2008 killing
spree are among the weapons used in Counterstrike. Kazmierczak
didn't need video games to teach him how to use a gun, however.
Like Kimveer Gill, Charles Whitman, and Alvaro Castillo, Stephen also
enlisted in the military, and like the others he was also purportedly
given a psychological discharge. He lasted only five months in the
army, from September 2001 to February 2002.

Kip Kinkel was so obsessed with excessively violent programming,
his parents had to disconnect their cable TV. Lieutenant Colonel
Grossman asserts that violent visual imagery is as addictive as alco-

hol or nicotine, and that this addiction is being knowingly marketed to youth. According to recent estimates, children view, on average, twelve thousand acts of violence a year on television alone, and over one thousand murders. *Operant conditioning (a repetitive process of stimulus-response) teaches you to kill,* Grossman wrote, *but classical conditioning (i.e., learning to associate pleasure with some neutral or disagreeable stimulus) is a subtle but powerful mechanism that teaches you to like it. Both methods are fully operational in the visual media industries.*

In classic movies of the past, death was usually presented as being fairly bloodless. Recent slasher films revel in the gory slaughter of innocents while allowing the mindlessly evil psychopath who butchers them to achieve immortality. Those movies may have an R rating, but kids still get to see them. For years, Freddie, Jason, and the *Scream* character costumes were best sellers at Halloween. The face masks may look scary, but by getting inside one and pretending to become the very thing they are afraid of, children feel powerful. Plus, there's an added bonus: by being able to "scare" others, they may even feel a satisfying little surge of pleasure.

This tradition has a long pedigree. Primitive tribes, dancing in bear, wolf, or lion skins, could overcome their fear of the creatures they hunted. School shooters may also imagine that they can "wear evil," as if it is a mask or a suit of camouflage, but eventually they become the role they play. The mask sticks to their face and they can't remove it.

In video games, the player can be resurrected interminably by the push of a button. A handful of teenagers don't get the message that real life doesn't work like that. Popular electronic media helps spread the myth that dealing out death is all part of a day's work for an action hero, and that is, in a sense, what most school shooters imagine they are. For the victims, it's quite a different story. "It's so awful and it's so forever," Thurston student Betina Lynn sobbed. "It's not like the movies. The hero doesn't get up and get the shooter and save the girl. You sit there and you bleed and you cry."

In the real world, gunshot wounds are a messy business. The *National Enquirer* was criticized for running color photos of the blood-soaked corpses of Harris and Klebold sprawled on the floor of the Columbine library, where they died, but the shock value of these gory pictures probably did more to dispel their admirers' image of a heroic or noble death than anything yet published.

Older games like Doom, Duke Nukem, and Mortal Kombat are ancient history to today's sophisticated players. The newer, far more realistic games require a deeper sense of planning and strategy, thus creating a stronger sense of involvement. Still, we have a choice. The U.S. Constitution enshrines our freedom to select the options we will live by, learn by, and grow with. As children, we're directed in our choices by parents. As adults, we're expected to know what's best for us. But in the middle world of adolescence, preferences are more complex. There are issues of self-esteem, hero emulation, temptations of awakening sexuality, projections of fantasies, a need for fulfillment, escape from real or imagined persecution, and living up to the expectations of peers. Those who market to youth are well aware of these psychological buttons. In the global, multibillion-dollar video and entertainment industry, the corporations also have the leverage to push them in whatever way they wish.

Young people do not just suddenly grow into school shooters overnight. Step by step, they develop within a family environment, and they mature within a shared culture. Although they may not represent the cultural norm, they are still an indirect product of that society. While an overwhelming percentage of youth involve themselves in worthwhile projects and positive endeavors, a minority of adolescents recognize only their own selfish and immediate desires, dismissing the valid needs of others as inconsequential. In a materialistic society in which marketing is king, they're often encouraged to do so. A handful of these troubled kids have ended up literally at war with society, resembling nothing less than suburban guerrillas. This generation did not invent teen rejection of parents, peers, and the establishment, but some among them are now able to access a frightening combination of firepower and cutting-edge technology. With semiautomatic weapons, a deficit of conscience, virtual training, a few homemade explosives, and some smoldering resentment, a young person can create his own limited edition of Armageddon.

• Chapter 19 •

Face Value

What a weird culture this is. We allow our children's hours to be saturated with violent images. We acquire guns as if they're tennis rackets or golf clubs—about 200 million firearms for 260 million people—and leave them lying around as if they're spare change. And we reserve a special recognition for the criminal who fascinates us even as he reviles.
—Cynthia Tucker, editorial page editor,
Atlanta Journal-Constitution

America prides itself on its achievements, and rightly so. Nevertheless, no honest appraisal of school shootings can take place if our society blinds itself to its own contributions in nurturing a culture that idolizes instant fame over the measured development of excellence, naively embraces superficial and misleading images of good and evil, thrills to the mass marketing of violence, condones the private accumulation of battle-ready assault weapons, and readily accepts shallow solutions to highly complex issues.

The late twentieth century witnessed the triumph of style over substance, the glorification of form over content, and the quite literal acceptance of "face value." Just before the husband of Laci Peterson was arrested in April 2003 and charged with the Christmas Eve murder of his wife and their unborn son, a woman called into a radio talk show that was discussing the crime. The caller told the program host she was convinced Scott Peterson could not possibly have killed his pregnant spouse. When asked why she was so certain, the woman replied, "Because he doesn't look like a murderer."

Our reliance upon stereotypical good guy/bad guy imagery has been reinforced by eighty-plus years of media conditioning, packaging, and public relations. Designing "surface appeal," be it on behalf of physical objects or people in the public eye, has become a major American art form. Attractive music stars who can barely sing, and actors whose chief talent is in their looks, are embraced by legions of adoring fans; spin doctors ensure that everything from overpriced pharmaceuticals to war enters our collective consciousness in the most acceptable way; and even presidential elections are miracles of make-believe. Superficial appearance substitutes nicely for any deeper interpretation.

These same kinds of illusory suppositions were at work prior to every school shooting in which the youthful "innocence" or buffoonery of the killer led people to assume that nothing terrible would really happen. If merely creating a likable image could be judged as the measure of one's virtue . . . but then, it very often is. In our time, we have seen high-profile celebrities literally get away with murder, solely on the basis of their popularity. Many serial killers are successful in concealing their crimes and obtaining new victims precisely because they're such charming, confident, or good-looking con artists.

Perhaps future historians will note that in the decade between 1998 and 2008, the single largest shift in the American perspective was a stunned realization that seemingly likable people can do abominable things, and that being a good and decent person is no defense against their crimes. It was a lesson that had been learned centuries ago by people in Europe, Africa, and Asia, but American optimism in the twentieth century had kept such knowledge at a safe distance—at least until the Oklahoma City bombing, 9/11, and a spate of school, workplace, and mall shootings altered that perception.

School shootings could only take root in a nation that wasn't prepared for such behavior from its own children, but even so, they didn't emerge out of a complete vacuum. They materialized within the context of the society that spawned them. Former Springfield (Oregon) superintendent Jamon Kent observed, "You can't expect our schools to be islands of safety when our communities are a sea of violence." A kindred view was embodied in a response to school shootings prior to 1996, when in the *Education Digest*, Mari McLean wrote, *Perhaps the greatest damage the negative focus on schools has done is to cause people to see schools as places that are the source of violence, rather than as places that reflect the violence of society as a whole.* British historian Henry Thomas Buckle wrote in the nineteenth century what is still true today: "Society prepares the crime; the criminal commits it."

School-shooting incidents came in waves that peaked and ebbed, leaving behind discernible currents and drifts. Yet, while it's true each one may have influenced several others, what about the initial cases at the very beginning? How did the crime of school shooting actually get started? It's widely accepted that the earliest cases grew out of an emulation of adult mass murder. The question, then, is, how did this "senseless slaughter of innocents" migrate from adult to juvenile hands?

In his paper "The Ecology of Evil," Reverend David Bumbaugh describes a mutually dependent symbiosis in the relationship between our society and the types of media we embrace. Because we hunger for it, he writes, *newspapers, magazines, radio and television all feed us a steady diet of stories detailing the existence of evil in our world.* He adds, *There is an ecology to evil, a structural relationship which involves the entire community.*

What changed in our society during the 1990s that could help explain the apparent acceleration of school-shooting incidents from a few infrequent occurrences into a national disease? Consider some of the other major news events that transpired during that decade: it began with the collapse of the Soviet Union, and then saw the rise of fledgling dot-coms, which promised untold riches to investors, a skyrocketing economy, and the growing belief that nearly all of America's enemies had been vanquished. In the midst of this optimistic period of relative peace and prosperity, tangible symbols of success were being enthusiastically embraced by those who shared in this euphoria of stability and economic achievement. This celebration of well-being was then passed on to our children.

Orchestrated almost exclusively by media-based role models, this new materialism manifested itself in prestige-based lifestyle choices, a nearly universal desire to purchase name-brand clothing fashions, and, at least among teens and preteens, in attitudes, gestures, and the latest expressions peppering youthful dialogue. For a while, it sounded as if every adolescent seen on TV came from Southern California, and millions of others wanted to imitate them.

Many youngsters became devoted to the cult of status and style at an early age, but for a small minority, ownership itself became a goal worth fighting for—or worse. Take, for example, a simple article of clothing like sneakers. Once conventional footwear, they became expensive, high-tech fashion statements. A few children who couldn't afford such luxuries took the property and—on several sad occasions—the lives of others who could. Yes, kids were actually murdered because others wanted what they wore. To their killers, possession of the physical item was deemed more important than life itself. Who was teaching these misguided children such values? In the sense that society condoned and even encouraged this new materialism, we all were.

The transfer of moral and cultural attitudes between generations may be accomplished either by conscientious parenting or by relinquishing that obligation, consciously or unconsciously, to other influences, such as schools, churches, playground companions, or mass media. In chapter 15, we considered the differences between narcissism and self-esteem, but social critic Dr. Gerald L. Rowles believes that these two traits are intertwined. The promulgation of "artificially induced" self-esteem during the past three decades, he asserts, should be held liable for the fostering of a national spirit of narcissism in this country. Rowles feels that the boomer generation's "fragile and ever needy sense of egotism" gave rise to the "self-esteem movement" that was billed by "nouveau-pop psychologists" as an antidote to the epidemic rise of depression, suicide, and substance abuse among America's teens. Instead of that result, he says, "The well-meaning efforts of self-appointed self-esteem gurus may be substantively responsible for the escalation of violence in our children."

Dr. Rowles connects current egoistic attitudes with the widespread popularity and acceptance of alcohol and drugs from the late '60s through the present day, and posits, "What were drug-indulging baby boomers self-medicating themselves against? The unequivocal answer is anxiety, a central precursor of addiction and a hallmark of withdrawal, that has generalized and broadened as the boomers have aged." He suggests that "the source of boomer anxiety is, paradoxically, freedom—not the traditional freedoms revered by America's Founding Fathers, but the unbounded, narcissistic, self-indulgent freedom to pursue one's own hedonistic needs—the freedom to always feel good, absolved of personal responsibility." Ironically, while Kip Kinkel protested he "had no other choice," Rowles suggests that having too many choices may lead to equally dire results for those who equate "freedom to choose" with "the absence of all restrictions."

We learn self-indulgence at an early age. In its role as universal babysitter and educator, television is now entering its fourth generation. For decades, a majority of American kids have spent more hours per week in front of the TV than they do at school, and certainly far more time there than they spend talking with parents. By default, TV programs give us the ideals we aim for, and advertisers give us the road maps we need to get there.

In shows like *Lifestyles of the Rich and Famous, How to Marry a Millionaire*, or Donald Trump's *The Apprentice*, materialism is wed to power. It's always difficult to step outside of contemporary civilization and view it objectively, and in the midst of affluence, no one questions our right to indulge. As an illustration, an interviewer asked a very obese man at an all-you-can-eat buffet if he felt he was making the right choice by gorging himself; to which the portly fellow replied, "Why should I deny myself?"

Why indeed? Living in a progressively acquisitive culture and saturated by its commercial reinforcements on a daily basis, vanity, gluttony, pride, and greed all went from vice to virtue within a single generation, and became so second nature we hardly noticed the change. The concept of being self-disciplined, eating just enough to satisfy, buying only what one needs, and saving up for purchases rather than getting into credit card debt seem today like the values of an antiquated civilization, good in their day but now thoroughly outmoded. Yet we're also aware that by not heeding the long-term consequences, individuals who overconsume wind up with financial and health problems. Likewise, overconsumption by an entire nation leads to problems in societal well-being.

In Michael Moore's 2002 documentary, *Bowling for Columbine*, Goth rocker Marilyn Manson, himself held responsible for inspiring several school shootings, blames much of American violence on a culture that promotes scare stories on TV and simultaneously sponsors them with messages of consumption. "You're watching the news, being pumped full of fear. . . . Cut to commercial . . . keep everyone afraid and they'll consume."

Sound far-fetched? Not according to recent studies in neuromarketing that make use of functional magnetic resonance imaging (fMRI), a technique for determining which parts of the brain are activated by different types of physical sensation or activity. These tests were not conducted for healing but rather for marketing purposes, and the results demonstrate that TV viewers are more susceptible to advertising when they are feeling anxious, frightened, or depressed. In a February 2005 report in the *Los Angeles Times,* Caltech researchers at the school's social cognitive neuroscience laboratory were investigating how clever marketing may brand the brain's preference for products—and politicians. They found that thought processes traditionally considered to be the result of deliberation and logic are actually driven by primitive brain systems that manage automatic, emotional responses usually tied to the elemental appetites of survival. The interconnected neurons that blend memory, emotions, and biochemical triggers to shape the ways that we process fear, panic, exhilaration, and social pressure also influence the choices people make.

Author Lauren Coleman, writing about *The Copycat Effect,* the title of his 2004 book, wrote: *Advertisers know that it works and use it as an accepted way to market their products. And the media knows it is real, too, using it to focus on the next epidemic, the next death story, or the next threat—and unconsciously triggering the next event they will be reporting on.*

One may feel justified in wondering if violence is endemic to the American psyche, a tradition as old as our nation. As *Bowling for Columbine* points out, paranoia can be a national trait as well as a personal one. In contemplating that characteristic, Moore cites the fact that Canadians have as easy access to guns as we do, they watch as many slasher films, and they play as many violent video games; yet, despite the handful of horrific Canadian school shooting incidents cited in this book, they kill far less frequently. Something is obviously wrong in America, Moore is saying, at a very deep level. An overabundance of defensive weapons owned by individuals, or gathered in a community, or propagated by an entire country, indicates a surfeit of fears.

As if to bolster this theory, after 9/11 the sale of personal firearms in the United States soared, as if handguns in the home would have any effect upon madmen crashing airplanes into skyscrapers or would help deter nefarious Islamic militants from assembling bombs in some basement. People didn't buy the guns because it actually made them safer, they bought them because they were scared.

Fear feeds the killing, and killing feeds the fear. A study of 626 fatal and nonfatal shootings in three widely separated states, published in the *Journal of Trauma* in 1998, found that only thirteen of these incidents could be legally considered justifiable or acts of self-defense. In other words, guns were twenty-two times more likely to be discharged in accidents, suicides, or criminal mischief than in self-defense, according to police and medical records. The only way to break the circle is to step away from it, to refuse to be a part of it. That requires far more courage, calmness, and rational thinking than overstockpiling weapons, be they Glock pistols or ICBMs.

Director Moore highlighted connections between the disproportionate number of gun deaths in this country, our post-1960s doctrine of solving international problems by aggressive military action, and news media that heighten ratings by marketing an agenda of fear. Jane Spencer and Cynthia Crossen, writing in the *Wall Street Journal*, also concluded that fear and paranoia are an accepted part of our daily diet. *Today, thanks to research labs, tort law and media hype, danger seems to lurk in every corner of life, from children's toys to McDonald's coffee, anthrax to secondhand smoke, West Nile virus to SARS,* they wrote in an April 24, 2003, editorial. *The past century also saw the flow of information about risk grow from a trickle to a tidal wave. Government officials, scientists, marketers and the media learned to use risk as a way to get people's attention.*

According to Reverend Bumbaugh, however, wholesale purveyors of anxiety have garnered a compliant audience in those who act as passive accomplices to the process by eagerly devouring each news bulletin in the hope that it will furnish a focus to their fears, and provide a label for the vague sense of dread that many people live with but cannot put a name to. *We feed ourselves on fantasies of fear and violence,* he wrote, *because it justifies our determination to spend our energies protecting ourselves and our property, and it excuses us from accepting responsibility.*

While living in fear or living fearlessly is still largely a personal choice, to a psychotic paranoid, there is "no choice"—for them, the world is populated by only two kinds of people: those who fear others, and those who are feared. While it's hard enough for a mentally unstable adult to maintain a sense of equilibrium, an unbalanced juvenile mind struggling with rejection and isolation might see the opportunity to be feared, rather than living in fear of others, as a step upward. The coward who's been bullied is most often the one who will seize an opportunity to bully others. The abused child, left unprotected, almost inevitably becomes an abuser.

• Chapter 20 •

Fame and Immortality

People will do anything to get on these reality shows and talent contests on TV. We're obsessed . . . trapped into programmed thinking that we're all expected to have a certain amount of material things to be perceived as worthwhile human beings.

—Madonna Ciccone, the original "Material Girl," following
her immersion in Kabbalah studies, April 2003

Popular philosophical writers and poets—like Erich Fromm, Kahlil Gibran, Leo Buscaglia, Deepak Chopra, and countless others—have cautioned us for years not to measure ourselves by what we own. Nevertheless, it has largely been a futile battle. Observe any shopping mall, and it seems that the goal so many young people still cherish is to become fully integrated into the most current vogue. To be a part of that is to be included in the fashionable cutting edge of youth culture. Anything less is . . . "like, so five minutes ago."

According to Boston College sociologist Juliet B. Schor, children are exposed to forty thousand commercials every year. By the age of eighteen months, they can recognize logos. By ten, they have memorized three hundred to four hundred brands. By the time they are young teens, students are well aware of the prestige attached to a show of material possessions and have learned what it takes to be part of the in crowd at school.

It follows that when youngsters who are cultural rejects get bullied or left behind, they feel emotionally devastated. The difference between present and previous generations, however, is that today the disenfranchised can easily obtain the means to exact heavy vengeance upon their real or imagined tormentors. Before his November 2006 shooting rampage in Germany, Sebastian Bosse (chapter 26), who'd been badly teased and ostracized, said on videotape, "Why is every kid who's different from the majority a loner? Because the fucking media tells the people what is cool and what is not."

But why aren't kids like Sebastian worried about the consequences? One of the simpler answers may be a four-letter word: fame. A British poll conducted in December 2006 found that kids rated being famous higher than any other value. In fact, they said, becoming a celebrity would be the "very best thing in the world." It is perhaps significant that Stephen Kazmierczak began and ended his 2008 rampage at Northern Illinois University up on the stage of a crowded lecture hall in front of between seventy and 100 students.

Young people—whose every material need is being met—will still long for something even more essential from their peers: recognition and admiration. The most direct course to that objective is achieving fame, and in a world of immediate gratification—the faster, the better. Being famous was once associated with hard-earned achievement, although that sentiment seems oddly antiquated today. In a society that values celebrity more than honor, and notoriety more than accomplishment, why work hard to be illustrious when you can just take a shortcut and be instantly infamous?

While schools are still the common training ground of youth, television is the common proving ground for the aspirations of our entire nation. The ultimate high for many of today's kids would be to appear on TV, preferably in some kind of positive light. Robert Thompson, director of the Center for the Study of Popular Television, said, "Humans have this almost pathological behavioral characteristic that makes them scream out, 'Look at me!' Given the choice between becoming fabulously wealthy and fabulously famous, most of them choose famous."

A young woman auditioning for a new TV reality show in Washington, DC, explained, "I think fame will give meaning to my life. I mean, who am I right now? A face in a million. If I become famous, then I really will feel like I am someone. I will be known."

While being a contestant on a kids' game show or a finalist in an *American Idol* contest would no doubt be awesome, even a negative portrayal on television might carry a lot of cool currency to an attention-seeking teenager with deeply rooted problems, access to guns, and more ammunition than common sense. If you can make it onto the six o'clock news, you can make it, period. The price might be high—perhaps life itself—but to a boy who's also considering suicide, being featured nationwide as a famous fatality could be seen as an acceptable trade-off. Gaining posthumous fame as a killer is better than no fame at all. In a wired world, however, self-destruction is only the beginning. Kip Kinkel, the Columbine boys, and dozens of other school shooters never intended to simply die and be forgotten, but it was more than just getting their fifteen minutes of fame. It was the attraction of being part of the cutting edge of a new American wave, one of the select few destined for immortality via the world news report.

This was a message not lost on adolescents who craved recognition at any cost. Among them were more than a few who, while not necessarily willing to pay for it with their own lives, were certainly willing to sacrifice the lives of others. After Clay Shrout murdered his whole family, and just before he drove to school, he happened upon a neighbor he'd never spoken to before. "You don't know me," he told the man, "but my name is Clay Shrout and you're going to hear a lot about me today. I'm going to be on CNN." His friends later said, "He wanted attention. He wanted to show everyone that he was someone. He did that. Now there's no more identity crisis. Now he knows who he is—a killer."

Just hours before he shot his English teacher to death, thirteen-year-old honor student Nathaniel Brazill told friends, *"Just watch. I'll be all over the news."* Brazill killed teacher Barry Grunow on May 26, 2000, at Lake Worth Community Middle School in Palm Beach County, Florida, with a .25-caliber semiautomatic pistol stolen from the home of his grandfather. A counselor had suspended him earlier that day (the last day of the school year) for tossing water balloons. Brazill told police that he returned with the gun and shot Grunow after the teacher refused to let him say good-bye to two girls in his class. Brazill was tried as an adult and convicted of second-degree murder in May 2001. On July 27 of that year, he was sentenced to twenty-eight years in prison.

I'm gonna be fucking famous were the words written on a suicide note left behind by nineteen-year-old Robert A. Hawkins, who killed eight people and wounded five others with an assault rifle before taking his own life in an attack upon an Omaha, Nebraska, indoor mall on December 5, 2007. While outside the immediate scope of this book, mass murder by young men at shopping malls has become more common. Although these violent acts have many parallels with both workplace rampage (targeting fellow employees or superiors) and school shootings (targeting fellow students, teachers, or administrators), they are true domestic terrorism, targeting the general population at large. Hawkins's parents had kicked him out a year earlier; he'd been in foster homes and had psychiatric sessions. He'd just lost his job at McDonald's, and his girlfriend had left him. However, it wasn't his coworkers, boss, parents, girlfriend, or fellow students that Hawkins targeted, it was society as a whole, which he felt had rejected him to the point that he was nothing more than, as he wrote, *a piece of shit my entire life.*

Earlier in 2007, on February 12, Sulejmen Talovic, an eighteen-year-old loner who lived with his mother, took a backpack full of ammunition, a shotgun, and a .38-caliber pistol to Trolley Square mall in Salt Lake City, Utah. Talovic, a siege of Srebrenica (Bosnia) survivor whose family moved to the United States as refugees in 2000 after his grandfather was killed by shellfire, almost always dressed in black. This day, he wore a trench coat as he fired randomly at customers, killing two men, two women, and a fifteen-year-old girl, and wounding four others before being shot to death by police.

But why target shopping centers? At the time of Talovic's massacre, Danny Ledonne wrote:

> What are the real causes of these shootings? I believe that far more than violent videogames, the entire system reduces empathy for other human beings. Shopping malls are the ultimate expression of meaningless consumption—they are places created for the explicit purpose of recreational shopping. The sources of these kids' seemingly inexplicable rage can be traced back to the empty pursuit of materialism that creates a "shopping mall mentality," to an educational system geared toward robotic memorization rather than opening minds, and to the dehumanizing influences of tech-

nology itself We have molded a society in which a tremendous number of young people don't feel connected, valued or driven by a sense of purpose in their lives.

Hawkins's suicide note seemed to confirm that assessment.

Take away the instant fame factor, and half the motivation for these shootings would evaporate. Statistics may be able to demonstrate how pervasive this cause-and-effect relationship between school shooters and the news media has proven to be. The killings did not happen randomly but were clustered in sets of kindred attacks linked by timing and/or location. Four of the seven shootings in 1995, for example, took place within a two-month period in the southeastern United States. In 1996, seven of thirteen attacks occurred in the three months between February and April. Two Georgia shootings in September of that same year ensued within ten days of each other.

There were ten school shootings or similar attacks (bombs, knives, hostage taking) in '97, nine in '98, and seventeen in '99 (including groupings of five events in April, three in May, and four in October). The 1999 events included three overseas and another in Canada. That assault, by fourteen-year-old Todd Cameron Smith, in Taber, Alberta, was Canada's first fatal *high school* shooting in twenty years. That it took place just eight days after Columbine was not coincidental. Smith had also been the subject of teasing and name-calling. He'd dropped out to do homeschooling, but returned to W. R. Myers High School at lunchtime wearing (déjà vu) a long dark blue trench coat. Some students asked sarcastically if he had a gun under his jacket. He did. Not knowing that, they continued to joke and laugh at him until he pulled out the .22-caliber sawed-off rifle and fired four shots, killing Jason Lang and injuring Shane Christmas, both seventeen.

Smith spent the rest of the year in a coma because of a congenital heart condition, but he later pleaded guilty to murder and attempted murder. In November 2000, he was sentenced to three years in a youth facility. At his trial, it came out that he'd written: *I did this because . . . ever since the shooting at Columbine . . . all I've been able to think about is doing this.* After serving his time, Todd was transferred to a Toronto halfway house, sparking protests amongst nearby residents. In October 2006, the Ontario Crown sought to have Smith, now twenty-two, incarcerated again, in an adult prison.

The thirteen actual and twelve barely prevented school attacks in 2000 included the youngest shooter thus far. On February 29, six-year-old Dedrick Owens had an argument with first-grade classmate Kayla Rolland in the playground of Buell Elementary School, in Mount Morris Township, near Flint, Michigan. He yelled, "I don't like you!" and she replied, "So?" Then he took out a .32-caliber semiautomatic handgun and shot her. Dedrick told investigators it was an accident—he was only trying to scare her. Prosecutors said he was too young to be held responsible, but they brought an involuntary manslaughter charge against Jamelle James, a nineteen-year-old man who had bought the stolen firearm and left it loaded under some blankets in a bedroom, where guns and drugs were exchanged. Dedrick's mother had been evicted from her home and had left her sons with their uncle at that house a week before the shooting.

Extremely young victims were again featured in two bizarrely similar European day care center attacks in May 2000, giving further credence to the idea that violent events that make headlines generate similar crimes. Remarkably, both incidents involved forty-year-old men wielding guns who held over two dozen children captive, and many hours later released them. The first was in Norway on May 15, the second in Luxembourg on May 31. The Norwegian said he was angry for being denied access to his sons after losing a custody battle to his ex-partner; the man in Luxembourg had two children, and they had attended that targeted day care center. Luckily, none of the children held hostage were injured in either episode.

The tally in 2001 was seventeen actual school shootings and eight prevented attacks. The clusters included ten in February and eight in March—but only one bona fide occurrence and one deterred assault after the 9/11 terrorist attacks that year. There were larger horrors occupying the news programs after the WTC towers collapsed.

Still, the question remains: did increased media coverage lead to more shootings, or were more shootings being reported (including some lesser events that might have been omitted previously) because they had become a "hot item"? Or, perhaps, it wasn't the reports themselves, but the "manner" of the reporting.

Before they became another form of entertainment, traditional news broadcasts used to present information in a timely and responsible manner without allowing it to deteriorate into tabloid sensationalism. During the '90s, however, there was a marked increase in the amount of dramatic "in your face" cable news coverage aggressively backed by a disco beat, framed by multiple message boards signaling a sense of urgency, enhanced by vibrantly colored text that screamed "anxiety," and delivered by attractive talking heads who seemed more interested in ratings than objectivity. News shows became high-stakes operations as networks competed for loftier audience numbers that generated phenomenal advertising revenue. Celebrity trials, frivolous alarms, and shallow distractions often proved to be more lucrative alternatives than credible news analysis.

Lauren Coleman wrote: *No one is asking the media to stop reporting the news. . . . It's about how the stories are being presented, how the current approach has backfired and triggered the copycat effect. In essence, the media has to stop using rampage shootings, celebrity suicides, bridge jumpers, and school shootings the way it uses tornadoes, hurricanes, and earthquakes to get people to watch their programs. Copycats are a consequence of a thoughtless, sensational media.*

Something akin to our current system of news broadcasting had been prophesied back in 1976 when Sidney Lumet directed *Network*. One of the four Oscars awarded to that film went to screenwriter Paddy Chayefsky for his sharp critique of the "hollow, lurid wasteland of TV journalism where entertainment value and short-term ratings were more crucial than quality in the ruthless tabloid-tainted television industry."

From a strictly practical viewpoint, school shootings were easily good for three to five days of eye-catching coverage. "If it bleeds, it leads" goes the well-known industry cliché. Jason Vest wrote in the *Village Voice* after Columbine, *it seems at least in bad taste, if not offensive, to crow over ratings spikes for such a tragedy.* In a passing moment of seriousness, Eugene, Oregon, *Comic News* editor Don Kahle wrote that *once news is treated like a consumable product, truth becomes a luxury, but getting and keeping people's attention remains essential.* TV columnist Kay McFadden suggested in the *Seattle Times* that, *in striving to beat the pants off the competition, most*

*[networks] seemed to forget that being a news leader incurs re-
sponsibility—and sometimes blame.*

Among the print media, only one major U.S. newspaper, the
Chicago Sun-Times, chose to move both the Thurston and Columbine
tragedies to the inside pages in order to avoid sensationalizing them.
Editor in chief Nigel Wade stated, "We see a danger that publicity
surrounding such attacks could be contributing to the phenomenon."
This action was condemned by some who saw it as a way of white-
washing the news, showing the public only what they feel comfortable with. Others praised the self-imposed restraint of the *Sun-Times.*
"The coverage is there, but it's not used to sell the paper," commented Michigan State University journalism professor Sue Carter.

Ultimately, as U.S. news regarding school shooters was reported
internationally to an ever-wider audience, the dilemmas we faced here
began to spread beyond our national borders. Because of our economic success, our social ills were sometimes magnified, exploited,
and derided by other countries, as was our apparent impotence to
stem the flow of school violence. People in a multitude of foreign
locations formed an image of the United States as a land where juvenile crime had spiraled out of control. Nevertheless, the American
problem turned into a global predicament when students and teachers overseas became increasingly common targets of rampaging killers.
While the phenomenon of school shooting may have originated on
our soil, it soon found fertile ground among like-minded adolescents
and unbalanced adults in other cultures.

While news media may have affected patterns of school shootings, the influence of cinema upon these crimes has been far less am-
biguous. When Harris and Klebold videotaped their perverse plans
for Columbine, they recognized their destruction would spark major
international coverage. They also discussed which famous director—
Tarantino or Spielberg—should make the film version of their story.
The code letters for their Columbine attack were *NBK,* standing for
the title of their favorite movie, *Natural Born Killers.* Eric wrote in
his journal, *NBK comes too quick. Everything I see and hear relates
to NBK somehow. Sometimes it feels like a goddamn movie.*

This 1994 film, a thinly veiled satire written by Quentin Tarantino and directed by Oliver Stone, features two social outcasts, molested and abused by their parents as kids, who become lovers and

brutal, psychopathic serial killers. The storyline follows Mickey Knox (Woody Harrelson) and Mallory (Juliette Lewis) as the couple graphically slay at least fifty people, just for the pleasure of killing. As their rampage seems unstoppable, the media glorifies them as legendary folk heroes, like Bonnie and Clyde. They become international celebrities with teenage fans from Paris to Tokyo gushing, "They're just so cool!" One girl holds up a sign, KILL ME MICKEY! They do get arrested but escape in the end, accompanied by a narcissistic, self-promoting television reporter, whom they execute.

Though Stone intended it to be a critique of society and the media, *NBK* has been cited as the inspiration for more rampage killers than any other film in history. Like a half-dozen other school shooters, Kimveer Gill (chapter 7) and Finland's Pekka-Eric Auvinen (chapter 26) listed it among their favorite movies. Alvaro Castillo (chapter 1) actually used up the bulk of his hour-plus video by aiming his camera at a TV playing the most brutal passages of *Natural Born Killers, Scarface, Predator* and the Discovery Channel documentary *Zero Hour: Massacre at Columbine High*. He laughs loudly at the most gruesome parts, and at other times narrates the scene or demonstrates his familiarity with the dialogue by chiming in, word for word, with the actors.

Tobin Kerns and Joseph Nee were part of a group of teenagers at Marshfield High, in Massachusetts, who called themselves the Natural Born Killers, a group Nee originally formed in 2004 to protect younger students who were being bullied. Instead, his Natural Born Killers compiled a hit list of about thirty students, administrators, and police resource officers who were marked for death. They tested handmade explosives, made maps of the school, and tried to order guns. Their attack was originally planned to take place April 20, 2005, on the sixth anniversary of Columbine, but that got pushed ahead because of school vacation. They were caught when mistrust between Kerns and Nee turned to betrayal.

So why all this affinity for a single movie? There've been thousands of violent films, but none has had quite the impact of *NBK*. Part of the reason may be that the story is partially true. The fictional kiss-and-kill characters, Mickey and Mallory, were based upon two real 1950s Midwest spree killers, Charles Starkweather and his underage girlfriend, Caril Ann Fugate. At least five feature films and the Bruce Springsteen song "Nebraska" were made about the pair. Rockstar, the company responsible for some of the most ferocious, shocking, and successful video shooting games in history (Grand Theft Auto series sold over 65 million copies), chose Starkweather as the name of their lead antagonist in Manhunt.

One can appreciate the experimental cinematic elements in *Natural Born Killers* that made it so appealing to film critics of its day (nominated for a Golden Globe, it was called "best movie of the '90s" by *Entertainment Weekly*), but those same innovative techniques—psychedelic special effects, segues into animation and sitcom sequences, facial distortions, alternating color with black and white—also pushed its popularity among a small but growing demographic of youth partial to gratuitous violence, hallucinogenic drugs, casual sex, and semiautomatic weapons. Not everyone in the audience was sophisticated enough to discern Stone's less than subtle mockery. The fact that both Mickey and Mallory had traumatized childhoods no longer seemed like an anomaly but rather the norm in a world where families were disintegrating, divorce rates had climbed to over 60 percent of all marriages, and even trusted clergymen were corrupting the innocent. Kids could relate. If ever there was a promotional film made for generating mayhem, this was it. The movie became a magnet for young, would-be sociopaths in the way it glorified the killers ("The nation caught Mickey and Mallory fire"), legitimized murder ("It's just murder. All God's creatures do it") and countenanced cruelty ("A lot of people . . . deserve to die").

Author Gerard Jones (see below)) has cautioned that "entertainment has its greatest influence when it's speaking to something that isn't otherwise being addressed in a child's life." We all look for heroes to emulate, and when those role models can't be found in close proximity, some seek them in media. The year *Natural Born Killers* came out, seventeen-year-old Nathan K. Martinez viewed it dozens of times. Obsessed with the film, he shaved his head like the Mickey character and wore the same style sunglasses. Then he shot and killed his sleeping stepmother and half sister at their home in a suburb of Salt Lake City.

In all, at least six major killing sprees have been attributed to the film. In April 2006, a dozen years after it was made, *NBK* was again implicated in the Medicine Hat, Alberta, triple murders committed by twenty-three-year-old Jeremy Allan Steinke and his twelve-year-old girlfriend, Jasmine Richardson (the youngest person ever charged with multiple murder in Canadian history). After Steinke watched *NBK* several times, together they slaughtered her parents and eight-year-old brother.

Barry Loukaitis, who carried out the Moses Lake school shooting in 1996, watched *Natural Born Killers* so often (renting the video seven times) that he frequently quoted lines from the movie to friends and told them it'd be "fun to go on a killing spree." Loukaitis also enjoyed director Scott Kalvert's 1995 film *The Basketball Diaries,* starring Leonardo DiCaprio. This movie was, likewise, popular among several other shooters. Michael Carneal claimed that watching it influenced him. It's based on the autobiography of Catholic prep school star basketball athlete Jim Carroll, who became a heroin addict. There's a dream sequence in the movie showing the DiCaprio character going to school dressed all in black, wearing a long trench coat to cover a concealed rifle, and then shooting his teacher and classmates. Harris and Klebold made a video for a film class emulating this scene, in which they portrayed themselves in trench coats, shooting athletes as they walk down their school hallway. In the video, the two had their friends pretend to be jocks. Eric and Dylan were the gunmen.

The video market version of *The Basketball Diaries* was later withdrawn from circulation. Parents at several school shooting sites sued New Line Cinema, the maker of the film, for over $100 million.

The horror movie *Saw* was significant enough to Stephen Kazmierczak that a month before his rampage at Northern Illinois University, he ordered a Champaign tattoo artist to cover his arm with a rendition of a macabre doll from that film riding a tricycle through a pool of blood. In the background were additional tattoo images of several bleeding cuts, significant because when depressed as a teen, he cut himself.

Violent imagery knows no national boundaries. A few of the photos Virginia Tech killer Seung-hui Cho sent to NBC News were perplexing until a connection was made to a brutal but critically acclaimed South Korean revenge movie by director Park Chan-wook called *Oldboy.* Cho, who was born in South Korea, watched the graphically violent film repeatedly prior to his killing spree. Two pictures that show Cho posturing in a threatening manner with a hammer and holding a gun to his head mimicked scenes of actor Choi Min-sik, who played a kidnapped character achieving vengeance. Cho's photo posing with two handguns may have been inspired by John Woo's *Bullet in the Head.*

It's not only feature films that have an impact. Rock group Pearl Jam's music video "Jeremy," winner of the MTV Video of the Year award in 1993, was cited as a negative influence on Barry Loukaitis, who had memorized all the words. The song is based upon the true story of a lonely Richardson, Texas, fifteen-year-old named Jeremy Wade Delle, who was ruthlessly taunted in high school and committed suicide in 1991, shooting himself in front of his class. The video revises the tale to show the boy killing his classmates as well.

Police found a copy of the "Jeremy" video in Loukaitis's bedroom, along with a collection of Stephen King books, including a well-worn copy of *Rage*, which King wrote in 1977 under the pen name "Richard Bachman." The significance was that when Loukaitis sauntered into his fifth-period algebra class and opened fire, he was reenacting the plot from *Rage*, in which a troubled boy in the novel kills his algebra teacher and takes his class hostage, just as Loukaitis did. With his math teacher, Leona Caires, and classmates Manuel Vela and Arnold Fritz both dead, another pupil critically wounded, and nearly two dozen other students crying around him, Loukaitis smiled and said: "This sure beats algebra, doesn't it?" This line came straight out of *Rage*.

A copy of this same book was also found in Michael Carneal's school locker after his rampage in Kentucky. King later apologized for writing the novel, saying he penned it during a distressing period in his life and wished it had never been published. In 1999, he had it pulled from bookstores and he told the publisher to eliminate it from their lists.

While King and several other celebrity writers and actors endeavored to have their work withdrawn from circulation after witnessing the chaos it inspired, the problem remains that once something is distributed, it cannot be fully purged. This is especially true for electronic media—it will be accessible somewhere. Many of us wonder why any kind of media that glorifies violence and has no redeeming social value is even made in the first place. And the answer, of course, is that it is profitable. Arousing our most ignoble emotions creates a demand for more of the same. The question then becomes, can any moral limits be applied to producing and marketing such products?

This question divides those who endorse unrestrained creativity in the media versus those who would safeguard underaged consumers from exposure to potentially harmful influences. In the former camp, we find defenders of First Amendment rights, many game designers, TV and movie producers, legal associations, media advocates, and people like Ed Nebb, a spokesman for Take-Two Interactive Software, who wrote, *We firmly believe that informed adults should be able to make their own choices about entertainment products for them-selves and their families.*

Those in the latter camp view such sentiments as corporate spin expounded not because its proponents are cheerleaders for unfettered freedom of creative expression and the right to choose, but because such noble-sounding rhetoric is a way to maintain astonishing earn-ings while circumventing ethics. The United States video game in-dustry sales had reached a record high of nearly $18 billion in 2007. If greed trumps all, the power of profits—even if earned appealing to our basest instincts—will overshadow all other considerations.

These opposing views on media violence constitute one of the most contentious issues of our times. A case in point: Manhunt 2 is a lurid first-person stalking game in which players use ordinary tools and implements to torture, kill, and maim opponents in order to es-cape from an insane asylum. Rockstar already had a reputation for pushing the moral bar of gaming ever lower, but if Manhunt 2 had any positive message, it wasn't obvious to the Entertainment Software Rating Board. Prior to its release in 2007, they tagged the game AO (adult only), which would have precluded sales at family retailers. A modified version released on Halloween earned an M (mature) rat-ing in the United States, but the British Board of Film Classifications continued to ban it completely, citing "the bleakness and callousness of tone," and the "visceral and casually sadistic nature" of its "exe-cution kills." Ed Nebb defended the game, writing that it was meant *specifically for those players mature enough to appreciate it.*

Fine thought, but how do you ensure these games do not reach the hands of younger people when some stores are known to sell them to buyers below the recommended age, and many parents just shrug off the ratings? More significant, at what point in a democratic, but materialistic, society does the right of free choice conflict with the necessity to protect children from their own bad decisions if parents abrogate that responsibility?

The fact remains that we as a nation do not condone the sale of hard-core porn, addictive drugs, assault weapons, and harmful explosives to children because we know these things are detrimental to their well-being. When those same items are packaged digitally in video games or DVDs, however, we tend to be less proscriptive. Perhaps we are simply awed by the technology or feel helpless in the face of "progress." We resignedly accept that while the kind of sensationally violent imagery contained in contemporary media was, in previous generations, restrained at the fringes of society, today it's gone mainstream, able to penetrate any home in America through the electronic portals of TV, PlayStations, and laptops.

Further, we should ask what the designated ratings of "adult only" and "mature," which Nebb defends, have to do with the actual meanings of those words. In each individual's personal journey toward enlightenment, brute violence is the most primitive stage. Almost every boy passes through it, but only those who fail to mature remain in it. How, then, can play that encourages mindless carnage be considered mature or adult?

Those who design ultraviolent video games intentionally excite young minds by reproducing the stimulating effects of killing without conscience. The more dysfunctional the family and the less involved the parents, the more absorbing these questionable influences can be. Ultimately the negative results of obsessive play spill into our schools and our society.

This is not to imply that appropriate forms of gaming and other media can't be a fun and integral part of growing up. As Ledonne has written:

> Just as not every commercially successful film is in the action or horror genre, not every (or even most) popular videogames are M-rated for violence. While a few attention-grabbing titles do have high levels of graphic brutality, the vast majority are far less vicious, yet remain extremely popular. When minors commit savage crimes and are found

to have come from broken homes or had negligent parents, the media they obsessed over is merely an indication of larger problems rather than being the problem itself. These games are not marginal aspects of our culture that only turn up in the hands of mentally disturbed individuals—a recent study suggests 98.7% of adolescents play videogames to greater or lesser degree. Yet, despite the increasingly pervasive presence of videogames, rampage shooting incidents by disturbed young men remain relatively isolated deviations in which the perpetrator happens to be of the same demographic as this emergent medium of entertainment.

In short, we need to consider that if so many kids play potentially harmful games, why have such a small percentage of them been so adversely affected?

Gerard Jones takes it a step further. In his book *Killing Monsters: Why Children Need Fantasy, Super Heroes, and Make-Believe Violence,* as reviewed by *Publishers Weekly,* he *argues that violent video games, movies, music and comics provide a safe fantasy world within which children learn to become familiar with and control the frightening emotions of anger, violence and sexuality,* and that *violent games and TV shows can help children conquer fears and develop a bold sense of self.* However, he also feels that *children clearly understand the difference between pretend and reality,* and as we've seen, that's not always so.

Most writers and filmmakers who take up the subject of youth violence are attempting to provide valuable insights into this crisis, with mixed results. A 2003 *Boston Globe* review of *Elephant,* Gus Van Sant's movie about a pair of school shooters, summarized the film's message by stating that it *measures tragedy not by what the shooters did but by the lovely, terrifying, ordinary world they destroyed.* While *Elephant* won both the Golden Palm and a Best Director award at Cannes, audiences there and nearly everywhere else were divided regarding its value as a deterrent. By contrasting the cold-blooded, casual planning of the two shooters with the routines of daily high school life seen from the view of ordinary students, *Elephant* builds into a quiet kind of horror. But by ending abruptly while the lead shooter is still on a euphoric high, and by including so much footage shot from the emotionless perspective of both killers, no moral statement is made at all. In this author's view, the climax of the film is just one last play on a video game.

Jeff Weise provided unfortunate substantiation of this analysis prior to his shooting spree at Red Lake, Minnesota. According to Sky Grant, Weise's friend since sixth grade, the would-be shooter brought a video copy of *Elephant* (the title refers to something unpleasantly obvious in a room that no one wants to talk about) to Grant's house on March 4, 2005, a little more than two weeks before his rampage. The early part of the movie familiarizes viewers with the personalities of several future victims and bystanders, impressing us with their recognizable, unremarkable humanity. However, Weise skipped ahead on this occasion to the sequence that shows the two students planning and carrying out the most violent scenes of their school shooting. Although Weise didn't say anything to make Grant suspect he had any plan to emulate the film, in twenty-twenty hindsight, it's clear that's exactly what Weise was contemplating. The movie in Weise's mind did not dissuade, it instructed.

Weise also created two of his own short animated films and posted them on the Internet. His first brief effort presented a deranged clown strangling a young man. The second—more complex but equally crude—contained several ugly scenes, including two men in a park shot through the chest, another being decapitated, a police car hit by a grenade, and a shooter putting a gun into his mouth and firing, ending this sorry cinematic effort with a blood-red screen.

In the DVD liner notes for director Ben Coccio's movie *Zero Day* (not to be confused with the documentary *Zero Hour*), Henry Jenkins, Director of the MIT Comparative Media Studies Program, wrote, *Culture warriors always ask what the media is doing to our children. Yet, it seems more productive to ask what our kids are doing with media.* In *Zero Day*, the fictional shooters Andre Kriegman and Calvin Gabriel use a camcorder *as a confessional, allowing them to examine themselves through its lens,* notes Jenkins. *At other times, they are performing for the camera, acting out their militarist fantasies. Having the camera in their hands seems to embolden them to take the next step, as if they were becoming the stars of their own action movie. . . . Zero Day invites us to see the boys as media pro-*

ducers as well as media consumers, shaping their own fantasies from the resources they have at hand rather than being shaped by mass culture's prefabricated fantasies.

What is most disturbing about Jenkins's observations is that they antedate Seung-hui Cho's NBC tapes, Alvaro Castillo's newspaper videos, Sebastian Bosse's good-bye speech on the Internet, and Pekka Auvinen's YouTube postings (chapter 26), all of which occurred in the years that followed. What *Zero Day* did have for reference, of course, were the videotapes made by Harris and Klebold, which the film follows slavishly, even down to imitating their laughter-filled target practice in the woods. The result is a Columbine pseudodocumentary, filmed as a home movie. The shooters come across as a couple of laid-back guys conspiring to kill in an offhand, casual way. They are almost-likable monsters, planning to take human lives as if it were a science project. Knowing the movie is fiction helps dull the cold-blooded edge of their dialogue, but knowing almost every passage in the film is based upon the actual videos and journals of Eric Harris and Dylan Klebold sharpens it again. It even ends with footage from the imaginary school's surveillance cameras, and a 911 voice-over, similar to recordings made at Columbine High. The final disclaimer that the work is fictional and "any similarity to real events is unintentional" seems ludicrous.

What makes this another questionable cinematic effort is that the actors give practical critiques on the mistakes other school shooters have made, suggest ways to keep homicidal intentions secret, and provide pointers on how to assemble actual bombs—though most would-be bomb makers probably know all that from the Internet anyway.

In fact, any discussion about limiting the effects of violent media is probably moot because that Pandora's box has been open for so long, it's way beyond containment. Both the products and the problems have gone global. Since 2002, nearly every foreign school-shooting event has been tied to some form of popular media.

Not surprising, the migration of our "American school-shooting problem" to other cultures brought with it at least one glaringly consistent element—a fundamental question that has more to do with testosterone than it does with TV, movies, consumption, or fame—namely, why is it almost always boys or men who do the killing and not females?

Chapter 21

The Female of the Species

Unprovoked and awful charges—even so
  the she-bear fights,
Speech that drips, corrodes, and poisons—even so
  the cobra bites. . . .
And She knows, because She warns him,
  and Her instincts never fail,
That the Female of Her Species is more deadly
  than the Male.
          —Rudyard Kipling, "The Female of the Species"

It should be obvious to anyone who has even a passing familiarity with school shootings that gender plays a pivotal role. Only a handful of shooters have been female, although on the opposite side, girls are more likely to be targeted. Part of the reason for such victimization may lie in the romantic frustrations some young male shooters have felt toward females in general because of one or two unpleasant personal experiences.

Among adolescent females, just as many girls must feel tormented by unrequited love as boys, yet they seldom act out their hostility with guns. Instead, they're more likely to turn their pain inward. When the very rare girls do kill at schools, it's just as often other girls they target—rivals, former friends, or someone who's been harassing them—though, of course, there are cases in school of young women shooting a former boyfriend who has "done them wrong." And while there have been no combined school shootings and par-

219

ricides among females comparable to those of the boys described in chapter 1, there's no shortage of daughters who slay one or both of their parents.

Among adult mass murderers and serial killers, hardly three in a hundred are women. The same lopsided gender ratio holds true for school shooters. On a list of over two hundred shooters, only six of the perpetrators were female.

The earliest incident involved a sixteen-year-old San Diego girl named Brenda Ann Spencer. On January 29, 1979, Brenda shot at children and employees at Cleveland Elementary School, across the street from her home, with a rifle. Principal Burton Wragg died trying to help children escape, and custodian Michael Suchar was killed, attempting to go to Wragg's aid. Eight kids and one police officer were also wounded. When asked why she did it, Spencer uttered her infamous "I just" explanation: "I just started shooting, that's it. I just did it for the fun of it. I just don't like Mondays. . . . I just did it because it's a way to cheer the day up. Nobody likes Mondays." Irish singer/songwriter Bob Geldof was touring the United States with the Boomtown Rats at that time and he penned their biggest hit, "I Don't Like Mondays," based upon the incident.

Spencer pleaded guilty and was sentenced to two 25-years-to-life prison terms. At a parole hearing in April 2001, Brenda admitted remorse, saying, "With every school shooting, I feel I'm partially responsible. What if they got their idea from what I did?" She claimed her violence grew out of an abusive home life in which her father beat and sexually abused her for years. "I had to share my dad's bed till I was fourteen years old," she said. The rifle she used was a Christmas present from her father. "I had asked for a radio and he bought me a gun," she said. "I felt like he wanted me to kill myself." She shot at the school in the hope that police would kill her. "I had failed in every other suicide attempt. I thought if I shot at the cops, they would shoot me," she confessed.

A woman nearly twice Spencer's age committed an almost identical act a decade later. Adult school shooters are a category in themselves, but on May 20, 1988, thirty-year-old Laurie Wasserman Dann became the only adult American woman to go on a shooting spree inside an elementary school. A resident of Winnetka, Illinois, Laurie began the day by starting a fire at Ravina Elementary School in High-

The Female of the Species   221

land Park about 9:00 A.M. No injuries occurred. She returned home, started a fire there, and then drove to Hubbard Woods elementary school, this time carrying three handguns she was able to purchase by simply lying about past treatment for mental illness. First, Laurie entered a second grade classroom and pretended to be a collegiate observer. After a short while, she walked out to the corridor, pushed a boy into a restroom, and wounded him with a .22 semi-automatic Beretta pistol. She tried to shoot two other boys with a .357 Smith and Wesson Magnum revolver, but it jammed and she threw it in the sink. As the boys ran out to the office, Laurie's nurturing side temporarily kicked in and she stopped in another classroom to report that a boy had been shot. Then she reentered the previous second grade classroom and forced children to line up against a wall, saying, "I'll teach you about life." She opened fire with a .32 Smith and Wesson, killing eight-year-old Nicholas Corwin and wounding two other boys and two girls. Laurie ran from the school, brazenly went into a nearby home, and wounded resident Philip Andrew. Finally, as police closed in, Laurie put a gun in her mouth and pulled the trigger.

College shootings are another category dominated by males, but, once again, a solitary American woman decided to enter that roster, on September 17, 1996. Jillian Robbins, nineteen, who lived near Penn State University, but was not enrolled there, quietly spread a tarp under some low-hanging tree branches in the northwest corner of the campus lawn, around 9:30 A.M. She took out a Mauser rifle and randomly fired at five students. One shot killed senior Melanie Spalla, 138 feet away. Another bullet from this high-powered military weapon traveled over three hundred feet to penetrate twenty-two-year-old Nicholas Mensah's abdomen (Mensah recovered). Just as she reloaded a second clip, student Brendon Malovrh tackled Jillian and wrestled the gun away. She pulled out a knife and tried to stab him, but missed, stabbing herself in her thigh, and slitting an artery. Brendon assisted her by applying a tourniquet with his belt until paramedics and police arrived. When asked why she did it, Jillian kept repeating, "I don't know."

An attack by a seventeen-year-old girl was apparently prevented in Haines City, Florida, when she was suspended in November 1999 for keeping a notebook filled with descriptions of killing people and a plan to bomb her school. On February 22, 2000, a schoolgirl in Germany was arrested for planning a copycat crime scheduled for the one-year anniversary of Columbine. And in the youngest female conspiracy yet, three first-grade girls were suspended from an elementary school in Lake Station, Indiana, after their murder plot was uncovered in April 2000.

Other incidents appeared to be crimes of passion, such as one on March 25, 1993, when nineteen-year-old Lawanda Jackson killed her seventeen-year-old ex-boyfriend, Tony Hall, with a pistol shot to the back of his head in the hallway of Sumner High School, St. Louis, Missouri. But female-to-female bullying was the cause of a school shooting just two days after Andy Williams's rampage in Santee, California. On March 7, 2001, a fourteen-year-old eighth grader named Elizabeth Bush shot a thirteen-year-old classmate during lunch in the crowded cafeteria at Bishop Neumann High School, in Williamsport, Pennsylvania. An argument between the two girls sparked the shooting. A witness who described Elizabeth as an "outsider," and the butt of constant teasing and abuse, commented, "She started walking around saying she didn't want to live anymore, and she should commit suicide right here." Her victim recovered after surgery, and Elizabeth was sentenced to an indeterminate term at a residential treatment facility for juveniles.

In March 2007, a seventeen-year-old student at another Catholic school, this time in Lawrence, Kansas, posted two lists in the bathrooms threatening to murder eighteen of her classmates. The first named eight boys marked as *kill* and a ninth labeled as *dismember*. The other was a list of girls tagged with *enjoy last days of life*. Her MySpace page also threatened Central Catholic High School students. However, Katherine Koontz wasn't arrested until a month later during a nationwide wave of copycat threats that followed the April massacre at Virginia Tech.

Six days before the Northern Illinois University shootings on Valentines Day, 2008, the first African-American female to commit a school shooting took two lives and then her own in a classroom at Louisiana Technical College in Baton Rouge. Latina Williams, 23, was estranged from her family in Mississippi and had been living out of her car. She began losing touch with reality and showing signs of paranoia, yet was able to buy a .357 revolver and a box of ammunition at a pawnshop in New Orleans the day before the shootings. The nursing student apparently called a crisis counselor anonymously on the morning of February 8, indicating she was planning to take her own life. Twenty other people were in the room when Latina killed two female classmates, aged 21 and 26, before turning the gun on herself.

Finally, in a bizarre twist on this genre that involved no firearms at all, two thirteen-year-old girls were charged with terrorist acts in Marietta, Georgia, after they baked a cake laced with bleach, clay, and an expired prescription drug and served it to at least a dozen of their classmates at East Cobb Middle School. The students who ate the cake on November 16, 2004, began to vomit and suffer from headaches and diarrhea. Everyone recovered, but both girls were charged with twelve counts of aggravated assault with intent to commit murder.

When it comes to parricide, the 97 percent to 3 percent gender imbalance begins to align more toward the center, probably because many of those who kill their fathers do so in retaliation for sexual abuse. In Kathleen M. Heide's book *Why Kids Kill Parents*, she states that 12 to 15 percent of parricides that occurred during the years 1977 to 1986 were committed by daughters, not sons.

Psychologists generally agree that, whether by nurture or nature, girls internalize, boys externalize. Girls statistically become more depressed than boys do, because they turn their anger inward. They're more likely to castigate themselves for problems rather than blame others, so they're less likely to kill other people and more likely to want to kill themselves. However, boys succeed at killing themselves more than girls, because they tend to use more certain means, such as guns, rather than overdosing on tranquilizers, cutting wrists, or ingesting poisons.

Aggression has always been part of human nature, and particularly masculine nature, but is there something about our present culture that fortifies this discrepancy in the violent actions and reactions of adolescent males and females? Perhaps we should consider the very fact of adolescence itself in the context of contemporary society. Both physically and psychologically, the onset of puberty is the most intense and tumultuous transition we experience during our lives. It is a period of dramatic sexual awakening and emotional confusion. Author Pamela Spence suggests that in our modern world, we've lost the sense of celebration that these psychobiological changes once engendered. In pagan times, she writes, this metamorphosis was glorified with holy rituals that commemorated the symbolic death of the "child-self," and for the male, it was his rebirth as a hunter-warrior (life-taker) and sexual procreator (life-giver). For the female, only the latter was required. For hundreds of centuries, this was the way of mankind, a human animal at one with the cycles of nature.

Danny Ledonne wrote of the frustrations modern youths face, commenting: *Men evolved to be hunters and warriors, yet we're living in a world of shopping malls and fast-food chains, put into a system of boxes and compelled to remain within the lines.* He suggests that while society as a whole has become more "civilized," our basic human nature cannot be so easily regulated.

The roots of American society are anchored deep in puritanical ethics inherited from the early colonizers of this continent. Under their patronage, paganism and nature worship were viewed as savage elements. Adolescent cravings associated with puberty came to represent a potential for chaos. Far from being celebrated, such yearnings were discouraged, ignored, or repressed.

Today, lacking much of substance to replace those ancient and profound rites of passage, adolescents tend to create their own ritual acts—some as harmless as piercing, tattoos, and spiked hair, and some much more destructive. A frustrated would-be hunter-warrior, longing for attention and admiration from his "tribe" of peers, but finding only rejection and ridicule, might seek redress for his isolation by lashing out at his symbolic enemy—or prey. Second in popularity to trench coats, a large number of male school shooters chose to dress in camouflage clothing or to wear hunting jackets.

Whether the above factors contribute to the alienation of young men any more than they do to young women, the fact remains that males decisively dominate school shootings, and often have a grudge against females. Marc Lépine (chapter 8) was the first to openly declare he was specifically targeting women, but from a Freudian perspective, every assault with a bullet, knife, or spear is, like rape, an act of forced penetration into another person's body by a violent aggressor seeking power, domination, and control.

Two classroom attacks that occurred in the autumn of 2006 swept this aspect of school shooting into an entirely new and frightening direction. First, on September 27, Duane R. Morrison, fifty-three, took six girls hostage for four hours and sexually molested them at Platte Canyon High School in the small mountain town of Bailey, Colorado. At least two of the six girls were raped.

Morrison had been arrested in Denver two months earlier for obstructing police, and in 1973 for larceny and marijuana possession. He'd been living in his car. The school parking lot's video camera showed him sitting in his Jeep for about twenty minutes before mingling with students as classes changed. Nearly thirty-five minutes before the siege began, Morrison, wearing a camouflage backpack, approached a pupil and asked questions about a list of female students. Then he walked unchallenged up to a second-floor college-prep English classroom. He stepped inside, wielding a gun, fired a warning shot at the floor, and ordered students to line up, facing the chalkboard.

"All the hairs on my body stood up," student Chelsea Wilson said later. "I guess I was praying it was a drill." Then Morrison tapped each teen with his gun, handpicking the ones he wanted to stay— all blond, smaller girls. The rest were ordered to get out. Chelsea, a tall brunette, was first to leave.

When word of the crisis reached the school office, the intercom announced a "code white," directing everyone to stay in their classrooms. Jefferson County authorities, who'd also handled the attack at Columbine about thirty miles northeast of Bailey, sent a bomb squad and SWAT team. Morrison claimed to have explosives in his backpack and threatened to set them off, telling police, "Leave me alone, get out of here." Negotiations led to the gunman releasing four girls, one by one, before suddenly cutting off contact with the warning "Something will happen at four o'clock."

In an effort to save the two remaining hostages, the SWAT team had no choice but to end the standoff by blowing a hole in the classroom wall in hopes of getting a clear shot. When they couldn't see the gunman through the gap, they blew the door off its hinges and started inside. Morrison hid behind the hostages, using them as shields, as he fired at the officers. One of the girls, sixteen-year-old Emily Keyes, was a member of the volleyball and debate teams. Smart and agile, she broke away rather than be caught in the cross fire.

Morrison shot her as she ran, then turned the gun on himself. Emily was rushed to a Denver hospital, critically wounded, but died en route. The final hostage was unharmed.

Detectives traced Morrison's handgun to one of his relatives, who gave them the killer's suicide note. Bailey residents were understandably in shock. Park County sheriff Fred Wegener said, "This is something that has changed my school, changed my community. . . . My small county's gone." Sheriff Wegener later shared with the author that "it could have been worse. We believe Morrison was planning an abduction as we found two caches of weapons traced back to him, one north of Bailey, one south, both in remote parkland areas." Another resident echoed the words of so many who'd been through this before: "I just never thought this would happen in this school, but it happens everywhere." That last phrase was prophetic, as was proven just five days later in Pennsylvania.

The Amish people who populate Lancaster County are among the most benign, inoffensive religious groups in the United States. Their stance as conscientious objectors grants them blanket immunity from military service. They learn from birth to follow the pacifist teachings of Christ and literally "turn the other cheek" if offended or attacked. Also known as the "Plain People," at least a third of them live without electricity, telephones, fancy clothes, automobiles, or other modern conveniences in order to remain true to their Anabaptist beliefs. In short, they symbolize something pure, simple, and innocent in the heartland of a nation with more than its share of moral compromise.

Among them, outsiders are tolerated, and those with good intentions are welcomed. Somehow, into the midst of this decency came a force of darkness unlike any they'd ever encountered. Charles Carl Roberts IV did not seem ill intentioned. He was a well-liked thirty-two-year-old milk truck driver who often picked up raw milk from Amish farms in the area. He lived quietly with his wife, Marie, and their three children. True, the couple had suffered the loss of a daughter in 1997 shortly after she was born, but it seemed they'd gotten over that. What no one yet knew was that Roberts had molested young relatives two decades earlier and had "dreams of molesting again." His fellow employees at the dairy noticed that his mood had clouded over recently and he no longer chatted or joked with them and his customers.

On Sunday night, October 1, 2006, Roberts had worked his usual night shift, finishing at 3:00 A.M., on Monday. He was scheduled to take a random drug test that afternoon. He seemed perfectly normal to his wife, at 8:45 A.M., as he escorted their children as usual to the school bus stop. However, when Marie returned home after her morning prayer group, she found suicide notes that her husband had written to each of their children explaining "what brought him to this point." It seemed he hadn't gotten over the death of their prematurely born child nine years earlier, after all. He wrote about *the tragedy with Elise. It changed my life forever. I haven't been the same since it affected me in a way I never felt possible. I am filled with so much hate, hate toward myself, hate towards God and unimaginable emptiness. It seems like every time we do something fun, I think about how Elise wasn't here to share it with us, and I go right back to anger.* It remains a mystery how this anger and emptiness could get intertwined with his sexual fantasies, and then be twisted into a plot to rape and kill young girls, while Roberts was still able to maintain an image of being a peaceful and mild-mannered fellow.

At eleven that morning, Marie was startled by a call from Charles's cell phone saying he was not coming home because he was involved with police in getting even for some long-ago offense. Even when it was all over, Marie would remember her husband as "loving, supportive, and thoughtful" and "an exceptional father."

After seeing his kids off, Roberts had driven a short distance to the one-room schoolhouse for Old Order Amish children, aged six to thirteen, in the village of Paradise, near West Nickel Mines, Lancaster County. Less than thirty students from ten families attended the neat white building surrounded by green fields and a horse fence.

Roberts then backed his truck up to the school and calmly began unloading his cargo. At first, it looked like a construction job: several pieces of lumber, a box with various tools, including a hammer, hacksaw and pliers, wire ties and rolls of clear tape, plus a five-gallon bucket holding a change of clothes, toilet paper, and earplugs. Then came the weaponry: a 9mm semiautomatic pistol, a 12-gauge shotgun, a bolt-action rifle, and a stun gun on his belt. He hauled out a range bag containing roughly six hundred rounds of ammunition, two cans of smokeless powder, and two knives. But there were some more disturbing items: a piece of wood with evenly spaced eye-bolts, flex ties and K-Y lubricant jelly, all of which could be used to secure ten girls to the board and sexually assault them.

The gunman entered the classroom around 10:00 A.M. and found fifteen male and twelve female pupils, a teacher, and several assistants ranging from teens to adults. He addressed them, brandishing his handgun. He told all the boys, a pregnant woman, and three young mothers with small infants to leave. One girl was able to escape with her brother. The teacher and another adult also fled to a nearby farmhouse. At 10:36 A.M., a call went in to 911.

Roberts secured the school doors by nailing two-by-fours and two-by-sixes into place. He piled up desks and flexible plastic ties to complete the barricade, sealing himself in with ten hostages, aged six to thirteen. The gunman then made the girls line up in front of the blackboard and restrained their ankles using wire and plastic cuffs. The children asked Roberts why he was doing this. He replied, "I'm angry with God."

Here there was true heroism. Thirteen-year-old Marian Fisher offered to be slain first, telling Roberts, "Shoot me and leave the other ones loose."

Outside, there was confusion. Police had arrived at 10:45 A.M. and surrounded the building, but they were unable to get a response using their car loudspeakers. Then a call came in from an emergency operator in Harrisburg. She'd been relayed a message from the gunman warning that if police didn't pull back, he'd open fire on the hostages. As this communication was being passed on, at least sixteen shots in rapid sequence rang out from the school. Police stormed in, smashing the windows, but when they entered, they found three girls and the gunman dead, and seven badly injured. Most had been shot in the head, execution-style. Two more girls died overnight. Those murdered were Naomi Rose Ebersol, 7; Anna Mae Stoltzfus, 12; Mary Liz Miller, 8, and her sister Lena Miller, 7; and Marian Fisher, 13, the girl who'd volunteered to be shot to free the others.

The fact that several of Roberts's key items had been purchased a week earlier suggests that he intended committing this offense even *before* the attack in Bailey, Colorado. What happened in the classroom, however, had all the signs of a copycat crime: taking students hostage, ordering the boys to leave, and making the girls line up in front of the blackboard, just as Duane Morrison had done. In the entire history of school shootings, only these two had an openly sexual motive and both happened five days apart. Could that be mere coincidence?

The dynamics of gender imbalance in school shooting is clearly not accidental, but can we simply attribute it to levels of testosterone? It's also possible that the dearth of female shooters up until now simply reflects the traditional passivity that our society has fostered among girls. Among the far more repressive Islamic societies of the Middle East, for example, women were only recently recruited to carry out homicidal bombings by Hamas, al-Qaida, and other terrorist organizations. The reason girls were previously excluded was not out of respect for their tender nature, but rather in disdain of their "lack of worthiness." In the new textbooks of terrorism, there are no rules.

Perhaps a burgeoning sense of feminist empowerment in the West will lead to a corresponding rise in cases of female rampage killers, but it hasn't happened yet. For every female who committed a school shooting, there were at least four others responsible for preventing such an event. Among the cases listed in 2001, for example, attacks at Southside High, in Elmira, New York; De Anza Community College; and Twentynine Palms, in California, were all staved off by courageous girls. In an aborted school-shooting incident in New Bedford, two months after 9/11 (chapter 26), it was the one girl in a group of five conspirators who, because of her sympathy for a teacher, put a stop to it by informing police.

Greater empathy may be a characteristically female trait, but there is one situation where, taken to an extreme, it becomes self-defeating. The reference is to those cases where women have chosen to ignore the crime and embrace the criminal, the subject of our next chapter.

Chapter 22

Love in All the Wrong Places

We are actually drawn to the very dangers, intrigues, dramas and challenges that others with healthier and more balanced backgrounds would naturally eschew.
—Robin Norwood, *Women Who Love Too Much*

The role of the sexes goes beyond victims and victimizers, for what are we to make of women (and seldom, if ever, men) who seek out convicted murderers as the objects of their romantic obsessions? If this category of interpersonal relationship were restricted to mature adults, it would not be included in this book. However, even youths such as Kip Kinkel have been on the receiving end of fan mail that is of a sexual or romantic nature. Some school shooters have gone on to get married while incarcerated to women with whom there is no possibility of consummating their wedding vows. In fact, the killer who has *not* received such offers of affection is the exception rather than the rule.

Jeanette Sereno, a criminal justice professor at California State University, Stanislaus, wrote that it's not uncommon for young men accused of terrible crimes to receive such mail from female admirers. "If you don't see him as responsible for the [murders], he's a very sympathetic young man, someone the whole world is against," Sereno said. "People out there have a need to come to the rescue of someone beleaguered." For example, Scott Peterson, in jail for murdering his pregnant wife and their unborn child, received stacks of romantic letters from women, including one serving time for slaying her husband.

Prior to the Thurston High shootings, probably the worst murder incident involving teenage victims in Lane County history was the slaying of three youths by twenty-two-year-old Conan Wayne Hale at a logging landing near Springfield in 1995. The trial of the killer was nearly over on May 21, 1998, the day Kip left the morning newspaper folded open to the page headlining Hale's story as he drove away to shoot up his school.

Kip's attack, of course, swept all other news off the front page, but on May 22, continued coverage of Hale's trial ran in section C of the Eugene *Register-Guard*. The newspaper had previously carried Deputy DA Bob Gorham's description of how Hale had brutally murdered the trio of youths, aided by his friend, Jonathan Susbauer. The victims were Kristal Bendele and Brandon Williams, both fifteen, and thirteen-year-old Patrick Finley. The girl had allegedly been Hale's lover. Prosecutors argued that Hale killed all three in a jealous rage when Kristal broke up with him and started dating Brandon. Susbauer's version of what took place clashed with Hale's as each vied to pin the blame on the other. The final consensus was that Hale knocked the two boys unconscious with a baseball bat, raped Kristal, and "forced" Susbauer to also rape her. Hale then shot the girl, and Susbauer did the same to the boys. After briefly leaving the scene, they returned to find one of the boys still alive, so they shot him and Kristal once again.

To paint a clearer picture of Mr. Hale's character, a neighbor testified that the perpetrator was a white supremacist who worshiped Satan, had swastikas carved into his arm, hanged cats regularly, dealt drugs, and was a serial rapist. Hale treated both sexes with equal disrespect. He had been arrested for beating and raping a man in 1991 when he was eighteen, and "often attacked his mom [and] punched her in the face."

Even so, four women who testified on his behalf claimed that the killer wasn't really such a bad fellow. They came to "show another side" of Hale to the jury. The two unmarried mothers of Hale's three kids told of the loss they'd suffer if he was executed. They made no mention of what others might suffer if he was freed. The mom whom he had beaten cried to release him. And then there was the inevitable woman who fell in love with him after his arrest: "And I think he fell in love with me," she sighed, informing the jury, "I have grown to respect him. He taught me how to respect God." Hale had sent her two hundred "wonderful" love letters from prison. Some contained autopsy photos of his victims. In a passionate plea for mercy, the woman exclaimed, "If he lost his life, I would lose part of my heart." The jury decided to side with the slain victims. Conan Hale was found guilty on thirty-three criminal counts, including thirteen charges of aggravated murder. He was sentenced to death by lethal injection.

The date of Hale's sentencing was May 27, 1998, less than a week after Kip attacked Thurston. It's conceivable the two killers had some tangential influence upon each other's fate. After their convictions, both shared in common that their weekly mail included not only messages of hate (disposed of before reaching their hands) but also messages of romantic affection (censored and selectively passed on).

Kinkel and Hale were hardly alone among convicted felons in attracting the attention of women who are convinced that their amorous obsessions for "misunderstood" prisoners will make up for what is missing from their lives. Just as there are teenage fan clubs for school shooters, so also are there abundant love letters written to these adolescents from women who want to marry them, have their babies, or, in respect of their youth, want to nurture them. No matter how vicious the crime, they conclude: "It couldn't have been his fault. It must have been his parents or his environment." They convince themselves that their motives are altruistic, but the truth is that both the criminal and the woman who wants to "save" him are selfishly using each other for their own gain. Their real sentiments often echo those of Kristin Kinkel, who so honestly expressed her continuing love for her brother: "Not because he needs me to, but because I need to. . . . It keeps me alive."

When Robin Norwood wrote her best-selling book *Women Who Love Too Much: When You Keep Wishing and Hoping He'll Change,* her intention was to help women who are attracted by emotionally unavailable or abusive men to reach a more rewarding state of self-awareness. Taking an empathic approach, she wrote, *The situations*

and people that others would naturally avoid as dangerous, uncom-
fortable or unwholesome do not repel us, because we have no way
of evaluating them realistically or self-protectively. She prescribes an-
tidotes for those who repeatedly follow patterns of fixation upon a
male they select for all the wrong reasons, desperately hoping that
the "love" they shower upon him will eliminate his history of abuse
of himself and others.

Journalist Sheila Isenberg took this concept a step further by examining one extreme culmination of this tendency in her book *Women*
Who Love Men Who Kill. Isenberg interviewed dozens of individuals who, on the surface, appeared to be quite conventional, yet became deeply obsessed with convicted murderers, eventually abandoning
all else, including, in some cases, their children and husbands, in order
to marry or devote their lives to their felonious lovers.

While these women came from every socioeconomic level, almost
all had in common a dysfunctional childhood in which they were
molested by fathers and/or saw their pain and pleas for help ignored
by passive mothers. They reacted by retreating into an idealized, illusory world based upon a romantic myth of love with a safe but
powerful man. Incarcerated men, safely locked up behind bars, allow
for a controlled relationship without ever truly becoming intimate.
Although some prisons permit conjugal visits, most of these marriages are never consummated, playing into the woman's fantasy of
chivalrous love and validating the nobility of her sacrifice. Isenberg
adds that *there is also the thrill of fame. Since many of these women*
have low self-esteem, the killer's notoriety provides a sense of worth:
The bigger his crime, the more important she feels.

Bridget Kinsella's book *Visiting Life: Women Doing Time on the*
Outside offers another view. Like Isenberg, she interviews women
who have husbands or boyfriends in prison for committing murder,
but she does so in a more personal way, for Bridget is one of them.
The man she cares for, however, fully admits his guilt and accepts
his punishment. An educated, perceptive writer, Kinsella is the first
to admit that nearly all of these women, herself included, are seeking a kind of deliverance from their own wounded lives. And while
the men they find romance with at the bottom of the dating pool
have "nothing more to lose," some of those prisoners also offer a

much-needed understanding of the pain they share, borne of isolation and despair. In Kinsella's book, that empathy enables her to
achieve closure and embark upon a life of renewal.

Still, it is hard for an average, healthy person to comprehend how
so many murderers—even after they are caught, been proven guilty,
and sentenced—are still pursued by legions of women writing love
letters, expressing a desire to be his next partner, despite the fact that
the offender may have murdered his last two partners. Included in this
category are the score of would-be lovers who lined up for the affections of infamous serial killers such as David Berkowitz, Ted Bundy,
John Wayne Gacy, and Hillside Stranglers Kenneth Bianchi and An-
gelo Buono.

While some of these women had only a grade-school education,
others had earned advanced college degrees. In nearly every case, the
woman's capacity for denial was as immense as her gullibility in
accepting her lover's declarations of innocence, often in spite of overwhelming proof and the prisoner's own previous confession to authorities. "He didn't really mean to do it," "He only wanted to scare
her," and "He had no idea the gun was loaded" are some of the
more common phrases they utter, according to Isenberg. Obviously,
the women's emotional needs transcended their ability to exercise intelligent judgment.

A case in point was Judge Charles Martel's removal of a well-
known Seattle public defender on August 14, 2002, for having sex
with her client, an accused triple murderer, in a semiprivate conference room at the King County Jail. Theresa Olson, forty-three at the
time, sacrificed her fifteen-year career to engage in a sexual liaison
with Glen Sebastian Burns, seventeen years her junior, who was awaiting trial for bludgeoning the parents and twenty-year-old sister of
his codefendant to death with a baseball bat at their suburban Seattle home in 1994. The murders took place when Burns was eighteen
years old. The teens allegedly planned to use a $350,000 life-insurance
settlement to help finance their moviemaking project. Guards had
suspected the attorney and her client were misbehaving for several
months because of seductive letters from Olson found in Burns's
cell encouraging him to have sex with her. A few weeks earlier in
an interview in Vancouver, Canada, Olson had declared, "He is innocent. . . . Those boys are not guilty." The question one might ask: Did

this belief in the prisoner's innocence emerge before or after the sexual attraction?

The point this chapter endeavors to make is, while many school shooters (and other murderers) were able to deceive those closest to them into believing they were harmless before their rampage, it's incredible that, even after their crimes, there are still some who see them as being blameless.

With over 250 witnesses in the Thurston cafeteria, no one could pretend that Kip Kinkel wasn't guilty. As in the case of most school shooters, however, it's the assumption of a different kind of innocence that's the main attraction to those women whose priority is nonjudgmental nurturing. Their core belief is that the boy who kills is a confused, helpless child caught in a drama not of his own making, in a situation compounded by the poignancy of an enigmatic mental disorder. As a visiting female professor from the Ukraine at the University of Oregon commented upon hearing about the letters of consolation Kip had received from many women: "I can relate to that. That is our feminine role in life, to succor, to comfort." She saw no contradiction in the fact that no such letters were sent to Kip's young victims, male or female, from women who wanted to succor or comfort them.

As long as Kip remained just another unexceptional youth among the crowd, he received less than average attention from the female sex. Ironically, once his crimes took him into prison and beyond the reach of sexual fulfillment, he was rewarded by needy women with the very promises of intimacy that he had so craved, but could now no longer benefit from.

• Chapter 23 •

Damaging Relations

Two filthy fags slaughtered thirteen people at Columbine High.

—Media alert sent out by the Westboro
Baptist Church, of Topeka, Kansas

Gender issues are not limited to heterosexuals. In school shootings involving two or more males, there's often some question regarding the underlying dynamics of those relationships. Were their shared fantasies of retribution a violent variance of "normal" male bonding, or did that sharing imply a more personal association? The same uncertainty came up in 2002 concerning "Beltline Snipers" Lee Boyd Malvo, seventeen, and his partner, John Allen Muhammad, forty-one, who together shot seventeen people in five states and DC, killing ten of them.

Individuals and organizations that have a fixed agenda will take almost any opportunity to promote their viewpoint by linking it to newsworthy events that catch the public imagination, especially when explanations for those events remain unclear. School shootings are no exception. When the shooters are associated in any way with intimations of homosexuality, that alone may become the focus for those who insist that any sexual orientation deviating from the norm is the basis for a criminal trajectory, despite a wealth of factual data to the contrary. Sometimes, however, it's the negative power of these very taunts—"fag, faggot, homo, queer"—that push a teen tottering on the brink of rage over the edge.

In Van Sant's *Elephant* (chapter 20), fictional protagonists Eric and Alex (unambiguously styled after Columbine's Eric and Dylan) play a violent video game together, watch a Hitler documentary, and then share a shower before they leave to spill blood at their school. In the shower, Eric says regretfully he's never kissed anyone, and Alex obliges. The camera cuts away as they embrace.

In actual fact, Eric Harris included gays on his hate list. That didn't prevent statements of antigay sentiment from arising among a few members of the extreme Christian right regarding Harris and Klebold, just as it would after 9/11 when Reverend Jerry Falwell blamed that devastating terrorist attack upon God's anger against America's "abortionists, feminists, gays, and lesbians."

Shortly after the Columbine shooting, journalist and author Dave Cullen noted that "law enforcement officials, the media, and the Christian right continue to track reports that at least one of the Columbine High gunmen was gay. . . . Harris and Klebold had endured repeated harassment due to rumors they were gay. Jocks especially taunted the pair with epithets like 'faggot' and 'homo.' Reverend Falwell described them as gay on *Geraldo Live* . . . but friends insisted that the young men were straight."

Instead of oversimplifying these relationships, it would be more meaningful to consider the deeper issues of complex team dynamics at work here. Paired shooters are very different from small shooter groups or cliques, such as those with up to a half-dozen members that were detained for plotting the New Bedford, Massachusetts, North Pole, Alaska, and Burlington, Wisconsin school attacks, among others.

The largest such gang may have been a covey of teenagers in Fort Myers, Florida, who called themselves the Lords of Chaos (LOC). Led by Kevin Don Foster, a charismatic eighteen-year-old dropout, this group of Riverdale High School students banded together to "cause chaos and destruction," including vandalism, arson, and armed robbery. One night in April 1996, they were attempting to burn down their school gymnasium when Mark Schwebes, the school's thirty-two-year-old bandleader, caught them and said he would file a report the next morning. Foster led three LOC members to Schwebes's home and shot him in the face. On the way back from the murder, he called for a group hug, telling the boys it had been a "job well done." Foster was sentenced to death, and the others received lengthy prison terms.

By contrast, when only two individuals set up a cooperative dyad (defined by Webster's as "two persons in a continuous relationship involving interaction"), their more intimate solidarity forms a "you and me against the world" cohesion. Obviously, Harris and Klebold, as well as Johnson and Golden, fit into this category, but the psychological theory that most closely defines their rapport is called "shared psychotic disorder" (also known as *"folie à deux,"* literally "double insanity" in French). SPD is an asexual condition whereby an abnormal fantasy develops in an individual directly as a result of his or her close relationship with another person who has a similar, already-established psychotic delusion. Although *folie à deux* is a very rare disorder, it often occurs in a forensic setting where shared delusional beliefs incorporate a heightened risk of violence. A more common, less extreme alternative is called *egoisme à deux,* representing a sort of communal ego as if the two individuals had become one mind.

While the two Columbine boys murdered an approximately equal number of students during their shooting spree, it's generally acknowledged that Eric Harris took the dominant role in their alliance. Describing how their dyad related to the rest of the population, they made it clear they were the only two "superior" beings in their venom-filled world. Their personal covenant was expressed in grandiose pronouncements such as, "We're the only two who have self-awareness," "Nobody else is like us," and "We're the only two people who seem to understand the meaning of life."

As to Johnson and Golden, while both lads later accused each other of being the instigator at Jonesboro, it's interesting to note that it was Mitch Johnson, the older one, who exhibited more remorse than the younger "sharpshooter," Andrew Golden, who remained stoically aloof and surprisingly unemotional during most of the trial proceedings. In an analysis of ninety-seven *folie à deux* cases in Japanese literature, professors H. Kashiwase and M. Kato found that younger subjects more often influence older ones. The Japanese study found the most common diagnosis for the dominant partner is schizophrenia, and for the submissive one, paranoid reaction. Delusion is the most common symptom shared by both partners. While the causes of *folie à deux* are not well understood, often the best course of treatment is simply to separate the two individuals.

In the aftermath of the Virginia Tech shootings, only one tabloid magazine (the *Globe*) cranked out a headline screaming that Seung-hui Cho's crimes were committed because he was a frustrated homosexual, who had allegedly been seen cruising gay bars in nearby Roanoke. Ironically, the antigay Westboro Baptist Church in Topeka (not affiliated with any national Baptist organization), founded and led by Fred Phelps, declared that Cho was sent by God to punish the Virginia Tech teachers and students who brought their fate upon themselves by not being true Christians. The proof of this, said Phelps's daughter Shirley Phelps-Roper, was that "God does not do that (i.e., mass murder) to his servants." Paradoxically, she also claimed that Cho was both fulfilling the word of God and burning in hell for violating God's commandment not to kill.

In the only school shooting that's been labeled a sexual-orientation hate crime, a fourteen-year-old boy at E. O. Green Junior High in Oxnard, California, shot an openly gay classmate twice in the head on February 12, 2008, in front of a classroom full of students. The victim, fifteen-year-old Lawrence King, often wore feminine clothing, makeup, high-heeled boots, jewelry and painted nails. King died the next day from his injuries. According to a 2002 California Department of Education survey, students thought to be gay were five times more likely to be threatened or injured by a weapon.

Mother-son relationships have figured into several school shootings. Luke Woodham's clinically overpossessive mother, Mary Ann, was described in chapter 12. The 1996 Moses Lake shooter Barry Loukaitis (chapter 20) also had a divorced mother whose judgment in shared intimacies was questionable. When earlier that year she revealed to her son a Valentine's Day plan to kidnap and kill her ex-husband and his new girlfriend, it was Barry who took the mature role of convincing her not to go through with it and instead write out her anger on paper. Unfortunately, his mother could not reciprocate because Barry didn't share his own deadly plans with her.

Shared secrets in the Kinkel home may have been deeper than outsiders imagined. The issue of sexual orientation took a surprising twist when a woman who claimed to have firsthand information concerning Kip's dad made a startling confession. Her disturbing report suggested an alternate rationale as to why this tragedy took place. Unfortunately, it's unlikely this particular revelation can ever be substantiated.

During a November 2002 phone call with the mother of a girl whom Kip had dated, the question of Kip's relationship with his father arose. "There was more going on than people knew," the mother hinted. The author acknowledged that while Bill Kinkel was an exemplary teacher, when frustrated by his son's learning disabilities, he'd reputedly been guilty of some verbal abuse against Kip at home, but never physical abuse, such as hitting. In fact, Bill never lifted a hand against anyone.

"No," the mother said, "a different kind of abuse." This remark not only went against the grain of everything known about Bill Kinkel's character, it was also something never mentioned in any psychiatric examination of Kip, as it surely would have been had the boy offered up such information. Further, if true, the defense team would have undoubtedly used this in Kip's favor. How, then, could it be possible that such an idea had been communicated to only one person and no other? I requested that the mother relate the exact circumstances. Hesitantly she replied, "One day Kip asked me, 'If my father is gay, does that mean I will eventually become gay as well?' So I asked Kip why he would think his father was gay, and he replied that his father had done some things to him." She was asked to be more specific. "No, I really don't want to go there," she answered, "but just look at the literature that's out there on patricide, why boys kill their fathers, and you'll find all you need to know."

Certainly, the bulk of patricide cases for both males and females do involve sexual abuse or similar physical mistreatment, and the results have produced children with much the same mind-set as "heartless" school shooters, like Brenda Spencer (chapter 21). As author Ann Rule wrote in her book *Small Sacrifices* about another major murder drama in Lane County, Oregon, *Studies show that sexually abused children learn to disassociate themselves from their bodies. They deal with the abuse by going away someplace—in their heads. . . . They learn to feel nothing at all. If one does not feel, one cannot be hurt. Nor can one feel anything for anyone else.*

Yet such general data proves nothing in this particular case. Obviously, the temptation to accept this report at face value was powerful simply because it would conveniently tie up so many loose ends and would make perfect sense from an analytical perspective. One child psychologist suggested, for example, that here would be the ideal solution to explain the unexplainable—namely, why an educated man who is aware his son is troubled, seeing a psychologist, and on medication might agree to buy that son weapons. "A father wanting to buy off his guilt?" the psychologist suggested. "Or a bribe to keep silent, or even a 'payment' for services?" In short, if true, this highly charged allegation would be the final blow to Bill Kinkel's dignity and reputation. If it could not be verified, it would have to be disregarded as mere gossip. Yet either of these alternatives were as difficult to *dis*prove as they were to prove.

Since nothing of this nature had ever been spoken of elsewhere, only two people knew the absolute truth: one of them was dead, and the other, incarcerated and protected by the rights of law, was beyond the reach of further private interrogation. One could therefore surmise in this circumstance only three possibilities:

(a) The mother's information was false. She made it up, embellished a partial truth, or had a faulty memory.
(b) Kip had lied to that mother.
(c) The information was true.

For either (a) or (b), what motivation would there be to lie? In Kip's case, his dishonesty is well-documented, yet all of his falsehoods adhere to one of two patterns: either he was denying something he'd done, or he was projecting the image of a character who was a little dangerous. This episode fits neither category. In fact, it contradicts both patterns. That still doesn't mean Kip was telling the truth. It's also possible he wanted to win points with the mother by gaining sympathy for his plight, or he wanted to set up his dad in her mind as a bad guy for some other purpose. Even so, it seems an odd and unprecedented admission from a young man who was already insecure about himself.

Then consider the mother's possible motivation in telling this tale. There seemed no way she could benefit from this other than gaining attention for herself. However, attention was the last thing she wanted. Unlikely as it was, if she knowingly told a lie, was it some form of revenge from the parent of an indirect victim against the parents of the victimizer? There was no way to ascertain this. A week later, I called the mother again. She stood by what she'd previously said, but added that she'd now spoken with her attorney and she would not step forward publicly, nor would she be able to speak of this again. End of story.

Like so many other intriguing leads in this case, this, too, had reached an impasse. There was no other information that could justify taking this woman's account seriously, and as for Bill, there was nothing to support the idea that he was wearing that sort of mask. Further, if he were, how wise would it be for him to buy a gun for a boy he supposedly "victimized"?

This impasse, however, altered somewhat in December 2006 when the author spoke with a person of indisputable reputation who has worked closely with Kip within the youth correctional system. Because professional ethics do not allow the divulgence of privileged information, this individual could only confirm that there was a period in Kip's life, between ages seven and nine years old, that carries memories for him in association with his father that are too painful even now for Kip to express without breaking down in tears and not being able to proceed further. In regard to the insinuations imparted by the mother of Kip's girlfriend, this individual suggested that they shouldn't be dismissed, and further agreed that if Kip had been more willing to share this aspect of his history with his attorneys, it might have helped his case, or at least contributed to the victims' understanding of the reasons Kip became the way he was. Still, it isn't hard to fathom, if these implications are warranted, why a son would want to keep private the shame of secrets that died with the murder of his parents.

Being called a "fag" or similar taunts is one of the most disturbing insults a teenage boy can hear, namely because many young males have moments of self-doubt. Both school and workplace shootings are usually preceded by a "final straw," one last crisis or insult, real or perceived, that pushes an already depressed gunman over the edge. For Barry Loukaitis, it was being called a "fag" by a member of his algebra class, and it was this same barb that sparked Michael Carneal's rampage at West Paducah. As mentioned earlier, it was also one of the indignities hurled at Ramsey and Harris and Klebold.

As for Kip, because of his small stature and lack of sports ability, he may have received this epithet in greater proportion than the average student, but he more often was known to use it against others whom he bullied. In chapter 16, however, it was mentioned that just after murdering his father, Kip told friends Tony McCown and Nick Hiaasen that he intended to kill Brian Havelock. Tony knew it was because Brian had called Kip a faggot, and he recalled that unlike Kip's usual belligerent and immediate response to that insult, this time his friend had not reacted at all. In fact, Kip had remained uncharacteristically silent. That alone proves nothing—Kip might have been too scared to respond, or he bottled up his anger for a delayed act of revenge with firearms later on.

Kip's hostile attitude toward his peers may also have simply been a reflection of a more prosaic but nevertheless damaging relationship with his father. Kip told his psychologist Dr. Hicks that he could sometimes talk about personal issues with his mother, but he "cannot discuss his feelings with his father for fear he will become angry with him." His real paranoia was not fear of foreign invasion but fear of being the unworthy son, never getting it right, or that he was "less of a man" than other boys. By extending that fear of inferiority to his peers, he would have been extremely sensitive to being mocked or laughed at by any students who echoed his father's verbal jabs. In keeping with the credo of the bully who is at heart a coward, Kip would have looked for weaker beings to project his own self-loathing and self-doubts upon, and this he did.

Guns made Kip a man. From a strictly Freudian perspective, his rifles, pistols, and knives could be symbolically viewed as phallic amplifications, but they were equally extensions of his wounded ego. They became his shell and armor, one that bristled with barbed daggers and bullet-shaped projectiles. His explosive personality found literal embodiment in his explosive bombs. Whatever dark mysteries were fermenting in the obscure regions of Kip's mind, his outward attitude regarding women remained well within the range of normalcy. Like every teen boy, he stumbled through the early stages of romantic involvement. He had not progressed very far when he committed the deeds that abrogated all such further pursuits.

• Chapter 24 •

Parents' Rights, Parents Wronged

You can't have the kind of saturation of violence that we have today without it manifesting itself somewhere. It's like a virus spreading through a large population of people. Not everyone gets sick. Just the most vulnerable, and then with varying degrees of illness.

> —Dewey Cornell, director of the University of
> Virginia Youth Violence Project

It's every parent's worst nightmare—knowing that your son or daughter is in harm's way, and may at this very moment be wounded or bleeding while you're unable to reach them or even discover what condition they're in. It has happened at every school where a shooting occurred. The Thurston High parents serve as a classic example. For many of them outside school that day, this waking horror lasted for over two agonizing hours. Theirs was not an isolated case. In Littleton, Virginia Tech, and elsewhere, the scenario was much the same. The narratives that follow describe the anguish these parents faced, whether their own child was physically injured or not.

Within thirty minutes of the shooting at Thurston, the scene both in and outside school was one of total chaos. The image that stayed in student Tony McCown's mind took place in the school's parking lot. He'd been walking onto the campus with Nick Hiaasen when two kids shouted, "Kip's got a gun in there!" It was the first he knew that his best friend had actually crossed that line of rationality and committed this appalling act. Nearby, a mother had just dropped her son off, and they were exchanging a few last words at the open window of her minivan. "Suddenly," Tony recalled, "she picks up on the fact that all these kids are streaming out of the school, yelling about a gun, and, still sitting in the drivers seat, she reaches her arm out the open window, grabs her son around his neck, and begins speeding out of the parking lot." McCown stared in amazement as the boy's feet scrambled to run as fast as he could, trying to keep up with the car while being held in a headlock. The mother's instinctual reaction to save her son came close to killing him. Seeing the world going insane around him, Tony felt a sudden emptiness open up inside.

Another mother was inside the school when the shooting occurred. Pam Case had been in the school library when some students ran in to say shots had been fired. When she was finally able to gain access to the cafeteria, Case faced a scene of mayhem. She discovered her son Tony among the wounded. He had taken three bullets through his back and one to his right leg. "As I knelt beside him," she reported, "it didn't seem so bad. He was pale, weak, and vomiting, but trying to smile and talk. Now I know that he was bleeding to death internally. There wasn't pain. Death was quietly coming to Tony. He was dead on the elevator going into the operating room." But after a week in the intensive care unit, Pam was told that Tony would, in fact, survive, although he required months of further care and surgery.

Assistant Principal Dick Doyle was also just leaving the library, where he'd been the keynote speaker at a Senior Men's Excellence Breakfast that morning. The uplifting event had just finished, and Doyle was feeling energized by the presentation as he strutted out across the open courtyard toward the cafeteria. Suddenly he was facing waves of panicked kids running directly toward him like a giant cascade of flailing bodies tumbling in fast-forward motion. The mind plays strange tricks at such moments, and for a few crucial seconds, Doyle's stunned senses became fixated upon an implausible sight.

"What I couldn't get over," he said, "was how they appeared to be running in unconscious coordination, left-foot, right-foot, lock-stepped as if all were being choreographed by some unseen demonic force." Doyle shook off this trancelike perception and dashed into the cafeteria. He didn't know how or why the carnage had occurred, but the smell of blood was overpowering, as if this were a battle-field. Doyle immediately started tending to the wounded. When some-one said they thought there might be a second shooter "still out there," he made a circuit of the building, returned, and got onto the public-address system to warn everyone of the danger.

Rebecca Lynn, a Springfield mom who had both a boy and a girl at Thurston, got a call from her son's cell phone and listened as the event unfolded. "I remember the absolute terror I felt when my son, Mikel, called me, in very hushed tones, to tell me there'd been a shooting," she would later tell a hearing. She ordered Mikel to stay put and asked if he knew whether his sister, Betina, was safe. Before he could reply, Rebecca "felt a chill unparalleled to anything I've ever experienced" as she heard the voice of Dick Doyle thundering over the loudspeakers: "All students, stay in the classroom! Close and lock the doors! Turn off the lights!" Mikel begged his mom not to come to Thurston because they didn't yet know where the shooter was, but Rebecca was already on her way out the door. As she raced toward the school in her car, well over the speed limit, two ambu-lances passed by twice as fast. She increased her speed.

Approaching Thurston, she met complete pandemonium. "I saw law enforcement vehicles from the city, the county, the state. I saw ambu-lances . . . fire trucks. I also saw Don Stone." Coach Don Stone was only trying to help. He'd been in the cafeteria with Doyle helping the wounded, but didn't realize he had blood on his hands. As he lifted them to direct traffic, one mother stared at his palms and nearly fainted.

As television and radio began reporting the disaster, distressed parents gathered in front of Thurston High desperately seeking in-formation regarding the fate of their kids. The situation became chaotic as frustration gradually gave way to panic. School and law officials shepherded them from one staging area to another, keeping them away from emergency services crews. Worried moms and dads, now numbering in the hundreds, were advised to pick up their kids at the auditorium. Apparently, it was just a ruse. The auditorium was empty.

The effect of this subterfuge upon the anxious assemblage was devastating. "People were shouting and asking questions, screaming and crying," Rebecca Lynn recounted later. They were given periodic updates, but little of it proved reliable. After apprehensive adults had counted twelve stretchers with bodies being carried to ambulances, an official told them that a list of the wounded would be posted on the door of a church across the street. The crowd rushed madly over, but again, the story was false; no such list was forthcoming. Police now restrained the terrified throng from recrossing the road back to the school.

Finally, two and a quarter hours after Kip's assault, Principal Larry Bentz came and told the group that a list of wounded would be read out at the back of the church. There was another frenzied dash to this new site. Rebecca continued, "To add insult to injury, the officer assisting Mr. Bentz advised that nothing would be read until we were absolutely still. . . . I thought [it] was inhumane, given the situation and the panic that each of us felt, wondering, wondering, 'Is my son or daughter okay? Are they shot? Are they dead?' It felt like we were reduced to the level of kindergarten children. If not compliant, we wouldn't get the information we all so desperately sought."

Despite appearances, authorities were not being deliberately cruel. Rather, they'd been stalling in order to gather a number of specially trained grief counselors, who would be in place when the terrible but inevitable news reached the ears of some of the parents assembled there. As the names of the injured were being read, "there was an instant eerie moan from the crowd as somebody recognized their child's name," Rebecca remarked. She guiltily admitted experiencing relief each time a name was called, because it was not one of her kids, and, at the same time, shame for feeling comforted as another parent took the blow. Then came her own.

"I think it was the twelfth name Larry read: Betina Lynn," she said stoically. "At first, it didn't register. . . . It was almost like an out-of-body experience. . . . I [saw] my hands were shaking uncontrollably. Then it was with almost an intellectual observation that [I understood] those hands were connected to my body. I next became aware of this very low, guttural, and primal cry coming from somewhere. Again, it took several seconds to realize it was coming from me."

Even those who did not lose a child to the violence that day were profoundly affected by this ordeal. Michael Crowley's son Ryan was not on the list, but another boy named Ryan was. Hearing that first name, and thinking for a second it was his son, was a shattering experience. Crowley described how "standing in the group of parents in the church parking lot, hearing name after name of all the people who had been shot, I can't describe the horror as each name was read. One of the last names read was Ryan Atteberry. It was not my son. It didn't matter. I lost it at that moment. I couldn't go on. I can't explain to you the effects this has had on my family and my marriage. The stress of having to deal with these issues on the son, the husband and wife, are immense."

Despite the passage of nine years, parents at Virginia Tech were just as stymied. A much larger campus, their cell phone calls soon overwhelmed the region's service capacity, forcing many to drive to the college for answers. The school was cordoned off, however; so they converged on the hospitals, creating security problems. No Tech officials showed up at the medical centers to help families cope. Parents searched for their sons and daughters in vain. One of the most poignant and wrenching memories burned into the souls of first responders is something that will haunt many of them for years—the sound of cell phones desperately ringing inside body bags as they carried out victims. That single image alone could sum up the entire tragedy of school shootings.

At Thurston, parents of wounded students had been taken on buses to two hospitals to try and locate their kids. Rebecca Lynn needed to find her uninjured son first. When they were finally reunited, she broke the news to him that his sister had been shot. She still had no idea how bad off Betina was. They raced to the first hospital, but no one there had any information about her. A chance meeting with a friend established that her daughter was at the second location. As mother and son jogged back across the parking lot, Rebecca noticed that Mikel, who stands six feet two inches and weighs 218 pounds, was sobbing like a small child. "Mom," he cried, "I can't imagine living life without Betina." She stopped, held him, and assured him with all the confidence she could muster, "You won't have to! I promise."

They made their way up to the trauma unit at Sacred Heart Hospital and were told that although the girl was not critically injured, they couldn't see her for another hour. When they finally entered her room and found her wrapped up in bandages and IVs, Betina cried,

"Mom, Mom! I thought he was going to kill me, I thought he was going to kill me!" over and over again as they tightly hugged.

As the long day crept bleary-eyed into the early hours of Friday, May 22, Springfield police chief Bill DeForrest finally got ready to leave the station house. Years later, he'd recall that after midnight only one other remained in that dimly lit room. Detective Al Warthen sat silently at his desk, his head cradled in his hands. DeForrest knew then that Warthen must have taken it harder than anyone else on the force, perhaps because he'd been the one to let Kip go on May 20.

Parents of students who'd been physically and/or emotionally wounded later had a litany of grievances concerning the responses of authorities and the effrontery of the national press. A few journalists had been so blatantly intrusive as to disguise themselves as medical personnel in order to gain access to emergency rooms to interview seriously injured students.

In the aftermath, what parents wanted more than anything was to corner Kip and demand he tell them why he targeted kids he hardly knew, why he felt such a need to destroy lives. It was hoped those questions would be answered during Kip's trial, but it never happened. Instead, at the sentencing hearing a year later, parents and victims alike were able to speak their minds to Kip in court. He wasn't allowed to answer, but he had to listen.

• Chapter 25 •

The Other End of the Gun

I am Jennifer Alldredge and you tried to murder me. . . .
I hate you. I hate what you have done. I hate what I have
become because of you. I hate living in fear each day. . . .
You made the rest of my high school life absolute hell. I
became someone other kids avoided because I reminded
them of you and the shooting. Other so-called friends tried
to use me to get attention. I became this story and no
longer a person. I became the object of people's pity, and
that sickens me. My name became 'victim.' "

—Jennifer Alldredge, spoken to Kip Kinkel
at his sentencing hearing

What if the dead could return and speak to their murderer, to tell
their side of the story? This was the subject of a play called *Bang,*
Bang You're Dead! written by William Mastrosimone, an Oregon
drama teacher, in response to Kinkel's attack. But in real life, the
physically and emotionally maimed of Thurston could come back
and verbally confront their tormentor toward the end of his sentencing hearing in November 1999. This was arranged to help them
achieve closure. While there was little that could compensate them
for their loss, at least they could express their feelings directly to the
person responsible.

In most murder trials, there are seldom more than one or two
survivors to speak out against the perpetrator. In Kip's case, more
than two dozen people he'd shot were invited to meet head-on with

the boy who'd tried to kill them. During a five-hour period, each of the wounded victims and their family members, as well as the families of the two boys killed, were given the chance to stand up and speak their minds.

Those who'd suffered the scars of this ordeal vocalized their feelings, as much to release their frustrations as to convince Judge Mattison to hand down the maximum possible sentence. Some spoke with anger, others with reasoned calm. A few forgave their attacker with surprising compassion, while many vented their wrath over the misery they'd endured at his hands. Several wanted Kip to suffer as they had.

Predicting this, Kip's sister, Kristin, urged him to "go to a safe place in his memory," and try not to listen if he could possibly tune out their words, "because they are angry and going to say things they really don't mean." Kip replied to Kristin that he "owed it to the victims to listen." However, for the most part, he kept his head lowered onto the table, cradled in his arms, only occasionally looking up when a speaker would demand his attention. One parent said, "Your sister told you to tune us out because we're angry. Well, that's true, I am angry. But that doesn't mean I'm irrational and I don't mean what I say."

These victim impact statements take up 150 pages of the hearing transcript. What follows is a small sampling. Those who suffered the greatest loss—the families of students Ben Walker and Mikael Nickolauson, who were both killed—were given the privilege of speaking first. Benjamin's dad, Mark Walker, instructed the judge that "the sentence you are about to render will send a message to other young people whether they can expect leniency from the law or that they will be held accountable for their actions. . . . If Mr. Kinkel is sitting in prison without possibility of release for the rest of his life, it might—just might—keep some other young person from taking a gun to school. That would be the only positive thing that could come from this tragedy."

Walker added that Kip, "was selective and warned people he thought to be friends away from school that morning. . . . Mr. Kinkel walked past my son in the hall, turned, put his gun to the back of my son's head, and killed him. This was cold-blooded murder, not a random act of rage. His actions were callous, calculated, premeditated, and with no regard for human life. Benjamin was sixteen years old. He lost sixty to seventy years of his life, as did the Nickolauson boy. Teresa Miltonberger will spend the rest of her life missing part of her brain. The scars and the trauma suffered by the other young people who survived will be with them for the rest of their lives as well."

Benjamin's mother, Linda Kluber, wondered how Kip could have the gall to promise he'd learned his lesson. She asked, "If your closest family and friends could not tell that you were capable of murder, and you even surprised yourself, how can we believe you when you say you won't [hurt anyone] again?" Another of her statements explains one of the reasons this book was written. "When the sentencing phase began," she said, "there was a chance that . . . we could try to understand what happened and learn why you did what you did. Unfortunately, that didn't happen."

Mikael Nickolauson's mother, Dawna, spoke of the immediate personal effect of the tragedy. "When something like this happens," she explained, "your life is put on hold. You lose track of time. You don't know what day it is. You don't remember to eat." She mentioned how the sorrow had spread to touch "everybody that we know." And rather than the death of their son being one isolated calamity, it came in the midst of others. Her husband's dad had died eighteen months earlier, his sister died two weeks after that, and then his cousin was lost to cancer; his grandmother and uncle went next, and then their son was shot. Following that, his aunt and Dawna's grandmother passed away. This was a family well-versed in grief.

The boy's father, Michael Nickolauson, retraced the stages of their son's life. "There is always something very special about a firstborn child. Mikael was that for us . . . but the real joys come when you realize they are beginning to change from a child to an adult. Mikael was at that point in his life. He had found somebody he wished to marry and was making plans. And suddenly that was taken away from him, and from us, and the places in our hearts that had been filled with happiness, joy, expectations, left an empty hole filled with nothing but pain and agony, which will never go away." Reading a letter from the boy's sister, he added, *"We were all killed a little when Mikael was murdered."*

Christina Osburn, who'd been shot two times, accused Kip of deciding to "play God with other people's lives," and asked him the questions everyone wanted to know: "Why were you so angry that you decided to kill so many people? What did these people do to you?" Of course, she included herself, adding indignantly, "I don't even know you!"

Jennifer Alldredge answered Christina's questions for Kip, who had to remain silent throughout. "You didn't care," she stated simply. "We were just more target figurines on your wooden (target practice) board." Jennifer's personal outrage against Kip for shooting her had inspired the injured girl to speak out in interviews and at a press conference in Washington, DC. Her goal was to promote stronger laws against juvenile felons, thus preventing killers, such as Kip, from getting early release or a transfer to a psychiatric hospital. In opposition to those who felt her indignation, while justified, failed to acknowledge the depth of Kip's mental illness, Jennifer remained unconvinced that this issue was pertinent or valid. She considered Kip to be a spoiled child of privilege, end of story. She told him straight, "I want you to know that I'm not falling for this poor little mentally sick rich boy. I don't buy that whole act of burying your head in the table. I'm not going to feel sorry for you, or claim you were misunderstood. Do you know that everyone felt depressed if they were not seen for who they really were in middle school and their freshman year? I don't buy that excuse."

Alldredge was also the most graphic in describing her personal injuries at the hearing. Her motive in doing so is easy to surmise. Assuming that mass murderers do not feel empathy or consider consequences, Jennifer likely wanted to drive home to Kip a lesson in cause and effect, a recognition that once a bullet leaves the barrel, the shooter gives no further thought to its aftermath. But it's a simple truth: every gun has two ends. The satisfaction, pleasure, fear, or dread a person feels in the presence of a weapon depends upon which end of it they happen to be positioned at. The individual pulling the trigger may feel excitement and even elation in the explosion of deadly firepower that his finger unleashes, but how would that same person react if his own face had been held up to the other end of the gun at that very moment?

Jennifer tried to force Kip to realize a measure of her experience at the receiving end, hence the uncompromising detail of her description. "I will have my hand deformed for the rest of my life," she said. "In the summer, when I wear a bathing suit or a tank top, people gawk and ask questions about the scars from the bullet holes, forty-two staples, three chest tubes, and hand scars. I feel as if I've done something to be ashamed of. As if I've done something to deserve to look the way I do."

While most school shooters were considered to be outsiders or losers, Alldredge and a number of others thought Kip was part of the in crowd. "The cafeteria side door opened and you walked in. There were strange noises, like fireworks, and I thought you were campaigning for class elections like the rest of the popular group you hung out with," she told him. "You were on the football team, and had it made."

Jennifer verbalized the loneliness and isolation that many surviving victims experience in the life-altering postscript to such a tragedy. "Everyone felt compelled to discuss every gory detail of the shooting and its aftermath with me," she said. "I felt alienated. Between therapy meetings, doctor appointments, surgeries, and dealing with my own fear that you'll one day try to hurt me again, I am so tired of having all of this run my life. I've had to continually deal with the consequences of what you've done. That, to me, sounds as if it's a harsh punishment just for sitting in the cafeteria. The fact that you'll spend at least twenty-five years in jail seems so inconsequential."

Her rebuke ended: "I never want to worry about you hurting my friends and me ever again. I never want to send my kids off to school one day and worry if you've been released. I'm tired of being scared. You shouldn't ever be able to have that power over me again."

David Alldredge, Jen's dad, spoke about the frustration of listening to defense psychiatrists argue that Kip might someday be well enough to be released. "For a father of one of the shooting victims," he said, "sitting through all of this was trying, and took a lot of patience. Basically, I wanted to stand up and scream."

Diana Alldredge, Jen's mom, compared the "kid-glove treatment" the perpetrator was getting in prison to the suffering of her child. Remembering how Kip's doctors were concerned about his pale skin, lack of appetite, anxiety, and depression, she reminded the court that when her daughter was shot, "her coloring was pale also. In fact, it was actually gray." With tubes in her body, "she couldn't eat at all." Unable to speak, Jen's anxiety was expressed in the first question she was able to ask: "Am I going to die?" Diana told of the "emotional roller coaster" that only a parent in this situation could comprehend. "When I heard the news that a mother of a Columbine shooting victim had committed suicide," she confessed, "I knew how close I'd come to the same end."

Doctors were amazed at the extraordinary number of injuries that came dangerously close to being fatal, but miraculously were not. Betina Lynn, for instance, was told that "I was so very lucky because the first bullet didn't paralyze me. It entered less than half an inch to the left of my spine. If I'd flinched, it would have severed my spinal cord and I'd be in a wheelchair today."

Melissa Taylor, shot once, was another "miracle child." The bullet lodged in her shoulder a half-inch from her heart. Similar to Ryan Atteberry, who was shot on the side of his face, Melissa is one of many students who still have bullet fragments embedded in their bodies. In most cases, these couldn't be removed because they're positioned so close to vital organs or nerves, that to operate would be more perilous than to leave them be.

Melissa's dad, Vietnam vet Ted Taylor (no relation to the *Eugene Weekly* editor of the same name), cautioned the court that "these kids . . . are going to suffer post-traumatic stress disorder." Mr. Taylor admitted that he himself had been enduring PTSD for the past thirty-five years and freely confessed that his own actions on the battlefield were the cause. He told Kip, "Like you, I, too, have murdered, over and over. And I go to bed every night, thinking of those faces every damn night. And that's something you can't shake, boy." Taylor was assuming that Kip had a conscience similar to his own.

The truth of Taylor's warning about PTSD became evident in the months following the shooting. In some cases, there was a delayed response. Betina Lynn explained how "emotionally, I didn't react for months. I understood what had happened, and I knew who'd done it, but I didn't feel anything. I didn't feel anger, I didn't feel sadness. . . . I was just happy to be alive, I could see my friends and even eat chocolate."

With time, Betina began showing the same PTSD effects as many of the others. "I can't handle large groups of people," she said. "I can't handle the Fourth of July [or] when a car backfires [or] when a door slams. I can't handle it when people come up behind me and don't tell me they're there, and I turn around. . . . I practically jump out of my skin."

Naturally, a lot of hostility was displayed. The only time Judge Mattison had to speak out to limit aggressive remarks, however, was when Ted Taylor began his diatribe by glaring at Kip and saying, "I wish I could redirect the energy I have in my body so I could come over and shake the shit out of you." The judge interrupted and Taylor calmed down enough to continue in a cooler manner.

Another dad had even more reason to feel belligerent, but he saved his hostility until the end of his harangue. It was Ryan Crowley's face that Kip was aiming at when he ran out of bullets. Serendipity saved Ryan's life, but his father, Michael Crowley, had witnessed firsthand how this terrifying brush with near-death had affected his boy. He explained, "After the shooting, my son told me about sitting across from Mikael [Nickolauson]. He told me about watching Mikael grab his thigh, where he had been shot. Looking into Mikael's face as it was in anguish and pain. He saw the gun go to the back of Mikael's head. He saw Kip pull the trigger. He described in detail—this horrifies me to this day—how Mikael's face changed as he died."

Now the father turned again to the defendant. "Kip," he said, "you're a bastard. You shot Ben, you shot Mikael, you shot Ryan Atteberry—all in the back. But with my son, you put the gun to his forehead. They didn't know they were going to be shot. My son knew he was going to be shot, and knew he was going to be killed. But you just pulled the trigger. When there were no bullets, you tried to reload. Kip, I'm a pacifist. I have endured many things without taking a blow back. But if the court allowed me, I would kick the shit out of you."

The ultimate expression of rage that day came from Jacob Ryker, who'd watched his future fiancée cut down before he himself was struck in the chest. "I think the victims should get to do to you what you did to them," he taunted. "I think you should have to suffer in the hospital like they did, with no painkillers while they cut open your chest. . . . You don't deserve to live. You don't deserve to breathe.

If I had my way, fifteen minutes . . ." Ryker paused, hardly able to control himself. Then, "Three months of discipline, my senior drill instructor told me that I was the most disciplined recruit that he has ever seen. But I can't stand here and look at you without wanting to kill you."

Despite their professional training, first responders to school shootings also become traumatized by their interface with the event. This fact was brought home in Detective Al Warthen's victim impact statement when he reminded the court that many emergency personnel are also parents of kids at the very schools that they're rushing to assist. "When we were all racing to Thurston High," he said, "I saw the fear in the faces of colleagues in both police and fire who had children at school that morning. One of those faces was our own chief of police, Jerry Smith."

One officer's elementary-school daughter told her parents that she feared going on to middle or high school, where someone like Kip could bring in a gun and harm her. There were scores of other small children in Springfield who echoed similar sentiments. A second grader wrote a card to a wounded Thurston girl saying, *I'm sorry for what happened to you, and now I'm afraid someone will do this to me.* The mother of a six-year-old boy reported that for months after the event, her son would ask almost daily, "Is Kip still in prison, Mom?" The youngest of Kip's victims could well be the unborn child of one of Faith Kinkel's former students and later her teaching assistant. Married and pregnant at the time Faith was killed, she was so distressed over the murder of her beloved teacher and colleague that she suffered a heartbreaking miscarriage.

Some adults reacted in other tragic ways. The very first TV cameraman to reach Thurston on May 21 was Barry Johnson, from KVAL News. He arrived just behind the medics. In the midst of the most harrowing news story he'd ever recorded, Johnson found himself facing "frantic parents, stunned and bloody students, and frightened classmates." When his first videotape finished, he "sat his camera down and cried. Then he put in another tape and started filming again." Johnson had been having personal problems, including substance abuse, for several years, but the havoc at Thurston, said friends, pushed him over the edge. He was unable to cover any story related to Kinkel after that. Ten days after the third anniversary of Kip's attack, Johnson jumped to his death from the top of a Eugene parking garage. At age fifty-one, he added one more fatality to this tragedy.

Something strangely similar but even more disastrous occurred in the aftermath of Barry Loukaitis's 1996 rampage (chapter 20). The cousin of Arnold Fritz, one of two students killed at Moses Lake, was so distressed that ten months later, he killed himself and his family using the same choice of weapon as Barry—a hunting rifle. Aaron Harmon was just fourteen and in ninth grade, but having lost the one relative he felt closest to, he decided to seek revenge on an unrighteous world by murdering his mother and nine-year-old stepsister before turning the gun on himself.

It did not end there. A few years later, Phil Fritz, Arnold's father, killed himself at the grave of his son. Grant County prosecutor John Knodell sees everything that grew out of the incident at Moses Lake emanating from a clear source. "What we have to recognize is there is such a thing as evil," he said. "Barry personified it that day." Since his imprisonment, Loukaitis has never talked about the shootings, declining all requests for interviews.

Another delayed gun death occurred in Springfield, but it was not intentional. Just a month before the sentencing hearing, a student who'd been slightly wounded in the cafeteria, but had escaped death, was killed in an unrelated hunting accident. Kip had fired at Richard "Ricky" Peek approximately thirteen times as the boy scrambled to escape out the front door. Only two of the bullets actually found their mark. One hit his arm, but another, aimed at his back, ended up slamming into his backpack, shredding his notebooks, and lodging on page 125 of his history text, very likely saving his life. After that, Ricky generally kept to himself and seldom spoke about the incident. When Columbine was attacked in April 1999, after he'd left Thurston, he took the day off work to watch the news on TV. "I remember watching his expressions," Carlene Peek, his sister told the courtroom. "He was reliving it then. He was imagining being there, and remembering how lucky he was to be alive. . . . Most of us have no idea how [the Columbine students] felt, but he did."

Six months later, on October 5, Peek was out deer hunting when a rifle held by his younger brother, who'd also been in the cafeteria that day, accidentally discharged, causing a round to hit Richard in

the head, killing him instantly. Ricky's death added still another pitiful postscript to this event.

Almost all the kids who were in the cafeteria that day suffered
from nightmares and missed school because they were frightened to
go, or couldn't stand being there. Their grades plummeted. They were
not the same people they'd been eighteen months earlier. As Michael
Crowley put it, "Your Honor, the effects of Kip's actions on my son
will last [his] whole life. Why should Kip's punishment be any less?"

Victim statements such as these were no doubt instrumental in
helping to persuade Judge Mattison that only life imprisonment would
assure the citizens of Oregon that they need never fear Kip could
harm them again. But before his pronouncement, both Kristin and
Kip were allowed to give their side of the story.

Kristin Kinkel described Kip as a normal teenage boy, compassionate, likable, sensitive, and hardworking, who loved animals, had
a great sense of humor, was a people pleaser, and who put others
first. She spoke of his middle-school academic problems, strains in
his relationship with their parents, his becoming withdrawn, and his
stage of dressing all in black. Kristin wrote a letter to Judge Mattison insisting her little brother *is a good person that came from a
good home.* She recognized her description seemed *so contradictory,
looking at what actually took place,* and she admitted that *only with
hindsight do I truly see the signs of someone who was in desperate
need of help, different help than any of us knew how to give.*

Kristin's positive spin on Kip's manipulation of others was that
"he found ways to learn what those around him wanted and made
every effort to become it. I believe that is how he dealt with his illness so well and with such subtlety for so long." She now felt that
her brother was "aware of the pain that he has caused, and is just
as shocked as the rest of us that he was capable of such horror."
Kristin appealed to the court to recognize that Kip "is hurting more
than any of us can imagine," and she marveled that he was "adapt-
ing to an extremely unpleasant situation better than most ever could."

As to allowing Kip to return to society someday, and the risk that
he'd cause more chaos, she declared, "There really should be no concern for this kind of thing to happen again." Finally Kristin gave
away the real reason she clung to these beliefs when she insisted,
"It's the truth, and it keeps me alive," and later stated, "I love my

brother more than I ever thought possible. And not because he needs me to, but because I need to." This, at least, made sense. Still, the question that remained in many peoples' minds is whether Kristin would have become an additional casualty had she been home at the time Kip shot his parents.

After all the victims had spoken to him in court, Kip offered his own statement to those whom he had hurt. He realized the futility of this effort, but declared, "I have spent days trying to figure out what I want to say. I have crumpled up dozens of pieces of paper and disregarded even more ideas. I have thought about what I could say that might make people feel just a little bit better. But I have come to the realization that it really doesn't matter what I say. Because there is nothing I can do to take away any of the pain and destruction I have caused. I absolutely loved my parents and had no reason to kill them. I had no reason to dislike, kill, or try to kill anyone at Thurston. I am truly sorry that this has happened. I have gone back in my mind hundreds of times and changed one detail, one small event, so this never would have happened. I wish I could. I take full responsibility for my actions. These events have pulled me down into a state of deterioration and self-loathing that I didn't know existed. I am very sorry for everything I have done, and for what I have become."

It is interesting to note that Mitchell Johnson spoke a nearly identical expression of regret at his trial in Jonesboro when he lamented, "I am so sorry. . . . If I could go back and change what happened on March 24, 1998, I would in a minute." It appears that Mitchell and Kip required total catastrophes to learn the most basic lessons of sympathy, if indeed they ever have. Perhaps some show of contrition was better than none at all, but from the point of view of the victims, words cost nothing and the sincerity of postcataclysmic regrets may be open to suspicion. There is little value in an apology to those whose entire lives have been ripped into fragments.

Jody Hardenbrook, father of one of Thurston's wounded, attended an antiviolence conference in Atlanta, where he rubbed shoulders with parents from Littleton and West Paducah who'd lost sons and daughters. He found corresponding patterns of disruption reported by others who'd lived through a school shooting. "One of the clear issues that came out from the parents," Hardenbrook said, "is how each community has changed as a result of the shootings. We can say that we won't let fear dominate our thinking, but how can it not, when you think that a young man that lived up the hill from us could open the door of fear in our community by one selfish, senseless tantrum. . . . A sense of innocence in our community has been lost. We are all a bit more cautious. We are all a bit more wary, and we are a lot more calloused."

Eric Koerschgen, foster father of a girl Kip shot, added, "You not only brought horror and violence into the lives of those you assaulted and their families, you took away the security of our community and other communities across this nation. . . . You taught us we aren't invulnerable, and that because of people like you, life can end at any moment."

The scope of the ruin had been immense. After every school shooting, the same pattern repeats itself. The circle of pain that begins with the impact of that first bullet ripples out like the slowly ascending shock waves of a rising tsunami. Within hours, the news echoes through the media and is heard around the world. At some point, the grieving of the few becomes the sorrow of the many. Fear, doubt, and suspicion spread to other schools. We all feel less safe than before. We all become victims.

• Chapter 26 •

The One Safe Place

I will have to live with the fact that I was shot at school, the one place I'm supposed to be safe.
—Elizabeth McKenzie, Thurston student

September 11, 2001. The new millennium had arrived, and with it, the sudden appearance of bona fide foreign enemies attacking our nation. The result, at least in the immediate aftermath, was a massive groundswell of patriotic solidarity.

In retrospect, it may seem naive, but in the weeks following the cataclysmic events of 9/11, some of us assumed that even teenage Americans who held a personal grudge against their peers—in other words, any potential school shooters—could fathom that we all had a larger challenge to attend to now than their private animosities. This premise, however, underestimated the self-absorption of those whose worldview does not extend beyond the limits of their own depression or shortsighted resentments.

On November 12, 2001, in the Michigan farming town of Caro, north of Detroit, seventeen-year-old Chris Buschbacher was despondent about some legal troubles and a recent romantic breakup with his girlfriend. Intending to harm her, he went to Caro Community School's Adult Learning Center about 3:00 P.M. with a .22-caliber rifle and a 20-gauge shotgun. He could not find his quarry, so he took a teacher and a fifteen-year-old girl hostage. Chris spotted Principal Erl Nordstrom and fired at him, but missed. After negotiating with police for ninety minutes, he let his last hostage go and then shot himself in the head.

Somewhat earlier—barely a month after the WTC and Pentagon attacks—five students, including one girl, began planning a deadly assault on their high school in New Bedford, Massachusetts. Three were arrested just after Thanksgiving on November 24, 2001, and charged with conspiring to commit murder by detonating a bomb and then gunning down teachers and students as they fled. The conspirators then planned to shoot themselves.

Michael McKeehan, fifteen, led the group called the "Trench Coat Mafia," mimicking a name used in reference to the Columbine killers. One of his followers, who wore a spiked dog collar, told a classmate he was "sick of all the jocks and preppies making fun of the way he dressed," again echoing Eric Harris. The bedroom walls of a third member, Steven Jones, were covered with graffiti such as *Everyone must die, I hate the world,* and *Kill Everyone,* all hauntingly similar to messages Kinkel had written in his journal and Harris had written on his Web site.

In fact, the number of identical expressions Kinkel and Harris had in common is striking. This becomes evident when one compares the passages from Kip's diary, which are quoted in earlier chapters of this book, with the following excerpts from the Internet home page that Eric Harris maintained. *I hate the fucking world,* Eric raved. *I say "Kill mankind." No one should survive. . . . After I mow down a whole area full of you snotty-ass rich motherfucker high-strung God-like-attitude-having worthless pieces of shit whores, I don't care if I live or die. . . ."*

Germany's Sebastian Bosse (later this chapter), who adored Harris, regurgitated these phrases, saying in his 2006 video, "Humans are sick. The earth is sick. I can't fucking wait until I can shoot every motherfucking last one of you." Bosse also said, "I hate you and the way you are! You've all got to die! Since I was six, you've all been taking the piss out of me! Now you're going to pay."

No surprise, then, when in 2007, Finland's Pekka Auvinen (later this chapter) also put his murderous plans on the Internet, stating, *Hate . . . I'm so full of it and I love it. That is one thing I really love. The faster the human race is wiped out from this planet, the better. . . . No one should be left alive. No mercy for the scum of the earth.*

In a hate message posted as "nghtmrchld26" on a Web site the morning of his double rampage in December 2007, church shooter Matthew Murray (chapter 3) didn't even try to disguise his word-for-word copy (including capitalizations) of an Eric Harris journal entry:

> I'm coming for EVERYONE soon, and I WILL be armed to the fucking teeth, and I will shoot to kill. Feel no remorse, no sense of shame, I don't care if I live or die in the shoot-out. All I want to do is kill and injure as many of you as I can especially Christians who are to blame for most of the problems in the world.

The only change Murray made was substituting "Christians" for the name of Harris's former friend Brooks Brown.

Harris's crude arrogance was over-the-top in such passages as: *My belief is that if I say something, it goes. I am the law. If you don't like it, you die. If I don't like you or I don't like what you want me to do, you die.* Similarly, Mitchell Johnson at Jonesboro told his "sometimes friend" Dustin Campbell, "Everyone that hates me, everyone that I don't like, is going to die." Kimveer Gill (chapter 7) listed his dislikes on his Internet profile as: *The world and everything in it,* and *All those who oppose my rule.* Among his "likes": *Massacres, trench coats and destruction, Crushing my enemies' skulls,* and *Super Psycho Maniacs roaming the streets freely.* In a long, vitriolic note left in his dorm room, Seung-hui Cho spoke of his peers as *deceitful charlatans,* claiming, *You caused me to do this.*

These rantings may have started out as a form of release for the pent-up hostility that these boys were experiencing, but at some point the spilling of hate became an end in itself. The "kiss my butt" conceit of these compositions revels in self-glorification. What the writers failed to realize, however, is that hatred can also be a narcotic. Like any drug, it's only a matter of time before it takes over the person who imagined he or she could control it. Inevitably they learn, as have so many others, that addiction, when embraced, becomes the sole focus of existence.

Eric was an equal opportunity bigot. On his Web site and journal he declared hatred of all *niggers, spics, Jews, gays,* but he also despised *Star Wars* fans and people who drive slow in the fast lane. Few humans met Eric's standards of worthiness, yet he incongruously listed racists among his pet peeves, writing, *You know what I hate? Racism. Anyone who hates Asians, Mexicans, or people of any race because they're different.* Still, the killers believed above all in their own superiority, as if they constituted a two-man master race. The date they chose to attack Columbine was Hitler's birthday, not by chance considering their outspoken admiration for the Nazi leader and his "final solution." As the slaughter began, Eric tore off his trench coat to expose a white T-shirt declaring, NATURAL SELECTION.

Pekka Auvinen originally chose the username "NaturalSelector89" on YouTube in homage to Harris, but later changed it to "Sturmgeist89," meaning "storm spirit" in German. His final online communication was titled "Manifesto of a Natural Selector," in which he announced, *I, as a natural selector, will eliminate all who I see unfit, disgraces of human race and failures of natural selection.*

Despite this rhetoric, Auvinen cared enough to leave a good-bye letter at home addressed to his musician parents and younger brother, explaining his contempt of society. Just as in the case of Seung-hui Cho's family, the Auvinens were later placed under police protection because of death threats from people who held them responsible for their son's behavior. In his final tape, Eric Harris said, "To everyone I love, I'm really sorry about this. . . . I know my mom and dad will be just fucking shocked beyond belief." Sebastian Bosse's parents both collapsed after hearing what their son had done and were hospitalized for shock. In all of these cases, why were the shooters' actions such an unexpected blow to their families? How could the parents be so blind to the buildup of their sons' wrath?

What the parents simply didn't get is that their children were living parallel lives. To their families, the kids were still "that sweet little boy" who'd grown up and was perhaps acting a bit strange. In the mind of the son, this artful charade of normalcy was something to be maintained, up until the final moment of releasing all that pent-up rage.

Case in point: The mothers of two of the teens charged in the New Bedford incident adamantly insisted, as have so many other parents whose kids were caught before they pulled the trigger, that allegations against their boys had been exaggerated. "My kids are good kids and this has really been blown out of proportion," Carol McKeehan told the *Boston Globe*. Susan St. Hilaire characterized the lads as "gentle" and "misunderstood." But sure enough, when police searched the boys' rooms, they found bomb-making instructions, four knives, a meat cleaver, two billy clubs, a flare gun, ammunition, pictures of the suspects holding handguns, and a gym bag containing "bomb-making components."

In their resolve to use handcrafted explosives, the New Bedford clique was once again imitating Harris and Klebold. While the five kids arrested there had boasted to friends that their attack would be "bigger than Columbine," just such a catastrophe actually took place a few months later in what was formerly East Germany.

On April 26, 2002, less than a week after the third anniversary of Columbine, a nineteen-year-old expelled student named Robert Steinhäuser went on a rampage at his school in Erfurt. Dressed head to toe in black, Steinhäuser roamed the hallways with a pistol and a shotgun. His rage was not directed at fellow pupils, but rather at those he held responsible for his expulsion. Thirteen teachers, two female students who were hit by stray bullets, a school secretary, and a policeman died in the assault before the attacker killed himself as commandos closed in. The final tally of seventeen deaths did indeed exceed the thirteen killed at Columbine, and remained a record number until Virginia Tech.

Germany, as it turned out, was becoming the European nation with the likeliest chance of hosting a school shooting. Just two months before the mass murder at Erfurt, a former pupil killed his headmaster and set off pipe bombs in the technical school he'd recently been expelled from in Freising, near Munich. The young man also slew his boss and a foreman at the company he worked for before turning the gun on himself, making him perhaps the first suicidal school shooter who was simultaneously a workplace avenger.

Less than a week after Erfurt, on April 30, a high-school student in Bosnia-Herzegovina shot and killed his history teacher and wounded a math teacher with a bullet to the neck. The teen then committed suicide by shooting himself in the head. Police in the eastern town of Vlasenica, about fifty kilometers northeast of Sarajevo, said seventeen-year-old Dragoslav Petkovic used his father's 7.65mm hand-gun to carry out the attack.

Germany again set a school shooting record on November 20, 2006, when eighteen-year-old Sebastian Bosse injured eleven students and teachers at a secondary school in Emsdetten. If we factor in an additional sixteen policemen harmed by smoke grenade inhalation, the total of twenty-seven exceeds the twenty-five wounded by Kinkel.

Sebastian had been planning a suicidal killing spree for at least two years, hoping to revenge himself against those whom he felt had humiliated him. In June 2004, he'd posted this threatening message on the Internet: *This fear is slowly turning to rage. I am consuming all this rage and will let it all out at some point to take revenge on all the arseholes who wrecked my life! For those who haven't understood it exactly: Yes, this is about a shooting.* The warning was unambiguous, but was ignored. Although he graduated in 2005 with decent marks, "Bastian" had repeated two years because of poor grades. That may have contributed to his alienation. One classmate later said, "It was clear he would flip out at some point, the way he used to talk. He was boiling with rage. He had a huge hatred of the world." Even so, everyone underestimated the direction his anger would take.

Like Alvaro Rafael Castillo (chapter 1) and Seung-hui Cho, Bosse also digitally recorded a farewell speech, but instead of sending his video to the media, he posted it on the Internet the morning of his rampage. It was recorded in his parents' living room in good but expletive-laden English. He was very precise. "There are two reasons for this massacre," he said. "One, the school, the teachers, and students, everything in that fucking building. Two, the politics. I want anarchy. It's the only thing where you are really, really free. No one has a right to tell me what to do. It's my damn life and not the life of my parents or any fucking teacher in the whole fucking world." One can assume that his choice of English, a global language, was partly to ensure the video would be universally accessible, and partly to imitate his American heroes. Likewise, he changed his diary writing from German to English three weeks prior to his attack. (Sample: *I am not a fucking psycho.*)

Pekka Auvinen also posted in English, and also stated, *You will probably say that I am insane, crazy, psychopath, criminal or crap like that. No, the truth is that I am just an animal, a human, an individual, a dissident.*

Still earlier, Sebastian had made films of himself costumed as an Eric Harris wannabe, exploding small bombs and feigning a phony execution with a friend in some woodland where he'd often gone hunting with his father, a postal worker. He posed for his camera outfitted for battle with a cluster of weapons. It reflected his dream of a career in the army, engaging in warfare in full combat gear. In his good-bye statement, he wrote, *Much of my revenge will be directed at the teachers, because they are people who intervened in my life against my will and helped put me where I am now: On the battlefield!* The final words on his video were, "It will be better if you can run on Monday because I've got guns, I've got bombs, I've got Molotov cocktails. You are in a war. This is war."

On July 6, 2007, a journal was found in a McDonald's parking lot, in Long Island, New York, which stated, similarly to Bosse, *I will start a chain of terrorism in the world. . . . I want to kill so many people in the war zone and the target. So many this will go down in history. Take out everyone there then turn the guns on the cops then on myself. Perfecto.* Plans were jotted down to shoot specific staff and students and ignite explosives at Connetquot High School, in Bohemia (a hamlet near Islip) on the ninth anniversary of Columbine in 2008. Police arrested the fifteen-year-old McDonald's employee who'd written the diary, then detained his seventeen-year-old co-conspirator, Michael McDonough. On the younger boy's computer, detectives noted several attempts to obtain weapons via the Internet, including an Uzi and five pounds of explosive powder.

That attack was prevented, but the students at Sebastian Bosse's school weren't so lucky. Bosse may have chosen that Monday to attack because he was due in court the next day for illegal weapons possession. Shortly before 9:30 A.M., during the first class break, Sebastian marched into the schoolyard of Geschwister Scholl wearing a long black coat, a backpack, and a gas mask. He looked ridiculous, and, at first, the students laughed. Then they noticed he was carrying two rifles with sawed-off barrels. Invisible beneath his jacket were a pistol, a gas-powered handgun, a knife attached to his leg, three homemade pipe bombs strapped to his body, and ten more, plus a petrol bomb, tucked into his backpack.

He entered his old school building with guns blazing, setting off smoke canisters and living out his sophomoric game fantasy at the expense of the real lives of former fellow pupils, a pregnant teacher, a janitor. . . . Miraculously, none of their injuries were life-threatening. As police flooded in, Sebastian killed himself with a shot to the head. His body couldn't be removed until hours later when experts unstrapped his explosive packs.

On November 18, 2007, German police in Cologne were able to thwart an attack by two teens using crossbows, air guns, Molotov cocktails, and pipe bombs to commemorate the one-year anniversary of Emsdetten. Their plot was foiled after classmates at Georg-Buechner High School saw them studying Columbine images on the Internet and alerted the principal. Clearly suicidal, one of the teens threw himself in front of a tram after his police interrogation and was killed.

The Cologne students' quick action in reporting this pair was likely due to the major school shooting in Tuusula, Finland, just eleven days earlier. On November 7, 2007, eighteen-year-old Pekka-Eric Auvinen killed eight people, including the headmistress at Jokela High School, before turning the gun on himself. Police arrived at the school eleven minutes after being summoned, at 11:43 A.M., but did not enter the building until three hours later. Pekka fired one shot toward them, then continued his rampage, using up sixty-nine of the nearly four hundred bullets he'd brought along. All who died were shot several times, as at Virginia Tech—an indicator that the killer was not just firing wildly, but methodically executing each victim. Auvinen also spread an inflammable liquid on the second-story walls and tried to start a fire, but it didn't take. When a SWAT unit finally reached Pekka, he was unconscious near several other bodies in the lower lobby where the shooting had begun. In critical condition, he died shortly after in the hospital.

Considering the destruction Auvinen caused using a small .22 semiautomatic Sig Sauer "Mosquito," purchased less than a month earlier, it's unsettling to learn he'd tried to get a license for a more potent 9mm. His application, based on a recommendation from his shooting club, was refused because the larger weapon was considered too powerful for his stated purpose of "target practice." After his attack, the Finnish government proposed raising the minimum age for buying guns from fifteen to eighteen, although Auvinen was already that old. With a strong hunting tradition, Finland stands behind only the United States and Yemen in civilian gun ownership.

Pekka Auvinen was soon dubbed "the YouTube Killer," because that's where he'd posted eighty-nine videos honoring Harris and Klebold, Jack the Ripper, Stalin, Hitler and other Nazi leaders, the Unabomber, Timothy McVeigh, and serial killer Jeffrey Dahmer. He also uploaded images of the '93 siege at Waco, the '95 sarin gas attack in Tokyo, the 2003 bombing of Baghdad, and similar examples of humanity at its worst. These tributes doubtless allowed him to justify the phrase printed on his T-shirt: HUMANITY IS OVERRATED. To make certain no one mistook his choice of films as sympathy for the innocent lives that were lost, he had the word "DIE" flash across scenes showing victims of these horrors, including clips from *Schindler's List* in which Jews are tortured or killed.

Auvinen next began posting videos of himself, including one called "Me and my gun, Catherine. I love her!" It's not unusual for men to give their weapon a woman's name—U.S. Marines do it often, and the tradition has a long pedigree—think of frontiersman Davy Crockett and his favorite rifle "Betsy" (the one lost at the Alamo was one of three he'd owned with similar names). Rather than having Freudian overtones, this practice might better be explained in terms of dependability—a man looking upon his gun as a reliable partner who helps extend his circle of power. School shooter Alvaro Castillo had a crush on a girl named Rose, and displayed her name on one of his guns. In a videotape made March 15, 1999, Eric Harris cradled the sawed-off shotgun he called "Arlene" in his arms, kissed it, and said, "It's going to be like fucking Doom. Tick, tick, tick, tick . . . Haa! That fucking shotgun is straight out of Doom!" He'd read all four Doom novels in the series (based initially upon the video game) that include the shotgun-loving character, Private First Class Arlene Sanders (she doesn't appear in the video game).

The idea of guns as surrogate love objects certainly predates the Beatles' "Happiness Is a Warm Gun" (a title John Lennon lifted from a shooting magazine's cover story "Happiness Is a Warm Gun in Your Hand," in turn borrowed from the Charles Schulz book *Happiness is a Warm Puppy)*. Individuals like Kinkel and Auvinen, who spoke of their love of guns, may have done so partially in jest, but at the same time, *none* of the shooters mentioned previously had any genuine success in their relationships with women. Instead, guns "made them a man."

In another clip, Auvinen imitates the Columbine boys' "target practice in the woods" video (Harris and Klebold shot at stuffed dolls and bowling pins) by doing one of his own, shooting an apple. He called it "Just Testing My Gun," and it ends with a friendly wave to the camera. But his final video, posted just before he left on his mission of destruction, left no doubt of his intentions. Titled "Jokela High School Massacre," it showed a picture of the school shattering into pieces and revealing two images of the shooter bathed in red, pointing a gun directly at the viewer, Seung-hui Cho–style. He also did a last-minute MySpace posting titled "Fuck You!" showing the same photo of the school and the message *BYE BYE!!!*

His final YouTube clip was backed by rock band KMFDM's song "Stray Bullet." The lyrics include the following: *I'm your nightmare coming true / I am your worst enemy / I am your dearest friend / Malignantly Malevolent / I am of divine descent / I have come to rock your world / I have come to shake your faith.*

It's no coincidence that Eric Harris had also posted lyrics to KMFDM songs, including "Stray Bullet," on his Web site. Auvinen's online name "Sturmgeist" was also the name of one of his favorite bands. Other groups he liked include Rammstein, Nine Inch Nails, and Alice Cooper, but for once, Marilyn Manson isn't mentioned.

When Auvinen added a call for a *revolution against the system* in his profile, he was again merely echoing Eric Harris, who wrote, *Maybe we will even start a little rebellion or revolution to fuck things up. . . .* Auvinen's statement that "I am prepared to fight and die for my cause" is not far distant from Cho's grandiose pronouncements of martyrdom. Perhaps Pekka-Eric even fantasized that the student body would rise up and join him, because bursting into the first classroom, he shouted: "Revolution! Smash everything!" No one did a thing except stare in shock, so Auvinen shot at the TV and windows to make a statement. He then ran into the corridor without harming any of those students, but surely he realized then that he wouldn't be inciting anyone to join his rampage that day.

Pekka-Eric was misguided, inhumane, and possibly insane, but he wasn't stupid. He had studied Orwell's *1984,* Huxley's *Brave New*

World, and Bradbury's *Fahrenheit 451,* all of which deal with a single individual confronting a repressive society. For Auvinen, these books no doubt reconfirmed his worst opinions about humanity as he cast himself in the role of antihero. He also delved into Plato's *The Republic* and all the works of Plato's philosophical opposite, existentialist Friedrich Nietzsche, who avowed that tragedy was an affirmation of life, and who was the first to declare, "God is dead."

To his friends, Pekka was "a normal happy guy, a smart student who was very well-informed about world events." He had no criminal record and had never threatened anyone at school, but friends, such as Tuomas Hulkkonen, said Auvinen had recently developed a darker side. He'd turned "weird, had begun making drawings of gun massacres, and withdrew into his shell." When Hulkkonen pressed him for an explanation, Auvinen said he was "only joking." His friend conceded, "I couldn't imagine that in reality he would do anything like this."

These too often repeated refrains were especially bitter to the author, who'd spoken five months earlier with Scandinavian book distribution reps at the BookExpo America conference in New York. "School shooting is not our problem," I was told. "It's an American concern." Now those blindly provincial words seemed as myopic as the familiar chants "We never thought it could happen here" and "We thought he was just joking." I wondered anew what it would take for people everywhere to understand that this expanding mind-set of "acceptable" (to the shooter) violence disassociated from reality is a global *and* a local issue, not a distant danger that always happens somewhere else.

In fact, soon after the Jokela High massacre, we learned once again how event-connectivity is still pertinent. On October 10, 2007, about a month *prior* to the Finland event, a fourteen-year-old suspended student with a history of mental illness opened fire at his high school in downtown Cleveland, Ohio. Asa H. Coon, armed with two revolvers, fired eight shots, wounding two teachers and two students, before placing a gun behind his own left ear and pulling the trigger.

Tragic though the Ohio event was, it had a positive result. Watching this incident unfold, a Plymouth Whitemarsh High School student in Norristown, Pennsylvania, decided he was "sick of hearing about all these school shootings," and he "didn't want another kid to do the same thing and keep this chain of events going on." After consulting with his father, Lewis Bennett III placed a call to police reporting that a bullied, overweight, homeschooled acquaintance, fourteen-year-old Dillon Cossey, was planning to pull off something similar. Police searched Dillon's bedroom and found a 9mm semi-automatic rifle with a laser scope, about thirty air-powered pellet guns modeled to look like high-powered weapons, swords, knives, a bomb-making book, videos of the Columbine attack, and violence-filled notebooks. This time, the mother could not claim that allegations against her son had been exaggerated. Michele Cossey was herself arrested for purchasing those weapons, plus a .22-caliber hand-gun and a .22-caliber rifle. She was "indulging the boy's interests," according to District Attorney Bruce Castor, "because he was un-happy."

This was a family affair. Dillon's father, Frank Cossey, had spent about six years in prison for manslaughter charges stemming from a 1981 drunk-driving incident in Oklahoma, and he was still on home confinement for violating parole in 2006 by trying to buy his son, who "had psychological issues," a .22-caliber rifle.

Then came the kicker. Police discovered that Dillon had been com-municating online about video games and the Columbine massacre, since at least September, with a teenager in Finland who used the name "Sturmgeist89"—Pekka-Eric Auvinen. Now in captivity and admitting he really was planning a school shooting, Dillon Cossey claimed he was "horrified" when he found out about the Finnish at-tack. He claimed he'd never suspected Auvinen might follow through with such a violent act. So why, then, were they talking about it?

Pekka-Eric also had his immediate imitators. Just hours after Jokela, a thirty-year-old plumber in Sydney, Australia, posted a mes-sage on YouTube threatening students at his former high school. Under the pseudonym "Killthemallnow" (from Eric Harris's motto "kill them all now"), Jason James Cousins acknowledged Auvinen's moment of fame, writing: *Im* [sic] *giving him the centre stage for 4 more days . . . then the cameras will be at cambridge park high in sydney australia. . . . Those students (at Jokela) got what they de-served.* When brought before the law, Cousins apologized. Four days later, Finnish police arrested a sixteen-year-old boy in the village of

Maaninka for posting his own copycat video on YouTube threatening his school. The boy predictably told police it was a joke.

Germany had experienced one more scare back in 2002 when, on October 18, a sixteen-year-old boy, identified only as Marcel, walked into a computer room full of sixth graders at the Friedensschule in Waiblingen in midafternoon and pulled out a pistol. He kept the teacher and four students hostage, releasing the others, but after four hours, exchanged one more hostage for a pizza, and another later for a cell phone. Marcel told police via telephone that he wanted 1 million euros and a getaway car. He eventually let the remaining hostages go and was arrested. The weapon turned out to be an air pistol.

Strangely, and further illustrating the point that publicity generates copycats, another European hostage situation, precisely one month later to the hour, also involved kids the same age, an identical demand for 1 million euros, and even a pizza! On November 18, an armed seventeen-year-old wearing a ski mask charged into the Casal de l'Angel middle school in Hospitalet de Llobregat, Spain, and held a classroom of twenty-five preteens and their teacher hostage. Maybe the Spanish cops also learned from the German event, because this incident ended when a policeman dressed as a pizza delivery-man overpowered the instigator.

These two episodes were resolved well, but others were not as lucky. There were nine events in the United States in 2002, and an equal number overseas. In addition to those described previously, a shooting occurred at Monash University in Melbourne, Australia, on October 22. Thirty-six-year-old Huan Yun "Allen" Xiang, a Chinese fourth-year commerce honors student who was facing failing grades, murdered two younger Chinese grad students and injured four other classmates and a lecturer. There was a mass school knifing in South Korea (chapter 27). The worst event was a terrorist attack—Muslim against Muslim—on October 15, in the Chief Region of Algeria. Fundamentalists raided a Koranic high school, forcing fourteen students to line up against a wall and then opening fire, killing thirteen. The last pupil was seriously wounded, but able to flee. The Algerian government blamed this heartless act on the hard-line Armed Islamic Group.

Such an organized massacre would not be seen again until the even more horrifying terrorist attack of September 1 through 3, 2004, in Beslan, Russia. At the start of an annual celebration marking the beginning of the school year, thirty-one Chechen militants seized Middle School Number One. Some of the masked male and female gunners wore bomb belts. They forced over 1,200 students, parents, and teachers into the gym. There, the Chechens had them tear up floorboards revealing a cache of weapons hidden during the summer. A dozen teachers and parents were killed trying to protect their kids against the attackers. Police arrived and the militants lined students up along the gym windows, announcing they would murder fifty kids for each Chechen killed and twenty kids for each one wounded. The militants placed bombs in the basketball nets and laid trip wire throughout the school, threatening to blow up everything and everyone if police stormed the building.

During the entire three-day siege, the Chechens refused to allow food, water, or medicine to be brought in. The hostages had to drink their own urine. The police maintained a position around the perimeter and established negotiations. On the third morning, all hell broke loose when emergency workers were allowed in to remove bodies of people killed earlier, and one of the basketball bombs fell accidentally and detonated, causing an explosive chain reaction. This caused the gym roof to collapse, crushing those who were below. Many other hostages, dehydrated, nearly naked and bleeding, took this chance to flee. As they ran for their lives, the cold-blooded militants continued firing at them, though at this point they had nothing left to gain. All of the Chechens were eventually rounded up and wiped out by Russian Special Forces, except for one the Russian government maintains was captured alive. The final tally was 334 hostages, 21 responders and 31 militants dead, plus 783 wounded, making this the deadliest act of school violence in history.

What these appalling episodes in Russia and Algeria represent—and one might also include the slaughter of children at schools in Israel before, during, and after the intifada—is the clear intent of established terrorist groups to attack the most vulnerable and innocent among us in order to force recognition of their power. This was clearly the case on March 6, 2008, when Palestinian gunman Ala Abu Dehein stormed the Merkaz Harav yeshiva seminary in Jerusalem, killing eight students and wounding nine others. In principle, this is no different from what school shooters are trying to accomplish. On a grim but practical level, however, the ability of mature yet fanatical or deranged adults to plan and execute school attacks obviously exceeds that of adolescents simply by dint of seasoned experience and organizational abilities.

A perfect illustration of this occurred back on August 1, 1966, in what remained the worst campus shooting in U.S. history until 2007. Like Virginia Tech, this incident took place at a college, and the perpetrator was an adult. Twenty-five-year-old Charles Joseph Whitman was a former U.S. Marine sniper who used his military service credits to enroll at the University of Texas. He was doing well—a junior with a B average majoring in architectural engineering. However, on the night of July 31, something snapped, and Charles was once again at war—but this time with his loved ones and the civilians surrounding him.

First he drove to his mother's apartment. Margaret Whitman was strangled by her son before he crushed her head from behind with a blunt object, and stabbed her chest. Charles then drove home and stabbed his sleeping wife, Kathy, twenty-four times in the heart with a hunting knife. His motive for committing these two murders was similar to that of Kip Kinkel in killing his parents, and just as illogical—Whitman murdered his wife and mother *after much thought,* he wrote in one of several notes left behind, so that they wouldn't be embarrassed by what he was about to do next.

That morning, Charles went shopping and filled his marine-issued footlocker with food, water, rope, a bowie knife, a machete, seven hundred rounds of ammunition, a 6mm Remington rifle, with a four-power scope, a .357 Magnum pistol, a 9mm Luger pistol, and two brand-new guns he'd just purchased that morning—a .30-caliber rifle with clips and ammunition from a nearby hardware store, and a 12-gauge shotgun from Sears, bought on credit. Strangely, he also packed deodorant and an alarm clock.

He then drove to the University of Texas, and at 11:30 A.M. carried the footlocker into the clock tower elevator, took it up to the twenty-seventh floor, and hauled his burden up one more flight of stairs. On the twenty-eighth-floor observation deck, Edna Townsley cheerily greeted Charles, as was her official duty, and asked him to sign the register. Instead, he struck the back of her head with his rifle butt and then pulled her body out of sight. She died of her injuries. Unfortunately, a visiting family arrived just then to see the view. Inside the tower's tight confines, Whitman quickly dispatched Marguerite Lamport and her nephew Mark Gabour, and critically wounded Mike and Mary Gabour, who escaped and got help.

Charles finished setting up his sniper's nest on the narrow observation deck by 11:45 A.M. and then began his planned assault in earnest, shooting around a 360-degree circle at any and all human targets below. He was totally indiscriminate in choosing victims—a youth on a bicycle, professors, students, police officers, a young couple recently engaged, and a baby still in his mother's womb. During his ninety minutes of madness, Whitman left fifteen dead and thirty-one wounded in a three-hundred-meter radius around the tower.

During that time, authorities weren't idle—they were simply unable to dislodge Whitman from his fortified position. Not only police, but also dozens of deputized gun-owning Texan civilians aimed their sites at the tower, sending back hundreds of rounds of retaliatory fire. Unassailable from below, two patrolmen entered the tower from an underground tunnel and made their way up the staircase to the top. Charles turned to face them, but one of the cops shot first. Wounded, Whitman fired back but missed, allowing the patrolmen to empty their weapons into the sniper, ending the Texas massacre.

Before going on his killing spree, Whitman left a note saying, *After my death I wish an autopsy to be performed to see if there's any mental disorder.* This was done, and doctors did find a pecan-sized tumor in his brain. They concluded this was enough to give Charles frequent headaches, but it couldn't be cited as a factor in the butchery. Whitman's carnage was the first in a series of sniper-style mass murders that occurred both in the United States and abroad over the next few decades. These became so pervasive that satirist Jules Feiffer wrote a dark comedy on the subject in 1967 (also a 1971 film) called *Little Murders*.

The relevance of these sniper attacks to our study is simply that by doing the previously unthinkable—targeting innocents in their own community who had done nothing whatsoever to cause offense—Whitman and others opened up the possibility of imitation and further destruction by like-minded individuals, including, of course, troubled adolescents.

The carnage at the University of Texas illustrates another extremely important point, because it differentiates Whitman, as well as our first U.S. high school shooter Anthony Barbaro (chapter 8) eight years later—from much of what followed. Mass murderers who perpetrate their killings in sniper style fully expect to die, yet they take precautions to protect themselves from retaliatory fire for as long as possible. From 1975 onward, we begin to see a pattern of suicidal students wading into the center of the carnage they create and then killing themselves. This began escalating in the 1980s, probably spurred on by numerous acts of adult workplace rage. The trend toward overkill crested with Marc Lépine's slaughter of fourteen female students at a Montreal college in 1989 (chapter 8), but it certainly didn't end there. Since then, these incidents have periodically peaked with spectacular shootings, like Thurston, Columbine, Red Lake, Erfurt, Virginia Tech, and Jokela High, but they've never really waned. In fact, they're likely to get worse.

One further point needs to be made regarding learning from history. The Whitman massacre had another parallel to the Virginia Tech shootings: two crime scenes. As described in chapter One and in reference to extinction behavior (chapter 15), mass murderers may have more than one agenda. A very personal act of destruction may be followed hours later by a more generalized assault. For this reason, the fact that authorities at Virginia Tech did not initiate a lockdown after the first two murders in a dormitory is reprehensible. Their erroneous assumption that the morning's first shootings were the result of a "domestic incident" should not have precluded warning all students and shutting down the college. They had not seized any weapons at West Ambler Johnston Hall, nor had they captured the perpetrator. He had to still be armed and at large, but they fatally presumed he'd left the campus.

True, Virginia Tech differed from previous double-crime-scene school shootings in that the first victim, Emily Jane Hilscher, an eighteen-year-old veterinary sciences student, was not involved in any deep emotional relationship with Seung-hui Cho. It's feasible she was only a "target of convenience," but previous examples of double-murder sites indicate the killer does not go to a specific place at a specific time—in this case room 4040—merely by chance. Since it's known that Cho had previously stalked women, it's possible Seung-hui had recently formed some kind of fixation upon Hilscher. Ironically, that may have occurred at a shooting range Emily and her boyfriend, Karl David Thornhill, had been frequenting, as Cho also was known to be attending target practice. Whatever the connection, Cho was sighted near Hilscher's dorm at around 7:05 A.M., the time Thornhill dropped off his girlfriend. The first 911 calls came in at 7:15 A.M., so the gunman likely followed her up to her fourth-floor room. The second person killed at the dorm, twenty-two-year-old Ryan Clark, a senior and a student resident assistant, was simply coming to Hilscher's aid.

As destructive as Virginia Tech was, there was one worse school-related tragedy that occurred about forty years before Whitman's Texas rampage. The highest number of students killed in a single incident in the United States was not the result of a school *shooting*, but a bombing. In 1927, a farmer driven insane by frustration and taxes used explosives to blow up a primary school filled with children in Bath, Michigan. The assassin was Andrew Kehoe, who held a grudge against the new school because of a higher tax assessment he'd received related to its construction, but couldn't afford to pay.

Kehoe began the slaughter on May 17 by murdering his ailing forty-five-year-old wife, Nellie, whose illness had added an extra burden of debilitating medical bills. The following day, May 18, after meticulous booby-trapping of his property, he blew up his farmhouse, barn, and orchards. Next he drove to the school, which he had secretly rigged from the ground up with dynamite over the past few months. The way Kehoe secretly set the explosives beneath floor boards and in ducts was the same method the Chechens would use in Russia more than three-quarters of a century later. When he was certain most of the students and teachers had entered the building, Kehoe detonated the explosives using a push box hidden in his car. As a stunned and staggering superintendent Emery Huyck approached him to ask if he was okay, Kehoe blew up the car as well, killing himself, the superintendent, and several bystanders who'd survived the first blast. Altogether 38 fourth, fifth, and sixth graders, plus seven adults lay dead, and nearly sixty others were injured. At his property, Kehoe had left behind a sign that said, "Criminals are made, not born." It was the worst act of domestic terrorism in U.S. history until Timothy McVeigh and Terry Nichols carried out the Oklahoma City Bombing in 1995.

Adults almost always attack elementary, not high schools, because those youngsters are least able to defend themselves, and because small children represent the best hopes and dreams of society. In effect, the shooters are acting out an ultimate act of bullying in the sense that, rather than strike back directly at the actual cause of their pain, they strike at others who are far more vulnerable.

After Kehoe, it was thirty-two years before another adult brought destruction to an elementary school in the United States. A tile contractor named Paul Harold Orgeron, who was in his late forties, had a couple of burglary and theft convictions in his past. Orgeron went to enroll his seven-year-old son, Dusty, at Poe Elementary School, in Houston, Texas, on September 15, 1959, but he also took along an unusual briefcase. After meeting the principal, Orgeron and Dusty headed out to the playground, where the father handed two notes, incoherent and nearly illegible, to a second-grade teacher. One of them read, verbatim, as follows:

> Please do not get excited over this order I'm giving you. In this suitcase you see in my hand is fill to the top with high explosives. I mean high high. An all I want is my wife Betty Orgeron who is the mother of son Dusty Paul Orgeron. I want to return my son to her. Their answer to this is she is over 16 so that [is] that. Please believe me when I say I gave 2 more cases, that are set to go off at two times. I do not believe I can be kill and not kill what is around me, and I mean my son will go to. Do as I say and no one will get hurt. Please. P. H. Orgeron. Do not get the police department yet. I'll tell you when.

Then, without waiting for any further response, Paul fired a shot from a .32-caliber pistol into the briefcase, which was filled with gelex, an explosive more powerful than dynamite. The resultant blast killed Paul, Dusty, two children, two adults, and injured seventeen more youngsters.

Sometimes the egocentric individuals who cause this kind of heartbreak don't even have the excuse of real or perceived wrongs. On May 16, 1986, David and Doris Young, both in their forties, took 150 students and seventeen adults hostage at Cokeville Elementary School, in Wyoming. Their motive was simply greed. The couple demanded $300 million in ransom, but their plans came to an abrupt end when Doris accidentally set off a bomb, killing herself and injuring seventy-nine hostages. In the ensuing chaos, David shot at a teacher who was trying to flee, wounding him. Finally recognizing the futility of his crime, David, the town's former marshal who'd been fired, then turned the gun on himself.

While there have been dozens of attacks by adults in the United States upon schools, playgrounds, and even fast-food chains, conditions overseas haven't been any better. In Russia, long before the Beslan massacre, a thirty-year-old man named Yurl Kardanoc set off two hand grenades in a Vladikavkaz kindergarten classroom on a cold December day in 1995, killing three children, three policemen, and himself in the blast, while wounding three other children.

Three months later, the worst school tragedy to hit the United Kingdom in modern times occurred in Dunblane, Scotland. Thomas Hamilton, forty-three, was nicknamed "Mr. Creepy" by boys in Dunblane because of his predilection for taking photos of them shirtless when he set tasks for them as a scoutmaster. This obsession led to his dismissal. Upset, this avid gun collector wrote a letter to the queen just one week before his deranged attack, complaining there was a campaign to ruin his reputation.

On March 13, 1996, Hamilton entered Dunblane Primary School's gym, just after 9:30 A.M., armed with four handguns, dressed in black, and wearing earmuffs to protect himself from the noise he was about to generate. His weapons sprayed 105 bullets into the kindergarten class assembled there, killing 16 five- and six-year-olds and a teacher, Gwen Mayor. Another adult and twelve other children were wounded, several seriously. The gunman then killed himself.

This was the last straw for those in the United Kingdom who'd long been opposed to personal ownership of weapons unsuitable for hunting. British bobbies still didn't carry guns, and they didn't want

England echoing the "fear begets guns begets fear" pattern of the United States. When the Dunblane Inquiry ended, any British citizens who owned handguns (larger assault weapons have *never* been legal there) were given three months to turn them over to local authorities or face a ten-year prison sentence. Nearly two hundred thousand handguns were turned in. The school in Dunblane was demolished after the massacre—the memories were too painful—and replaced by a garden with a play area.

Ironically, the limitation on guns did not apply to another attack on British elementary-school children four months later. St. Luke's Primary School, in Wolverhampton, was sponsoring a teddy bear picnic on July 8, when thirty-three-year-old Horrett Campbell, wielding a machete and laughing like a maniac, appeared at the school fence. He jumped into the playground and slashed three children and four adults. Horrett fled the scene, but was found a day later hiding in a cupboard on the ninth floor of an apartment building a few yards from the school. During his trial, Horrett said he heard children taunt him as he walked past. He was diagnosed with paranoid schizophrenia, convicted of attempted murder, and ordered held indefinitely.

A little over a year after Dunblane, the Middle East experienced a comparable school shooting, which reflected the region's Islamic culture. Mohammed Ahmad Misleh al-Naziri was furious because one of his daughters was kidnapped and raped earlier that March in San'ā', Yemen. However, a medical examiner's report showed no evidence of rape. Not accepting that, Mohammed sought revenge on school officials, who, he believed, were involved in the crime. Armed with an assault rifle, he went to the Al-Tallai Private High School, where he gunned down the headmistress, a cafeteria employee who attempted to cover her body, and a bystander who tried to stop him entering the school. Once inside, Mohammed fired wildly, hitting students and teachers indiscriminately. He then raced a short distance to another school and opened fire again. Security forces wounded the gunman in a brief shoot-out. Six children and two others died. Justice is swift in the Mideast. Mohammed was executed by firing squad one week after the incident.

In considering the various types of mass murder, Dr. Palermo summed them up thus:

The revengeful act of an adult against groups of innocent people; the altruistic killing in which the perpetrator annihilates his own family or others to deliver them from imaginary suffering, often followed by the suicide of the killer at the site of the homicide; the pseudocommando action in which the killer, to achieve the maximum number of victims, accepts his own death, which he views as a form of sacrifice for a higher cause (e.g., terrorists); and recently, the mass murders perpetrated by young people on groups of other youngsters, usually in or around schools. This type of violence has become ubiquitous, spreading from city to rural areas.

The author would add that when Dr. Palermo differentiated adult mass murderers (the first three "types") from adolescents, he was writing pre-Columbine. It can now be postulated that all of these categories—revengeful, family annihilator, and pseudocommando—have been observed among teenage school shooters as well. Kip Kinkel and possibly Jeff Weise may have embodied all three.

• Chapter 27 •

The Cutting Edge

*I am not forgetting revenge for the compulsory education
that has produced me as an invisible existence. . . . Well,
this is the beginning of the game. Stupid police, stop me
if you can. It's great fun for me to kill people.*
—Taunting note written to police by the fourteen-year-old
"Kobe Killer," Japan, 1997

Conditions regarding school attacks overseas do not differ much in
terms of the homicidal/suicidal link, especially in Europe, where, despite tighter gun controls, students still manage to access firearms.
It's slightly different in Asia, where guns in private homes are few
and far between, blades are commonplace, and suicide has histori-
cally been viewed with more acceptance.

Japan is a perfect example. While that nation does not encourage suicide, neither is there the same stigma of immorality that we
in the West attach to it. In fact, for hundreds of years, suicide was
considered the only honorable way out of an insurmountable dilemma.
While Japan's technical prowess equals or exceeds the United States,
the historical, religious, and cultural outlook of its people offers a
complete antithesis to the American model. While Americans value
rugged individualism and competition, whether in school or in the
marketplace, the Japanese prefer to maintain overall social harmony
by limiting individuality and idealizing conformity. Citizens in Japan
function at their best when they adhere to the timeworn social institutions and preset standards of behavior that infiltrate every as-

pect of daily life. The renowned cleanliness, public safety, efficiency, and elegance of Japan depend upon this fact.

However, the downside of this principle is that those who don't fit in, and this is truest among younger people, may be subject to merciless bullying. Whereas in the West, bullying frequently takes the form of taunts and threats, in Asia, shunning and exclusion are more typical forms of harassment. As an inward-looking society, bullying in Japan is more likely to result in the victim committing suicide than striking back at his or her tormentors. Hundreds of kids do so every year, with many leaving notes as a last, futile protest.

As to more aggressive forms of violence, a determined psychopath will not allow a dearth of firearms to deter him from creating mayhem—as the machete incident in Wolverhampton, England, pointed out. In less violent societies and countries that discourage gun possession, adults and adolescents have found methods and means to vent their fury that differ only in weaponry from their American counterparts.

In May and June 1997, the main news topic in Japan was the grisly murder committed by a fourteen-year-old boy in Kobe. The decapitated head of an eleven-year-old mentally handicapped boy, who'd been missing for several days, was found one morning in front of the Tomogaoka Junior High School gate before students arrived for classes. The victim's body was later found on a hill five hundred yards away. Two messages had been crammed into Jun Hase's mouth expressing hatred for Japan's education system, which is renowned for its quality and discipline, but also for the bullying that often occurs among students. The notes also mocked the police, as if this were a game.

Police finally found the young killer, who immediately confessed, because he'd been kept home from Tomogaoka for killing a cat, cutting it into pieces, and leaving that at school. He'd admitted at that time, "I did it to threaten my teacher." As is usual in these kinds of situations, the school covered up the incident to save face, informing neither parents nor students. Investigators determined that this cover-up led the boy to kill Jun Hase, because with the cat, his whole intention had been to cause a stir and no stir was created. By not making waves and playing it safe, the school actuated a much greater danger.

The boy was also accused of attacking four schoolgirls in the same neighborhood, variously using a hammer or knife on 2 twelve-year-olds, a nine-year-old, and a ten-year-old named Ayaka Yamashita, who died after several blows to her head. None of these actions aroused an urgent sense of alarm in his docile neighbors, so the boy just continued on that path.

The teen killer reportedly owned more than one hundred horror movie videotapes, and many of his methods were supposedly learned from them. It's interesting to note that in 2006, Montreal police found 174 DVD horror films and a homemade disc entitled *Shooting sprees ain't no fun without Ozzy and friends LOL* in Kimveer Gill's CD player after his rampage at Dawson College. Jeff Weise at Red Lake also fixated upon violent scenes in violent films, as did Alvaro Castillo (chapter 1) and Seung-hui Cho.

In a psychiatric evaluation, doctors concluded that "the Kobe Killer," as he was branded, derived pleasure, including sexual satisfaction, from inflicting injuries upon people and animals. Under Japanese juvenile law, anyone aged sixteen and under cannot be prosecuted as a criminal defendant. The boy was sentenced to juvenile medical prison and treated for mental illness, but was released on probation in March 2004 at age twenty-one because he had expressed remorse. In Japan's highly organized social system, merely expressing remorse (whether it's sincere or not) is generally the key to forgiveness in most matters.

Young delinquents at Japanese schools correspond closely with U.S. school shooters who mainly come from homes relatively free from material want. Four-fifths of juveniles charged with crimes there reported being from middle-class families with both parents living at home. Although those aged fourteen to nineteen comprise only 9 percent of Japan's population, they accounted in a recent survey for 34 percent of serious crimes (murder and robbery), and 45 percent of violent crimes, including assault.

Explosives disquieted the Japanese educational system on June 10, 2005, when an eighteen-year-old seeking revenge against one student tossed a homemade bomb into his high school classroom in Hikari, Yamaguchi Prefecture. Fifty-eight students were hospitalized, but none seriously wounded by the device made of a glass container filled with gunpowder and nails.

As in the United States, the youngest and most merciless reap the most media attention, especially if they're girls. Japan's biggest murder story in June 2004 concerned a twelve-year-old female Okubo Elementary School student named Satomi Mitarai, in the town of Sasebo. Satomi had a close relationship with an eleven-year-old classmate, sharing lessons, sports, and an Internet bulletin board. Notes Satomi posted about her friend included critical comments about her weight and appearance. The piqued eleven-year-old began plotting revenge while watching a murder-mystery TV show. In an empty classroom, the younger girl slit Satomi's neck and arms with a box cutter, and left her to bleed to death. Afterward, she did express remorse.

Another elementary school, this time in Neyagawa, Osaka, was the scene of a knife attack by a seventeen-year-old boy on Valentine's Day, 2005. Holding a grudge against one of his former teachers, the young man entered the school, but stabbed a different teacher to death and seriously wounded two others. The teen then lit a cigarette in the teacher's room and waited calmly for police. No students were injured.

Four years earlier, in a different part of Osaka Prefecture, the worst school attack in modern Japanese history rocked that nation when a thirty-seven-year-old former janitor forced his way into Ikeda Elementary School, armed with a six-inch kitchen knife, and killed seven girls, aged seven and eight, and 1 six-year-old boy. Mamoru Takuma also wounded 13 first and second graders and two teachers before being subdued by faculty members.

Upon his arrest, officials discovered Mamoru had a long history of mental illness. He'd previously been arrested in March 1999 for spiking the tea of four teachers with tranquilizers at another school, where he'd worked. Ironically, he falsely claimed the cause for his deadly assault on June 8, 2001, was an overdose of medication he'd taken. In December of that year, he pleaded guilty, explaining as his rationale that he'd wanted to kill himself, but knew no one would mourn if he died alone.

Even this unloved and heartless child killer found romance in prison, however; and true to form, a sympathetic woman married Mamoru just before he was sentenced to death in August 2003. Yet, unlike the Kobe boy or Sasebo girl mentioned earlier, Takuma never expressed remorse. In fact, as he sat in his cell in 2004 waiting for his September 14 execution, one of his final statements was "I should have used gasoline, so I could have killed more than I did."

The September 4, 2002, knifing in Seoul, South Korea, mentioned in an earlier chapter was eerily akin to Mamoru's attack in Japan. A fifty-three-year-old man with mental illness, identified only as Hwang, heard voices telling him he would be killed unless he killed others. He decided the easiest path was to kill children at the Neung Dong Church Elementary School as they ate lunch in the school's canteen. Wielding two knives, Hwang yelled threats at the kids before he started slashing, inflicting multiple facial wounds on nine students. A courageous woman, Bang Eun-kyung, thirty-six, walked into the canteen and cried out, "Take me instead, you lunatic!" as she maneuvered to stop him. Police arrived and subdued Hwang with tear gas.

The pattern having been established, it was only a matter of time before a third East Asian nation would see the same crimes repeated. Even so, no one could have predicted that China would witness an astounding five fatal elementary-school and kindergarten knife attacks by deranged men within the final five months of 2004.

This was the Chinese equivalent to the late '90s wave of school shootings in the United States, and the root cause of this clustering may also be related. Americans unfamiliar with the rapid changes that have taken place in China during the last decade might be surprised at the advances in technology and standards of living that have swept through the urban centers and coastal regions of that nation. Communism may still be the official face of government, but an entrepreneurial spirit and the pursuit of wealth and material goods is an accepted fact of daily life. Television news no longer reports only the latest glowing reports from Farm Cooperative Number 17. When bad stuff related to the well-being of society occurs, people are informed. The intention is to shame the perpetrator and his family, and to discourage such events from recurring. Unfortunately, it seems there are always a few twisted souls who see these tragedies as an inspiration rather than as an admonishment.

The chain began in the capital, Beijing. Xu Heping, the fifty-two-year-old doorman at the kindergarten attached to Beijing University

Number One Hospital, had a history of schizophrenia, including institutionalization for his illness. On August 4, 2004, he was distraught because he'd heard the facility would be closing soon. He locked an iron door to prevent youngsters from escaping, pulled out a kitchen knife, and "just began hacking." It took eight police officers to overpower Xu and arrest him, but not before he'd wounded fifteen children and three teachers, and killed a four-year-old boy.

With that news still fresh, forty-one-year-old Yang Guozhu broke into a day care center for migrant workers' children on September 11 in Suzhou City, Jiangsu Province, armed with a knife, some gasoline, and homemade explosives. He slashed twenty-eight children and was about to light up the explosives and gasoline when police arrived and stopped him. All the wounded survived.

All twenty-five children survived the next attack as well, at Juxian Number 1 Experimental Primary School, in Shandong Province, just nine days later, despite cuts to their arms and faces. This time it seemed two neighbors, Jia and Shen, were involved in a long, drawn-out feud and Jia wanted revenge. Frustrated at not finding Shen at the school his son attended, Jia lashed out at other children with a kitchen knife. He held a nine-year-old girl hostage for an hour until police could rescue her. Sick of this string of identical crimes and calling the thirty-six-year-old's actions "especially cruel," the court ordered Jia to be put to death quickly. Accordingly, he was executed on November 24 as a warning to others, but on the *very next day* an even worse crime occurred in Ruzhou, Henan Province.

That night, a twenty-one-year-old man broke into three separate dormitories of Number 2 High School, in Pingdingshan City, Henan Province, and stabbed nine boys to death as they slept. He also wounded four others, two seriously. Yan Yanming escaped and hid at home, but when he tried to commit suicide, his mother turned him in to police. Yan's execution was scheduled for January 18, 2005, but before he'd been in custody even ten days, thirty-year-old Liu Zhigang scaled the Central Primary School fence in Panshi, Jilin Province, and stabbed 5 first-grade boys and seven girls with a kitchen knife, seriously injuring but not killing them. He then cut his own throat, but was rushed to the hospital, along with the kids. Since doctors determined Liu suffered from schizophrenia and depression, he escaped execution and wasn't held responsible.

China is the world's most populous country; so with that in mind, perhaps we shouldn't be surprised this series of copycat crimes could occur, one after another. And while it seems unlikely that anyone in the United States, save for serious Sinologists, was paying rapt attention to this overseas news, it seems almost uncanny that on November 25, the day after the Pingdingshan dormitory murders, James Lewerke, a fifteen-year-old at Valparaiso High, in Indiana, pulled a machete and a serrated knife out of his pants in first-period Spanish and stabbed seven of his classmates. Their injuries were severe, but not life-threatening.

Oddly enough again, on the very same Valentine's Day as the 2005 knife attack in Japan, a sixteen-year-old boy attacked his Lamar High School classmates, in Arlington, Texas, in samurai fashion with two swords, each having two-foot-long blades. One fourteen-year-old was cut on the face before the screams of students were heard by an unarmed school guard, who was also cut while tackling the boy and putting him out of commission.

Obviously, knives can kill just as guns do, but because they require closer range, they've proven less lethal when the victims are above elementary-school age. They're also more personal in the sense that with a gun, there's an intermediary object—a bullet—flying the distance between the killer and his intended target. However, one errant seventeen-year-old student in New South Wales, Australia, found an insidious way to combine the impersonal nature of a gun with a small stabbing projectile by ordering a crossbow on the Internet.

On May 21, 2004—the sixth anniversary of Thurston High—Martin Jackson, who'd apparently been the victim of constant bullying for years, brought the weapon to Tomaree High School and shot his former girlfriend, Tamara, in the chest. The force was such that the arrow passed through her and impaled the leg of another girl beside her, pinning them together. The boy then took out a couple of gasoline bombs he'd prepared to burn the girls and the school. Acting quickly, another student, named Joel Peddet, was able to prevent the bombs being set off. The arsonistic archer was sentenced to nine years in prison, and Joel received an award for bravery.

Mass murder overseas is just as lethal as in the United States, or more so, when guns can be substituted for sharp blades. In fact, just as the worst school shooting in history was carried out by a man of South Korean origin at Virginia Tech—by an unfortunate coincidence—the worst shooting spree perpetrated by a single individual in all of history took place in 1982, in South Korea. That doesn't imply South Koreans are predisposed to violence any more than other races, but as an advanced technological nation, they live with the added stress of having a bellicose North Korea next door.

In this case, access to firearms was due to the culprit being a police officer. Woo Bum-kon had got into an argument with his girlfriend and was drunk when he raided the police armory at headquarters. Armed to the teeth, he began knocking randomly at houses. Most people who see a cop at their front door don't hesitate to answer. In this case, it was the last thing they ever did. Woo did not hesitate to shoot anyone who opened their door, male or female, young or old. He detonated several grenades, wiping out entire families. In this fashion, he made his way overnight through five small villages during an eight-hour period before he was challenged by other police. At that point, he tried to hold three people hostage, but knowing it was all over, he blew himself up, along with his captives. A total of fifty-seven people lost their lives that night, and thirty-five were wounded.

In that situation, South Korea's strict gun laws had little effect, because Woo *was* the law. In other circumstances, laws based on common sense can make a huge difference. Similar to the United States, Australia had a spate of mass shootings in the 1980s and '90s, including thirteen large-scale events, culminating in the slaughter at Port Arthur Historical Site, in Tasmania, of thirty-five people by Martin Bryant in 1996. Bryant was armed with a legally purchased AR-15 assault rifle. Lacking the influence of a powerful gun lobby to cow politicians, the Australian government enacted a strict ban on semiautomatic rifles within twelve days. There hasn't been a single mass shooting in Australia since then.

While all of the discussed incidents varied widely in terms of geographic location, weaponry, and the age of the perpetrators and victims, the single element that all had in common (apart from the last

two incidents mentioned) is the fact that these crimes were committed in schools. While that much is obvious, it is neither accidental
nor coincidental. Whether insane, fanatical, in a rage, or merely jealous, each of the attackers chose a school as the scene of his crime
deliberately, and with an express purpose. It would profit us to examine why.

Chapter 28

Why the School?

Two surveys estimated 300,000 to 350,000 students take guns to school every month. Why, then, are there so FEW school shootings? Of America's 2,500 monthly shooting deaths, only one or two occur in or around a school.

—Mike Males, *Framing Youth: Ten Myths About the Next Generation*

Descriptions of violence at schools may make for discomforting reading, but the purpose of this book has never been to sensationalize these disasters. Rather, the objective has been to delve deeper below the surface than can be done viewing fleeting images on news bulletins, and to highlight the common threads that underlie each supposedly random act. And while it's hardly news to any clear-thinking person that the shooters had no right to do what they did, no matter how terrible their personal suffering, it seems there are still a few youngsters who haven't quite gotten that message from those who are responsible for their upbringing. Consider the Kinkels, the Shrouts, the Klebolds, the Harrises, the Bosses, the Chos, the Gills, and so many others. Despite being loving parents and educated people, they were unable to instill in their wayward sons this most basic respect for human life. That alone should give us pause for thought.

On May 16, 2004, speaking with columnist David Brooks, of the *New York Times,* in their first interview since the Columbine massacre, Dylan Klebold's father, Tom, said their son "did not do this because of the way he was raised. He did it in contradiction to the way he was raised." His mother, Susan, added, "People need to understand this could have happened to them." Are there other boys similar to Kip, Clay, Dylan, Eric, Sebastian, Seung-hui, and Kimveer still out there? Undoubtedly. Is there anyone exactly like them? Unlikely. A thousand others may grow up in comparable circumstances, yet they will never come close to killing people. It's the 1 in 100,000 that we're still trying to recognize.

In point of fact, less than 1 percent of all homicides among school-aged children occur in or around schools. The likelihood of being involved in a school-shooting event is minuscule. The National School Safety Center's *Report on School Associated Violent Deaths* detailed only 245 shooting deaths in or around schools during the ten-year period from 1992 to 2002. Although that is 245 too many, the number pales in comparison with shooting deaths in other nonschool locations.

During that same period, the *only* shooting deaths reported in Oregon schools were the two student victims of Kip Kinkel. In short, despite the huge number of guns that were and are smuggled onto campuses across the nation, schools are still one of the safest places a child could be. More children are killed at home than in any other location. In 2000, for example, there were sixteen school-associated violent deaths. By comparison, approximately sixteen children die at the hands of their parents or guardians *every three days* in America. From all sources, including family violence, around sixteen youths die specifically from gunfire each *two* days, mostly at the hands of adults. According to the National Center for Education statistics, crime in schools declined in the past decade, though the number of juveniles in custody continued to grow annually. The reason? Longer prison terms and more serious sentencing account for part of it.

Before many students reach the point of committing crimes, their rebelliousness at school often lands them in hot water, and not a few get kicked out. A tiny minority among them seeks violent redress. The "expelled student seeking revenge" syndrome had been seen often enough in America (and one could say that Kip Kinkel's expulsion on May 20, 1998, was the precipitating factor that set off his killing spree), but in 2002, almost every significant school attack in the United States was of that nature, as was the first bona fide school shooting in 2003. Two of the 2002 German school shootings (Erfurt and Freising) were also carried out by expelled students. Students on the brink of flunking out initiated several other attacks during this period, especially at colleges. This was the U.S. lineup:

- On January 11, 2002, a seventeen-year-old student in Raymond, Mississippi, who had just been suspended returned to school and held the principal and assistant principal at gunpoint for about three hours before releasing them.
- On January 16, 2002, a forty-three-year-old graduate student at the Appalachian School of Law, in Grundy, Virginia, went on a shooting spree at his campus. Peter Odighizuwa, a Nigerian national, had just met with the dean concerning his suspension over his failing academic performance. He left briefly, then returned to shoot him dead. He also killed a professor and a student and wounded three others before classmates tackled him. College officials were aware that Odighizuwa had a history of mental instability, having been diagnosed with paranoid schizophrenia. First-year student Justin Marlowe said that Peter "was a real quiet guy who kept to himself. He didn't talk to anybody, but he gave no indication that he was capable of something like this." These words are prophetically analogous to descriptions of Seung-hui Cho at Virginia Tech, five years later. A twelve-year-old pupil in Emsdetten, Germany, also reiterated them, almost word for word, after the 2006 shootings by Sebastian Bosse (chapter 26). "No one liked him," the boy said, "but we didn't think he'd be capable of something like this. He somehow always seemed so shy, never laughed and always stood on his own in the schoolyard." Some of Odighizuwa's victims and family members sued the law school for $23 million, but they eventually settled for $1 million. Cho and Bosse died in their rampages, but Odighizuwa is serving six life terms today.
- One of the most unlikely events of 2002 happened on February 12 in Fairfield, Connecticut, when a legally blind former student at Fairfield University held his professor and around two dozen students hostage. Patrick Arbelo, twenty-four, ordinarily brought a seeing-eye dog to class, but this day he came on his own,

wielding a knife and telling classmates that his bag had a bomb inside. During negotiations over the next six hours, he released one hostage after another and then surrendered peaceably.

• Another expelled student, another knife hostage, on May 13 in Arlington, Virginia, as a teenager returned to Lakewood High wielding a pair of kitchen knives. Although the principal was unable to talk the boy into letting his hostages walk free, after an hour, the school's resource officer trumped the teen's two knives with a gun, eliciting his surrender.

• On October 28, Robert Flores, a student flunking out of the University of Arizona Nursing School, shot three of his professors to death, then killed himself. Before his rampage, he mailed a twenty-two-page suicide note to the *Arizona Daily Star,* which began, *Greetings from the dead.* University president Peter Likins commented that the letter provided some insight into the thought processes that take place in the mind of a school shooter just before he strikes. "When people do horrible things," Likins said, "we always ask ourselves after the fact, 'What could he have possibly been thinking? How could he justify such atrocities in his own mind, or was he so deranged he wasn't thinking at all?'" But the letter is a thoughtful, intelligently written, step-by-step history of the slow buildup of economic, marital, and educational setbacks that caused Flores to seek, in his words, "a reckoning." (It may be read in its entirety at cgi3.azstarnet.com/specialreport/page2.html.) Flores's final solution was horribly wrong, but reading this, college administrators, health professionals, and government workers might benefit from noting how small factors can combine like volatile chemicals to cause an explosion in a man's life.

• Gasoline and a shotgun were the weapons of choice for eighteen-year-old Anthony "Tony" Cipriano when he walked into his former school on November 15, in Scurry, Texas. Tony had been suspended by the principal two years earlier for stealing a teacher's car. He was out for revenge, but he wasn't aware that Scurry-Rosser High School now had a new principal, named Richard Sneed. When he found out, he took a can of gasoline from his backpack and sprayed it over the hallway walls. Tony weighed in at three hundred pounds; so when he ordered students into the cafeteria, no one went up against him. Cipriano poured more gasoline around the students and splashed a few as he prepared to burn the school down, but Principal Sneed showed up and somehow wrestled Tony to the ground, forcing the gun to point in a safer direction. Two teachers and two football players joined in dog piling the supersized arsonist, pinning him down until police arrived.

- On April 24, 2003, Principal Eugene Segro was gunned down by fourteen-year-old James Sheets, as described in Chapter 4.

If we include the May 9, 2003, shooting by Biswanath Halder at Case Western's business college in Cleveland, mentioned earlier, we find that half of the eight U.S. attacks during this period were at universities instead of elementary or high schools.

The Appalachian School of Law event was similar to a 1991 shooting on the University of Iowa city campus. There, a distraught graduate student from China killed five people and permanently injured a sixth before fatally shooting himself in the head. Gang Lu, a doctoral candidate in physics, was upset over not receiving an academic award for his dissertation. This rampage was uncannily similar to the 2002 Monash University incident in Australia (chapter 26), also involving a Chinese grad student. These three events, among others, suggest a subclass of campus violence perpetrated by adults who, unlike Cho at Virginia Tech, are upset over academic rather than social failures. They blame faculty, not other students, though there is often collateral killing. In addition, overseas students face the further stress of possible deportation, second-rate job prospects back home, or even being required to repay university fees prefunded by their government.

This profile applied to the case of Nikhil Dhar, twenty-four, an Indian national who was a popular student government leader at UMass-Lowell. On December 22, 2005, despondent over a failing grade that might get him deported, Nikhil followed his hematology professor to her home and, after a brief but boisterous confrontation, hit her and stabbed her neck. She survived, and he was sentenced to a minimum of four years.

As University of Arizona president Likins's comments demonstrate, however, the questions being asked in 2002 were still the same as they were after every school shooting since 1974. Obviously, no one had found all the answers, or at least not enough to effectively prevent the continuation of these crimes, as we discovered once again at Virginia Tech.

One of the most frequent questions asked about rampaging students is why they choose to shoot up their schools and not, for instance, a theater, sports club, or hotel lobby. Former Thurston High principal Larry Bentz, speaking about this wave of young shooters in general, gave this response: "What's their frame of reference? What's the context for their life? It's school. If they're going to do damage, they're going to find someplace where there are people [similar to them] to damage."

One could take that deduction a step further. School is a teenager's personal stage, a social theater, and the place they're branded by their peers as winners or losers. School may not be entirely representative of the "real" world, but school plus home plus church or clubs may serve as the entire cosmos for young people whose perspective of life is limited by age and inexperience.

Furthermore, Americans are, broadly speaking, a very insular people. We generally don't excel in foreign-language skills compared to Europeans, and as any expatriate can affirm, there's little curiosity among the general population here about what goes on beyond U.S. borders, except perhaps for wars in which we're involved, or earth-shaking natural disasters. Even then, the focus is often "How many Americans were killed?" as if that's all that really matters. International travel or relocation is not a priority for many of our citizens. So for those who remain most of their lives within the geographic confines of a single community, schools represent the common ground that nearly all one's acquaintances pass through. The younger the resident, the more this is true.

Schools, therefore, take on tremendous symbolic value to a would-be mass murderer. Mayor Jimmy Foster, of Pearl, Mississippi, said in relation to Luke Woodham's 1997 school shooting there, "Ask most anyone who has lived around here for any time, and they will tell you: That school *is* this town. Everybody in town, either grand-parent, was tied to that school. If they had a grandchild, nephew, or niece, they went to the high school. That's the reason the tragedy affected this whole community. The community was tied to the school in a thousand ways."

For some kids, the school they are tied to represents nothing but hurt and humiliation. Before his 1997 shooting attack in Bethel, Alaska, Evan Ramsey (chapter 16) was the target of constant bullying. When the U.S. Secret Service asked Ramsey, "Why the school?" he replied, "That's where most of my pain and suffering was."

Sebastian Bosse put that in more detail on his videotape. "Life was beautiful until I went to school," he said. "I was picked on since first grade. They punched me, they spit at me, they knocked me down, they laughed at me, and I will shoot them. Where is the problem? There is no problem. I can shoot whomever I want. It's my life. It's my gun. I can do with it whatever I want."

Kip Kinkel may have had it in for one or two particular "jocks" he allegedly hated for their taunts, but if he'd truly wanted to target them exclusively, he could have stealthily waylaid them in the gym, the locker room, or on the sports field, rather than in the crowded cafeteria, where there was scant chance of spotting them. And if Kip did not, according to his own admission in court, hold a particular grudge against anyone who was in the cafeteria that day, why, then, did he launch an attack upon hundreds of students at a place and time when he could be assured only of inflicting maximum indiscriminate damage?

Many other school shooters could be classified as classroom avengers acting out of pure hurt and anger, but Kip may have had an additional reason to lash out at Thurston High. Here, after all, was the symbolic, emotionally charged arena where his questionable behavior consistently embarrassed his mom and dad in front of their peers and colleagues. A part of Kip seems to have thrilled at the idea of causing his parents the ultimate shame of committing a mass murder in school. In doing so, he would finally fulfill what he perceived as his father's expectation of him as a completely hopeless son, a "bad kid with bad habits," as Kip told Dr. Hicks.

Kip's outward social focus was divided between his Shangri-La home and Thurston High, the two settings that backdropped all of his problems with his teacher-parents. When he set out to destroy himself and everyone who interfaced with his life, Kip began with those closest to him and then spread his fury to encompass the rest of his small universe. He sprayed the cafeteria with bullets as if he were demolishing his world even as he himself was disintegrating. In the very institution where so many young people sought to expand their horizons, Kip sought to reduce his to zero. Perhaps he was acting out the lyrics to one of his favorite Marilyn Manson songs, "The Reflecting God": *Can you feel my power?/Shoot here and the world gets smaller.*

We still aren't learning the right lessons. On November 8, 2005, fifteen-year-old Ken Bartley Jr. walked into Campbell County Comprehensive High, in Jacksboro, Tennessee, and shot to death Ken Bruce, an assistant principal who'd turned to education after a stint as a lieutenant colonel in the army. In addition, Bartley wounded the principal and another assistant principal. He'd carefully chosen the three men as targets, and no students were injured. The boy was grazed in the hand by a bullet from his own .22-caliber handgun as the administrators and a teacher wrestled his weapon away. Once again, his classmates echoed those sickeningly familiar themes. One girl told reporters, "He's a big jokester. He's been in trouble before, but I just wouldn't expect something like this out of him."

Hearing this same mantra again and again is exasperating, but when it comes from a source that has prior experience with a deceptive student committing a school shooting, it's beyond upsetting. Principal Larry Bentz had been publicly lauded for his handling of the Thurston High tragedy and was awarded $25,000 in 1998 as Oregon "Principal of the Year." Shortly after, he became principal at Springwater Trail High School in Gresham, near Portland. Incredibly, six days before the massacre at Virginia Tech in April 2007, his new school was once again the scene of an attack by an armed, slightly built, fifteen-year-old freshman boy.

What are the odds that in a state that's had only three high school shootings in its entire history, two of them would fall under the jurisdiction of the same principal? Although there were only minor injuries this time, what makes this incident especially galling is that Principal Bentz, who of all people in Oregon should have known better, had not fostered an atmosphere at his school in which pupils would immediately come forward if they heard a threat. It was on his watch that Thurston was torn apart despite numerous forewarnings. Yet, in Gresham as well, Chad Antonio Escobedo told several students that he was planning to shoot at the school and they did not take him seriously. Even though Escobedo said exactly what he would do, and showed two students a bullet, none of them informed an adult.

Three days earlier, Escobedo had gotten the idea of using a gun to "punish" two teachers after watching a TV documentary on Columbine. One teacher had notified Chad's parents his grades were falling; another he disliked because she was "mean." After lunch on April 10, Chad went to a nearby field to retrieve a case holding his stepfather's Winchester .270-caliber bolt-action rifle. He'd hidden it that morning, along with three boxes of cartridges. From there, he fired two shots sniper-style at what he thought were the classrooms of the teachers he disliked. Flying glass and metal injured ten students. Two required surgery.

School officials claimed they were taken off-guard. Superintendent Ken Noah said, "This doesn't appear to be a story like those that have been told in other school-shooting episodes . . . where there were very visible signs of some troubled activity and behavior." Maybe they haven't been paying attention.

Students, as well, chose what they wanted to believe over what they knew in their gut to be true. That same day, a freshman girl had asked Escobedo to come to her party. "I can't," he replied as he pulled something out of his pocket, "I'll probably be in juvie." It looked like a gold bullet, but it didn't occur to her he'd harm anyone, as Chad "never seemed angry and he was always trying to make people laugh." Even so, when the shots were fired, she said, "In that moment, I knew. I just knew." It's called intuition.

Another girl admitted, "He was really a sweet kid and I didn't think he'd be able to do this, but he told me about it, like, yesterday morning, and I thought he was bluffing 'cause sometimes he lies. So when I heard the bang, I was, like, oh my God, he actually did it." Another freshman knew him better. "It really didn't surprise me that he'd do something like this," she said. They'd been close friends, sharing video games and scary movies, but a year earlier Escobedo asked her, "Do you ever imagine shooting something? I think about it sometimes." A junior student thought Escobedo was nice, until a few months earlier, when Chad confided, "I just might bring a gun to school and stand one hundred yards off campus and start shooting." That's exactly what he did. The morning of the shooting, he also showed her the gold cartridge. "What are you gonna do with that?" she asked, but he didn't answer. Later she recalled thinking, "You don't really take that kind of thing seriously like, 'I'm gonna shoot the school today.' That's kind of twisted. But then again, you always hear, 'He was such a nice guy' when things like this happen." Yet she, too, had failed to report anything.

The final irony in all this? Principal Bentz himself was the one counseling Escobedo about troubles the boy was having at home.

The violence and plans for mayhem have continued unabated. An earlier version of this book was published in March 2006, but events continued moving too quickly to keep up with. By April of that year, sixteen deadly new Columbine-style plots had been hatched by twenty-five students arrested across the United States from the heartland up to North Pole, Alaska. That last incident saw the detention of six middle school pupils working as a "death squad." Each of those attacks was only prevented because a few alert students (and in one case an adult) tipped off police.

Then came autumn. The fall semester of 2006 was the worst opening season on record: twelve dead and thirty-four wounded in twenty-five shooting incidents at or near schools from mid-August up till the Amish incident in October. Some of these events were covered earlier, but just to summarize:

This semester began with the death of an elementary-school teacher in Vermont on August 25, before classes had actually begun. The deranged adult shooter was on a general rampage, so the school itself was not a target. The first killing of a student was in Kimveer Gill's Montreal attack on September 13. The next day, in Green Bay, Wisconsin, two seventeen-year-olds were arrested for plotting a shooting spree at their school. Both were obsessed with Columbine, both had written suicide notes. One had just been rejected in an Internet love affair, and he was enraged. Authorities said these boys were "one bad day away from something happening." When police searched their homes, they found guns, bombs, detailed plans, and hundreds of rounds of ammunition. A third eighteen-year-old was arrested three days later.

On August 30 came the Alvaro Rafael Castillo shooting in North

Carolina. The Bailey, Colorado, rape and murder of high-school hostages occurred on September 27, and two days later, Eric Hainstock killed his principal in Cazenovia, Wisconsin. Then came the siege at the Amish school in Pennsylvania. The immensity of this last disaster, the disgust it engendered, and its tragic conclusion were, we hoped, strong enough to forestall any further violence. However, on October 9, a thirteen-year-old student, wearing a black trench coat, in Joplin, Missouri, entered his middle school with an AK-47 and several clips of ammunition, shot a hole in the ceiling, and told two administrators, "Please don't make me do this." Police safely disarmed him, but after all that had happened, the future was looking bleak. Virginia Tech was just six months away.

To see each incident we've covered as an isolated piece of a puzzling conundrum leaves us blind to a wider reality. Criminologists, psychologists, neurologists, sociologists, and a host of others have offered many valid and intriguing theories as to the roots and causes of these terrible events, but each scientific discipline by definition maintains its own limited perspective. By taking a broader approach, we're better able to recognize how school shooters were molded by the society that surrounded them, how they deviated from it, and how they have forever transformed it. That is the purpose of this book.

• Chapter 29 •

Conclusions

He kind of had a natural high, pulling the trigger, like it was some kind of game to him, like he was having a good time.
—ABC News, describing shooter T. J. Solomon, who on May 20, 1999, wounded six classmates in Georgia

A book should be more than just the sum of its parts. It's the author's hope that the astute reader will have grasped what lies not only between the lines but also between the chapters, filling in the inevitable gaps with his or her own observations and opinions of recent events. A nonfiction work should be interactive in the sense that the ideas presented here are but a jumping-off point for one's own resolve and a personal commitment to remain aware of both the problem and prevention of adolescent violence. Because school shootings show no sign of waning, and human wisdom has yet to overcome our built-in urge for self-destruction, this work is by necessity open-ended.

In this book, I've endeavored to make the insanity of school shootings and other forms of terror and mayhem less of an enigma by examining some of the common determinants and underlying themes that interconnect what at first appear to be senseless acts of violence. Clearly, it's not just one factor that sets the stage for mass murder, but the combined effect of multiple ingredients. Like a sickness that affects some people but leaves others unscathed, this disease also requires a ready host—in this case, a disturbed mind willing to accept the conditions that make mass murder not only a possibility, but a desirable option. Or for some, "the only choice."

As we have seen, the children who commit these acts are *not* normal kids, despite a superficial appearance of normality. Because they're generally clever enough to disguise their thoughts, plan covertly, and deny convincingly or jokingly any ill intent, they manage to "blend in" as easily as a terrorist in a Balinese nightclub or on a London bus.

Who among us is best qualified to recognize these young sociopaths for what they really are? One might assume that parents would be on the front lines of any defense because they live in closest proximity to the troubled teens. Unfortunately, many parents proved to be woefully unprepared and underinformed when it came to discerning just how hazardous the situation might become. Blinded by an understandable reluctance to suspect their own children, and by a natural desire to protect them, or simply by their denial of any real danger, a few of them paid for this naiveté with their lives. Some might call them gullible, but they were dealing with master manipulators who excelled in duplicity. Testimonies presented here have demonstrated that even professional counselors can also be fooled, as were police and psychologists, who were accustomed to dealing with far more obvious juvenile delinquents.

Teens are naturally more inclined to open up to those within their own inner circle. Might we hope, then, that acquaintances of a would-be killer could recognize and report disturbing speech, disquieting writings, or alarming behavior from their peers? Here again we observed that in almost every school shooting, the assailants were quite willing to candidly share their lethal plans with close companions— yet, too often, those friends tended to dismiss such warnings as empty bragging, wishful thinking, or dark humor, and some actually encouraged them.

There's been some progress. Through the many tragedies that have convulsed our nation over the past decade, Americans generally have more awareness now regarding what constitutes a legitimate threat. Obviously, there's still a way to go before recognition of the warning signs becomes universal among legal and medical professionals, as well as among ordinary citizens.

Most of all, we need to reassess what kind of people commit such crimes, and to understand that modern rampage killers, be they domestic schoolboys or foreign agents, are seldom obvious. It's a lesson we're learning with every terrorist attack, mass murder, and school shooting, but it's still a lesson that's difficult for some to accept: seemingly good people may do terrible things. Must we then suspect everyone or live in a constant state of fear? Nonsense. We need only be vigilant in our social environment, train our instincts to look beyond the superficial, and judge others not by what we wish to believe, but by what their words *and* their actions are really telling us. We need to truly listen.

This, of course, is easier said than done, but that doesn't mean we can't make an effort in the areas over which we do have some semblance of control. One of the most salient points made by Lieutenant Colonel Grossman was his assertion that society has now been conditioned to embrace violence as entertainment. Maybe that's a good place to start. An April 2005 research report from the University of Washington concluded that the more TV four-year-olds watch, the more likely they'll become bullies later in school and have increased risk of obesity, inattention, and exhibit types of aggressive behavior. That's only one among dozens of studies that demonstrate how the choices we make for our children during the primary stages of their development can affect their entire lives.

There's still much to be said about school shootings and their causes—subject matter that, for lack of space, was barely touched upon here, such as mental-health issues, the influence of various electronic media, and the use and effect of prescription drugs upon youngsters—a practice that conditions them to depend upon external, synthetic solutions to their problems rather than nurturing an inner strength to deal with dilemmas.

Further, although we urgently need to reconsider how young people so easily obtain high-powered weapons, the arguments and emotions attached to gun control legislation will no doubt prevent this subject from being rationally discussed for a long time to come. Under the George W. Bush administration, the NRA scored another big victory in Congress by allowing the ban on assault weapons to lapse. Access to firearms has now become less restrictive to permit more lethal guns in our home arsenals, the leading source of most school shooters' weaponry. Right or wrong, the view from outside this country is that America's gun laws seem designed to favor criminals, street gangs, drug smugglers, the Mafia, and homegrown militias, while putting police at a disadvantage. "How," I am constantly asked when abroad, "does this make sense? Who really controls your government?"

If guns were, as I suggested in an earlier chapter, a religion to Kip Kinkel—something he believed in, depended on, and could not imagine living without—then this is a religion embraced by many millions of Americans. To its most zealous adherents, criticizing their faith in guns is like criticizing a passionate Islamic extremist for his belief in Koranic authorization to kill nonbelievers. It can be dangerous. Restricting gun possession was one of Oklahoma City bomber Timothy McVeigh's gripes against the U.S. government when his carefully planned explosion ended the lives of 168 people and injured more than five hundred in 1995.

McVeigh had made it clear in letters written to newspapers before his attack that he blamed the federal government for a number of ills, including attempts to restrict private gun ownership. Reminiscent of Kip Kinkel, McVeigh began collecting guns while still in school, and according to an ex-army buddy, "He showed more interest in cleaning his collection of guns than in girls or beer."

Radical defenders of the doctrine of unrestricted gun ownership proudly proclaim they're willing to lay down their own lives to safeguard the sacredness of their belief. "From my cold, dead hands!" bellowed actor Charlton Heston as he raised an antique Revolutionary War musket above his head while seeking a fourth term as president of the NRA, on May 20, 2001—by chance, the third anniversary of the day Kip killed his parents.

Let's look a bit closer at this issue, because there's a supposition here that's truly mind-boggling. When this subject comes up on radio interviews, there's always a caller who says something like, "If a crazed student ran over a bunch of kids with an SUV, would we ban SUVs?" The stupidity of this comparison defies belief. Guns are *made* for killing. Unlike SUVs, ropes, knives, or baseball bats that can and have been used as murder weapons, guns have only one purpose. That purpose is to destroy life. That is why they're manufactured, and that's why people buy them. They may be used in defense, they may be used to put food on the table, or they may be used to massacre people. That's up to the user. But nothing can change the fact of what a gun is, which is a killing machine. To compare them to any other tool of murder is ludicrous.

After Virginia Tech, rock guitarist, gun rights activist, and NRA board member Ted Nugent argued that the policy of zero tolerance gun-free zones at schools and campuses "enabled the unchallenged methodical murder of thirty-two people," and should be eliminated. He suggested that if all the students and teachers at Virginia Tech had been allowed to carry concealed weapons, the killer would have been taken down immediately. He seemed to forget that the shooter *was* a student. Other gun advocates maintain that at present only "bad guys" have guns in schools; so arming the "good guys" will solve the problem. This simple-minded binary thinking—presuming the world is populated with easily recognized "good guys" and "bad guys," or that people who appear "good" today would never be "bad" tomorrow—is what got us into this situation in the first place. It works in fairy tales, but we expect more mature thinking from adults.

It's been said that if those who contend "having more guns makes us safer" were right, America would be the safest country in the world. Clearly, it's not. The argument is not about challenging the Second Amendment or making the right to bear arms illegal. It's about responsible gun ownership and not feeding the frenzy of ever more massive killing sprees. It's no accident that Virginia Tech was bigger than anything seen before. Until we address our addictions, expect worse to come.

The conditions that first created school shooters have not diminished—in fact, they've magnified. Kids are salivating for fame and publicity, more saturated now than ever with violent images in movies and electronic media. Parents working several jobs to make ends meet are often too preoccupied to supervise their son's and daughter's Internet wanderings or TV choices. Most important, schools continue to be "soft targets." Children are the most vulnerable members of society, and the shooter knows that's where he can inflict the maximum psychic and emotional damage upon a community he blames for marginalizing or rejecting him.

Much is being done at schools today in terms of prevention, but more must be done. Antibullying programs have been set up across the nation, yet school counselors report it's often the parents of the most at-risk adolescents who decline to be involved in meetings designed to prevent bullying and suicide, probably because, like the Kinkels and Klebolds before them, they are in at least partial denial that such problems exist within their own home. It's not enough to get bullies to temporarily suspend their insensitive, arrogant attitudes and feign contriteness. Schools need to be tenacious in working through the issues with those who intimidate others to identify the genuine source of their behavior. Was there a recent divorce? Abuse? Whatever the reason, kids need to realize that passing their inner pain on to others weaker than themselves is never right.

Perhaps books like Jodi Picoult's *Nineteen Minutes* should be required reading. In an interview with the New York *Daily News*, Picoult said, "I'm hearing from the popular kids themselves, who tell me that after reading the book, they sort of understand that what's a joke to them might not be a joke to another person—and if they forget it immediately, the other person might remember what happened forever."

What goes around, comes around. We have to wonder, when we hear that fellow students and church youth group members back in Chantilly, Virginia, used to tease Seung-hui Cho, to "push him down and laugh at him," whether today they feel they were justified in picking on that geeky kid who mumbled, or if they feel a tinge of guilt for being a part of the process that led to the deaths of thirty-two victims and the gunman himself. Will they, and thousands of other students whose harassment led to the lonely suicides of less aggressive bullied victims, teach their own children that a little kindness may be more important than just fitting in or trying to win points by putting down the less popular kids? There's a fifty-year gap between the publication of William Golding's *Lord of the Flies* and the making of the movie *Mean Girls*, but the underlying concept is still the same: in an environment devoid of altruism and higher moral influences, the fear of ostracism and the desire to belong don't bring out the best in human nature. It's up to each parent to instill that respect so deeply in their children at an early age, that no amount of peer pressure later on can erase it.

Considering those students who've been tormented, they need to be guided into programs that will rebuild their confidence and reverse their low self-esteem. Their concerns must be taken very, very seriously, not dismissed as normal passages of adolescence. They may not be the best communicators, but counselors and parents have to hear them out. Consider the price when we do not. Kids who are experiencing overwhelming frustration, anger, or depression should be monitored closely, especially if they're on prescription drug treatments.

Sometimes schools themselves, as defined by their administrators, may also be practicing a form of denial. In 1999, Columbine principal Frank DeAngelis said, "Now there have been accusations made that Columbine has a 'jock culture' in which athletes rule and outsiders are ostracized. In my twenty-two years at the school as a coach, teacher, and administrator, I've never heard of any such persecution. If there was any of this bullying going on, I think I would have received a phone call." Yet even now, Danny Ledonne reports, "I recently got an e-mail from a student claiming to be attending Columbine High, saying that the situation with the elite students who bully the rest, the cliques, the ostracism, and the unwillingness to address kids who are isolated and depressed is much the same as it was in '99. The e-mail concluded that another school shooting at Columbine is not impossible. Clearly, this problem is not going away."

A question often asked is: why is this happening now in smaller, rural schools? To answer simply, as urban and suburban schools step up their security programs, we'll see more attacks upon rural schools, where such events are least expected. School security nationwide is spotty and inconsistent. If we know terrorists may hijack a plane, we don't screen passengers at only the largest airports. It should be the same with schools. Living in a small and isolated location does not guarantee safety, but neither does being a student on an immense campus. Size is not the issue.

Just like at airport security, every single threat must be taken seriously—even if the student making it is known to be a joker, "a nice kid," a constant liar, or a big talker. *Never* assume they "wouldn't really do something like that." The notion that it can't happen here must go the way of cheap gasoline—it belongs to another era. That doesn't mean we should live with trepidation, just exercise caution.

Fostering a willingness among students to report legitimate threats in the interest of their self-preservation is a tried-and-true solution. It's already resulted in the prevention of dozens of potential school shootings. If a student sees or overhears anything that even resembles a gun or bomb threat, they should know that their school has provided a safe place to impart that information in confidence (see resource appendix on page 331). At the start of each school year, and again at the beginning of spring semester, every student should be reminded of these facts again, via lectures, assemblies, or e-mail.

Under current safeguards, anyone who hints to authorities that he's considered doing a school shooting may be arrested. If a desperate student is that close to the edge, but willing to share his feelings candidly, he needs to know there's a number he can call to get the help he needs without necessarily being locked away. School districts can set up something like this, modeled on suicide prevention lines.

At least once every couple of months, intruder or gun-on-campus drills should be conducted with the same regularity as fire drills. As Grossman pointed out, "Last year, dozens of students died from school violence in America, and a quarter of a million kids suffered serious injuries. We have fire sprinklers, fire alarms, fire extinguishers, and fire-retardant material in the ceiling. We prepare for fire, but not a single kid's been killed by a school fire in half a century. We need to be as prepared for violence." Each administrator, teacher, office staffer, SRO, and counselor should know exactly what to do in such an emergency and who they need to contact. Postevent strategies should also be worked out in case the worst should happen. These are just a few commonsense suggestions, but links to professional organizations that specialize in these areas are listed at the back of this book. There are dozens of commentaries, inquiries, and evaluations now available in electronic and printed form.

The sciences, as well, are constantly reexamining and updating our knowledge on how it is that some children manage to lose the natural sense of compassion that everyone possesses at birth. In April 2005, neuroscientist Marco Iacoboni, of the University of California's Los Angeles School of Medicine, suggested that "mirror neurons," a cluster of cells in the area of the brain responsible for planning movements, may also determine an individual's ability to learn empathy. They are called mirror neurons because these cells reflect actions, sensations, and emotions observed in others.

"Mirror neurons suggest that we pretend to be in another person's mental shoes," Iacoboni explained. "In fact, with mirror neu-rons . . . we practically *are* in another person's mind." If the mirror neuron systems are impaired or deficient, the result may be a kind of "mind-blindness" that prevents people from replicating the experiences of others—in other words, they lose all sense of empathy. For such individuals, emotional experience is observed rather than lived, causing the natural responses that govern much of our human behavior to become inaccessible. The end result is a mechanical and impersonal understanding of others, devoid of any genuine perception of their motives or emotions. In this way, intelligent boys like Kinkel and Klebold may have learned how to cleverly mimic and flatter the perceptions of others, without actually being able to know what others feel.

In defining the attributes of sociopaths, former policewoman and true-crime author Ann Rule wrote something similar: *An antisocial personality has not the slightest concern for the rights of others. A brilliant mind with no conscience to guide it . . . it mimics "real" people, giving back only what it must to receive gratification.* Such people, she says, *cannot love. They cannot even understand love.* She adds that sociopaths have no empathy, show no remorse, and view others as objects or possessions. When they cannot manipulate others to do what they wish, they react with indignation and rage—justifying *lying, cheating wheedling . . . even murder* to attain what they want.

Concepts such as impaired mirror neurons, intermittent explosive disorder, the binary mind, splitting, a media-driven copycat effect, and extinction behavior give us potential tools to explore the why and the how of school-centered domestic terrorism. By considering these, we might heighten our awareness of the psychological states of those who could once again pose a threat to our communities.

Hopefully, history may eventually record that those who experienced school shootings were among an unfortunate and extremely small minority whose lives were disrupted during a brief period in humanity's cultural evolution. However, for the ones who were there on the front lines, the reality of what they encountered became a turning point in their existence. Statistics give little comfort to those who actually interfaced with the violence.

The one thing recent events have taught us is that it's difficult to be prepared for each and every eventuality. Perhaps the fear of danger at schools has been exaggerated, and nothing more will happen. Maybe school shootings will end; terrorists will realize that they gain nothing by killing innocent people; workplace frustrations that boil over into deadly rage will be prevented by timely counseling; potential mass murderers will seek psychiatric help before they strike; and parents will spend more time listening to their kids' problems, taking charge of the media they're exposed to, and controlling their access to firearms. Or maybe not. Without succumbing to an obsession with fear, perhaps it's still prudent to sometimes imagine the unimaginable and have that emergency or contingency plan for the "worst possible scenario" ready in the school storeroom, just in case.

Sins of Compassion

If I can prevent someone from having the experience I went through, I want to do that. I killed people. There's no hope for me now, but there is hope for you. . . . No matter how bad things may seem, violence is not the answer. It will only make things worse. Sometimes life may seem horrible to us at the moment, but that may not be the case in the future. High school is just four years. It's not your whole life.

    —Advice given by convicted school shooter Evan Ramsey
      to some of the more than seven hundred students
      who've written to him in prison, expressing a desire
      to follow a similar self-destructive path

As weeks passed in the aftermath of Virginia Tech, authorities there were baffled. "We still haven't found a motive," they said. They just didn't get it. For a school shooter, the rampage itself *is* the motive. The paroxysm of violence, the payback, the instant fame, the lust for blood, the shooting game. They do it because they can. They're not motivated in the usual sense, like a jealous husband poisoning his wife or a slumlord arsonist out for insurance money. There may be a small triggering event, but the agony, the resentments, the descent into an isolated world of self-delusion, the cold-blooded planning, and the volcanic rage take years of buildup.

Seung-hui Cho was the culmination of thirty-three years of school shootings. He learned all the basics from those who came before, and improvised a few of his own. The twenty-three-year-old English major confided in no one, dropping hints only about his mental instability, not his final course of action. The two disturbing plays he wrote for playwriting class (*Mr. Brownstone* and *Richard McBeef*) aroused disgust, but we still don't know if his references in them to pedophilia were autobiographical. The forty-three photos and thirty minutes of video he sent to NBC News didn't really tell us who he was, but rather the scripted image of who he wanted us to see. He mistook violence for a symbol of masculinity. He called himself an "antiterrorist," yet his intention was to terrorize.

The story of what happened at Virginia Tech is by now familiar to most people, but to summarize with some more recent information:

Cho's family had worries about Seung-hui even before they came to the United States from South Korea, when he was eight. He seemed cold and distant and seldom communicated. Later he was diagnosed with autism. His parents were very religious and their pastor urged his mother many times to get him medical help, but she declined. No doubt the stigma of mental illness ran counter to the family's projected vision of success.

In Blacksburg, on the morning of April 16, the day started off with just a hint of snow in a light breeze. By 7:15 A.M., Cho had committed his first two murders at West Ambler Johnston Hall (chapter 26), using a 9mm Glock pistol, which shoots five rounds per second. Other students in that residence hall would later report being astonished they didn't hear any gunfire.

Cho returned to his room, finished preparing his media kit, and mailed his package to NBC at 9:01 A.M. from the campus post office. Sam Riley, a communications professor, remembered passing him on the steps and, noting his "dazed and slack-jawed" appearance, thought, *Good Lord! That's the most deranged-looking individual I've seen in a long time.* Between his two crime scenes, Cho may have been simply waiting to see if there'd be any reaction from campus police, but he also needed to organize the chains and weapons he'd carry to the engineering building.

One theory as to why the college did not lock down during that two-and-a-half-hour gap relates to the opening day of classes in August 2006. It was not an auspicious beginning. A prison inmate named William Morva killed a hospital guard and escaped to an area near the college. Before being recaptured, Morva also murdered a sheriff's deputy on a trail just off campus. The school was locked down and classes were canceled during the manhunt. It's possible administrators didn't want a repeat of that situation, as it could damage the school's reputation as a safe campus. If so, what occurred next was much worse.

Once inside Norris Hall, Cho first peered into some occupied classrooms to calculate the situation. Then he chained shut and padlocked the main doors. By taking time to do this, he demonstrated a chilling methodology. Cho knew this barricade would ensnare students within his trap and delay police, maximizing the number of deaths. He even taped notes on the exits saying, *Open the doors and a bomb will go off.* He probably chose Norris, an older building, because classroom doors had no locks, many windows were too small for people to escape through, and there were fewer escape routes. In August 2007, police revealed that *two days before the massacre,* a suspicious man wearing a hooded sweatshirt, and corresponding to Cho's description, was seen in Norris Hall—and soon after the exit doors were found chained shut! Was Cho practicing locking the doors in a dry run, or was he actually planning to shoot on that day, but then backed out?

There's something especially malicious and heartless about this strategy of ensuring innocent victims have no hope of escape, but Cho wasn't the only school shooter to think of it. Charles Carl Roberts (chapter 21) barricaded the Amish school doors by nailing thick wooden boards into place. Kinkel (chapter 16) planned to lock the two front doors of the cafeteria before he started executing students. At his trial, Tobin Kerns (chapter 20) admitted that among items he and Joseph Nee intended to purchase for their attack were bicycle locks to secure exit doors at Marshfield High and prevent anyone from leaving. Dillon Cossey (chapter 26) in Pennsylvania confessed that he tried to recruit another boy into his scheme to chain shut the doors at Plymouth Whitemarsh High and then back a car up to block the entrance. Intentions such as these go beyond a personal vendetta. To massacre trapped and helpless people is a barbaric crime against humanity.

At about 9:50 A.M., Seung-hui Cho burst into the first of four classrooms on the second floor of Norris, stood a few feet inside with "a very serious but calm look on his face," and shot the German professor in the head. Then he started firing at everyone else as students screamed and dropped to the floor. During his nine-minute rampage, Cho repeated this pattern in three more classrooms. He killed thirty-two people, and an additional twenty-five others had direct (gunshot wounds) or indirect (leaping from windows) injuries.

Cho displayed a calm exterior, but inside his killing instinct was seething. He didn't just spray his shots wildly; he viciously pumped at least three bullets into every victim. When he left one classroom, the desperate students who remained pushed their bodies up against the door (it wouldn't lock) so Cho couldn't get back in, but the killer persisted like a predator mad for blood, firing through the door and trying three more times to force his way in.

At the building's entrance, police used a shotgun to blow their way through the chained doors. Cho heard them rushing upstairs, put a gun to the side of his forehead, and sent a bullet through his brain. Next to Cho's body, police recovered a Walther .22-caliber semiautomatic, the Glock, and a note about a bomb threat. This last was of interest because the previous week there'd been two separate bomb threats at Virginia Tech. One was directed at the engineering buildings. Perhaps Cho had been probing the school's defenses.

The words "Ismail Ax" were written in red ink on one of Cho's arms. The same epithet was scrawled on his suicide note. The paired words have since been interpreted in dozens of ways, none of them satisfying. Earlier as well, Cho seemed to be cultivating an image of himself as a "silent man of mystery" when he sent out a series of e-mails signed "Question Mark." That's also the name he used to introduce himself to a girl he approached in his dorm. She reacted adversely, but Cho told his roommate, "I saw promiscuity in her eyes."

Late at night when Cho rode his bike in small circles around the dorm's parking lot, it seemed like a reflection of his state of mind. He played his favorite song, "Shine," by Collective Soul, interminably, and scribbled the lyrics on his dorm room wall. He titled his play *Mr. Brownstone* (drug abusers' slang for hashish) after a Guns N' Roses song, and used their lyrics verbatim in his dialogue. (Sample: "But that old man he's a real muthafucker.") That's the kind of talk other school shooters favored, but the song "Shine" is very different. It begins: *Give me a word/Give me a sign/Show me where to look/Tell what will I find,* and the chorus is *Oh, heaven let your light shine down.* Collective Soul denies being a Christian rock band, but admit their lyrics are often spiritual in nature. It's likely Cho's love of this song was a manifestation of his notion of himself as a martyr in a noble cause.

Self-styled martyrs seem to abound in this new millennium. In July 2005, the author was in London during the aftermath of the terrorist bombings that crippled that city's urban transportation system. The identities of the four bombers had been revealed, and Londoners were appalled to learn that, beyond the horror of their homicidal deeds, all these young men had been living for years in public housing on generous handouts of rental assistance, had collected unemployment and welfare benefits, and had used multiple identities to defraud the government of large sums of money. GRATITUDE! proclaimed the headline of one British tabloid. Like unappreciative and contemptuous children, the terrorists had murderously turned on those who'd considerately fed, clothed, and sheltered them. Somehow it all sounded so familiar.

During that same July, just across the English Channel, the trial of Mohammed Bouyeri was under way for the shooting and stabbing death of Dutch filmmaker Theo van Gogh. Bouyeri, a twenty-seven-year-old with dual Dutch-Moroccan citizenship, had very publicly murdered Van Gogh on November 2, 2004, because the filmmaker had been making a documentary critical of Islamic fundamentalism. Van Gogh had pressed ahead despite receiving death threats from Muslim zealots.

During the trial in Amsterdam, Van Gogh's mother and sister read out emotional victim statements. When permitted to reply, the killer stated, "I don't feel your pain. I don't have any sympathy for you. I can't feel for you because you're a nonbeliever." Bouyeri had opened fire on police after murdering van Gogh, hoping to die in a gun battle. In a condescending voice, he told the packed courtroom, "You cannot understand. I shot to kill and be killed."

Total lack of empathy. Suicide by cop. Extreme violence against others who disagree with or criticize one's own personal choices. All themes that have been interwoven into our examination of school shooters and mass murderers. But there was one more reminder of the similarities, as if we needed reminding: in the aftermath of every terrorist killing lies the same shadow of incomprehension that follows each school shooting—trying to fathom the minds of those whose vision of cause and effect is limited to whatever immediate destruction they might bring about, assigning guilt to their victims simply because they imagine those individuals' convictions may run counter to their own.

Self-glorification for an act of murder is an obscenity. The 9/11 attackers and other so-called Islamic martyrs (called *shuhada*) believed they would be rewarded in the afterlife with tickets to heaven for the entire family, seventy-two beautiful virgins (*houris*), plus "boys of perpetual freshness," water, wine, fruits, and wealth. In a mythical universe, one can promise anything. It's not difficult to envision how those who are disenfranchised or destitute, or whose lives lack meaning, might find comfort and brotherhood in such promises and in the radical forms of religion that promulgate them. Like addicts working their way up to hard drugs, they might start off with sincerely pious convictions, but eventually embrace hard-core fanaticism. When an individual becomes seduced by rabid extremism, exterminating nonbelievers becomes not only an imaginable act, but an obligation in some cases.

However, lest we in the West feel smug or superior about such uncivil religious convictions, consider that Paul Hill, the former minister who gunned down a Pensacola, Florida, abortion doctor on July 29, 1994, also stated the day before he was put to death that he was sure he'd be rewarded in heaven for his actions. Hill said he'd been following God's instructions when he murdered the doctor and a woman standing near him, as well as wounding the doctor's wife. The two females weren't intended targets but simply "collateral damage"—or what we used to call innocent bystanders. While one lone gunman, or even a small faction of extreme fundamentalists who advocate killing in a "just cause," can hardly be compared to a global terrorist organization, the point is not scale but motivation. Condoning murder in the name of righteousness is never an acceptable choice, no matter what the religion. Several school shooters were anarchistic idealists who used exactly the same excuse to justify their actions.

Hill was executed by lethal injection on September 3, 2003, but two weeks earlier, threatening letters containing bullets were sent by those ironically calling themselves pro-life to top Florida officials involved with carrying out the sentence. While we know that devout Muslims and Christians cherish the precepts of the Ten Commandments, we wonder what part of "Thou shalt not murder" these particular individuals don't understand.

Oklahoma City bomber Timothy McVeigh was, likewise, executed by lethal injection at a U.S. penitentiary in Terre Haute, Indiana, on June 11, 2001. In his case, it was nineteen children whom he called "collateral damage." McVeigh admitted in prison that he knew there were kids at a day care center inside the Alfred P. Murrah Federal Building. He decided to blow it up on April 19, 1995, anyway, because he didn't want to miss the symbolic second anniversary of the fatal U.S. Bureau of Alcohol, Tobacco, and Firearms raid on the Branch Davidian cult headquarters in Waco, Texas.

At first, authorities thought this worst-ever act of domestic terrorism (prior to 9/11) was carried out by Islamic radicals. When it was proven that twenty-six-year-old McVeigh and his accomplice Terry Nichols had truly done the deed, the nation was shocked that an "outstanding" former soldier and expert army marksman who had served in the Gulf War could turn on his own people. Few recalled that ex-marine sniper Charles Whitman (chapter 26) had done something akin to this in 1966, in Texas.

A more bizarre coupling came later when some investigators claimed McVeigh had met with Ramzi Yousef, the al-Qaida operative who had planned the 1993 World Trade Center bombing. The same sources also contend that McVeigh interfaced several times with the Philippines-based Abu Sayyaf Islamic terrorist group. Perhaps it was a twist on "The enemy of my enemy is my friend." What is more certain is that McVeigh had loosely been involved with right-wing antigovernment militia and a white supremacist movement.

According to his prison psychiatrist, Dr. John Smith, McVeigh was bullied at school and later created a fantasy world, where he imagined himself as a heroic warrior who would vanquish his persecutors—a comic book daydream. In Dr. Smith's opinion, his patient was a "decent person" of above average intelligence who allowed rage to build up inside until he exploded IED-style in "one terrible, violent act." According to McVeigh himself, the army taught him how to turn off his emotions so that he could kill even children in cold blood.

Again we hear familiar terms that apply equally to mass murderers, terrorists, school shooters, and others who slaughter innocent lives. As author Ann Rule wrote in *Lust Killer,* her narrative of Oregon's cross-dressing serial killer Jerome Brudos, violent sociopaths view other humans as mattering only in ways that fulfill or deny the killer's needs, and *only their needs matter, only they are real—their victims are not.*

So it was for Kip Kinkel, Seung-hui Cho, and dozens of other school shooters when their narcissistic needs prevailed over any respect for human life. Today, while most of those killers are either incarcerated or lying in graves, the interrupted lives of those who survived go on. In Springfield, Oregon, a closure of sorts was attained on May 21, 2003, five years after the Thurston High tragedy, when a memorial to the victims of the shooting was unveiled in a landscaped area of the school campus. The day of dedication was the first time many of the students who survived that ordeal had ventured back. Ryan Atteberry attributed his recovery to an ability to maintain a positive attitude, not dwell on the past, and recognize the healing power of laughter. Some students joined the forces of law and order. Aaron Keeney became a member of the sheriff's department. Jake Ryker became a combat engineer in the U.S. Marine Corps Reserve. He and Jennifer Alldredge got married in 2001.

Mikael Nickolauson's father, Michael and his mother, Dawna, helped plan the memorial. Michael still thinks about the things he never got to do with his son, but he tries to focus on his three other kids. Ben Walker's mom, Linda Kluber, could not bring herself to attend because she was still struggling with the loss, even while trying to prioritize her life around her husband and two children. Still, things have improved since the first few years when she visited Ben's grave every single day to let him know she was there for him.

Crystal, the student I'd first met in the LCC cafeteria, had desperately wanted to know why Kip had spared her life after looking into her eyes. We e-mailed briefly following that initial meeting, but she admitted having nightmares about the shooting because of our talk, and was concerned about her emotional well-being. Then she ceased correspondence. Several months later, her friend confided that Crystal had, in fact, been treated professionally for paranoid schizophrenia *before* the attack on Thurston. Ironically, this girl who'd constantly imagined herself being threatened by others almost became a victim in a real-life school shooting. No wonder she'd so calmly accepted that she was about to die. She'd been expecting something like this to happen most of her life. It's intriguing to conjecture whether Kip, also diagnosed as a paranoid schizophrenic, saw something in her eyes that he recognized in himself and turned the gun away.

Former assistant principal Dick Doyle still requires medication and counseling. He'll never be able to work in a school again, but he has regained a semblance of normalcy. Regarding the detective who allowed Kip to go free on May 20, his good intentions have never been in question. However, as an officer sworn to serve and protect the community, a more hard-nosed and objective assessment of the situation would have been appropriate in those circumstances.

The Kinkel family home in Shangri-La was sold to a deputy in the sheriff's department. Kristin used her share of the money from that sale to provide a lawyer for Kip's appeals. "It's what our parents would have wanted," she told a friend. The Kinkels were good people and they meant well, but they raised a son who killed. If we expected to find evidence that Bill and Faith had taught their boy "the Golden Rule," we fail to discover any sign of this in his concept of mercy. If, on the other hand, we consider Kip's own perspective, then it becomes clear that, by his logic, his shooting spree was very much "doing unto others" what he would have others "do unto" him. He shot them expecting to be shot in return. Because he lacked the willpower to go through with his own suicide, he tried to use others to do it for him, even after his arrest. Selfish to the end, Kip's entire worldview revolved around his own needs to such an astonishing degree that murdering his parents before completing his game plan of terrorizing Thurston High was simply an activity he squeezed in between phone calls, eating cereal, and watching TV.

There's no question that Kip was mentally ill, be it from IED, paranoia, schizophrenia, or some combination of the above, but ultimately, did the exact nature of his disturbance really matter? He purposely kept his infirmity hidden, refusing to expose it despite being given opportunities to do so. His parents, counselors, and teachers unconsciously abetted him in this masquerade; for whatever they may have suspected, the fact is they did not *want* to believe Kip had a mental problem. Even the psychologist at the Skipworth Juvenile Facility seems to have accepted that Kip was just passing through a rebellious stage, and Dr. Hicks never reached the depth of analysis that would have exposed the true nature of Kip's deviancy.

As for Kip's friends, they did not have the maturity, wisdom, or experience to fathom Kip's true intentions. Like most students, they conducted their peer relationships in the daily "communal theater" of school as if they were players in a sitcom world, a place where everything could be a joke and "serious" problems seldom extended beyond transitory glitches on their uphill journey through adolescence. None of the kids at Thurston were really prepared for this kind of intrusion upon their take on reality. Few children in America are.

I have come to view school shooting as the equivalent of small, personal civil wars being fought by a scattering of individuals against their own families, communities, and peers. The rationale of this book has been that by factually documenting each battle, analyzing its causes, and recording its consequences, we come a little closer to comprehending the larger picture, and knowing what part we all play in it.

Of the revelations I came across while writing this book, the largest was the denial I encountered in confronting difficult truths about things we as a society find pleasurable. I know several enthusiastic gamers who fit this bracket. I get it that role-playing in some virtual fantasy world (violent or not) can provide a controlled outlet for relieving stress, dealing with disagreeable emotions, taking time out for alter-ego-tripping as a surrogate avatar, or even building a bolder sense of self. I myself don't partake, not because I wouldn't enjoy building a Sims city, playing a Wii, or chasing dragons through some imaginary kingdom, but simply because I don't have the time to spend on entertaining diversions that are not especially productive. It's a personal choice, not a condemnation. However, insisting that hours of compulsive play can't be harmful is just another way to say, "It can't be bad because I like it." In that case, habitual gamers may as well stand in line behind smokers who think cancer is a myth, shopaholics who drive their family into debt, potbellied gluttons who take a fifth swipe at the buffet table, sofa spuds who can't turn off the TV, gun nuts who kiss their AK-47 good night, and hordes of alcoholics, sexaholics, and drug addicts who don't believe they have a problem. Affluence certainly offers us lots of choices.

I also noted how what goes around comes around. On February 24, 2006, about the time the first version of my book *The Shooting Game* was going to press, Oregon experienced its second-ever high school shooting. A fourteen-year-old Roseburg High freshman named Vincent Wayne Leodoro, enrolled in an at-risk program, had a long-running feud with sophomore Joseph Monti, sixteen. At 7:42 A.M., in the school's crowded courtyard, Leodoro's anger reached critical mass and he shot his classmate four times without warning at close range from behind. His Wyoming Arms 10mm semiautomatic handgun loaded with hollow-point bullets was, as in many previous shootings, smuggled out of his own home. After three hours of intensive surgery, Monti was in stable condition.

After the shooting, Leodoro casually walked out of the schoolyard as students scrambled away, screaming. Six armed policemen confronted him in front of a restaurant. The shooter brought his gun up to the side of his head, put his finger on the trigger, and threatened to kill himself. Inside the restaurant, customers shouted, "Don't do it, kid!" Police convinced him to put down the weapon, and seconds later, he was swarmed by officers, tackled, and handcuffed.

On the same day as the Roseburg shooting, four youths, ranging from thirteen to sixteen, were scheduled for mental evaluation at a juvenile court in Charlottesville, Virginia. All four were part of a plot to blow up Albemarle High School and Western Albemarle High School sometime before the end of the year. County police seized shotguns from their homes. The four planned their attack in Internet chat rooms.

A week later, four teens (including one girl) were arrested for bringing a gun to Springfield High, the very school where Faith Kinkel had taught. On the same date as the Springfield bust, seventeen-year-old Joseph Titus was arrested with explosive devices at his home in Muscatine, Iowa, one day before a threatened attack on his school. A week later, on March 10, Zaccaria Combs and Dillon Lucas, both fifteen, were charged with threats to commit terrorism at Southeast Warren High School, also in Iowa.

These and other events in the spring of 2006 (chapter 28) became so commonplace that a week without a serious threat or actual school shooting became the exception rather than the rule. Autumn, as we know, got even worse. Then it got personal. On September 27 (the same day as the deadly Bailey, Colorado, event—chapter 21), an angry fifteen-year-old dropout with two loaded, stolen handguns and extra ammunition showed up at my own daughter's high school in Eugene.

My girl had only started attending there two weeks before. Suddenly I was not just the author of a book on school shooting—I was also the father of a student about to be involved in one. An imaginative screenwriter composing a fictional script involving such a scenario would probably toss it out as being too far-fetched—but, in fact, it was all too real. I heard the news of the lockdown on the radio and sped over to her campus. Just five days earlier, Willamette High, in Eugene, had been locked down because of a gun threat from a former student. Here was that same copycat pattern again, but now it was on my doorstep.

When I arrived, I saw that police and Assistant Principal Mike Johnson already had the situation under control. Josiah Christian Trigg had been captured and cuffed near a sports shed without harming anyone. Sergeant Mike Gaylik, who assisted in the arrest, said, "There were some tense moments when Trigg was ordered to drop the guns and get down, but he just stood like a zombie holding them. We told him twice we were about to fire. He came within one short breath of losing his life. He didn't care. He was potentially suicidal."

Trigg was number four of ten children, nearly half of whom had different fathers. His mom claimed that Josiah's dad, an ex-con who'd allegedly done time for murder, had raped her. Right after birth, she gave him up for adoption. A year later, she got married to another man and took him back when his adoptive mom failed a drug test. Josiah didn't know all this until thirteen years later. When he found out, he said, "My mom gave me away," and became depressed. He twice threatened suicide. His sister found a note he'd written saying he wished he'd never been born. He was diagnosed with "attachment disorder"—not bonding with anyone, never smiling, bottling things up inside. Meanwhile, his mom took out a restraining order on her husband, who, it turned out, had physically, verbally, and emotionally abused the four oldest children, including Josiah—who were not biologically his. Then they got divorced.

Josiah turned to video games for comfort, but more the Pokémon type. He became interested in guns, but never fired one until he practiced the day before bringing the stolen weapons to school. He was angry because some friends had stolen his cherished backpack full of personal goods.

Sergeant Gaylik commented, "I've been on the force thirty years, dealing with adolescents. Teenagers often can't differentiate between the emotions that upset them and their response. It's like there's no pause to consider the consequences. It's just feelings, bang, action! No separation. And when something's bugging them, they get no closure until they act on it."

The judge who remanded Josiah into youth custody was named Kip Leonard. Just a mild coincidence, but the chaplain who oversaw Josiah's spiritual development was Al Gaines, the same pastor who'd undertaken Kip Kinkel's successful conversion to evangelical Christianity. He'd also ministered to Conan Hale (chapter 22). Gaines had been abused by his dad as a child and became a drug user at thirteen, a drug dealer by fourteen. "I should have been dead," he said, "but at twenty-eight I found Jesus." He was now sixty.

Later I spoke again with Assistant Principal Mike Johnson. "I need to learn from this," I said. "How did you guys get things done so smoothly?"

He replied, "Well, that was partly due to you."

"Why, what do you mean?" I asked. "I was nowhere near here. You people did all the work."

"My uncle is Dick Doyle," he said. My jaw dropped. "He gave me a first copy of your book. I read it three times—once for the big picture, once for details, and a final time to figure out what we'd do if any of those situations happened here. Our school district has its own *Emergency Procedure Manual* on every teacher's desk, but based upon my past experience and what I'd read, I initiated monthly four-in-one drills (intruder, lockdown, earthquake, and fire). I formed a campuswide Crisis Response Team, where everyone—admin, teachers, custodians, the school resource officer—knows their roles and responsibilities inside out. The police officer who'd been on the scene said we had the most efficient reaction to a gun at school they've ever seen."

I was impressed and told him so. As I got up to leave, he said, "One more thing. Did you ever imagine when you wrote this book that one day it might save your daughter's life?" I realized at that moment my involvement in researching school shootings had come full circle. Whatever else happened, everything I'd given to create this book was now returned a thousandfold.

As for the communities that experienced school shootings, while the rest of the nation may assume the story of these tragedies is over, the people who live there know better. These unhappy events affected everyone, leaving scars that may diminish but never disappear. Each new shooting incident rubs them raw again. For the parents of those who were slain, no passage of years can alleviate the pain or loss.

In my neighboring town of Springfield, there were no real villains in the true-life drama of Thurston High, outside of the maliciously pathetic figure of Kip Kinkel. There were only people of responsibility caught up in events beyond their comprehension. At worst, their errors in judgment might be described as "sins of compassion." Acting out of kindness or respect for a single family, those who had the power and authority to do so failed to fully consider the welfare of the larger community.

While at MacLaren Youth Correctional Facility, in Woodburn, Oregon, Kip received his general equivalency diploma (GED) and received intensive therapy specifically developed to help violent adolescent offenders. All who came in contact with him called the young man a model inmate. On June 11, 2007, two and a half months shy of his twenty-fifth birthday, Kip was transferred to the Oregon State

Correctional Institution, a medium-security 880-bed adult facility in Salem, where he was initially being housed among the general-inmate population. By exercising and pumping iron, he'd increased his weight to 220 pounds and stood five feet ten inches.

On August 7, 2007, a county judge denied Kinkel's request, made through his attorney, Larry Matasar, for a new trial, on the basis that he'd been mentally ill at the time he agreed to plea-bargain in 1999. Matasar argued the original defense attorneys and trial judge should have ordered a mental competency evaluation before proceeding. The attorney general's office rebutted that Kinkel understood what was happening and was intelligent enough to calculate that his best chance for a reduced sentence was the plea deal. He didn't want the trauma of a trial, and assumed he'd be found guilty, ending up with a life sentence and no hope of early release. From here, the case will move to federal courts, where further appeals may drag on into the future.

Just as the boy from Shangri-La had once dropped rocks onto cars from a highway overpass, Kip Kinkel dropped a heavy stone indeed into the quiet pond of Lane County life on May 20 and 21, 1998. The shock waves hit dozens of people immediately and hundreds in the next few hours and weeks. As years have passed, some peace has returned, but closure will never be complete until the last disturbing ripple has been absorbed into the forgiving sands of time.

Appendix 1
Warning Signs of Potential School Shooters (Based upon Information Presented in This Book)

A red flag should be raised whenever the student(s) in question exhibits at least *two* of the following (suggested response in parenthesis):

- Has been bullied or badly teased, and feels their concerns are being ignored. (Address those concerns with care and determine the seriousness of the situation.)
- Has been depressed to the point of suicidal and/or homicidal ideation. (Refer for immediate counseling.)
- Is a loner who seems locked into his (her) own world and rejects communication. (Try counseling to encourage hidden talents and offer alternative means of social networking.)
- Has been prescribed antipsychotic or antidepressant medications. (Cross-network with mental-health professionals and school counselors if other factors on this list are present.)
- Has access to weapons at home or with relatives, even if those are kept in a lockbox. (Confer with parents regarding safety, and suggest removal of firearms if other factors on this list are present.)
- Has a preference for violent media such as bloody action films and first-person shooter video games rated M or AO (targeting humans). (Determine the cause of this preference and whether this is addictive behavior.)

- Has a history of writing about disturbing, macabre subjects, or drawing excessively violent images. (Determine the cause of this disposition, and if other factors on this list are present, recommend counseling.)
- Downloads bomb-making recipes or detailed information on other school shootings from the Internet. (Immediately determine the cause and purpose of these actions.)
- Has purchased bomb-making equipment or chemicals. (Immediately determine the cause and purpose of these actions.)
- Seems obsessed about knives, guns, and other weapons. (Determine the cause of this disposition, notify parents, and if other factors on this list are present, recommend counseling or intervention.)
- Expresses admiration for other school shooters. (Determine the cause of this disposition, and if other factors on this list are present, recommend counseling.)
- Made a hit list of enemies or drew plans of the school. (Immediately determine the cause and purpose of these actions.)
- Has talked of plans for mayhem, but when questioned, says he (she) was only joking. (Suggest to parents they further investigate contents of student's room and closets, and what Web sites are being visited on the Internet.)

Appendix 2
Further Research and Assistance

The author recommends the following Web sites and resources, among many others that are available, for those interested in pursuing subjects brought up in this book:

- Reporting a threat to a school: dial 1-866-SPEAK-UP [773-2587].
- To get a copy of Oregon assistant principal Mike Johnson's plans for initiating the 4-in-1 emergency drill procedure and forming a campuswide Crisis Response Team, go to www.campusprep plan.com. The drills assist school personnel with preparing staff and students for emergency situations that happen on school campuses throughout the world every day. Situations that involve intruders, fights in and out of the classroom, weapons, accidents, earthquakes, fire, and other disruptions on campus can prove to be difficult to manage. With an organized plan for responding to campus disruptions, injuries would be fewer and order could be restored more efficiently. The 4-in-1 drill procedure would be performed at least once a month and would take seven to eleven minutes to complete.
- The Center for Safe and Responsible Internet Use: Effective strategies to assist young people in acquiring knowledge, decision-making skills, motivation, and self-control to behave in a safe, responsible, and legal manner when using the Internet and other

information technologies. Learn about stopping cyberthreats and cyberbullying at www.cyberbully.org.

- To order copies of the Oregon 4J school district *Emergency Procedure Manual,* you need to call their risk management program at 541-687-3335.
- *Early Warning, Timely Response: A Guide to Safe Schools* offers research-based practices at www.ed.gov/about/offices/list/osers/osep/gtss.html and is designed to help school communities identify these warning signs early and develop prevention, intervention, and crisis response plans.
- Dr. Kathy Seifert, a forensic psychologist, has identified the key childhood risk factors that cause young people to grow up into violent adults. Get the complete story at www.drkathyseifert.com.
- For a serious look at both legal (government-directed) and illegal (criminal) taking of lives, consider Lieutenant Colonel Dave Grossman's work on killology, the psychology of conditioning and desensitization related to the destructive act of killing. In particular, killology focuses on the reactions of healthy people in killing circumstances (such as police and military in combat) and the factors that enable and restrain killing in these situations: www.killology.com.
- Internet and video gaming addictions are real; they can break up homes and cause job losses. Dr. Maressa Hecht Orzack, a clinical psychologist, treats such addictive behaviors at McLean Hospital, where she is founder and coordinator of the Computer Addiction Service and a member of the Harvard Medical School faculty. Go to www.computeraddiction.com.
- Although on temporary hiatus and at times overwhelmed by current events, webmaster Alan Lampe's www.columbine-angels.com still offers the most complete chronological listings of *all* acts of school violence worldwide.
- Kill Thinking is an online aid community created by Joel Kornek, a Dawson College school-shooting victim. It contains information and insight into school violence and bullying, and also provides an online discussion forum that offers quick support from like-minded youth on a variety of topics: www.killthinking.com.
- The Bullying Project presents practical research-based strategies to reduce bullying in schools at www.stopbullyingnow.com.

- *A Guide for Preventing and Responding to School Violence.* This project, sponsored by the International Association of Chiefs of Police (the world's oldest and largest nonprofit membership organization of police executives) can be found at www.theiacp.org/pubinfo/pubs/pslc/svindex.htm. It's supported with funding from the U.S. Department of Justice.
- The University of Oregon's Institute on Violence and Destructive Behavior empowers schools and social service agencies to ensure safety and facilitate the healthy social development and academic achievement of children and youth, at darkwing.uoregon.edu/~ivdb.
- The mission of The Lion & Lamb Project is to stop the marketing of violence to children. The organization itself is no longer active, but their Web site is still useful, at www.lionlamb.org.
- Freedom States Alliance is a project to reduce gun injury and death in the United States. Their focus is on public awareness campaigns intended to change the way Americans think about guns, gun violence, and the gun industry. They also provide Web-based capacity-building resources for grassroots organizations and others working to address this important public-health issue: www.freedomstatesalliance.org.
- Susan Magestro is a criminologist and consultant for parents and teens in areas of anger management/antibullying strategies. If you know of a youth who is a victim of bullying, contact her at sulamaestra@gci.net, phone 907-529-7151, or write to P.O. Box 221993, Anchorage, Alaska 99522. There are skills students can learn so as not to be a victim. www.susanmagestro.com.
- The Ribbon of Promise National Campaign to Prevent School Violence can now be found at various regional centers and websites throughout the country. Visit www.citizenpreparedness.org/Ribbon%20of%20Promise.htm, for example. Also see the By Kids 4 Kids (BK4K) Student Program, which provides an avenue for students to create and implement their own solutions to school violence.

Appendix 3
Chronology of Major School Shootings, 1974–2008

December 30, 1974 (Olean, New York): *Major school shooting*. Anthony Barbaro, 18, honor student brought guns and homemade bombs to his high school, set off fire alarm, shot at janitors and firemen who responded, killed 3, wounded 9.

May 28, 1975 (Brampton, Ontario, Canada): *Major school shooting*. Michael Slobodian, 16, kills teacher and student, wounds 13 others at Centennial Secondary School, then kills himself.

October 27, 1975 (Ottawa): *Major school shooting*. Robert Poulin, 18, militia sharpshooter, shoots 6 people at St. Pius X High School, then kills himself. A wounded student dies later. Killed a girl at a youth home before school rampage.

May 19, 1978 (Austin, Texas): *School shooting*. John Christian, 13, honor student, son of LBJ's former press secretary George Christian, shot and killed 1 teacher.

October 1978 (Winnipeg): *School shooting*. Seventeen-year-old shot and killed other student at Sturgeon Creek Regional Secondary School.

January 29, 1979 (San Diego): *Female/major school shooting*. Loner

Brenda Ann Spencer, 16, uses rifle to shoot children and employees at Cleveland Elementary School across street from her home.

January 7, 1980 (Stamps, Arkansas, same town December 15, 1997): *School shooting.* Sixteen-year-old Evan Hampton, Stamps High School, shot Mike Sanders 3 times, killing him.

January 27, 1984 (Fayetteville, Arkansas): *College shooting.* James Howard Taylor, 19, former freshman at University of Arkansas, held 2 UAPD officers at gunpoint. Sergeant Houser drew revolver, shot Taylor 3 times. Taylor died at the scene.

March 19, 1982 (Las Vegas): *School shooting.* Bullied student Patrick Lizotte, 18, fatally shot psychology teacher Clarence Piggott and wounded 2 students at Valley High School with a Sturm/Ruger revolver.

January 20, 1983 (St. Louis, Missouri): *School shooting.* Unnamed 8th-grade student shot 2 classmates at Parkway South Junior High School, then committed suicide.

February 24, 1984 (Los Angeles): *School shooting by adult.* Tyrone Mitchell, 28, opened fire on the playground of Forty-ninth Street Elementary School. His rampage killed 1 and injured 10 other students. Tyrone then committed suicide.

January 21, 1985 (Goddard, Kansas): *Shot principal and 3 others.* James Alan Kearby, 14, claimed he had been bullied and beaten by students for years. He killed his junior high school principal and wounded two teachers and a student.

January 9, 1986 (Durham, North Carolina): *School shooting / girlfriend.* At Northern High School, David Mancuso gunned down popular cheerleader Norma Russell with 7 shots. David was routinely picked on and insulted by his fellow classmates.

May 16, 1986 (Cokeville, Wyoming): *Hostage / school shooting by adult couple.* David and Doris Young, in their 40s, took 150 students and 17 teachers hostage at Cokeville Elementary School, demanding a $300 million ransom. Doris accidentally set off a bomb, killing herself and injuring 79 students and teachers. David then shot himself.

December 4, 1986 (Lewiston, Montana): *School shooting.* Kristofer Hans, 14, threatened to kill his French teacher for giving him a failing grade, but shot and killed her substitute, injured a vice principal and 2 students.

March 2, 1987 (DeKalb, Missouri): *School shooting.* Nathan D. Faris, 12, was teased about being chubby and a walking dictionary. He brought a gun to school, killed classmate Timothy Perrin, 13, and committed suicide.

February 11, 1988 (Pinellas Park, Florida): *Shot principal and others.* Jason Harless, 16, and Jason McCoy, 15, opened fire on assistant principals Richard Allen and Nancy Blackwelder. Richard died from his wounds on February 18.

May 20, 1988 (Winnetka, Illinois): *Adult female school shooting–suicide.* Laurie Wasserman Dann, 30, shot 6 students at a Winnetka elementary school, killing 1. Later she killed herself.

September 26, 1988 (Greenwood, South Carolina): *Elementary-school shooting.* James William Wilson Jr., 19, opened fire with a pistol in Oakland Elementary School cafeteria. His gunfire killed 2 third-graders and wounded 9 other children and a teacher.

December 16, 1988 (Virginia Beach): *Major school shooting.* Nicholas Elliot, 16, came to Atlantic Shores Christian (High) School carrying 3 firebombs, a semiautomatic pistol, and 200 rounds of ammunition. He killed 1 teacher, wounded another.

January 17, 1989 (Stockton, California): *Major school shooting by adult.* Patrick Purdy, 26, opened fire on a playground at Cleveland Elementary School with an AK-47 assault rifle. Five children died, 29 kids and 1 teacher wounded. Purdy put a bullet to his head.

September 18, 1989 (McKee, Kentucky): *Hostage/ school shooting.* Dustin Pierce, 17, walked into Jackson County High School, fired 2 shotgun blasts and took 11 classmates hostage. He peacefully surrendered to the police.

October 5, 1989 (Anaheim, California): *Hostage/ school shooting.* Cordell "Cory" Robb, 15, shot 1 student who taunted him after he took a drama class hostage with a shotgun and semiautomatic pistol. Cory surrendered and was sentenced to 9 years.

December 6, 1989 (Montreal): *Major college shooting.* Marc Lépine at University of Montreal, École Polytechnique. In 20 minutes, Marc brought death to 14 (all female) and injuries to 27 more people.

May 1, 1992 (Olivehurst, California): *Hostage/ major school shooting.* Eric Houston, 20, killed 1 teacher and 3 students, and wounded 13 in an armed siege *(holding hostages)* at his former school—Lindhurst High.

August 24, 1992 (Montreal): *Adult college/workplace shooting.* Valery Fabrikant, 52, returned to Concordia University, his former place of employment, and opened fire. He killed 4 faculty members and wounded another.

September 11, 1992 (Amarillo, Texas): *School pep rally shooting.* Six students were shot and 1 was trampled when 17-year-old Randy Earl Matthews pulled a gun at a pep rally at Palo Duro High School.

December 14, 1992 (Great Barrington, Massachusetts): *Major school shooting.* Wayne Lo, 18, killed 2 people (a student and professor) and wounded a security guard and 3 others at an exclusive college-prep boarding school, Simon's Rock College.

January 18, 1993 (Grayson, Kentucky): *Major school shooting.* Gary Scott Pennington, 17, took a class with 22 students hostage at East Carter High. He shot to death teacher Deanna McDavid and custodian Marvin Hicks; sentenced to life.

May 1993 (Neuilly-sur-Seine, France): *Hostage/ preschool students.* Police finally ended a 46-hour hostage situation for 21 preschool students held by gunman Eric Schmitt, 42, in this Paris suburb, by shooting Eric dead.

May 24, 1993 (Red Hill, Pennsburg, Pennsylvania): *Shot 1 classmate.* Jason Michael Smith shot dead a schoolmate at Upper Perkiomen High School. Michael Swann had been bullying Jason since the 7th grade. Jason calmly waited for police.

December 1, 1993 (Wauwatosa, Wisconsin): *Shot associate. principal.* Leonard McDowell, 21, former student, returned to kill Associate Principal Dale Breitlow, who'd been handling his long history of discipline problems at Wauwatosa West High.

December 16, 1993 (Chelsea, Michigan): *School shooting by teacher.* Chelsea High chemistry and physics teacher Stephen Leith left a staff meeting, returning soon with a pistol. He killed the superintendent, wounded the principal and another teacher.

April 12, 1994 (Butte, Montana): *School shooting.* James Osmanson, 10, had been teased at Margaret Leary Elementary School. He shot at a classmate, missed his target, and hit 11-year-old Jeremy Bullock. Jeremy died the next day.

May 26, 1994 (Union, Kentucky): *School attack and family slaughter.* Clay Shrout, 17, took his Larry A. Ryle High School trigonometry class hostage after shooting his whole family to death at home. After 30 minutes, Clay released his hostages.

October 12, 1994 (Greensboro, North Carolina): *Shot assistant principal and suicide.* Nicholas Atkinson, 16, returned to Grimsley High School with a 9mm pistol after being suspended and shot and wounded the assistant principal, then killed himself.

October 1994 (Bluffdale, Utah): *Family slaughter.* Nathan K. Martinez, 17, became obsessed with the violent film *Natural Born Killers*, and shot and killed his stepmother and half sister while they slept.

November 7, 1994 Wickliffe, Ohio): *Adult shot custodian and others.* Dressed in camouflage and armed with a shotgun, 37-year-old Keith A. Ledeger storms the office of Wickliffe Middle School. He kills a custodian, teacher, and assistant principal.

January 23 1995 (Redlands, California): *Shot principal.* John Sirola, 13, shot/wounded Principal Richard Facciolo at Sacred Heart School. As John flees the principal's office, he trips and drops the gun. It went off and the shot killed John.

October 12, 1995 (Blackville, South Carolina): *Shot teachers and suicide.* Toby Sincino, 16, shot and killed 1 math teacher, wounded 1 more math teacher, then killed himself at Blackville-Hilda High School. Claimed he had been picked on by other students.

November 15, 1995 (Lynville, Tennessee): *Major school shooting.* Jamie Rouse, 17, at Richland High, walked up to 2 female teachers in the hall and shot each in the head. A student, Diane Collins, 16, was accidentally shot and died.

December 1995 (Vladikavkaz, Russia): *Adult attack/elementary school.* Yurl Kardanoc, 30, set off 2 hand grenades in a kindergarten classroom. He killed 3 children, wounded 3 other children, 3 policemen, and himself in the blast.

February 2, 1996 (Moses Lake, Washington): *Major school shooting.* Barry Loukaitis, 14, wearing a trench coat, opens fire in his junior-high algebra class with a deer rifle and 2 handguns; he killed the teacher, Leona D. Caires, and 2 boys.

February 8, 1996 (Palo Alto, California): *School shooting–suicide.* Douglas Bradley, 16, drove onto the playground and began throwing money out the window. He opened fire and wounded a 14-year-old boy in the leg. Douglas then committed suicide.

March 13, 1996 (Dunblane, Scotland): *Major overseas school shooting.* Thomas Hamilton, 43, dressed in black, entered an elementary school and sprayed 105 bullets into the gym, striking 29 people before killing himself. Sixteen small kids and a teacher died.

March 25, 1996 (Waynesville, Missouri): *School killing by trio.* Anthony Rutherford, 18, Jonathan Moore, 15, Joseph Burris, 15, all 3 fatally slashed and bludgeoned a student at Mountain Park Baptist Church and Boarding School.

April 29, 1996 (Fort Myers, Florida): *Murder of teacher by gang.* Kevin Don Foster, 18, a dropout, and other members of a gang named the Lords of Chaos, from Riverdale High, carried out a wave of crime, including murder of the school's band teacher.

July 8, 1996 (Wolverhampton, England): *Primary school attack by adult.* St. Luke's Primary School, Blakenhall. Machete-wielding maniac Horrett Campbell attacked 3 children and 4 adults. Later he was found in an apartment a few yards from the school.

September 17, 1996 (State College, Pennsylvania): *Female college shooting.* Jillian Robbins, 19, on Penn State University campus, pulled out a high-power military weapon, killed senior Melanie Spalla, and wounded 22-year-old Nicholas Mensah.

February 19, 1997 (Bethel, Alaska): *Major school shooting.* Evan Ramsey, 16, opens fire with a 12-gauge shotgun in a common area at the Bethel Regional High School. Killed are school principal Ron Edwards and basketball star Josh Palacios.

March 30, 1997 (San'ā', Yemen): *Major foreign school shooting by adult.* Mohammed Ahmad Misleh al-Naziri, 48, opened fire with an assault rifle on hundreds of students at 2 schools. Six children and 2 others died. Mohammed was executed by firing squad 1 week later.

October 1, 1997 (Pearl, Mississippi): *Major school shooting and parricide.* Luke Woodham, 16, killed 3 (his mother and 2 students), wounded 7. Sentenced to 3 life sentences, plus 20 years for each assault conviction.

December 1, 1997 (West Paducah Kentucky): *Major school shooting.* Michael Carneal, 14, killed 3 students, wounded 5 (2 partially paralyzed). Benjamin Strong, leader of the prayer group he shot into, talked Michael into dropping the gun.

December 15, 1997 (Stamps, Arkansas): *School shooting.* Joseph "Colt" Todd, 14, was charged in the sniper shooting of 2 students. Both recovered. Todd claimed he had been humiliated by teasing; wanted "somebody else to hurt."

March 24, 1998 (Jonesboro, Arkansas): *Major school shooting.* Mitchell Johnson, 13, and Andrew Golden, 11, at Westside Middle School. Four girls and a teacher killed; another teacher and 10 students wounded when the 2 boys open fire from the woods.

April 24, 1998 (Edinboro, Pennsylvania): *Major school shooting.* Andrew Wurst, 14, shot to death a science teacher and wounded 3 students at a James W. Parker Middle School prom. The boy is serving 30 to 60 years in prison.

May 9, 1998 (Memphis Tennessee): *Attack averted.* A 5-year-old Memphis kindergarten student with a loaded pistol in his backpack wanted to kill his teacher for punishing him. The teacher confiscated the .25-caliber semiautomatic pistol.

May 19, 1998 (Fayetteville, Tennessee): *One student killed.* A classmate killed an 18-year-old high school student in the school's parking lot.

May 20–21, 1998 (Springfield, Oregon): *Major school shooting and parricide.* Kip Kinkel killed his 2 parents at home, then left 2 students dead and a record 25 wounded next morning at Thurston High.

May 21, 1998 (Onalaska, Washington): *School bus hostage and suicide.* Miles Fox, 15, boarded a high school bus with a gun, ordered his girlfriend off the bus, took her to his home, then fatally shot himself as the girl's father was breaking down the front door.

May 21, 1998 (St. Charles, Missouri): *Attack averted.* Copying Jonesboro, 3 sixth-grade boys with a "hit list" were accused of plotting to kill their classmates on the last day of classes at Becky-Davis Elementary School.

June 15, 1998 (Richmond, Virginia): *School shooting.* Quinshawn Booker, a 14-year-old student, opened fire in a hallway of Armstrong High School while the kids took final exams. A coach and a volunteer were wounded.

September 29, 1998 (Miami): *School shooting.* North Miami Senior High School. Two teens smuggled a gun past the school's security, and opened fire in a hallway outside the cafeteria. Two students and 1 teacher wounded.

November 16, 1998 (Burlington, Wisconsin): *Attack averted.* Police foil a plot by 5 teenagers, ages 15 and 16, to kill classmates and teachers. They had specifically targeted 15 students, 2 administrators, and 1 faculty member.

April 16, 1999 (Notus, Idaho): *School gun incident.* Shawn Cooper, 16, a high school sophomore, fired 2 shotgun blasts in a school hallway after pointing a gun at a secretary and students. No one was injured.

April 20, 1999 (Littleton, Colorado): *Major school shooting.* Dylan Klebold and Eric Harris killed 12 students and 1 teacher, wounded 23 others, and killed themselves at Columbine High School.

April 23, 1999 (Wimberly, Texas): *Attack averted.* Four 14-year old 8th-grade boys arrested for a planned attack with guns and explosives on their high school in Wimberly.

April 28, 1999 (Taber, Alberta, Canada): *School shooting.* Todd Cameron Smith, 14, bullied by classmates, opened fire at W. R. Myers

High wearing a dark trench coat, killing one 17-year-old and injuring another.

May 3, 1999 (Costa Mesa, California): *Attack by adult in car.* Steven Allen Abrams, 39, drove his Cadillac into children playing in the yard of Southcoast Early Childhood Learning Center. His act killed 2 and wounded several other kids.

May 20 1999 (Conyers, Georgia): *Major school shooting.* Thomas "T.J." Solomon, 15, entered affluent Heritage High, firing at legs and feet, wounding 6 classmates. Assistant Principal Cecil Brinkley disarmed T.J. and talked him into surrender.

November 1999 (Meissen, Germany): *School violence.* After taking bets from classmates he would dare to commit the crime, a 15-year-old boy stabbed his 44-year-old high school teacher to death. The betting had reached $500.

December 6, 1999 (Fort Gibson, Oklahoma): *Major school shooting.* Seth Trickey, 13, fired a semiautomatic pistol at least 15 times outside Fort Gibson Middle School. Five of his classmates were wounded.

February 29, 2000 (Mount Morris Township (Flint), Michigan): *Shot 1 classmate.* A 6-year-old boy brings a .32-caliber semiautomatic handgun to Buell Elementary School and shoots to death fellow 1st grader Kayla Rolland because they had a fight on the playground.

March 5, 2000 (Branneburg, Germany): *Shot teacher and suicide.* A 16-year-old pupil at a private boarding school shot a 57-year-old teacher, who later died from injuries. The teenager—who also shot himself—was facing expulsion from school.

March 10, 2000 (Savannah, Georgia): *School dance shooting.* Darrell Ingram, 19, was arrested and charged with murder and aggravated assault after he killed 2 teens and wounded 1 after a school dance at Beach High School.

March 16, 2000 (Rosenheim, Germany): *Overseas school shooting.* An expelled 16-year-old boy returned and encountered the school's 57-year-old director, pulled out a gun, and killed him. He then fired several more shots into his own head.

April 2000 (Lake Station, Indiana): *Attack averted.* Three girls were suspended from an elementary school after a murder plot was uncovered; all 3 were only in 1st grade.

May 26, 2000 (Lake Worth, Florida): *Shot teacher.* Nathaniel Brazill, 13, a Lake Worth Community Middle School honor student, is taken into custody in the fatal shooting death of his English teacher, Barry Grunow.

August 28, 2000 (Fayetteville, Arkansas): *College shooting.* Student James Easton Kelly, 36, was seeking a Ph.D. from the Fulbright College of Arts and Sciences, University of Arkansas. Dismissed, he shot and killed his faculty adviser.

January 29, 2001 (San Jose): *Attack averted.* Al DeGuzman, 19, accused of planning a "Columbine-style" attack on De Anza Community College. Police found 30 pipe bombs, 20 Molotov cocktails, plus other weapons and ammunition.

February 6, 2001 (Hoyt, Kansas): *Attack averted.* Three students were charged with planning a massacre at Royal Valley High. Police found firearms, 400 rounds of ammunition, bomb-making materials, and a floor plan.

February 8, 2001 (Fort Collins, Colorado): *Attack averted.* Three 9th-grade teenagers charged with plotting an attack on Preston Junior High School, 60 miles from Columbine. Police found weapons and detailed plans.

February 14, 2001 (Elmira, New York): *Attack averted.* Student Jeremy Getman, 18, was arrested after he carried 18 bombs and 2 guns into Southside High School.

February 23, 2001 (Portland, Oregon): *School attack (knife).* Three people are wounded in the school's cafeteria as a 14-year-old student brings a knife to the school and begins stabbing people at random.

February 24, 2001 (Isla Vista, Santa Barbara): *College attack.* David Edward Attias, 18, the son of TV director Daniel Attias, plowed his black Saab into classmates at the University of California Santa Barbara. Four students dead, 1 wounded.

March 5, 2001 (Santee, San Diego): *Major school shooting.* Santana High School. Charles "Andy" Williams, 15, killed 2 students and wounded 13 in an 8-minute shooting spree. Within 48 hours, 23 American school kids arrested for threats.

March 7, 2001 (Williamsport, Pennsylvania): *Girl shot 1 classmate.* Teasing victim Elizabeth Bush, 14, shot Kimberly Marchese, a 13-year-old classmate, during lunch at Bishop Neumann High School. The victim recovered.

March 22, 2001 (El Cajon, California): *Major school shooting.* Jason Hoffman shot at students outside Granite Hills High, wounding 5 people before police shot and injured him. Hoffman pleaded guilty and hung himself in jail on October 29.

March 2001 (Twentynine Palms, California): *Attack averted.* Victoria Sudd, 17, watched Santee and told her mom she'd heard 2 boys talk about killing people. Authorities found a rifle and list of 16 students whom the boys were going to target.

May 15, 2001 (Ennis, Texas): *Class as hostages and suicide.* Jay Douglas Goodwin, 16, took over Ennis High School teacher Andrea Webb's English class with a .357 Magnum. Jay fired 1 shot into the room, and then a 2nd shot into himself.

June 8, 2001 (Osaka, Japan): *Major overseas school attack.* At Ikeda Elementary School, Mamoru Takuma, a 37-year-old armed with a 6-inch kitchen knife, killed 7 girls, ranging in age from 7 to 8 years old, and one 6-year-old boy.

November 12, 2001 (Caro, Michigan): *Two hostages and suicide.* Chris Buschbacher, 17, took 2 hostages at the Caro Community School's Adult Learning Center before killing himself.

January 16, 2002 (Grundy, Virginia): *Major college shooting.* Nigerian graduate student Peter Odighizuwa, 42, at the Appalachian School of Law, went on a campus shooting spree. He killed the dean, a professor, and another grad student.

February 12, 2002 (Fairfield, Connecticut): *Blind student/bomb/ hostage.* Former student Patrick Arbelo, 24, said he was carrying a bomb in his bag and held a professor and about two dozen students hostage. Blind, he left his seeing-eye dog at home that afternoon.

February 19, 2002 (Freising, Germany): *School shooting.* A man, 22, killed his boss and a foreman at the factory where he'd been working. He then killed the headmaster of his former school, set off pipe bombs, and blew himself up.

April 26, 2002 (Erfurt, Germany): *Major overseas school shooting.* An expelled student, Robert Steinhäuser, went on a shooting rampage at Johann Gutenberg secondary school. Eighteen people died in the terrifying assault, including the 19-year-old attacker.

April 29, 2002 (Vlasenica, Bosnia-Herzegovina): *Student kills teacher, self.* Dragoslav Petkovic, 17, shot and killed his history teacher, Stanimir Reljic, 53, in front of Vlasenica High School in this east Bosnia town. The teen then committed suicide.

September 4, 2002 (Seoul, South Korea): *Adult attack on school.* A 53-year-old man with mental illness attacked children at the Neung Dong Church Elementary school with 2 knives. Nine students were wounded.

September 22, 2002 (Spokane, Washington): *School attack.* Police shot and wounded a 17-year-old boy who brandished a gun at Lewis & Clark High School in downtown Spokane.

October 15, 2002 (The Chlef Region of Algeria): *Overseas terrorist attack.* Muslim fundamentalists raided a Koranic high school and forced 14 students to line up. They opened fire, killing 13 students between 14 and 20. The last child was wounded but able to flee.

October 18, 2002 (Waiblingen, Germany): *School attack and hostage.* A teenage boy wielding a pistol and wearing a bulletproof vest seized 4 sixth-graders at Friedensschule (Peace School) and held them hostage for nearly 7 hours.

October 21, 2002 (Melbourne, Australia): *Major overseas college shooting.* Huan Yun "Allen" Xiang, 36, on the Clayton campus of Monash University, with 4 pistols and a knife strapped to his body, opened fired inside a classroom, killing 2 of his fellow classmates.

October 28, 2002 (Tucson): *Major college shooting.* A 41-year-old Gulf War veteran Robert Flores, a student flunking out of the University of Arizona Nursing School, shot three of his professors to death, then killed himself.

November 15, 2002 (Scurry, Texas): *School attack/gasoline.* Anthony "Tony" Cipriano, 18, walked into his former high school with a can of gasoline and a shotgun, trying to burn the school down. Principle Richard Sneed wrestled him to the ground.

November 18, 2002 (Hospitalet de Llobregat, Spain): *School hostage.* An armed man wearing a ski mask charged into the Casal de l'Angel middle school and held a classroom of 25 preteens and their teacher hostage for hours.

Apr. 24, 2003 (Red Lion, Pennsylvania): *Principal killed/suicide.* James Robert Sheets, 14, pulled a .44 Magnum from his backpack and fired a bullet into the principal at Red Lion Area Junior High School. He then committed suicide.

May 9, 2003 (Cleveland, Ohio): *College shooting.* At Case Western Reserve University, Biswanath Halder, 62, a native of Calcutta, India, shot and killed a graduate student while wearing camouflage, a bulletproof vest, and army helmet.

September 24, 2003 (Cold Spring, Minnesota): *School shooting.* Two teens critically wounded when 15-year-old John Jason McLaughlin walked out of a locker room at Rocori High and shot them with a .22-caliber gun he had in his gym bag

May 21, 2004 (New South Wales, Australia): *School crossbow attack.* Using a crossbow, a 17-year-old student went to school and shot his former girlfriend in the chest. The arrow passed through her and lodged in the legs of another girl, pinning them.

June 1, 2004 (Sasebo, Japan): *School stabbing.* An 11-year-old girl, upset about her friend Satomi Mitarai, 12, posting critical Internet notes, slit Satomi's neck and arms with a box cutter at Okubo Elementary School, killing her.

August 4, 2004 (Beijing, China): *School attack by adult.* Xu Heping, 51, doorman at a nursery school, pulled out a kitchen knife and began "hacking people up." Xu wounded 15 children and 3 teachers, and killed a 4-year-old boy.

September 1–3, 2004 (Beslan, North Ossetia, Russia): *Terrorist school attack.* Chechen militants took over Middle School Number One. A tragic end with 335 dead (plus the militants) and 704 wounded, making this the deadliest act of school violence ever.

September 11, 2004 (Suzhou City, Jiangsu, China): *School attack by adult.* Yang Guozhu, 41, broke into a day care center with a knife, gasoline and explosives. He slashed 28 children and was about to light up the explosives when the police stopped him.

September 20, 2004 (Shandong Province, China): *School attack by adult.* Jia Qingyou cut 25 children on their arms and faces in a rage, but all survived. The 36-year-old was executed for this crime.

September 2004 (Marshfield, Massachusetts): *Attack averted.* Tobin Kerns and Joseph Nee were part of a group at Marshfield High called the Natural Born Killers. Their attack was planned to take place April 20, 2005, Columbine's 6th anniversary.

November 16, 2004 (Marietta, Georgia): *School poisonings by 2 girls.* Two 13-year-old girls baked a poisoned cake and served it to at least 12 classmates at East Cobb Middle School. The girls were charged with terrorist acts and intent to commit murder.

November 24, 2004 (Valparaiso, Indiana): *School knife attack.* James Lewerke, a 15-year-old student at Valparaiso High School, in northern Indiana, pulled 2 large knives out of his pants and stabbed 7 of his classmates.

November 25, 2004 (Ruzhou, Henan Province, China): *School knife attack by adult.* Yan Yanming, 21, broke into the dorm of Number 2 High School at night and stabbed 9 boys to death as they slept. He also wounded 4 others. He was soon executed.

December 3, 2004 (Panshi, Jilin Province, China): *School knife attack by adult.* Liu Zhigang, at the Central Primary School, Mingcheng Township, stabbed 12 1st graders and then cut his own throat before being restrained by school staff and police.

February 14, 2005 (Osaka Prefecture, Japan): *Foreign school attack on teachers.* A 17-year-old boy returns to Chuo Elementary School, Neyagawa, and attacks 3 teachers. Mitchiaki Kamozaki, a 52-year-old teacher, was transported to the hospital where he died.

February, 14, 2005 (Arlington, Texas): *School attack with swords.* A 16-year-old boy arrived at Lamar High School with 2 swords, each with 2-foot-long blades. He attacked his classmates and cut a 14-year-old on the face.

February 25, 2005 (Salluit, Quebec): *School shooting.* Peter Keatainak, 18, was expelled from his high school. He returned with a gun and shot teacher Hassina Kerfi-Guetteb in the neck and then committed suicide.

March 21, 2005 (Red Lake, Minnesota): *Major school shooting.* Jeff Weise, 16, shot to death his grandfather and grandfather's girlfriend, then went to his school. He killed a security guard, teacher, 5 students, and wounded 7 before killing himself.

February 24, 2006 (Roseburg, Oregon): *Shooting at school.* Roseburg High freshman Vincent Wayne Leodoro, 14, shot his classmate 4 times without warning at close range from behind. The victim survived.

February 24, 2006 (Charlottesville, Virginia): *Attack averted.* Four youths, ranging from 13 to 16, were on trial for a plot to blow up Albemarle and Western Albemarle high schools sometime before the end of the year.

March 3, 2006 (Muscatine, Iowa): *Attack averted.* Joseph Titus, 17, was arrested with explosive devices at his home the day before a threatened attack on his school.

March 10, 2006 (Liberty Center, Iowa): *Attack averted.* Zaccaria Combs and Dillon Lucas, both 15, were charged with threats to commit terrorism at Southeast Warren High School.

April 2006 (North Pole, Alaska): *Attack averted.* The arrest of 6 middle school pupils working as a death squad to create a school massacre.

April 23, 2006 (Saskatchewan, Canada): *Family slaughter.* After 23-year-old Jeremy Allan Steinke watched *Natural Born Killers* several times, he and his 12-year-old girlfriend, Jasmine Richardson, killed her parents and 8-year-old brother.

August 25, 2006 (Essex, Vermont): *Shooting at school.* The death of an elementary-school teacher. The adult shooter was on a rampage in that area, and the school itself was not a target.

September 13, 2006 (Montreal): *Major school shooting.* Kimveer Gill opened fire at Montreal's Dawson College. At the end, 18-year-old Anastasia DeSousa lay dead, 19 others wounded, many critically, and Kimveer shot himself in the head.

September 14, 2006 (Green Bay, Wisconsin): *Attack averted.* Two 17-year-olds arrested for plotting a shooting spree at their high school. Police found guns, bombs, detailed plans, and hundreds of rounds of ammunition. A 3rd teen was arrested later.

August 30, 2006 (Hillsborough, North Carolina): *Patricide / shooting at school.* Alvaro Rafael Castillo, 19, killed his father, videotaped himself, loaded his car with pipe bombs and weapons, then drove to Orange High. Two students injured, Castillo arrested.

September 27, 2006 (Bailey, Colorado): *Adult attack/major school shooting.* Duane R. Morrison, 53, took 6 girls hostage and sexually molested them at Platte Canyon High. He shot Emily Keyes, 16, as she ran, then turned the gun on himself. Both died.

September 27, 2006 (Eugene, Oregon): *Guns at school.* Josiah Christian Trigg, an angry 15-year-old dropout with 2 loaded, stolen handguns, and extra ammo, came to the high school, but was stopped by plans prepared by an assistant principal.

September 29, 2006 (Cazenovia, Wisconsin): *Shooting at school.* Special-ed student Eric Hainstock shot and killed his principal.

October 2, 2006 (Paradise, Pennsylvania): *Adult attack / major school shooting.* Siege at Amish schoolhouse by 32-year-old milk truck driver Charles Carl Roberts IV. Police stormed in and found 3 girls and Roberts dead, 7 badly injured. Two more girls died overnight.

October 9, 2006 (Joplin, Missouri): *Shooting at school.* A 13-year-old student wearing a black trench coat entered his middle school with an AK-47 and extra clips of ammunition. He shot a hole in the ceiling, but was safely disarmed by police.

November 20, 2006 (Emsdetten, Germany): *Major overseas school shooting.* Sebastian Bosse, 18, videotaped his suicide speech, then injured 21 students and teachers at his secondary school, before killing himself.

January 3, 2007 (Tacoma, Washington): *Shooting at school.* Douglas Chanthabouly, 18, fatally shot a fellow student in Henry Foss High School on the beginning day of class in the new year.

February 12, 2007 (Salt Lake City, Utah): *Teen shooting at mall.* Sulejmen Talovic, 18, took a trench coat, ammunition, shotgun, and .38 pistol to Trolley Square mall. He fired at customers, killing 5 and wounding 4, before being shot by police.

February 15, 2007 (New Britain, Connecticut): *Attack averted.* Frank Fechteler, 16, admits to plotting a shooting at Newington High School, targeting 20 students. YouTube footage showed him and others firing weapons and detonating explosives.

March 2007 (Lawrence, Kansas): *Threats at school.* Katherine Koontz, 17, arrested for bathroom lists threatening to murder 18 at Central Catholic High School. Her MySpace Web page also threatened students.

March 16, 2007 (Riner, Virginia): *Attack averted.* Two teens were charged with conspiracy to commit murder after 1 allegedly took a gun to school and 1 discussed shooting the principal and others.

April 10, 2007 (Gresham, Oregon): *Shooting at school.* Chad Antonio Escobedo, 15, charged with attempted aggravated murder after shooting into windows trying to kill 2 teachers at Springwater Trail High School.

April 13, 2007 (Calgary, Canada): *Attack averted.* Cops arrested a 14-year-old boy who had access to an assault rifle for designing an elaborate plan to murder 2 Calgary teachers on the anniversary of the Columbine massacre.

April 16, 2007 (Blacksburg, Virginia): *Major school shooting.* Seung-hui Cho, 23, opens fire in Virginia Polytechnic Institute and State University. Thirty-two people, plus Cho, died in the deadliest mass shooting in U.S. history. Many others injured.

May 23, 2007 (Toronto, Ontario): *School shooting.* A shooting at C. W. Jefferys Collegiate Institute in north Toronto left a 15-year-old student dead.

July 14, 2007 (Bohemia, Long Island, New York): *Attack averted.* Two students—age 15 (name not released) and age 17 (Michael McDonough)—arrested for plot to ignite explosives and shoot staff and students at Connetquot High on Columbine's 9th anniversary.

September 28, 2007 (Oroville, California): *Hostage/school shooting.* A 17-year-old student held a high school drama class hostage at Las Plumas High School, firing shots and holding 3 students more than an hour before police persuaded his surrender.

October 10, 2007 (Cleveland): *School shooting–suicide.* Asa H. Coon, wearing a Marilyn Manson shirt and black nail polish, opened fire with 2 revolvers, wounding 2 students and 2 teachers, before killing himself at SuccessTech Academy.

November 7, 2007 (Tuusula, Finland): *Major overseas school shooting.* "YouTube" gunman Pekka-Eric Auvinen, 18, killed 8 people, including the principal at Jokela High School, then shot himself.

November 18, 2007 (Cologne, Germany): *Attack averted.* Police thwart a plot by 2 teens to attack Georg-Buechner High with crossbows, air guns, and pipe bombs. One teen died throwing himself in front of a tram after questioning.

December 5, 2007 (Omaha, Nebraska): *Mall shooting and suicide.* Robert A. Hawkins, 19, wearing black, kills 8 people, wounds 5 others, with an assault rifle before taking his own life in an attack at a shopping mall.

February 8, 2008 (Baton Rouge, Louisiana): *School shooting / suicide.* Nursing student Latina Williams, 23, the first African-American female to commit a school shooting, killed two female classmates, aged 21 and 26, before turning the gun on herself.

February 11, 2008 (Memphis, Tennessee): *Shooting at school.* Corneilous Cheers, 17, a sophomore at Mitchell High School, shot senior Stacey Kiser, 19, multiple times during a gym class in the cafeteria, leaving him in critical condition.

February 12, 2008 (Oxnard, California): *Shooting at school.* A 14-year-old boy shot Lawrence King, 15, twice in the head in a classroom full of students at E. O. Green Junior High, because King wore feminine clothing and was openly gay.

February 14, 2008 (DeKalb, Illinois): *Major school shooting.* 27-year-old former graduate student Stephen Kazmierczak burst through a stage door in Cole lecture hall at Northern Illinois University and murdered 1 male and 4 female students, wounding 16 others before committing suicide.

March 6, 2008 (Jerusalem, Israel): *Overseas terrorist attack.* Eight students died and 9 others were wounded when Palestinian gunman Ala Abu Dehein stormed the Merkaz Harav yeshiva seminary with an automatic weapon and a handgun.

Index

Abrahamsen, David, 28
Abrams, Steven Allen, 343
Ad Astra Oasis, 22
Age limits, and juvenile justice system, 46–50
Agiler, Esme, 171
Albemarle High School, 324–25, 350
Alcohol (alcoholism), 119–20, 197–98
Allaway, Edward, 80
Alldredge, David, 254
Alldredge, Diana, 254–55
Alldredge, Jennifer, 14–15, 111–12, 250, 253–55
Allen, Richard, 336
Allgood, Justin, 37–38
Al-Naziri, Mohammed Ahmad Misleh, 282, 340
Al-Qaida, 152–54, 229, 320–21
Al-Tallai Private High School, 282
American Ideal Family, 51–63
Amish Schoolhouse shooting, 226–29, 351
Anarchist Cookbook, The, 54–55, 56–57, 118
Andrew, Philip, 221
Animal cruelty, 105–8
Antibullying programs, 308–9
Anti-Christian shooters, 20–23, 154
Antidepressants, 32–36, 39
Appalachian School of Law, 35, 295, 297, 346
Arbelo, Patrick, 295–96, 346
Armstrong High School, 68–69, 342
Arney, Len, 88–89
Atkinson, Nicholas, 338

Atlantic Shores Christian School, 77, 81, 336
At-risk adolescents, 308–11
Atteberry, Ryan, 13, 248, 255, 256, 321
Attias, Daniel, 345
Attias, David Edward, 345
Auditory hallucinations, 122–40
Auvinen, Pekka-Eric, 155, 263–64, 265, 267–74, 353

Baadsgaard, Cory, 34
Bad guy/good guy imagery, 194–96
Bang, Bang, You're Dead! (play), 250
Bang, Eun-kyung, 288
Barbaro, Anthony, 39–40, 75–77, 334
Barta, Richard, 69
Bartley, Ken, Jr., 300
Basketball Diaries (movie), 212
Battan, Kate, 111–12
Baty, Jessica, 34, 112–13
Baumeister, Roy F., 146
Beach High School, 343
Beard, Jay, 112
Beatles, 270
Becky-Davis Elementary School, 50, 342
Bendele, Kristal, 231–32
Bennett, Kelly, 171
Bennett, Lewis, III, 273
Bentz, Larry, 88–89, 247, 298, 300–302
Bernall, Cassie, 20–21, 22–23, 71–72
Beslan, Russia, 275, 348
Bethel Regional High School, 159–60, 340
Binary mind, 140, 149–56
Bingham Middle School, 37–38

Bishop Neumann High School, 222, 345
Black, David, 76
Black box warnings, 39
Black trench coat, 8–9, 11–12, 19, 107–10
Blackville-Hilda High School, 38, 339
Blackwelder, Nancy, 336
Blame, politics of, 85–92
Blanket amnesties, 46–47
Bogost, Ian, 180
Bolstad, Orin, 115–19, 125–37, 164–65
Bombs (bomb-making), 54–57, 77–78,
    91–92, 161–62
Bonner, Keith, 63
Booker, Quinshawn, 68–69, 342
Books, 213, 271–72
Boomtown Rats, 220
Bosse, Sebastian, 154–56, 267–69, 352
    black clothing, 109
    family reaction, 265
    farewell video, 97, 154–56, 203, 263,
        299
    video games, 191
Botts, Mark, 8
Bouyeri, Mohammed, 318
Bowling for Columbine (documentary),
    121, 198–200
Boyer, Peter, 53, 54–55
Boyette, Marshall Grant, 105–8
Bradley, Douglas, 37, 339
Bradley, Richard, Jr., 172
Brain, 184–85, 199, 311–12
Brathwaite, Christopher, 158
Brazill, Nathaniel, 204, 344
Breitlow, Dale, 338
Brewer, Alyssa, 141
Brinkley, Cecil, 32, 343
Brooks, David, 293–94
Brooks, Natalie, 48–49
Brown, Brooks, 71, 142, 188–89, 264
Brown, Richard, 3, 4, 109, 160
Bruce, Ken, 300
Brudos, Jerome, 321
Brun, Derrick, 19
Brunell, Sam, 34
Bryant, Martin, 291
Buckle, Henry Thomas, 196
Buell Elementary School, 207, 343
Bullock, Jeremy, 338
Bullying, 38–39, 202–3, 308–10
    antibullying programs, 308–9
    Eric Hainstock and, 176
    Jeff Weise and, 38–39
    Kip Kinkel and, 60, 165–66, 186,
        242–43
    in the West vs. Asia, 285

Bumbaugh, David, 196, 200–201
Bum-kon, Woo, 291
Burlington, Wisconsin, averted attack,
    69–70, 342
Burns, Glen Sebastian, 234–35
Burris, Joseph, 340
Buschbacher, Chris, 262–63, 346
Bush, Elizabeth, 33–34, 222, 345
Bush, George W., 22, 306
Bushman, Brad J., 146
Bushnell, Dick, 62–63, 93, 98, 100–101,
    110
Butterworth, Robert R., 10

Cacioppo, Joseph, 190
Caires, Leona D., 213, 339
Caldwell, Michael, 141
California State University, 80
Camouflage society, 182
Campbell, Dustin, 264
Campbell, Horrett, 282, 340
Campbell County Comprehensive High
    School, 300
Cannon, Jesse, 104–5
Capital punishment, and juveniles, 43
Carneal, Michael, 29–30, 341
    animal cruelty, 105
    "fag" epithet, 242
    "guilty but mentally ill" plea, 124
    media influences, 212, 213
    video games, 189–90
Caro Community School, 262–63, 346
Carrie (King), 152
Carroll, Jim, 212
Carter, Gary, 69
Carter, Sue, 209
Casa de l'Angel School, 274, 347
Case, Pam, 245
Case, Tony, 245
Case Western Reserve University, 146,
    347–48
Castaldo, Richard, 71
Castillo, Alvaro Rafael, 6–9, 210, 270,
    302–3, 351
Castor, Bruce, 273
Centennial Secondary School, 77, 334
Central Catholic High School, 222, 352
Chanthabouly, Douglas, 352
Chapman, Mark David, 65
Chayefsky, Paddy, 208
Chechens, 46–47, 275
Cheers, Corneilous, 354
Chelsea High School, 338
China, 288–90, 348, 349
Cho, Seung-hui, 41–43, 314–18, 353

double-crime scene, 278–79
family life, 52, 315
guns, 9, 152–53
involuntary psychiatric admittance,
    117
media influences, 212–13
persecution complex, 22, 41, 107,
    153–54
school lockdown and, 278–79,
    315–16
sequence of events, 315–18
sexual orientation, 239
suicide ideas, 31, 41–42
terrorists vs. school shooters, 152–54
video games, 190–91
writings and videos, 150, 152–54
Christian, George, 79, 334
Christian, John, 79, 334
Christianity, 20–23, 107, 154, 237
Christmas, Shane, 206
Chronology of school shootings, 334–54
Chuo Elementary School, 349
Cipriano, Anthony "Tony," 296–97, 347
Cleckley, Hervey, 147
Cleveland Elementary School, 81–82,
    220, 334–35, 336
Close, Dan, 103–4, 140, 144–50, 156,
    163–64
Coccio, Ben, 217–18
Code of silence, 169–70
Cokeville Elementary School, 281,
    335–36
Coleman, Lauren, 199, 208
Collective Soul, 317–18
Collins, Diane, 124–25, 339
Columbine High School, 70–73, 77–78,
    342. See also Harris, Eric; Klebold,
    Dylan
  fan clubs, 178–80
  "God question," 20–23
Combs, Zaccaria, 325, 350
Comic books, 177–81, 185–86
Commercials, 198–99, 202–3
Complicity by inaction, 169–70
Concordia University, 83, 337
Connetquot High School, 268, 353
Consent to treatment, 8
Coon, Asa H., 272–73, 353
Cooper, Shawn, 70, 342
Copycat Effect, The (Coleman), 199
Copycats, 64–70, 74–84, 274
Cornell, Dewey, 244
Corwin, Nicholas, 221
Cossey, Dillon, 273, 316
Cossey, Frank, 273

Cossey, Michele, 273
Counterstrike, 190–91
Cousins, Jason James, 273–74
Criminal justice system, 42–50
Crossen, Cynthia, 200
Crouse, Roy, 117
Crow, Kim, 37
Crowley, Michael, 103, 256, 259
Crowley, Ryan, 16–17, 103, 247–48,
    256
Cruel and unusual punishment, 43
Crumbley, John, 58, 116
Cullen, Dave, 237
Culver, Bonnie, 76
Curnow, Steven, 71–72
C.W. Jefferys Collegiate Institute, 353

Dahmer, Jeffrey, 115, 270
Dang, Khoa Truc "Robert," 36–37
Dann, Laurie Wasserman, 33, 220–21,
    336
Dawson, Rachel, 105
Dawson College, 64–67, 332, 351
DeAngelis, Frank, 7, 310
De Anza Community College, 171–72,
    344
Death penalty, and juveniles, 43
DeForrest, Bill, 85–87, 164, 249
DeGuzman, Al, 171–72, 344
Dehein, Ala Abu, 275–76
Dehumanization, 184–86
Delle, Jeremy Wade, 40, 213
Demons, 20–23, 105–10
DePooter, Corey, 72
Depression, 29
DeSousa, Anastasia, 67, 351
Devil, 20–23, 105–10
Dew, Lydia, 108
Dhar, Nikhil, 150, 297
DiCaprio, Leonardo, 11, 24, 94, 212
Dietz, Park, 44, 75, 105, 115–16, 136,
    151
Doom, 181–82, 188–89, 193, 270
Doyle, Dick, 61–62, 87–92, 99–101,
    245–46, 322, 327
Doyle, Jennifer, 72
Draher, Bill, 78–79
Drill procedures, 311, 327, 331
Drug companies, 32–36
Duke Nukem, 189, 193
Dunblane Primary School, 281–82, 340
Duy, De Kieu "Lisa," 127–28

Early onset antisocial kids, 144–46
East Carter High School, 83–84, 337–38

East Cobb Middle School, 223, 349
Ebersol, Naomi Rose, 228
Edmond, Oklahoma, Post Office, 141
Edwards, Ron, 159–60, 340
Effexor, 32–36
Egocentricity, 146–47, 182–87, 197–98
Egoisme à deux, 238–39
Eighth Amendment, 43
Electronic media, 177–93, 213–18
Elephant (movie), 216–17, 237
Eliezer, Occi, 69
Elliot, Nicholas, 77, 81, 336
Elmira High School, 68
Empathy, 184–87, 229, 232–35, 311–12
Ennis High School, 37, 345
E.O. Green Junior High School, 239, 354
Escobedo, Chad Antonio, 301–2, 352
Eubanks, Austin, 72
Eugene High School, 325–27
Everett High School, 78–79
Evil, 18, 196
Ewert, Korey, 60–63, 88–92, 161–62, 167–68
Ewing, Charles Patrick, 74, 102
"Expelled student seeking revenge" syndrome, 294–97
Extinction behavior, 140, 151, 157

Fabrikant, Valery, 83, 337
Facciolo, Richard, 36, 339
Face value, 194–201
"Fag" epithet, 165, 242–43
Fairfield University, 295–96
Falwell, Jerry, 237
Fame, 194, 202–18
Fan clubs, 176–79, 182–85, 187
Fan mail, 230–35
Faris, Nathan D., 38, 336
Fascism, 173–74
Fechteler, Frank, 352
Feher, Michael E., 158
Feiffer, Jules, 277
Female fan mail, 230–35
Female shooters, 219–23, 229
Ferguson, Todd, 14
Finkbeiner, Kat, 81
Finley, Patrick, 231–32
Firearms. *See* Guns
First Amendment, 214
Fisher, Marian, 228
Fleming, Kelly, 72
Fletcher, Justin, 68
Flores, Robert, 296, 347

Folie à deux, 238–39
Fort Gibson Middle School, 35, 343
Forty-ninth Street Elementary School, 335
Foster, Jimmy, 298–99
Foster, Kevin Don, 237–38, 340
Fox, Miles, 36, 341–42
Franks, Bobby, 79
Fritz, Arnold, 213, 258
Fritz, Phil, 258
Frontal lobe, 184–85
Frontline (TV show), 53, 54–55, 110, 129, 139
Fugate, Caril Ann, 210–11

Gabour, Mark, 277
Gaines, Al, 326
Gang Lu, 297
Gang members vs. school shooters, 143–45
Gangsta rap, 161
Garbarino, James, 112
Garcia, David, 34
Gardner, Neil, 71
Gates, Bill, 191
Gaylik, Mike, 325–27
Geldof, Bob, 220
Gender issues, 219–43
    fan mail, 230–35
    male bonding, 236–43
Georg-Buechner High School, 268–69, 353
Getman, Jeremy, 172, 344
Gill, Kimveer, 64–67, 107, 109, 155, 264, 351
Gill, Parwinder, 65
Gillette, John, 68, 121
Girlfriends, 95–97
Girl shooters, 219–23, 229
God, 20–23, 152–56, 156, 237, 319–20
"Going postal," 140–41
Golden, Andrew "Drew," 48–50, 341
    animal cruelty, 105
    fire alarm ploy, 78
    lack of emotions during trial proceedings, 238
    medications, 33
Golden, Dennis, 49
Golden, Doug, 49
Golding, William, 309
Good guy/bad guy imagery, 194–96
Goodwin, Jay Douglas, 37, 345
Gorham, Bob, 231–32
Goth culture, 25–26, 65–66, 105–10, 121, 179, 181, 198–99

Graham, Marcia, 97–98, 126
Grand Rapids High School, 75–76
Grand Theft Auto, 64, 211
Granite Hills High School, 171, 345
Grant, LeeAnn, 19
Grant, Sky, 217
Graves, Reggie, 19–20
Graves, Sean, 71
Grayson, Wilbur, Jr., 79
Grimsley High School, 338
Griswold, Tami, 56
Grossman, Dave, 176, 185, 191–92,
    306, 311, 332
Grunow, Barry, 204, 344
"Guilty but insane," 43–46, 139
Gun lobby, 8–10, 306–8
Guns, 143, 199–201, 306–8
    Kimveer Gill and, 65–66
    Kip Kinkel and, 55–56, 59–62, 91–92,
        104, 110–11, 156–57, 243, 307
    as surrogate love objects, 269–71
Guns N' Roses, 318

Hadley, Nicole, 29–30
Hainstock, Eric, 141–42, 176, 303, 351
Halder, Biswanath, 146, 297, 347–48
Hale, Conan Wayne, 25, 231–32
Hall, Makai, 71–72
Hall, Tony, 222
Hamilton, Thomas, 281–82, 340
Hampton, Evan, 80, 335
Handguns. See Guns
Hans, Kristofer, 336
Hanson, Michelle, 34
Harcleroad, F. Douglas, 85–87
Hardenbrook, Jody, 260–61
Hare, Robert D., 182–83, 186–87
Harless, Jason, 336
Harris, Eric, 263–65, 342
    bomb-making, 77–78
    fan clubs, 178–80
    "God question," 20–23
    love crushes, 97
    media influences, 209–10, 212, 218
    medications, 33
    Nazism and, 174
    sequence of events, 70–73
    sexual orientation, 237, 238
    video games, 188–89, 193
Hartle, Cody, 68
Hase, Jun, 285–86
Hate messages, 262–83
Havelock, Brian, 165–66, 243
Hawkins, Robert A., 150, 204–6, 353
Heath High School, 29–30, 124

Heavy-metal music, 56–57, 108–9,
    125–26, 213, 317–18
Heide, Kathleen M., 223–24
Henry Foss High School, 352
Henson, Melinda, 49
Heritage High School, 31–32, 343
Herring, Paige Ann, 48–49
Hess, Rudolf, 174
Heston, Charlton, 307
Hiaasen, Nick, 132, 165–66, 243,
    244–45
Hicks, Jeffrey, 58–59, 116–17, 243, 323
Hicks, Marvin, 84
Higgs, Carlene, 114
Hill, Paul, 319–20
Hilscher, Emily Jane, 278–79
Hinckley, John, Jr., 115
Hit lists, 158–70
Hochhalter, Anne Marie, 71
Hoffman, Jason, 34, 40, 171, 345
Hoffman, Jens, 158
Homosexuality, 236–43
Houghton, Cheyenne, 166
Houser, Reggie, 81
Houston, Eric, 83, 337
Hubbard Woods Elementary School,
    220–21
Huyck, Emery, 279–80

Iacoboni, Marco, 311–12
Ikeda Elementary School, 287–88, 345
Ingram, Darrell, 343
Insanity, 114–18, 122–40
Insanity defense, 43–46, 139
Intermittent explosive disorder (IED),
    139–57
Internet, 177–93, 263–65
Intruder drills, 311, 327, 331
Ireland, Patrick, 71–72
Isenberg, Sheila, 233–34
Islamic Jihad, 152–54, 200, 229,
    274–76, 282, 319, 320–21
Israel, 275–76, 354
Ivey, London, 6

Jackson, Lawanda, 222
Jackson, Martin, 290
Jackson County High School, 337
James, Jamelle, 207
James W. Parker Middle School, 67–68,
    341
Japan, 284–88, 348, 349
Jenkins, Henry, 217–18
Jesus Christ, 22, 107, 154
Jia Qingyou, 348

Jock culture, 310
Johann Gutenberg Secondary School, 346. *See also* Steinhäuser, Robert
John Glenn High School, 37
Johnson, Barry, 257–58
Johnson, Michael (student), 71
Johnson, Mike (assistant principal), 325–27
Johnson, Mitchell, 48–50, 264, 341
  fire alarm ploy, 78
  medications, 33
  remorse during trial proceedings, 238, 260
Johnson, Stephanie, 48–49
Jokela High School, 155, 269–73, 353
Jones, Gerard, 211, 216
Jones, Steven, 263
Jonesboro shootings. *See* Golden, Andrew "Drew"; Johnson, Mitchell
Joseph, Mike, 148
Jourdain, Floyd, Jr., 174–75
Jourdain, Louis, 174–75
Juvenile justice system, 42–50

Kahle, Don, 208
Kaltenbach, Tim, 124
Kalvert, Scott, 212
Kamozaki, Mitchiaki, 349
Kardanoc, Yurl, 281, 339
Kashiwase, H., 238–39
Kato, M., 238–39
Kaye, Neil, 150–51
Kazmierczak, Stephen, 203, 354
  firearms of, 9–10
  media influences, 212
  medications, 34
  "monster" comparison, 112–13
  video games, 191
Keable, Gavin, 57–58, 67, 104–5
Kearby, James Alan, 335
Keatainak, Peter, 39–40, 349–50
Kechter, Matt, 72
Keeney, Aaron, 161–62, 321
Keeney, Scott, 60–63, 90, 103
Kehoe, Andrew, 279–80
Kehoe, Nellie, 279
Kelly, James Easton, 81, 344
Kelly, Judy, 95
Kennedy, Anthony, 43
Kent, Jamon, 88–89, 98, 195–96
Kerfi-Guetteb, Hassina, 39–40, 350
Kerns, Tobin, 210, 316, 349
Kessinger, Berry, 103, 105
Keyes, Emily, 225–26, 351
Killing Monsters (Jones), 216

King, Lawrence, 239, 354
King, Stephen, 152, 213
Kinkel, Bill, 1–3, 24–27, 51–63, 93–94, 99–105, 110–11, 114–21, 128–29, 133–34, 147–49, 165, 239–43
Kinkel, Faith, 1–3, 24–27, 51–63, 93–94, 95, 101–5, 110–11, 114–21, 125–37, 147–49, 166–67, 257
Kinkel, Kipland "Kip," xii–xiv, 321–23, 341
  arsenal of, 55–56, 59–62, 91–92, 104, 110–11, 156–57, 243, 307
  disciplinary problems of, 60–63, 85–90, 110–11, 125–27
  family history and life, 10, 51–63, 93–94, 99–105, 118–20
  fan clubs, 176–77
  fan mail, 230–35
  farewell note, 2–3, 25–26, 93–94, 125
  insanity defense, 43–46, 139
  intermittent explosive disorder and, 139–57
  Jonesboro shootings and, 67, 138–39
  lack of probable cause, 85–92
  "love sucks," 93–98
  medications, 33, 58–59, 104
  paranoid delusions, 114–23, 125–40
  personal journal and essays, 26–27, 94–98
  police confession, 24–27, 129–32
  prison sentence, 327–28
  school as setting for, 299–300
  school hit list, 161–70
  sequence of events, 1–3, 11–18, 23–26, 244–47
  sexual abuse charges, 239–43
  stolen gun incident, 60–63, 85–90
  "suicide by cop," 137–39
  victim impact to shooting, 247–61
  video games, 188, 191–92
  warning signs, 93–101, 145–47, 158–70
Kinkel, Kristin, 1, 52–55, 232, 251, 259–60, 322–23
Kinsella, Bridget, 233–34
Kintgen, Mark, 72
Kipling, Rudyard, 219
Kirklin, Lance, 71
Kirsten, George, 21
Kiser, Stacey, 354
Kitzhaber, John, 92
Klang, John, 141–42, 176
Klang, Sue, 176
Klebold, Dylan, 342
  bomb-making, 77–78

family life, 111–12, 293–94
fan clubs, 178–80
"God question," 20–23
love crushes, 96–97
media influences, 209–10, 212, 218
Nazism and, 174
sequence of events, 70–73
sexual orientation, 237, 238
video games, 188–89, 193
warning signs, 30, 95, 142
Klebold, Susan, 294
Klebold, Tom, 293–94
Kluber, Linda, 252, 321
Knives, 56, 59–60, 156–57, 191, 290
Knock on Any Door (Motley), 66
Knodell, John, 258
Koerschgen, Eric, 261
Konkol, Richard J., 115
Koontz, Katherine, 222, 352
Kornek, Joel, 332
Kreutz, Lisa, 72
Kroth, 105–8

Lakewood High School, 296
Lake Worth Community Middle School,
     204, 344
Lamar High School, 349
Lampe, Alan, 71–73, 332
Lamport, Marguerite, 277
Lane Community College, xiii–xvi
Lang, Jason, 206
Larkin, Ralph W., 122
Larry A. Ryle High School, 3–5, 338
Las Plumas High School, 353
Late onset antisocial kids, 144–46
LeBlanc, Russ, 6
Ledeger, Keith A., 339
Ledonne, Danny, 65, 171, 179–82,
     205–6, 215–16, 224, 310
Lefevre, Greg, 168
Leith, Stephen, 35, 338
Lennon, John, 65
Leodoro, Vincent Wayne, 324, 350
Leonard, Kip, 326
Leopold, Nathan, 79
Lépine, Marc, 82, 224, 278, 337
Levin, Jack, 141
Lewerke, James, 290, 349
Lewis & Clark High School, 346
Lewis, Dorothy, 118–19, 128–29, 134,
     136
Likins, Peter, 296
Lindhurst High School, 83, 337
Little Murder (play), 277
Liu Zhigang, 289–90, 349

Lizotte, Patrick, 335
Lo, Wayne, 123, 337
Loara High School, 82
Locke, John, 81
Loeb, Richard, 79
Lopez, Anthony, 82
Lord of the Flies (Golding), 309
Lost love, 36–38, 93–98
Louisiana Technical College, 222–23
Loukaitis, Barry, 258, 339
     black clothing, 109
     "fag" epithet, 242
     family life, 239
     media influences, 40, 212, 213
Lucas, Dillon, 325, 350
Lumet, Sidney, 208
Lund, Nissa, 105
Lussier, Chase, 20
Lussier, Daryl "Dash," 5–6
Lussier, Roland, Jr., 20
Lussier, Shelda, 5–6
Lust Killer (Rule), 321
Lynn, Betina, 192, 247–49, 255–56
Lynn, Mikel, 246–47, 248–49
Lynn, Rebecca, 246–47, 248–49

Mabe, Bryan, 12–13, 139
McClain, Scott, 172
McCown, Tony, 105, 110–11, 118, 132,
     138–39, 156–57, 165–68, 243,
     244–45
McCoy, Jason, 336
McDavid, Deanna, 83–84
McDonough, Michael, 268, 353
McDowell, Leonard, 338
McFadden, Kay, 208–9
McGraw, Phil, 181
McKeehan, Carol, 266
McKeehan, Michael, 263, 266
McKenzie, Elizabeth, 15–16, 262
McKissack, Fred, 75
McKissick, Robert, 119
McLaughlin, Jason, 348
McLean, Mari, 196
McMahan, John, 83
McVeigh, Timothy, 307, 320–21
Madonna Ciccone, 202
Male bonding, 236–43
Males, Mike, 293
Malovrh, Brendon, 221
Malvo, Lee Boyd, 236
Mancuso, David, 335
Manson, Charles, 25
Manson, Marilyn, 25–26, 109, 121,
     158, 198–99

"Man That You Fear" (song), 158
Marchese, Kimberly, 345
Margaret Leary Elementary School, 338
Marks, Sean, 67
Marlowe, Justin, 295
Marshfield High School, 210, 349
Martel, Charles, 234–35
Martinez, Nathan K., 211, 338–39
Martyrdom, 20–23, 317–18
Mask of Sanity (Cleckley), 147
Mass media. *See* Media
Mastrosimone, William, 250
Masuzoe, Yoichi, 185
Matasar, Larry, 328
Materialism, 194–203
Matthews, Randy Earl, 83, 337
Mattison, Jack, 44–46, 251, 256
Mauser, Daniel, 72
Mayor, Gwen, 281
Mean Girls (movie), 309
Media, 142–43, 177–93
    copycats and, 75–84
    face value, 194–201
    fame and, 202–18
    rating systems, 214–17
Medications, 32–36
Medved, Michael, 184
Menefee, Christina, 5, 31, 106–8
Mensah, Nicholas, 221, 340
Merritt, Rob, 142, 188–89
Metcalf, Earl, 76
Metzger, Josh, 165–66
Military service, 67, 191
Miller, Lena, 228
Miller, Mary Liz, 228
Miltonberger, Teresa, 15–16, 252
Mirror neurons, 311–12
Mr. Self-Destruction, 25
Mitarai, Satomi, 287, 348
Mitchell, Tyrone, 335
Mitchell High School, 354
Monash University, 274, 347
Montes, Mark, 167–68
Monti, Joseph, 324
Moore, Devin, 64
Moore, Jonathan, 340
Moore, Michael, 121, 198–200
Morgan, Buddy, 68
Morris, Chon'gai'la, 20
Morrison, Ashley, 19
Morrison, Duane R., 225–26, 351
Mortal Kombat, 193
Mortimore, Kent, 44, 162
Morva, William, 316

Mother-son relationships, 239–40
Motley, Willard, 66
Mountain Park Boarding School, 340
Movies, 177–81, 192–93, 209–13,
    216–18
Muhammad, John Allen, 236
Mullen, Richard, 43–46
Muniz, Brandon, 67, 162, 163
Munson, Stephanie, 71
Murchison Junior High School, 79
Murder-suicides, 28–43
Murdoch, Cindy, 99
Murray, Matthew J., 21–22, 33, 123–24,
    264
Murry, Tina, 167
Myrick, Joel, 108

Naffziger, Joyce, 119
Narcissism, 146–47, 197–98, 321
Natural Born Killers, 210, 349
Natural Born Killers (movie), 155, 209–12
Nazism, 78–79, 172, 173–75, 265
Nebb, Ed, 214–15
Nee, Joseph, 210, 316, 349
Needham, Roger, 78–79
Network (movie), 208
Neung Dong Church Elementary School,
    288, 346
Newington High School, 352
News reports, 208–9
    and copycats, 75–84
Nickolauson, Dawna, 252
Nickolauson, Michael, 252, 321
Nickolauson, Mikael, 16, 251–52, 256,
    321–22
Nicoletti, John, 1
Nielson, Patty, 23, 71, 72
Nietzsche, Friedrich, 112, 272
9/11 terrorist attacks (2001), xi, 200,
    207, 262–63, 320–21
Nine Inch Nails (NIN), 25, 125–26
Nineteen Minutes (Picoult), 309
Noah, Ken, 301
No Easy Answers (Brown and Merritt),
    142, 188–89
Nordstrom, Erl, 262–63
Northern High School, 335
Northern Illinois University, 9, 34,
    112–13, 354
North Miami Senior High School, 69,
    342
Norwood, Robin, 230, 232–33
"Not guilty by reason of insanity"
    (NGRI), 43–46, 139

Nowlin, Nicole, 72
NRA (National Rifle Association), 306–8
Nugent, Ted, 308

Oakland Elementary School, 81, 336
O'Dell, Derek, 62
Odighizuwa, Peter, 35, 295, 346
Okubo Elementary School, 287, 348
Oldboy (movie), 212–13
Olean High Scool, 75–77
Olson, Theresa, 234–35
Operant conditioning, 192
Orange High School, 6–9, 351
Orgeron, Paul Harold, 280
Orzack, Maressa, 189, 332
Osborne, Tom, 124
Osburn, Christina, 252–53
Osmanson, James, 338
Oudemolen, Bill, 20–21
Owens, Dedrick, 207

Palacios, Josh, 159–60, 340
Palermo, George B., 10, 40, 41–42, 186, 282–83
Palestinians, 275–76, 354
Palm Harbor Middle School, 172
Palo Duro High School, 83, 337
Paradise Amish Schoolhouse, 226–29, 351
Paranoid delusions, 114–23, 125–40, 238–39
Parenting, 10, 51–53, 102–5, 110–13, 305
Parents Under Siege (Garbarino), 112
Park, Chan-wook, 212–13
Park, Jeanna, 72
Parkway South Junior High School, 335
Parricide, 223–29
Paxil, 32–36
Pearl High School, 5, 105–8
Pearl Jam, 40, 213
Pearse, Adam, 12, 118, 156–57
Pearson, Joshua, 16–17
Peddet, Joel, 290
Peek, Carlene, 258–59
Peek, Richard "Ricky," 258–59
Pennington, Gary Scott, 83–84, 337
Penn State University, 221, 340
Perrin, Timothy, 38, 336
Persecution complex, 20–23, 38–39, 117–18, 153–54
Pet cruelty, 105–8
Peterson, Laci, 194–95

Peterson, Scott, 194–95, 230–31
Petit-Frere, Felly, 69
Petkovic, Dragoslav, 346
Pharmaceutical industry, 32–36
Phelps, Fred, 239
Phillips, David, 75
Piasecki, Joseph, 35
Picoult, Jodi, 309
Pierce, Dustin, 82, 337
Piggott, Clarence, 335
Plato, 272
Platte Canyon High School, 225–26, 351
Poe Elementary School, 280
Politics of blame, 85–92
Port Arthur Historical Site, 291
Post-traumatic stress disorder (PTSD), 255–56
Poulin, Robert, 77, 334
Prescription drugs, 32–36
Preston Junior High School, 172, 344
Prevatte, Billy Ray, 75–76
Privilege, 30, 47, 79–80, 145, 153–56
Probable cause, 85–92
Prozac, 32–36, 39, 58–59, 104, 116–17
Psychosis, 44, 114–40
Purdy, Patrick, 35, 81–82, 109, 336

Rage (King), 213
Ramsey, Amber, 15
Ramsey, Evan, 158–60, 299, 314, 340
Rating systems, 214–17
Ravina Elementary School, 220–21
Raynor, Rodric "Rick," 88–92
Reagan, Ronald, 115
Red Lake High School, 5–6, 18–20, 173–75, 350
Red Lion Area Junior High School, 36, 347
Religion, 18, 20–23, 156, 319–20
Reljic, Stanimir, 346
Richardson, Jasmine, 211–12, 350
Richland High School, 339
Riley, Sam, 315
Ritalin, 32–36
Riverdale High School, 340
Robb, Cordell "Cory," 82, 337
Robbins, Jillian, 221, 340
Roberts, Charles Carl, IV, 226–29, 316, 351
Rocori High School, 348
Rogers, Neva, 19
Rohrbough, Daniel, 71
Rolland, Kayla, 207, 343
Romano, Nick, 66

Romeo and Juliet (movie), 11, 24, 94
Rose, Anna, 8
Roseburg High School, 324, 350
Roth, Kevin, 76
Rouse, Jamie, 124–25, 339
Rowan, Kevin, 125–26, 132–33
Rowles, Gerald L., 197–98
Royal Valley High School, 172, 344
Ruegsegger, Kasey, 71–72
Rule, Ann, 240, 312, 321
Rupp, Shelly, 142
Russell, Norma, 335
Rutherford, Anthony, 340
Ryker, Jacob "Jake," 14, 16–17,
    114–15, 176–77, 256–57, 321

Sabitt, Mark, 43–46
Sachs, Brad, ix–xi
Sack, William, 115, 123
Sacred Heart School, 36, 339
Sadoff, Robert, 121
Safeguards, at school, 310–12
St. Hilaire, Susan, 266
St. Luke's Primary School, 282, 340
St. Pius X High School, 77, 334
Sanders, Dave, 71, 72
Sanders, Mike, 80, 335
Santana High School, 169–71, 345
Satan (Satanism), 20–23, 105–10, 161
Saul, Destry, 163
Saw (movie), 212
Schizophrenia, 44, 122–40
Schlessinger, Laura, 184
Schmitt, Eric, 338
Schnurr, Valeen, 21, 72
Schoenfeld, James and Richard, 79
Schor, Juliet B., 202–3
Schulz, Charles, 270
Schwanz, Diane, 19
Schwebes, Mark, 237–38
Scott, Craig, 72
Scott, David, 104
Scott, Rachel, 20–21, 22–23, 71
Scurry-Rosser High School, 296–97
Second Amendment, 306–8
Segro, Eugene, 36, 297
Seki, Darrell, 174
Senn, Phyllis, 38
September 11th terrorist attacks (2001),
    xi, 200, 207, 262–63, 320–21
Sereno, Jeanette, 230–31
Sexual orientation, 236–43
Shakespeare's Romeo and Juliet (movie),
    11, 24, 94

Shapiro, Rami, 18
Shared psychotic disorder (SPD), 238–39
Shared values, 183
Sheets, James Robert, 36, 297, 347
Sherrill, Patrick, 141
"Shine" (song), 317–18
Shoels, Isaiah, 72
Shooting Game, The (Lieberman),
    xiii–ixv, 324
Shrout, Clay, 3–5, 56–57, 338
    animal cruelty, 105
    black clothing, 109
    bomb-making, 56–57
    fame and media, 204
    hit lists, 160
    occult subjects, 109
    parents and family life, 3, 51, 56, 111
Shrout, Harvey, 3–5, 56
Shrout, Kristen, 3–4, 56
Shrout, Lauren, 4
Shrout, Rebecca, 3–5
Shryer, Shannan, 12–13
Sigana, Michelle, 5–6
Simon's Rock, 123, 337
Sincino, Toby, 38, 339
Sirola, John, 36, 339
Sisler, Jacob, 164–65
Slasher films, 192–93
Sledge, Justin, 106–8
Slobodian, Michael, 77, 334
Small Sacrifices (Rule), 240
Smith, Jason Michael, 338
Smith, Jerry, 257
Smith, John, 320–21
Smith, Marian, 98
Smith, Todd Cameron, 34–35, 206–7,
    342–43
Smith, Valerie, 188
Sneed, Richard, 296–97, 347
Sniper (play), 76
Sniper attacks, 276–79
Social privilege, 30, 47, 79–80, 145,
    153–56
Social status, 196–97, 203–4
Solomon, Thomas "T.J.", 31–32, 343
Sommers, Christina Hoff, 184
Southcoast Early Childhood Learning
    Center, 343
Southeast Warren High School, 325, 350
South Korea, 288, 291
Southside High School, 172, 344
Spalla, Melanie, 221, 340
Spence, Pamela, 224
Spencer, Brenda Ann, 220, 334–35

Spencer, Jane, 200
Sperry, Denny, 103, 104
Splitting, 150–51
Springfield High School, 325
Springwater Trail High School, 300–302, 352
SSRIs (selective serotonin reuptake inhibitors), 32–36, 39
Stamps High School, 335
Starkweather, Charles, 210–11
Status, 196–97, 203–4
Steepleton, Daniel, 71
Steinhäuser, Robert, 109, 174, 191, 266, 346
Steinke, Jeremy Allan, 211–12, 350
Stevens, Josh, 170
Stoddard, Kari, 162
Stoltzfus, Anna Mae, 228
Stone, Don, 60–63, 89–90, 246
Stone, Oliver, 209–12
Strand, James, 68
"Stray Bullet" (song), 271
Strong, Benjamin, 29–30, 341
Sturgeon Creek Regional School, 334
SuccessTech Academy, 353
Suchar, Michael, 220
Sudd, Victoria, 171, 345
Suicidal ideation, 152–53
"Suicide by cop," 18–19, 137–39
Suicide-murders, 28–43
Suicide rates, 28–29
Sumner High School, 222
Super Columbine Massacre RPG!, 65, 179–82
Superheroes, 177–81, 185–86, 216
Supreme Court, U.S., 43
Susbauer, Jonathan, 231–32
Swann, Michael, 338
Symbolic value of schools, 298–99

Takuma, Mamoru, 287–88, 345
Talovic, Sulejmen, 205–6, 352
Tarantino, Quentin, 209–10
Tate, Sharon, 25
Taylor, James Howard, 80–81, 335
Taylor, Janet, 122–23
Taylor, Mark, 71
Taylor, Melissa, 15, 255
Taylor, Ted, 255, 256
Television (TV), 183–93, 198, 203–4, 208–9, 306
Terrorism (terrorists), xi, 46–47, 152–54, 156, 229, 274–76, 319
Thetford, Lynette, 49

Thomas, Gabe, 15
Thompson, Dave, 142
Thompson, Jack, 180–81, 191
Thompson, Johnny, 38
Thompson, Robert, 203
Thorn, Jesse, 162
Thornhill, Karl David, 279
Thunder, Cody, 19
Thurston High School, xii–xiv, 341. See also Kinkel, Kipland "Kip"
  hit list, 161–70
  memorial, 321–23
  politics of blame, 85–105
  sequence of events, 11–18, 23–26, 244–49
Titus, Joseph, 325, 350
Todd, Evan, 71, 72
Todd, Joseph "Colt," 80, 341
Tomaree High School, 290
Tomlin, John, 72
Tomogaoka Junior High School, 285–86
Tough guy image, 109–10
Townsend, Lauren, 72
Townsley, Edna, 276–77
Toy guns, 142–43
Tracy, Caren, 125–26
Trammell, Justin, 50
Tran, Catherine, 37
Trench Coat Mafia, 263
Trickey, Seth, 35, 343
Trigg, Josiah Christian, 325–27, 351
Tucker, Cynthia, 47, 194
Tury, Jacob "Jake", 68

University of Arizona Nursing School, 296, 347
University of Arkansas, 80–81, 335, 344
University of California, Santa Barbara, 345
University of Montreal, 82, 337
University of Oregon, xiii, 158
University of Texas, 276–79
University of Utah, 127–28
Upper Perkiomen High School, 338
Ure, David, 17
Ure, Douglas, 17

Valley High School, 335
Valparaiso High School, 349
VampireFreaks.com, 65–66
Van Gogh, Theo, 318–19
Van Sant, Gus, 216–17, 237
Varner, Brittheny, 49
Vela, Manuel, 213

Velasquez, Kyle, 71
Vest, Jason, 208
Victim impact statements, 250–61
Video games, 64–65, 179–93, 213–18, 323–24
Violent media, 177–93, 198–200, 209–14, 285–86
Virginia Tech, xiii, 248, 314–18, 353. *See also* Cho, Seung-hui
   gun advocacy after shooting, 308
   lockdown issues, 278–79, 315–16
   sequence of events, 315–18
   Whitman massacre parallel with, 278–79
Visiting Life (Kinsella), 233–34
"Voices in my head," 122–40
Voluntary consent to treatment, 8

Wade, Nigel, 209
Wahluke High School, 34
Walberger, Adam, 17
Walker, Benjamin "Ben," 12–13, 85, 251–52
Walker, Mark, 182, 251–52
Walters, Barbara, 52, 55
War Against Boys (Sommers), 184
Warner, Brian, 121
Warning signs, 329–30
Warthen, Alan, 23–27, 60–62, 86–92, 97, 100–101, 120, 129–32, 249, 257
Warthen, Sherrie, 101
War toys, 142–43
Wauwatosa West High School, 338
Weaponry. *See* Guns; Knives
Weaver, Travis, 17
Webb, Andrea, 37, 345
Webb, Bob, 34
Web sites, 331–33
Wegener, Fred, 226
Weigand, Joe, 120
Weise, Jeff, 5–6, 173–75, 350
   black clothing, 109
   bullying and teasing, 38–39
   demons, 108–9
   media influences, 217
   medications, 33, 39
   parents and family life, 5–6
   sequence of events, 18–20
Werner, Richard, 123–24
Westside Middle School, 48–50, 341
Whitaker, Julian, 32–33
Whitman, Charles Joseph, 8–9, 35, 117, 276–79

Whitman, Kathy, 276
Whitman, Margaret, 276
Why Kids Kill Parents (Heide), 223–24
Wickliffe Middle School, 339
Wiley, Forest, 76
Willard, Nancy, 135, 187–88
Williams, Brandon, 231–32
Williams, Charles "Andy," 169–71, 345
Williams, Latina, 222–23, 354
Willis, Vanessa, 170
Wilson, Chelsea, 225–26
Wilson, Eloise, 69
Wilson, James William, 81, 336
Wilson, Tom, 78–79
Without Conscience (Hare), 182–83
Woloszyn, Ben, 191
Women Who Love Men Who Kill (Isenberg), 233–34
Women Who Love Too Much (Norwood), 230, 232–33
Wood, Jerame, 61–62, 89–90
Woodham, Luke, 5, 105–8, 298–99, 340–41
   animal cruelty, 105, 106
   bullying, 153
   on death, 30–31
   demons, 105–8
   medications, 33
   parents and family life, 5, 106–7, 239
Woodham, Mary Ann, 106–8, 239
Woods, Frederick Newhall, IV, 79
Workplace rage, 140–41
World of Warcraft, 189
W.R. Myers High School, 206–7, 342–43
Wragg, Burton, 220
Wright, Shannon, 49
Wurst, Andrew, 67–68, 109, 121, 341

Xanax, 32–36
Xiang, Huan Yun "Allen," 274, 347
Xu Heping, 288–89, 348

Yamashita, Ayaka, 286
Yang Guozhu, 289, 348
Yan Yanming, 289–90, 349
Young, David and Doris, 281, 335–36
Young, Mickell, 111
Yousef, Ramzi, 320–21
YouTube, 218, 270–74

Zemcik, Robert, 68
Zero Day (movie), 66, 155, 217–18
Zoloft, 32–36